Robotic Process Au Projects

Build real-world RPA solutions using UiPath and
Automation Anywhere

Nandan Mullakara
Arun Kumar Asokan

Packt>

BIRMINGHAM - MUMBAI

Robotic Process Automation Projects

Commissioning Editor: Pavan Ramchandani
Acquisition Editor: Heramb Bhavsar
Content Development Editor: Divya Vijayan
Senior Editor: Mohammed Yusuf Imaratwale
Technical Editor: Deepesh Patel
Copy Editor: Safis Editing
Project Coordinator: Kinjal Bari
Proofreader: Safis Editing
Indexer: Tejal Daruwale Soni
Production Designer: Joshua Misquitta

First published: May 2020

Production reference: 1220520

Published by Packt Publishing Ltd.
Livery Place
35 Livery Street
Birmingham
B3 2PB, UK.

ISBN 978-1-83921-735-7

www.packt.com

To everyone out there striving to make work more fun!

To my mother, Vijayalakshmi, and to the memory of my father, Vasudevan, for their unconditional love and support.

To my wife, Anjali, for being my loving partner throughout our life journey.

– Nandan Mullakara

To my loving wife, Harini, and my beautiful daughter, Nakshatra, for supporting me in completing this book in the most difficult and uncertain period of my life.

To my parents, Asokan and Selvi, for their love, support, prayers, and inspiration throughout my life.

To all the brave souls fighting the COVID-19 virus head-on, risking their lives for others.

– Arun Kumar Asokan

Contributors

About the authors

Nandan Mullakara is the CEO of Innomatiq, an automation consulting firm that is helping organizations to discover, develop, and deploy automation with **Robotic Process Automation** (**RPA**) and **Artificial Intelligence** (**AI**).

He was most recently the head of RPA consultancy at Fujitsu America, where he helped enable the Fujitsu Digital Workforce offering. He blogs on RPA and technology at *nandan.info*.

> *I want to thank my wife, Anjali, and son, Adarsh, for their cooperation and support while I wrote the book. A special thanks to five-year-old Ashish, without whose love and encouragement the book could have been completed a bit earlier.*

Arun Kumar Asokan is an Assistant Vice President (AVP) at EXL Service. He is an intelligent automation consultant and business process management professional. Currently, he is helping clients design and operate RPA **Centers of Excellence** (**CoEs**) and build AI and **Intelligent Document Processing** (**IDP**) capabilities. He has previously worked for different digital consulting groups in HCL, Infosys, and Wipro, helping clients in different parts of the world. In addition to this, Arun promotes RPA and AI technologies by educating junior RPA developers with demo videos and thought leadership articles.

> *I would like to first and foremost thank my parents, Mr Asokan and Mrs Selvi, for their unquestionable support for all my life decisions, and my lovely wife, Harini, and daughter, Nakshatra, for their continued support, patience, and encouragement throughout the long process of writing this book. Thanks to my friends and colleagues who shaped my professional career, to all the people out there fighting COVID-19, and to God Almighty for this opportunity and allowing me to complete this book.*

About the reviewer

Rameshwar Balanagu is an experienced enterprise architect leading intelligent automation practice and is an active speaker about and supporter of the use of automation to enable rapid digital transformation.

He has led in various roles in enterprise architecture, analytics, and intelligent automation. He has worked in various areas, such as databases, middleware, **Enterprise Resource Planning (ERP)**, **Software as a Service (SaaS)**, **Business Intelligence (BI)**, cybersecurity, and more. He also runs the sixth-largest intelligent automation meetup in the US.

In his spare time, he likes to teach and blog, and he loves playing badminton and ping-pong.

Packt is searching for authors like you

If you're interested in becoming an author for Packt, please visit `authors.packtpub.com` and apply today. We have worked with thousands of developers and tech professionals, just like you, to help them share their insight with the global tech community. You can make a general application, apply for a specific hot topic that we are recruiting an author for, or submit your own idea.

Packt>

Table of Contents

Preface

RPA is an exciting new technology seen as the first step for using advanced new technologies to automate enterprise processes. We will see how RPA brings advances to automation compared to earlier techniques, which involved scripts and macros.

In this book, we will carry out a few real-world **Robotic Process Automation** (**RPA**) projects.

By the time you complete this book, you will be equipped with the knowledge, techniques, and mindset that you need to work on RPA projects of simple to medium complexity with UiPath and Automation Anywhere, with minimal guidance.

Who this book is for

This book is for anyone who would like to get started with a few real-world RPA projects. Building these projects is like getting an on-the-job training on Automation. They may seem a bit tough to get through at first, but if you can use the book along with the supporting code, you will have completed some robust projects in the way that they would be executed in enterprises.

You will benefit from this book if you are any of the following:

- An IT professional looking to build your first RPA project
- A technology-savvy business professional (perhaps in finance or HR) seeking to explore automation via RPA
- An IT or Business line manager, director or executive (any managers or directors in these areas) who would like to understand applied RPA

What this book covers

Chapter 1, *Getting Started with Robotic Process Automation*, gives you a quick introduction to RPA, its types, and its benefits. We walk you through the installation of UiPath and Automation Anywhere, the tools we will use for our projects.

Chapter 2, *Help Desk Ticket Generation*, shows you how to automate helpdesk support tickets using spreadsheets. This is an *attended automation*, which you can invoke using a shortcut.

Chapter 3, *CRM Automation*, demonstrates automating a typical "swivel chair activity" wherein you look up data from one application and use it to update another system. Here, we look up customer information and update that information in our CRM system.

Chapter 4, *Moderating Social Media Using AI*, teaches you to use AI to automatically moderate images that are uploaded to social media sites. The automation uses the Google Vision API and sends the administrator a spreadsheet with its moderation recommendations.

Chapter 5, *Purchase Order Processing with UiPath ReFramework*, uses the advanced UiPath ReFramework to process purchase orders. We read the purchase orders from a spreadsheet and input them into a purchase order application.

Chapter 6, *Completing an RPA Challenge*, sees you solving the RPA challenge at rpachallenge.com using both UiPath and Automation Anywhere A2019.

Chapter 7, *Sales Order Processing*, shows you how to take sales order data from an Excel spreadsheet and create orders on a web-based business application using Automation Anywhere A2019.

Chapter 8, *ERP User Administration*, sees you building a bot that automates new user creation. The bot looks up user information from a user creation request and creates the user in a SaaS application.

Chapter 9, *Employee Emergency Notifications*, shows how organizations can be enabled to send notifications to employees in the case of pandemics, hurricanes, floods, and so on. We look up a list of employees and send them a mass text message (SMS).

Chapter 10, *Using AI and RPA for Invoice Processing*, teaches you to use Automation Anywhere's IQ Bot to convert invoice data from an unstructured format into a structured format that we can use for automation.

To get the most out of this book

Since RPA is a productivity tool, you mainly need the right version of the RPA tools.

In this book, we are using UiPath and Automation Anywhere, so ensure that you have the right version installed.

You also need access to a few SaaS applications and APIs, as documented in the *Technical requirements* section of each chapter.

Here is a summary of the software and hardware used:

Software/hardware covered in the book	OS requirements
UiPath Community Edition, version 19+	Windows 10
Automation Anywhere A2019 Community Edition	Windows 10

This book is compatible with the latest version of UiPath at the time of publishing (UiPath 2020.x).

If you are using the digital version of this book, we advise you to type the code yourself or access the code via the GitHub repository (link available in the next section). Doing so will help you avoid any potential errors related to the copying and pasting of code.

Download the example code files

You can download the example code files for this book from your account at `www.packt.com`. If you purchased this book elsewhere, you can visit `www.packtpub.com/support` and register to have the files emailed directly to you.

You can download the code files by following these steps:

1. Log in or register at `www.packt.com`.
2. Select the **Support** tab.
3. Click on **Code Downloads**.
4. Enter the name of the book in the **Search** box and follow the onscreen instructions.

Once the file is downloaded, please make sure that you unzip or extract the folder using the latest version of:

- WinRAR/7-Zip for Windows
- Zipeg/iZip/UnRarX for Mac
- 7-Zip/PeaZip for Linux

The code bundle for the book is also hosted on GitHub at `https://github.com/PacktPublishing/Robotic-Process-Automation-Projects`. In case there's an update to the code, it will be updated on the existing GitHub repository.

We also have other code bundles from our rich catalog of books and videos available at `https://github.com/PacktPublishing/`. Check them out!

Code in Action

Code in Action videos for this book can be viewed at https://bit.ly/2Zo0s1u.

Conventions used

There are a number of text conventions used throughout this book.

CodeInText: Indicates code words in text, database table names, folder names, filenames, file extensions, pathnames, dummy URLs, user input, and Twitter handles. Here is an example: "We will start by adding a new Sequence within the Main Sequence."

Bold: Indicates a new term, an important word, or words that you see onscreen. For example, words in menus or dialog boxes appear in the text like this. Here is an example: "Once you've done that, click on **Save and Exit** on the **Recorder** panel."

Warnings or important notes appear like this.

Tips and tricks appear like this.

Get in touch

Feedback from our readers is always welcome.

General feedback: If you have questions about any aspect of this book, mention the book title in the subject of your message and email us at customercare@packtpub.com.

Errata: Although we have taken every care to ensure the accuracy of our content, mistakes do happen. If you have found a mistake in this book, we would be grateful if you would report this to us. Please visit www.packtpub.com/support/errata, selecting your book, clicking on the Errata Submission Form link, and entering the details.

Piracy: If you come across any illegal copies of our works in any form on the Internet, we would be grateful if you would provide us with the location address or website name. Please contact us at copyright@packt.com with a link to the material.

If you are interested in becoming an author: If there is a topic that you have expertise in and you are interested in either writing or contributing to a book, please visit authors.packtpub.com.

Reviews

Please leave a review. Once you have read and used this book, why not leave a review on the site that you purchased it from? Potential readers can then see and use your unbiased opinion to make purchase decisions, we at Packt can understand what you think about our products, and our authors can see your feedback on their book. Thank you!

For more information about Packt, please visit packt.com.

Getting Started with Robotic Process Automation

1

Hello there! In this book, we will be guiding you through a few real-world **Robotic Process Automation (RPA)** projects. Thanks for joining us. By the time you complete this book, you will be equipped with knowledge, techniques, and the mindset to work on simple to medium complexity RPA projects with UiPath and Automation Anywhere with minimum guidance.

RPA is an exciting new technology that is being seen as the first step to using new and advancing technologies to automate enterprise processes. We will learn how RPA brings a level of advancement to automation that is much more evolved than the earlier automation process through its use of scripts, macros, and so on.

RPA is advancing rapidly and is part of a bigger movement to low code and no-code tools. Compared to traditional coding, these tools are easier to use and faster to deploy. Organizations are now using these rapid development tools with emerging technologies such as process mining, **artificial intelligence (AI)**, and analytics to enable end-to-end process automation. We'll take an in-depth look at the future of RPA in the *Appendix – Looking Forward and Next Steps*.

In this first chapter, we will cover the following topics:

- A quick introduction to RPA, its benefits, and the types of RPA
- Overview of top RPA platforms – UiPath and Automation Anywhere
- Installing and setting up UiPath and Automation Anywhere

Technical requirements

To set up the RPA tools for this chapter, please ensure that you have the following:

- A machine that is running Windows 7 or above.
- At least 4 GB RAM, though ideally, your machine should have 8 GB or more.
- The Google Chrome and Internet Explorer web browsers installed.

If you have your hardware and software ready, then let's get started!

What is RPA?

Robotic Process Automation (**RPA**) excels at automating manual and repetitive tasks. RPA, therefore, gives us a tool that we can use to automate all the unexciting work you may have been doing so you can do some exciting work! With this tool, you have more time to spend on unique human activities such as delighting your team, boss, and customers.

So, let's have a quick look at what exactly RPA is and the amazing benefits that makes it the hot technology that it is today.

A quick definition

RPA allows software robots to carry out tasks on a computer just like a human would.

The best way to visualize RPA would be to think of someone working on the computer and doing their daily work by clicking through computer screens, sending emails, and so on. Now, what if the computer clicks through, enters the required data, and performs the same work automatically? That is what RPA helps us do.

Here is an example of what RPA can do for you.

Let's say you are responsible for processing invoices in an **Enterprise Resource Planning** (**ERP**). You would log in to your ERP, go to a specific screen, and enter the invoice details one by one. Now, if you'd like to automate this task with RPA, you would configure these task sequences to create a "bot." Once this bot has been deployed, it would carry out the same tasks automatically – it would log in automatically and carry out the tasks without you having to do this repetitive work!

RPA doesn't just automate ERP transactions. As we will see later, throughout our projects, there are many business areas where RPA comes in handy and automates business and IT processes. This results in some great benefits to businesses. Let's have a look at a few of them.

Benefits of RPA

The benefits of RPA are as follows:

- **Improved productivity:** More than 60% to 90% of the repetitive effort can be removed, with RPA increasing the output for each of your employees.
- **Rapid results and in-year benefits:** Rapid implementation and results are a key promise of RPA as you can conceive, design, develop, and deploy in weeks, not months or years.
- **Low startup costs:** Each of the bot licenses is less costly compared to other software tools and the bot can perform the work of about two to three **Full Time Equivalent (FTE)**, ensuring the startup costs are low.
- **Reduced processing costs:** The costs of processing are reduced drastically as the bot costs around one third to one fifth the cost of an employee, depending on location.
- **Improved quality and accuracy:** Your bots perform assigned work with 100% accuracy, thereby reducing any rework that may have been required.
- **Improved compliance:** RPA activities are logged and can be reviewed at any time. This gives you a greater degree of oversight and control over your operations.

You can gain these benefits using two types of RPA that have emerged so far – one runs on your desktop and the other type runs on a server.

We will complete projects with both types of RPA in this book. Now, let's take a look at what these types of automation are.

Types of RPA

We have two kinds of RPA automation that are based on how the RPA tool helps you automate. One of them is like an assistant that you call upon to help you complete the tasks, while the other is a kind of automation that's mostly used for back-office work. What does that mean? Let's find out.

Attended automation

These are the assistants that run on your computer and help you complete parts of the tasks that you are performing. For example, if you usually copy and paste data from one application to multiple applications, you can invoke an attended RPA to take over just these sets of activities. The control is then returned to you by RPA to carry out the next set of tasks.

> Attended automation solutions are installed on individual workstations. Sometimes, these desktops differ in terms of resolutions, display settings, and even graphics cards. This may lead to failure in terms of automation on a desktop, even though it was working well on another one.

This type of automation is popular with agents at call centers. With this, the long, repetitive processes that an agent does are replaced with single clicks! This greatly reduces the time it takes to train your representatives. Therefore, attended RPA can reduce the average handling times, improving your customer experience.

You would use attended bots for the following reasons:

- Tasks that need real-time human-system interaction
- To augment your employee's day-to-day work, enabling them to do it faster and better
- To help your employees understand and embrace automation

Unattended automation

If you don't need a representative or worker interaction to execute a process, you can usually run the process on a backend server. This is known as unattended automation, which can be used to automate back-office work.

In unattended automation, workflows are self-triggered and run on servers. They usually run to a predetermined schedule and are available 24/7. For example, you can batch your invoices and process them at certain times during the day. The bot would later send you a report, indicating the invoices that could not be processed automatically. You can review the report and only work on the invoices that need your intervention.

These automated tasks can be scheduled or started through control rooms. You can allocate tasks, adjust priorities, manage queues, and intervene, in the case of performance issues, through the control room.

Usually, unattended automation gives you more control over the automation process. It follows your rules to complete a process automatically. You would use unattended automation for the following reasons:

- Tasks that are structured and can be fully mapped
- To replace entire roles where possible
- To gather, sort, analyze, and distribute large amounts of data

You can use both unattended and attended automation either by themselves or together to implement use cases that give your business a distinct advantage. Most of the top tools give you the capability to implement both types of RPA. Let's look at two of them – UiPath and Automation Anywhere – both of which we will be using for our projects.

Our RPA tools – UiPath and Automation Anywhere

RPA tools help you automate business processes using multiple technologies. It all started with screen scrapping and workflow configurations to automate BPO processes. The emergence of AI technologies has helped the RPA tools include cognitive aspects. RPA, along with AI, is now being called "Intelligent Automation."

UiPath and Automation Anywhere are two of the top RPA platform vendors, as per the rankings from respected analysts such as Forrester and Gartner. They have taken different paths, as we will see, and have evolved into the top RPA platforms that we see today. In this book, we will be using these two platforms for our projects. So, let's understand a bit about them and their makeup before we dive into the projects.

UiPath

UiPath is a top RPA platform by many measures. The company is one of the most funded in this space and gives you a sense of what investors consider the best RPA tool in the long run.

It is quite popular and has a big community. The secret to this is that Uipath made the platform easily accessible quite early. It is also one of the easiest RPA platforms with a comparatively low learning curve. This is why we have selected UiPath as one of the platforms for our projects in this book.

UiPath started as DeskOver in 2005. They first started by building automation libraries and software development kits for companies such as IBM, Google, and Microsoft. These libraries are still part of some of the products from these companies.

UiPath, which was DeskOver at that time, launched the first UiPath Desktop Automation product line around 2012. This product specifically targeted the RPA market. They worked with BPO providers to realize the market fit with RPA.

Fast forward to today, and UiPath is a top enterprise RPA platform. The UiPath platform helps you develop automation rapidly while being secure and scalable.

The platform has three main components:

- UiPath Studio
- UiPath Orchestrator
- UiPath Robot

Let's check out each of these components.

UiPath Studio

You design and configure your process workflows in UiPath studio. It is a low-code environment where you drag and drop prebuilt components. These components are provided by UiPath and are called Activities. The following is a screenshot of UiPath Studio:

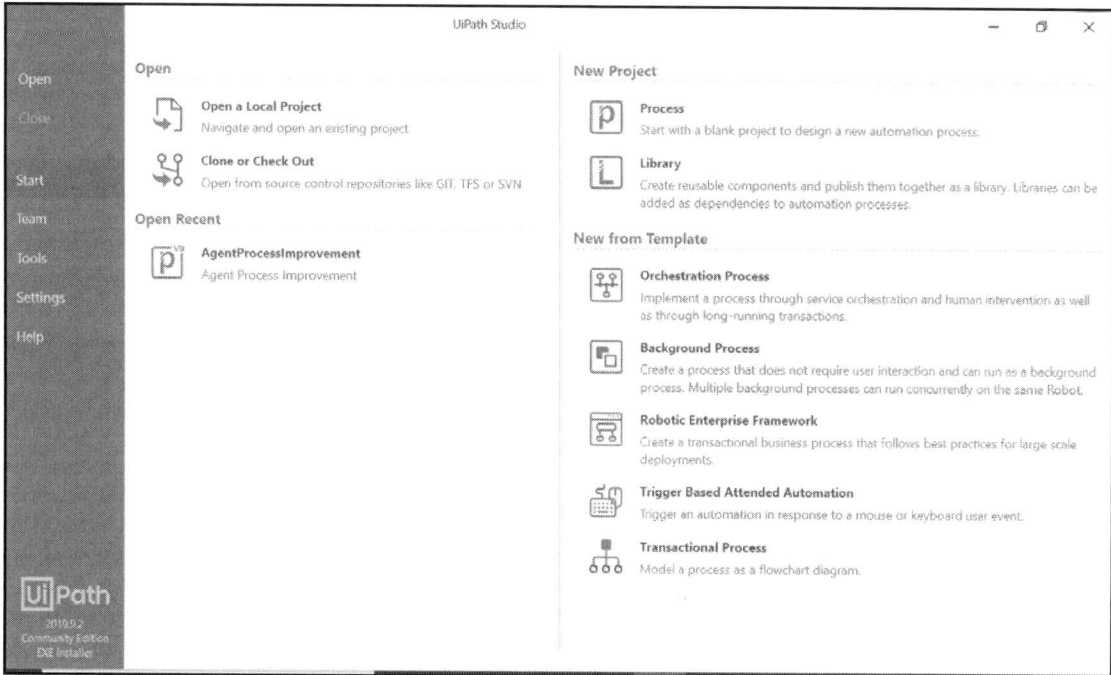

You can also create your custom components if the Activity that you need is not available. All these Activities enable you to create bots that automate processes. When you have many bots, you can manage them with an Orchestrator.

UiPath Orchestrator

Orchestrator, as the name suggests, is the central place where you manage the UiPath bots.

You can deploy and keep track of all your bots from this interface:

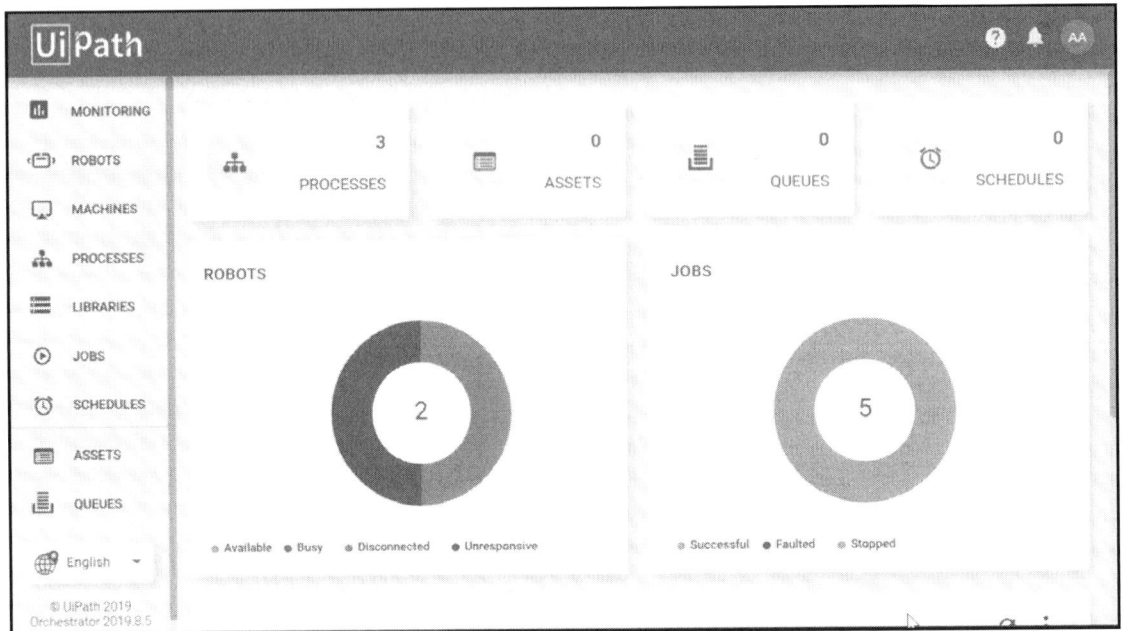

The Orchestrator is conveniently accessible through your browser and also through mobile apps. At the time of writing this book, UiPath has apps for iOS (Apple App Store) and Android (Google Play Store).

The Orchestrator allows multi-tenancy, allowing you to scale easily and enable discrete departmental RPA initiatives. The bottom line is that you can build your first bot and scale up to thousands of bots with this architecture.

UiPath Robot

UiPath Robot is your runtime executable and allows you to run workflows built using Studio. It runs on your local machines and can be accessed from the Windows Tray:

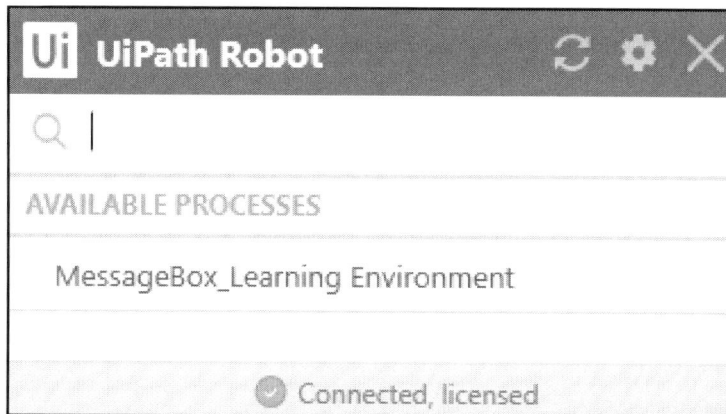

Robot can be run with or without people's supervision – attended or unattended, as we saw earlier. These robots need to be connected to UiPath Orchestrator to execute processes or you have to license them locally. The license you choose determines the capabilities of the robot.

UiPath – an integrated view

The UiPath components we described previously work together to provide you with a rapid development environment where you can create your automation projects. Here is an integrated view of how these components work together to build, deploy, execute, and monitor both attended and unattended automation:

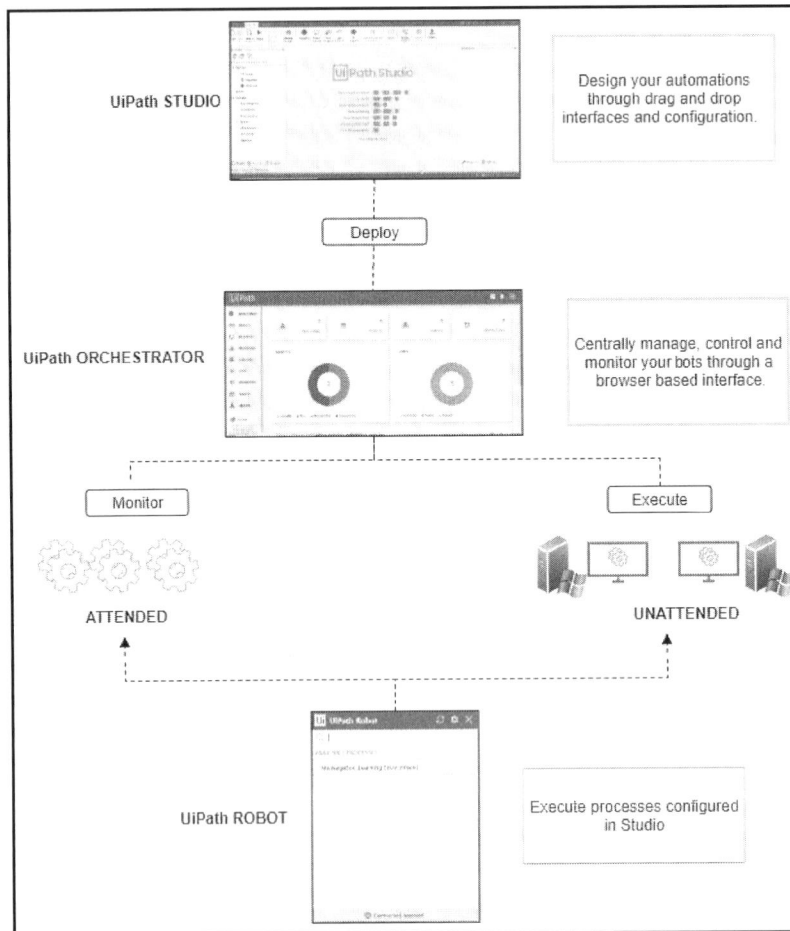

UiPath is an easy-to-use RPA tool that is easily accessible to developers through its Community Edition. Next, we'll look at Automation Anywhere, which is another top platform in the RPA space. We will be completing a few projects with Automation Anywhere A2019 as well.

Automation Anywhere

Automation Anywhere is another top RPA tool. It has a good depth of functionality and features while being mostly user-friendly. You can get started fairly quickly and scale easily with this decently robust tool.

Automation Anywhere started in 2003 with a vision to replace manual scripting applications with process automation that could be designed by the user. Their focus was to support all aspects of automating business processes, including end-to-end processes.

Fast forward to today, and the current version of Automation Anywhere, known as A2019, can be deployed on the cloud or on-premise. It has a web-based Control Room where you can develop and deploy bots. The Control Room connects to a bot agent on your Windows desktop to execute the automation process. We will be using the A2019 cloud-based Community Edition for our projects.

Let's have a look at the primary components of A2019.

Enterprise Control Room

Automation Anywhere's Control Room is a central place where you can develop, configure, and monitor your bots using a collection of specialized web-based services. Here is a screenshot of the Community Edition Control Room that we will be using:

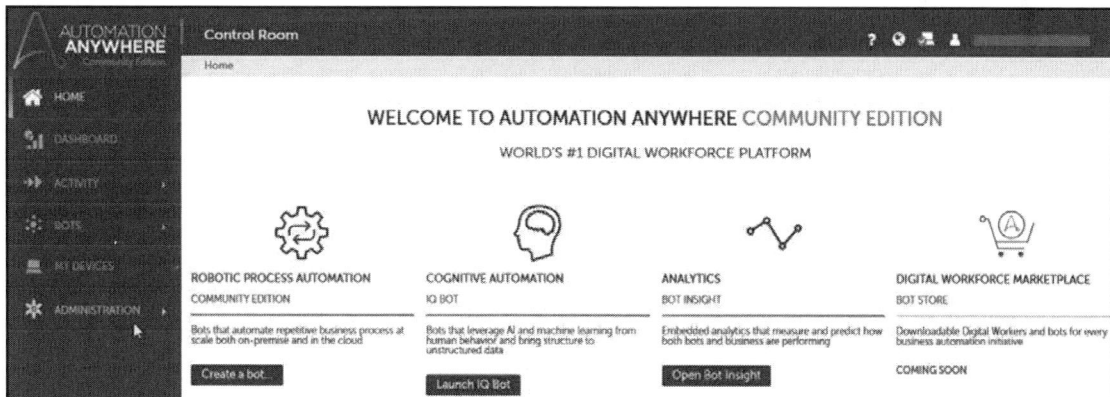

The Control Room connects to a local bot agent to run your bots. It is a plugin that can be installed on your computer that accesses the Control Room.

The Control Room provides us with the ability to build, manage, and analyze bots. Let's look at each of these aspects.

Build

Automation Anywhere's web-based Control Room can be used to create and edit bots from anywhere you have access to a web browser. You can access the bot editor from the Control Room by navigating to the **My bots** section, as shown in the following screenshot:

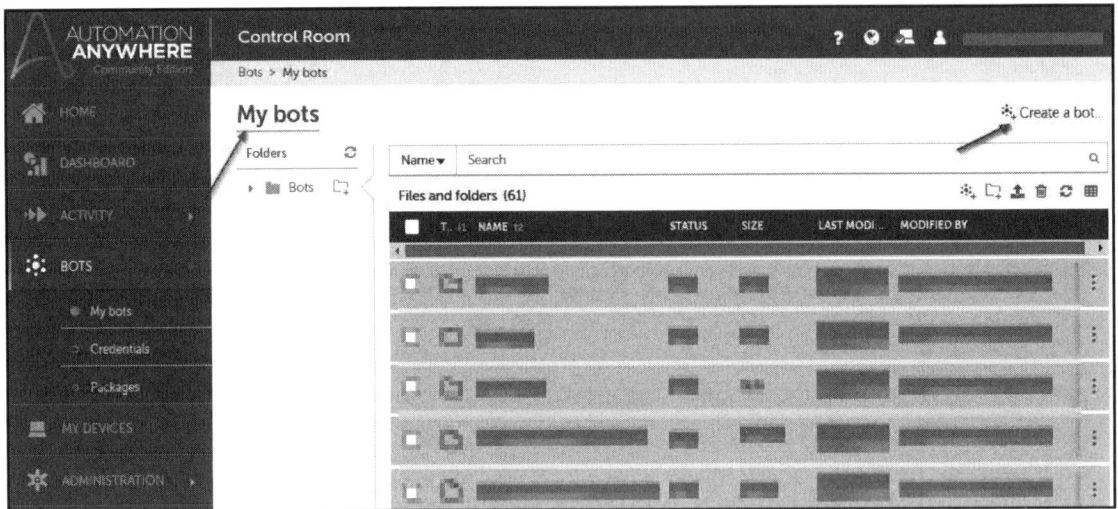

You can also manage your usernames and passwords securely using the **Credentials** option. The packages that you can use to develop your automation are listed under the **Packages** option. Next, let's explore the **My Devices** and **Administration** tabs.

Manage

You can also configure your client machine and users using the Control Room.

The client machine that you use to connect to the Control Room to create or run your bots is called Devices. You can manage these devices from the **My Devices** option. In the Community Edition that we are using, we can run one bot agent, as shown in the following screenshot:

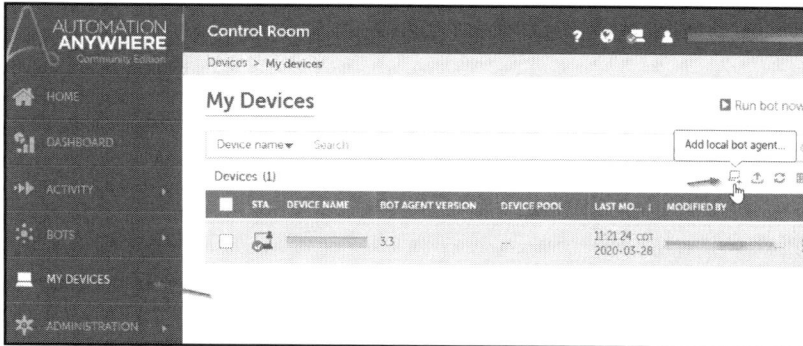

Enterprise administrators can manage various aspects such as databases, the credential vault, users, roles, packages, licensing, and so on using the Control Room. In the Community Edition that we will be using, we can only view registered users. If you'd like to find out more about the Enterprise Control Room features, visit the Automation Anywhere website at `automationanywhere.com`.

Analyze

You can analyze the performance of your bots with the help of Automation Anywhere Bot Insights. This option, which can be found in the Control Room, provides real-time and interactive insights into your automated business processes:

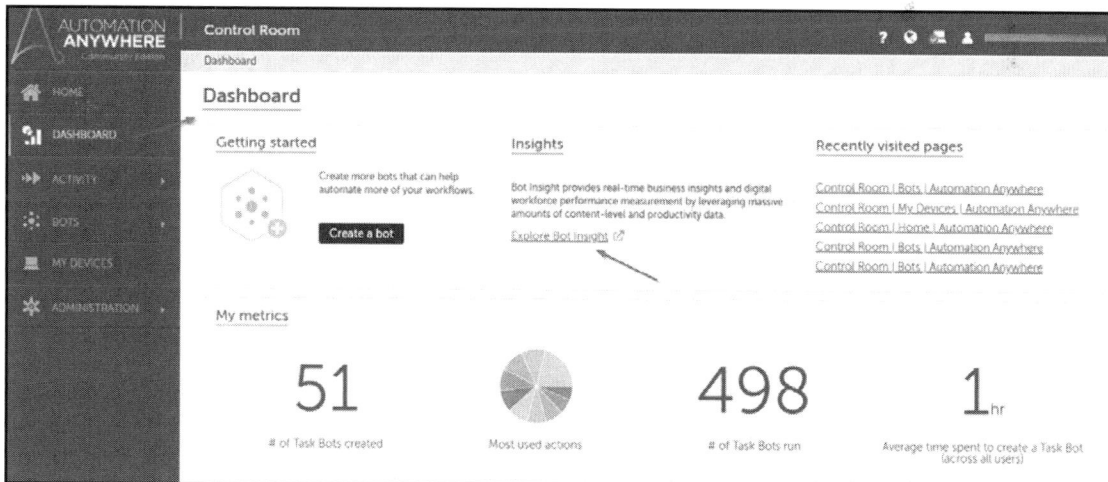

You can explore the **Explore Bot Insight** option from the Control Room for your bots once you have deployed a few of them.

Automation Anywhere also offers an AI-based bot option called IQ Bot. Let's have a quick look at that.

IQ Bot

Automation Anywhere's IQ Bot uses different AI techniques such as computer vision, **natural language processing** (**NLP**), and **machine learning** (**ML**) to digitize semi-structured or unstructured data. This means it can help us extract data from documents, forms, images, and emails.

We will be using IQ Bot in one of our projects, so you'll get a more in-depth understanding of it by the end of this book.

With that, we have provided an overview of both UiPath and Automation Anywhere. Now, let's have a quick look at what we will be doing together.

Our projects

We have many use cases that we can automate with RPA. Usually, processes that have a lot of tedious manual work are ripe for RPA automation. We have identified nine use cases or projects that we will be completing as part of this book. These projects are as follows:

- Helpdesk ticket generation using UiPath
- CRM automation using UiPath
- Moderating social media using AI with UiPath
- Purchase order processing with UiPath's RE framework
- Completing an RPA challenge with UiPath and Automation Anywhere
- Sales order processing with Automation Anywhere
- ERP user administration with Automation Anywhere
- Employee emergency notifications using Automation Anywhere
- Using AI and Automation Anywhere for invoice processing

These projects are in the order they will be covered in this book, and go from being simple to more complex. It is our endeavor that you should be able to replicate these projects easily.

We have chosen tools with free community versions and a growing community so that you can implement and get help for these projects. Even the supporting software such as ERP, Helpdesk, and so on have free versions available for you to download.

While we have used SaaS software with Freemium versions for these projects, the licensing terms may vary based on location and other conditions. Make sure you through the licensing conditions carefully before using them.

Also, as you probably know, there are many more RPA tools out there. You may find that some are better than UiPath and Automation Anywhere for certain situations. For example, Blue Prism is a very widely used tool and one of the most robust ones around. You may want to explore this RPA tool too, depending on your interest and need.

Now, as the first step to completing our RPA projects, we're going to install and set up our RPA tools.

Installation and setup

In this section, we will go through the step-by-step installation and setup of UiPath and Automation Anywhere. This will enable us to configure and run the projects in this book.

Before we get into the installation process, ensure that you have the hardware and software specified in the *Technical requirements* section, which can be found at the beginning of this chapter.

Installing UiPath

In this section, we will walk you through the steps you need to follow to install UiPath Studio and Robot. We will be using the Community Edition for our projects, so the installation process we'll follow will be for that version.

UiPath Community Edition has an auto-update feature, which means it's automatically updated to the latest version. While there may be some changes, the setup and concepts that will be covered in this book's projects should still be applicable to future versions.

UiPath Studio and Robot

Follow these steps to install UiPath Studio and UiPath Robot:

1. First, go to the UiPath website (`https://www.uipath.com/`) and find the link to access the Community option.

2. Choose the **Always free** community option from the available choices.
3. You will be asked to sign up with UiPath. If this is your first time registering, you may be asked for a few more details before you can sign up.
4. Once you've signed up, you should be on the UiPath Portal, as shown in the following screenshot. Click on the **Resource Center** in the left-hand panel and download the **Community Edition**:

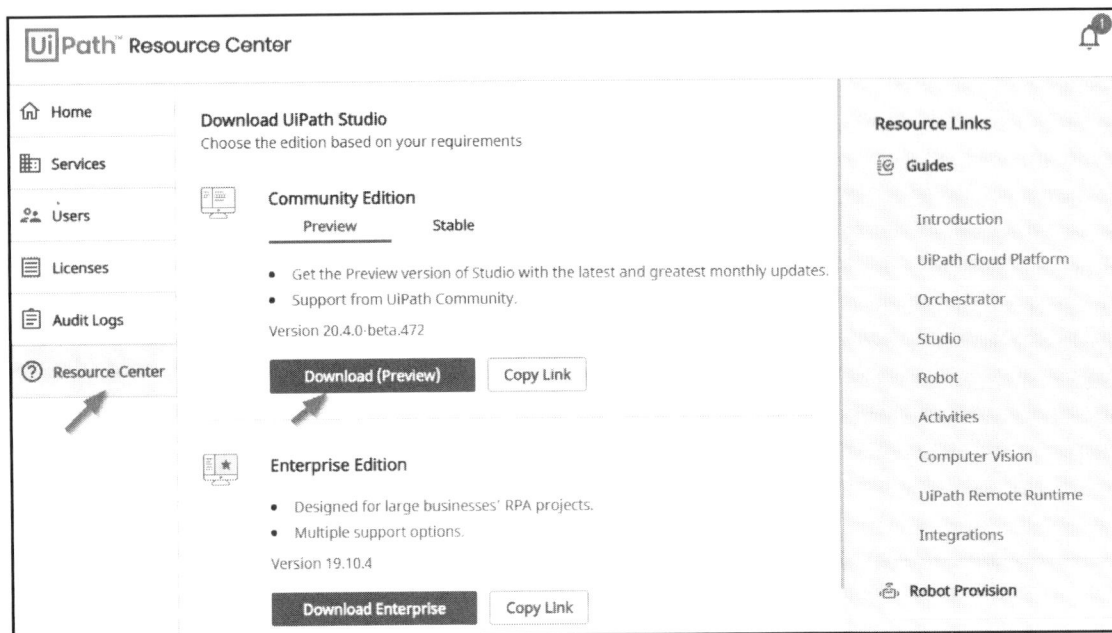

5. Download the latest version of UiPath **Community Edition** (**CE**) from the Resource Center. Note that we are downloading the **Community Edition** and not the **Enterprise Edition** since our purpose is to learn.
6. The executable setup file should start to download. Once the file has downloaded, locate it in your downloads folder and run it by double-clicking it.
7. UiPath will take a few minutes to complete the installation, depending on your system configuration. UiPath Studio should automatically launch after the installation is complete.
8. At the top of Studio, there should be a pop-up license screen. On that screen, click on **Activate Community Edition**. Note that the licenses for both UiPath Studio and Robot will be activated:

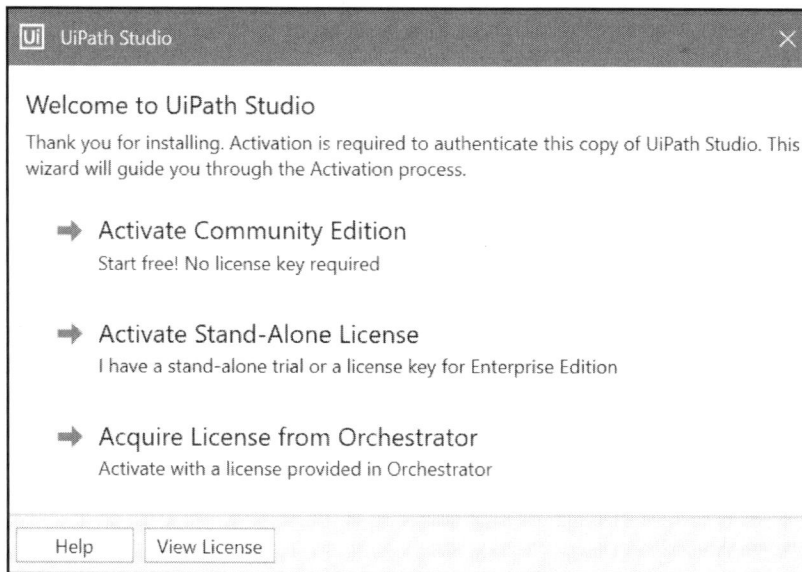

9. The installation process will open the browser and indicate that **UiPath was successfully activated on your computer**.

> **TIP**
>
> Please check for UiPath Studio and UiPath Robot in your Windows programs. If you're unable to find UiPath Studio and/or UiPath Robot in your programs, restart the machine and try to rerun the `UiPathStudioSetup.exe` file.

Congratulations! Your Community Edition of UiPath Studio and Robot is ready for use. Studio is where we will configure projects, while Robot is where we will execute the automation.

Next, we will learn how to install Automation Anywhere A2019.

Configuring Automation Anywhere

We will be using Automation Anywhere A2019 Community Edition for our projects. Let's learn how to access and configure the Control Room for our projects.

Registration and setup

Let's register and activate A2019 community Edition trial account. To do that, follow these steps:

1. Go to the Automation Anywhere website at `automationanywhere.com` and find the **Community Edition.**
2. Sign up for it by providing your details, such as name, email, and so on.
3. You should receive an email from Automation Anywhere with the details you can use to access the Control Room. Look for the **Control Room URL** and the credentials in the email:

Control Room URL: https://community.cloud.automationanywhere.digital/
Username: a⬛⬛⬛⬛⬛⬛⬛⬛⬛u
Password: ⬛⬛⬛⬛⬛9-

4. Click on your **Control Room URL** in the email. This should open your personalized Control Room in the web browser.
5. Log in to your Control Room using the username and password from the email. When you access the Control Room for the first time, you will need to change your password.
6. Once you've logged in, you will be on the home page of the Automation Anywhere Control Room. With that, you are all set to build and run your automation with A2019.

You should get a prompt to build your first bot. You can follow along with that to verify the setup.

Installing the bot agent and verifying the setup

Let's create a simple first bot to complete the setup process:

1. Click on **Create a bot...**, as shown in the following screenshot, and provide a name for the bot:

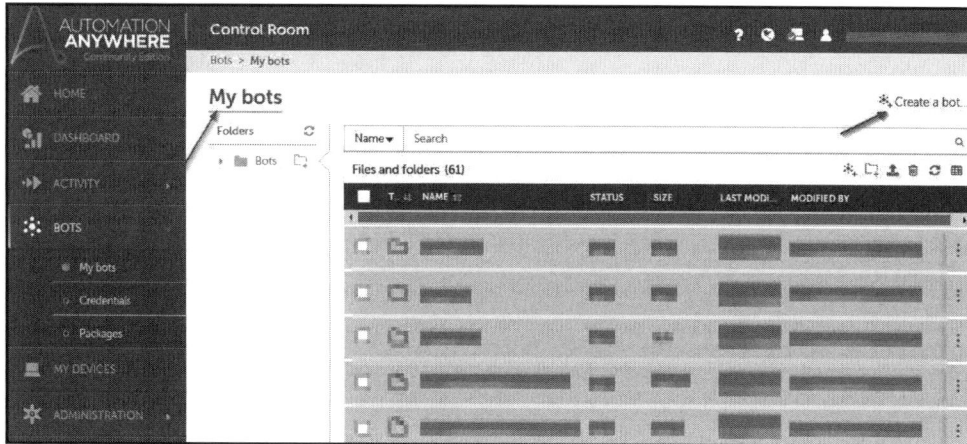

2. On the development canvas that comes up next, search for **Message box** in the **Actions** search box. Drag and drop this action in-between the **Start** and **Stop** buttons. Update the message that you wish to display and click **Apply** and **Save**, as shown in the following screenshot:

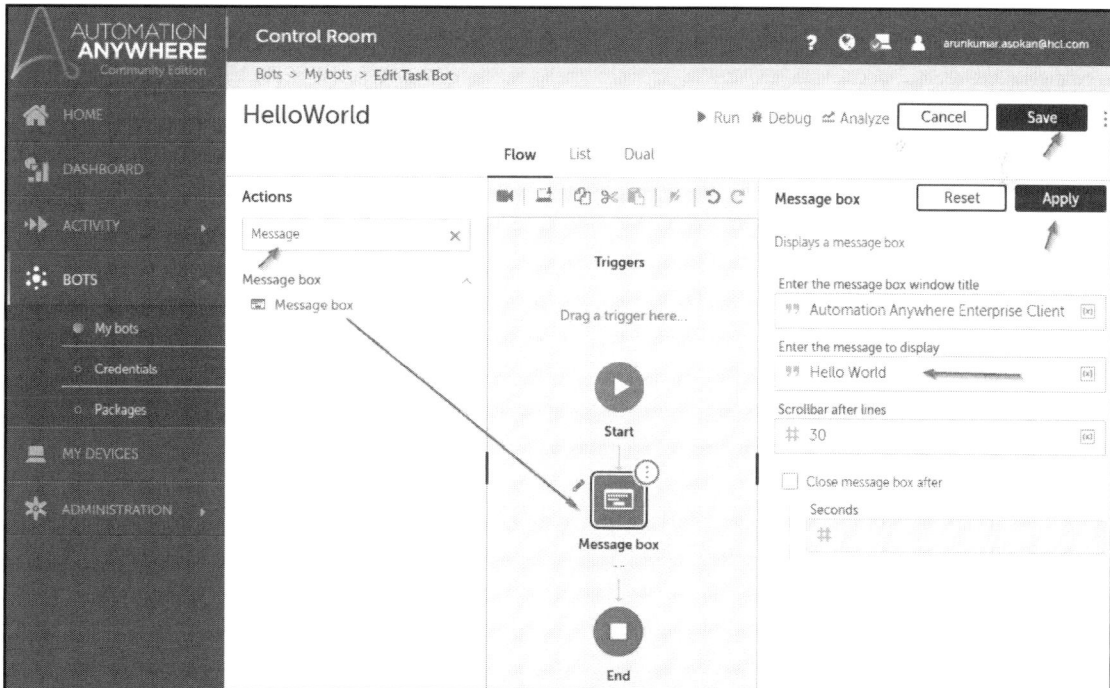

3. Click on **Run** in the top menu to run the bot. At this stage, the bot needs to connect to your local computer to execute the automation. As this is the first time you're doing this, you'll be prompted to install the bot agent. Go ahead and save the executable and run the installable file. The installation process should be quick and will be followed by a prompt where you can enable the browser extension.

4. Once this process is complete, A2019 automatically detects the agent and the Chrome extensions. It connects to your computer and runs the automation. You should now see a message box with the message you added.

When you go to **My Devices**, you should see that your device is now connected. This is indicated by a green checkmark. If not, you can use the **Add local bot agent** option, as shown in the following screenshot, and follow along to add the bot agent:

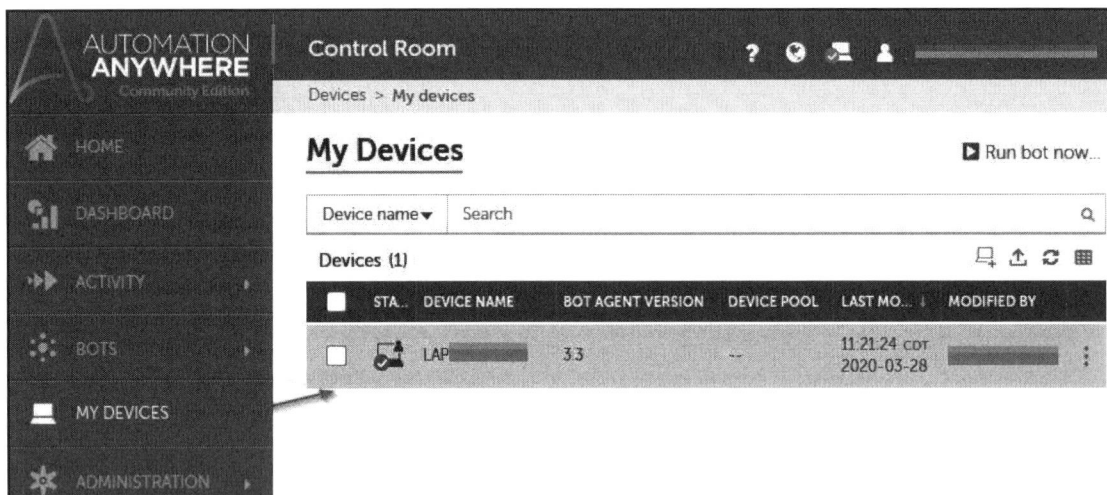

That completes the setup for A2019. We will be using this for the A2019 projects later in this book.

Before we start our exciting journey, let's quickly recap the first chapter.

Summary

RPA excels at automating manual and repetitive tasks. It is a capability that allows software robots to carry out tasks on a computer, just like a human would.

We saw that there are two types of RPA – one runs on your desktop and the other runs on a server. Most of the top tools give you the capability to implement both types of RPA. We looked at two of them – UiPath and Automation Anywhere – both of which we will be using for our projects.

UiPath is one of the easiest RPA tools with a comparatively low learning curve. This is why we have selected UiPath as one of the tools for our projects in this book. It has three main components: UiPath Studio, UiPath Orchestrator, and UiPath Robot.

Automation Anywhere is another top RPA tool and the latest A2019 community edition is cloud-based. We can create and deploy bots with a web browser. With the Control Room, we can build, manage, and analyze our bots.

Finally, we installed and set up the Community Editions of UiPath and Automation Anywhere. It's time to get started with our projects. Sound exciting?

In the next chapter, we'll get started with an Attended Automation Helpdesk project with UiPath.

Help Desk Ticket Generation 2

Let's get started with our first project – a simple help desk automation with UiPath.

Help desk agents get inputs from a variety of channels, including phone, email, and spreadsheets, to create and update support tickets. Support tickets are the requests that you raise by calling help desk agents to get your issues resolved; for example, your laptop is not working, or you have internet issues.

For this project, we will only be covering the automation of inputting tickets from spreadsheets that a requester places in a certain folder. We are assuming a very simple use case of ticket creation for this first project. All you have to do in this project is to input support ticket data in a spreadsheet and place it in a folder. The bot, once invoked, automatically creates a support ticket within the help desk system for you.

If you noticed, we are invoking this bot. This means that we will be building an attended automation that behaves like an assistant – an assistant that raises tickets automatically!

This project will help you understand the following topics:

- Attended RPA concepts
- UiPath Excel automation
- UiPath automation for web-based apps
- Creating automation workflows and invoking them
- Using `Try` and `Catch` for exceptions

Technical requirements

The hardware and software that will be required for this project are as follows:

- A PC with UiPath Community edition version 19+ installed (we covered the hardware relating to installation in `Chapter 1,` *Getting Started with RPA*).
- A Chrome browser with a UiPath add-on.
- A Zoho Desk SaaS application. You can sign up for free at `https://desk.zoho.com`.
- Microsoft Excel 2007 and later.
- Check out the following video to see the Code in Action: `https://bit.ly/36gX89C`.

You can find the code files present in this chapter on GitHub at `https://github.com/PacktPublishing/Robotic-Process-Automation-Projects/tree/master/HelpdeskAgentAttendedAutomation`.

Project overview

We will automate the creation of help desk tickets using data from an Excel sheet.

In this project, once the bot is invoked, it will check whether there are new request files available to process. If available, the bot will read the ticket data from this spreadsheet. The data is then used to create support tickets in the Zoho Desk application.

Here is the high-level workflow for the project:

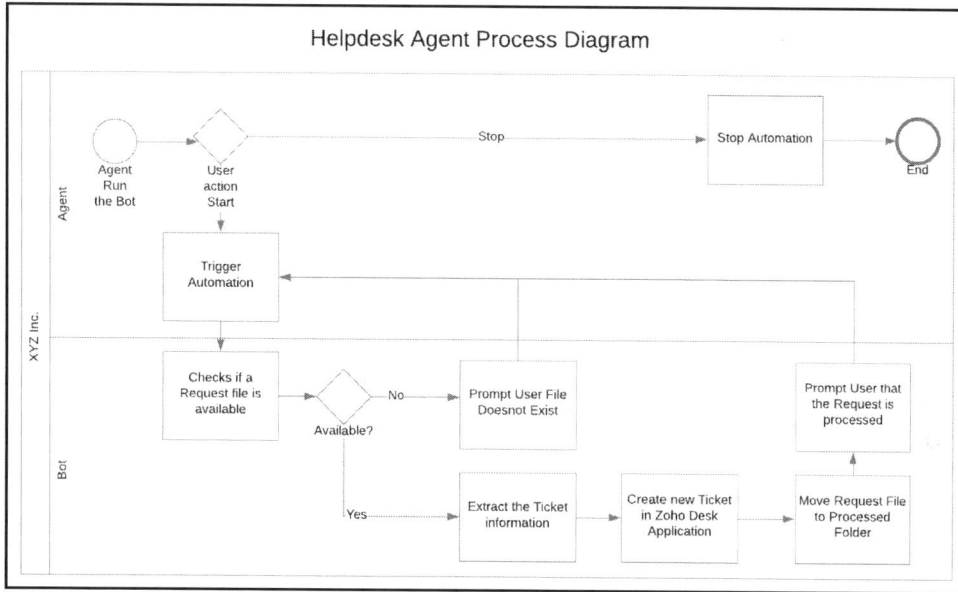

We believe it should take you around **1 hour** to build and run this first project. Obviously, the amount of time it will take will vary depending on your background.

Now, let's dive into the details and step through the creation of the automation.

Project detail

Let's now look at the overall flow for this project in terms of the components we will be building and their interaction.

We will have a main workflow called `Main.xaml`, which will invoke other workflows and orchestrate the automation. Within this workflow, we will keep checking for the trigger *Alt + S*. Once triggered, we will check whether the `Request.xlsx` file is available. If the file is available, then we will invoke `ReadRequestExcel.xaml` from `Main.xaml`.

Within `ReadRequestExcel.xaml`, we will use the file path as an input argument to open the Excel file, read the content, and store it in three output arguments – `Name`, `Email`, and `Subject`.

Next, `Main.xaml` invokes `ZohoAutomation.xaml` with these three arguments (`Name`, `Email`, and `Subject`) to create the ticket in the Zoho desk. If all goes well, a `Successful` message is returned.

Finally, once the `Successful` message is received, `request.xlsx` is moved to the `Processed` folder and the bot is ready to process new requests:

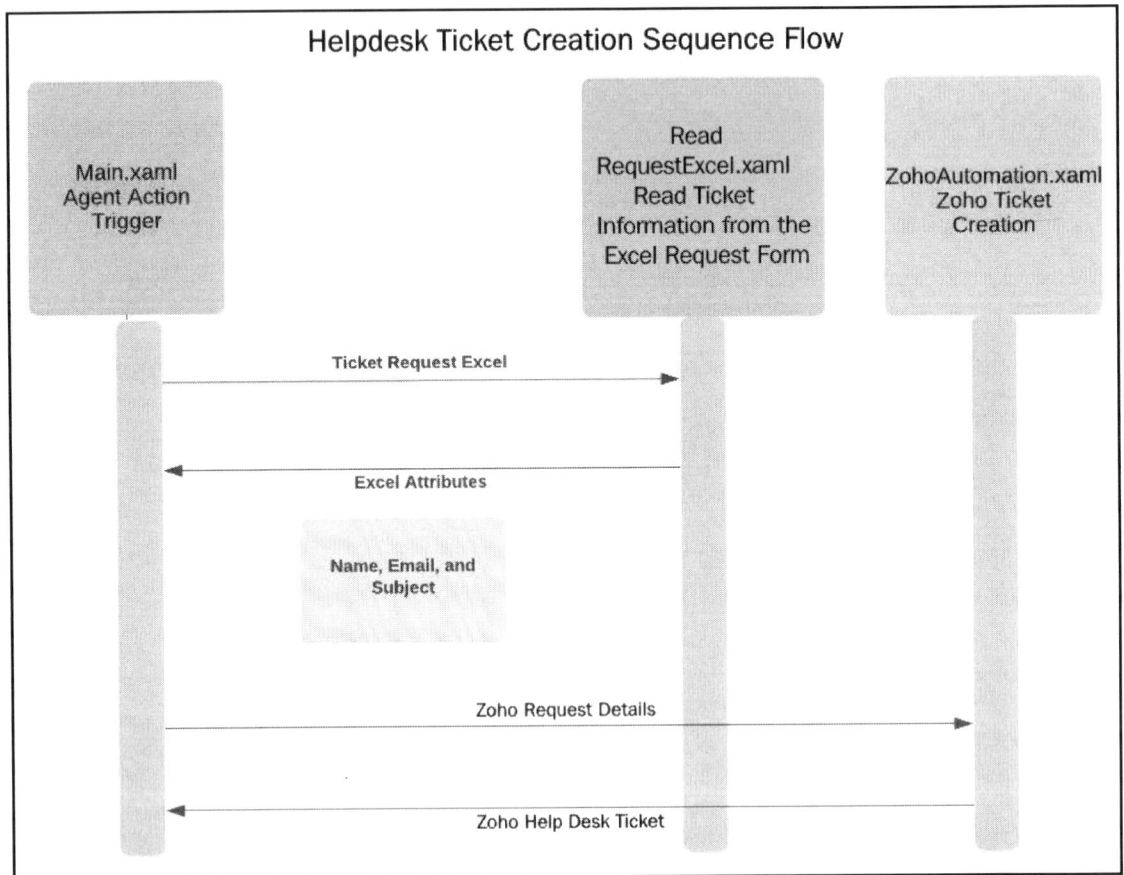

This was an overall flow to give you a high-level view of what we will be doing to create this automation.

Before we configure our main workflow, let's undertake some groundwork that is required for the project.

Project groundwork

As part of the project groundwork, we will create the project folders, along with a spreadsheet for the ticket data, and also log in to the Zoho SaaS application.

Creating project folders

Let's create two folders, one to accommodate the spreadsheet containing the data to process, and the other to accommodate the processed spreadsheets:

1. Open Windows Explorer on your machine and create a folder for the project.
2. Within this project folder, create two folders, called Requests and Processed, as shown in the following screenshot:

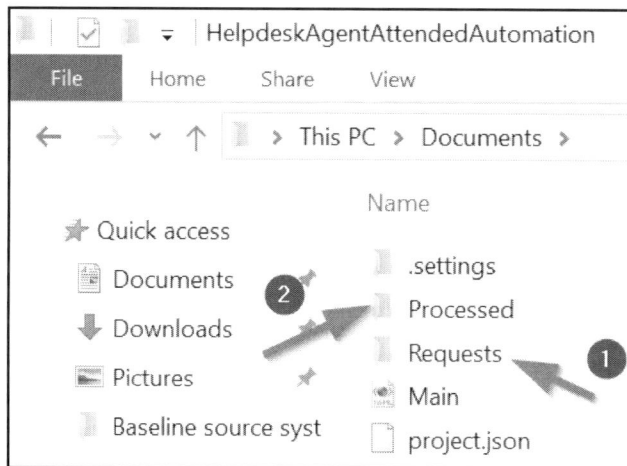

We will place the spreadsheet in Requests, and then the bot will move the processed sheets to the Processed folder.

Next, let's create the requests spreadsheet.

Creating an Excel sheet with ticket data

Now, let's create a simple spreadsheet with ticket data:

1. Open Excel and create a sheet with three rows and two columns, as shown in the following screenshot:

The first column contains the data labels, and the second column contains the data you like for your support ticket.

2. Save this file as `Request.xlsx` in the `Requests` folder that we created in the previous section.

Let's now log in to the Zoho application.

Registering and logging in to Zoho Desk

Perform the following steps:

1. Go to `desk.zoho.com` and choose the option to log in. You should be directed to a page to log in or sign up if you do not have an ID. Create a free desk account by filling in the details if you do not have one:

2. Once you register with your details and company name, you will be walked through the steps to get started. You should eventually end up on the Zoho Desk view with the current tickets:

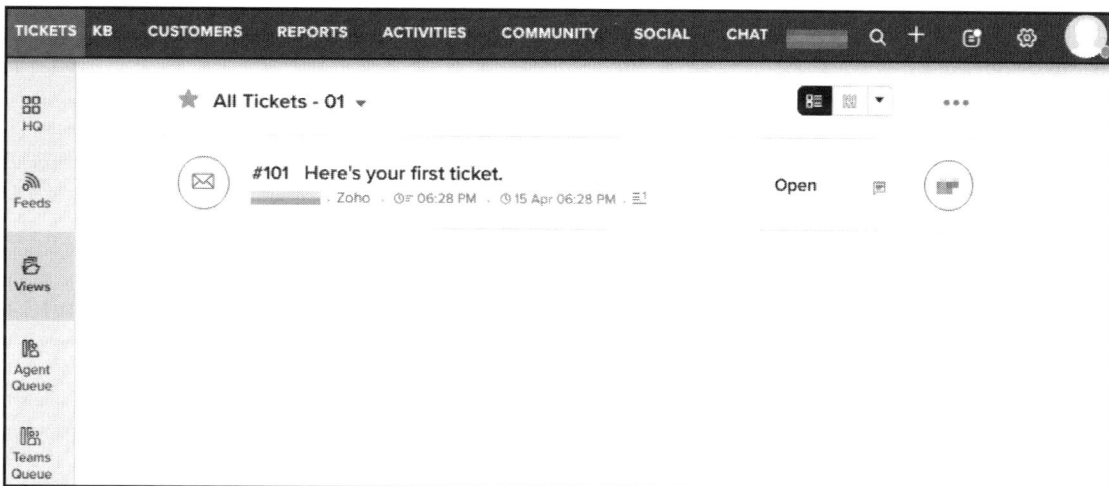

Leave the tab open with the application logged in for the automation.

That was all the project groundwork we needed to implement.

Now, as mentioned in the *Project detail* section, we will create the workflows for the automation. Let's start with the main workflow.

Main workflow

Let's start by opening the UiPath Studio. This is one of the UiPath components we installed in Chapter 1, *Getting Started with RPA*. On your Windows machine, you can go to **Start** and then select **UiPath Studio**.

Project setup

Let's create a new project for our automation using the UiPath template:

1. On the first UiPath studio screen that pops up, select the project called **Trigger Based Attended Automation**. This will use a predefined UiPath template to create an attended automation project:

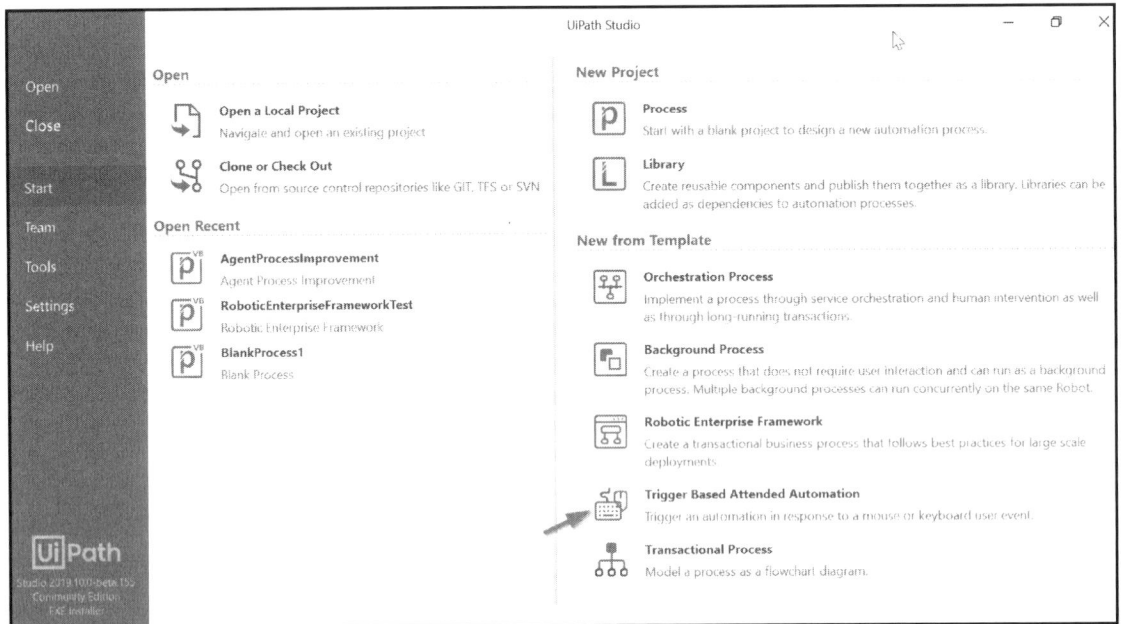

2. Next up, provide a name for your project and an optional description and click on **Create**:

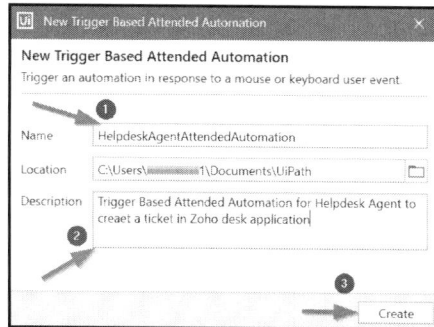

3. On the Studio main screen, click **Open Main Workflow** to get to the main workflow.
4. Your initial workflow should look like the following. Go ahead and remove the five unwanted activities highlighted in the following screenshot by right-clicking and selecting **Delete**:

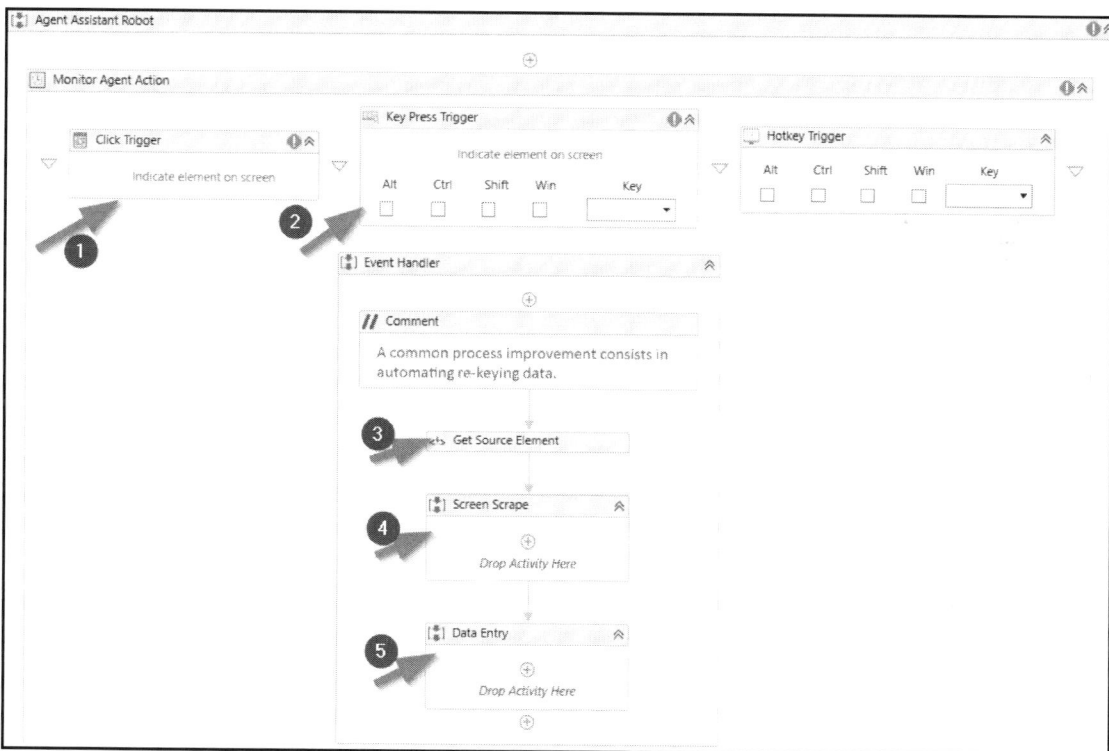

5. Once done, ensure that you save the project and keep doing so periodically.

The project is now set up. We are now ready to configure the initial part of the automation.

Configuring the initial part of the main workflow

We will add a few UiPath activities to initiate the attended automation.

> UiPath activities are puzzle pieces that we use to create any UiPath automation. The activities are automation actions, such as clicking, typing, and message box. We can use these activities to create with Excel, email, and the web.

Let's now look at the steps to add the activities:

1. We'll start by adding a message box. To do this, go to the **Activities** panel and search for message box:

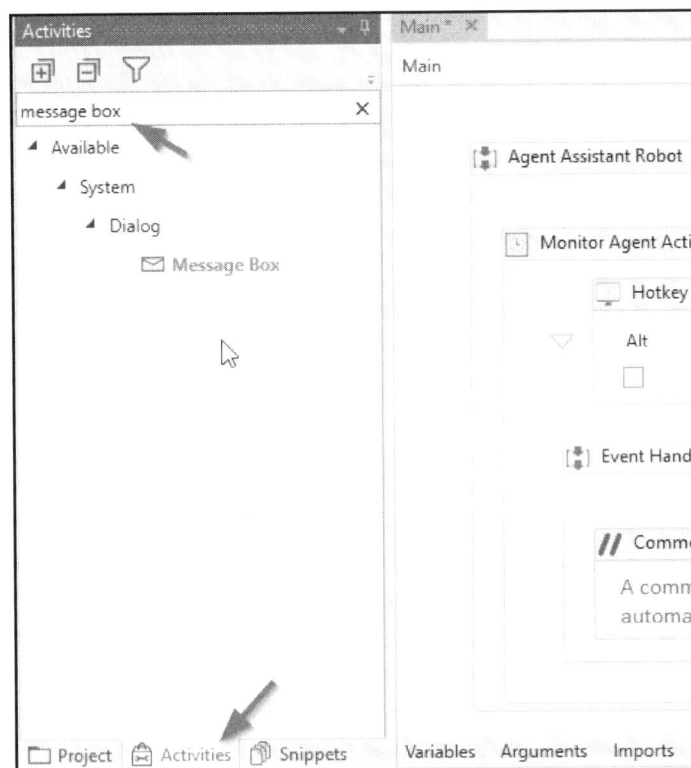

You can then drag and drop the activity to where you want it in the workflow.

2. Once added, click on the box for the message and type `"Agent Ready. Please use ALT + s to trigger the Automation"`. Note that you must keep the quotes as you input the message. Please refer to the image in step 4.

3. Next, let's tell UiPath which hotkey we will use to trigger the automation. Luckily, UiPath has provided the activity within the template to do just that. In the **Hotkey Trigger** activity, choose **Alt** and type in *s* for the key, as shown in the screenshot in *Step 4*.

4. It is always a good idea to add adequate comments for people to facilitate understanding of your workflow "code". Within **Event Handler**, let's start by adding a **Comment** to say `Create a Zoho desk Ticket from the Request excel file.`:

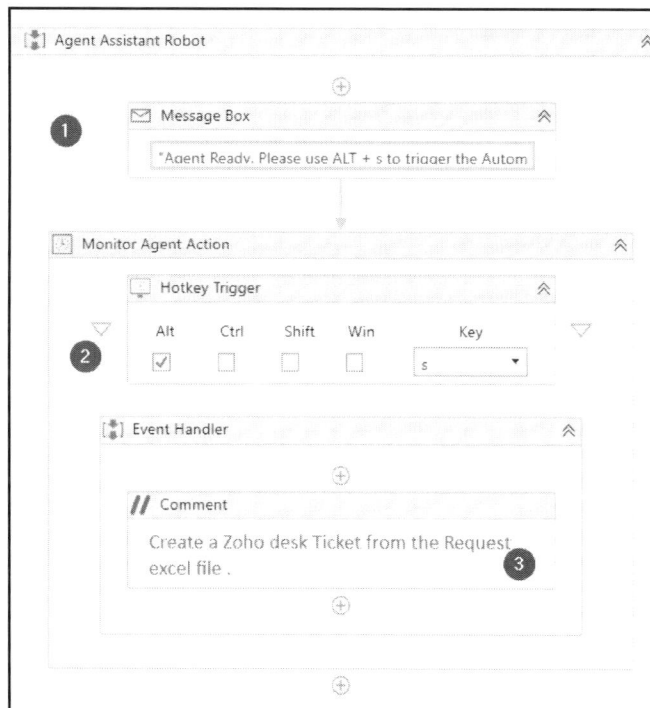

5. As the first activity in **Event Handler**, we will be checking the `Requests` folder to see whether there are any new requests. For that, we will use the **Path Exists** activity. Follow the same steps as before to find the activity in the left-hand panel and drag and drop to the main workflow.

6. Now, for this and all activities, there are UiPath properties that are displayed on the right pane. Let's use the following **Properties** for the **Path Exists** activity we added:

- **Path**:
  `Environment.CurrentDirectory+"\Requests\Request.xlsx"`
- **PathType**: **File**
- **Exists**: Create a `boolean` variable (use *Ctrl + K* or right-click) and create a new variable called `boolFileExists`.

UiPath properties are the parameters and settings for the selected activity. The properties pop up on the right panel of your Studio interface. You can go to the panel and add or update properties for the selected activity.

Your sequence and properties should look like this:

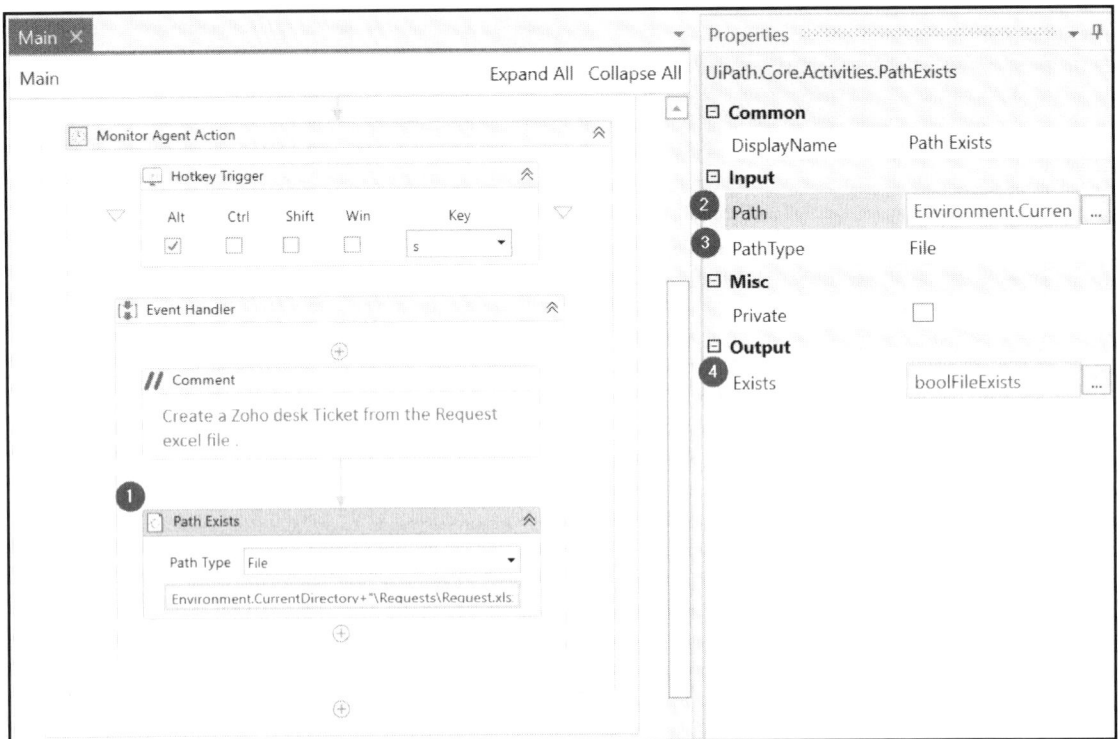

7. Next, let's display a message to let the user know whether the bot found a request and whether it will process this request. We will use an **If** activity from the activities panel to do that. Add the **If** activity below the **Path Exists** activity.

8. Let's use `boolFileExists`, which we created in the earlier step as the condition to check. Within this **If** control, add two messages boxes with messages as per the following screenshot to display an appropriate message to the agent:

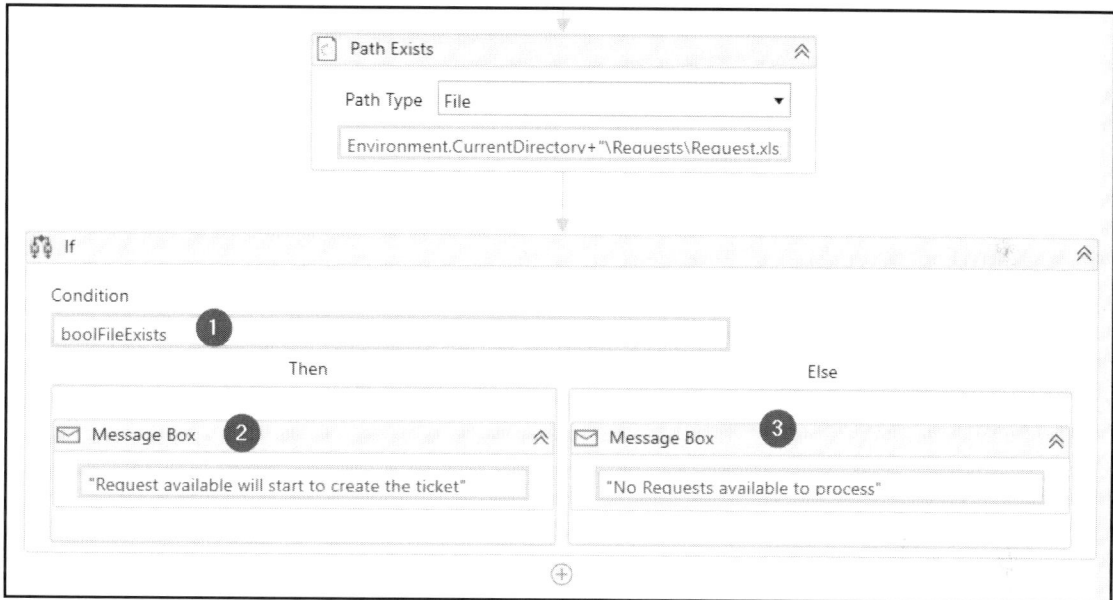

This is all for the main workflow for now. We will revisit the workflow later to call the `ReadExcelRequest` and `ZOHOAutomation` workflows, which we will create in the next two sections.

Reading from Excel

In this next workflow, we will pick up the `Request` Excel file from the folder we created, read the ticket data, and incorporate them in variables for the next workflow to process. This will help you get your feet wet with Excel-based automation:

1. Let's start by creating a new **Sequence** in the project. This will create a new workflow for us to work on:

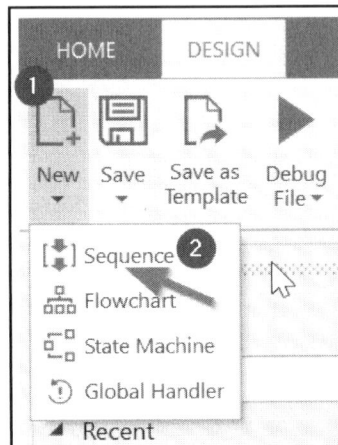

2. Let's name it `ReadExcelRequest` and click **Create.** The studio will create a default sequence for you:

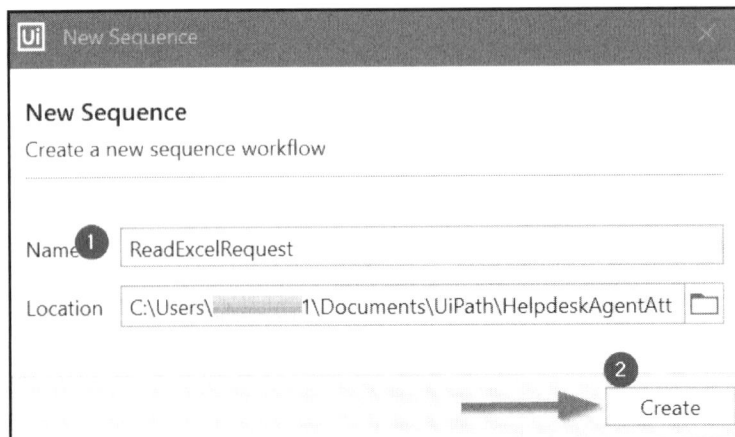

3. Within the workflow, let's first add the arguments using the **Arguments** tab at the bottom of Studio (refer to the following information box). **Arguments** will enable us to input and output data from this workflow to the main workflow. Proceed and create four arguments, as shown in the following screenshot:

Name		Direction	Argument type	Default value
RequestFilePath	1	In	String	*Enter a VB expression*
ContactName	2	Out	String	*Default value not supported*
Email	3	Out	String	*Default value not supported*
Subject	4	Out	String	*Default value not supported*
Create Argument				
Variables Arguments Imports				🖑 🔎 100%

Note **Direction** and **Argument type**.

The difference between a variable and an argument is that variables pass data to other activities, while arguments pass data to other workflows. The **Arguments** tab is next to the **Variables** tab at the bottom of the Studio screen.

4. We will always use a `Try-Catch` block to handle any exceptions gracefully. So, let's add the **Try Catch** activity to this sequence. Then, within the **Try** block, add the **Read Range** activity under Workbook to read the specified Excel file. The **Read Range** activity reads the value of a specified Excel range and stores it in a **DataTable** variable.

5. For the **WorkbookPath**, specify the `RequestFilePath` argument that we added in step 2. This argument should be populated with the path to `Requests.xlsx` when we invoke this workflow from **Main**. Your sequence and properties should look like this:

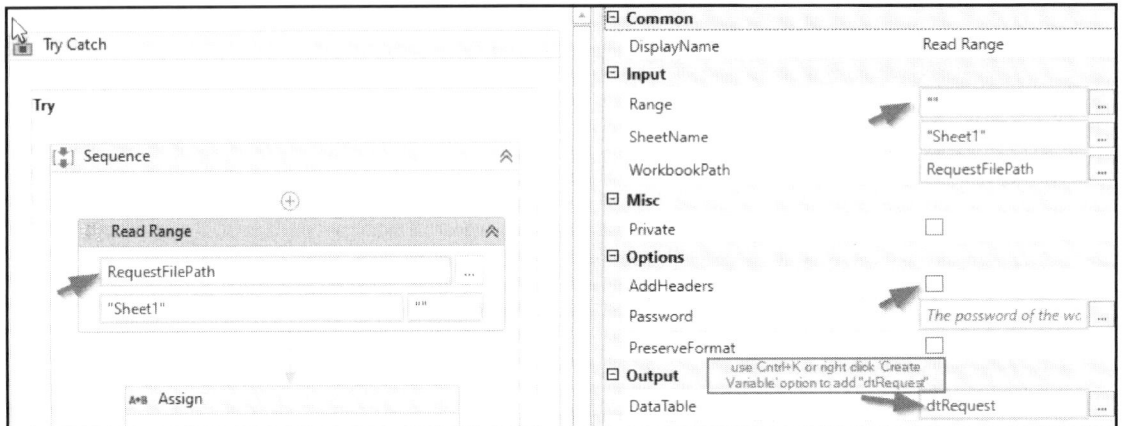

In the properties for the **Read Range** activities, perform the following steps:

- Remove the range to cover the entire sheet. To do that, add "" to the **Range** property on the right pane.
- While there, uncheck the **AddHeaders** property as we don't have header in our input file.
- Add an **Output** variable to store the data table. Use *Ctrl + K* to add the `dtRequest` variable within the **DataTable** property.

6. Next, we will use three **Assign** activities in the workflow to read from Excel and store the data for `ContactName`, `Email`, and `Subject` in respective arguments.

7. Use the arguments we just created on the left-hand side of the activity. You can start typing the argument names and the argument names should pop up for you to select:

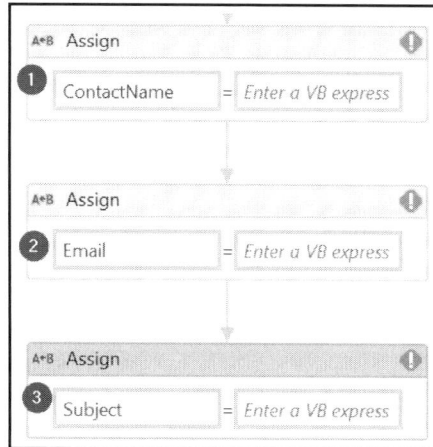

8. We will use the `dtRequest.Rows(row)(column)` data table to read Excel values and map them to the arguments. For example, `dtRequest.Rows(0)(1)` means the first row and second column value in Excel. Since the output variable only accepts the values of the `String` type, we have to add `.tostring` at the end of this formula; for example, `dtRequest.Rows(0)(1).ToString`:

9. After the **Assign** activities, add a **Log Message** activity to update the Excel read options in the system logs. This will help us to debug the workflow if needed:

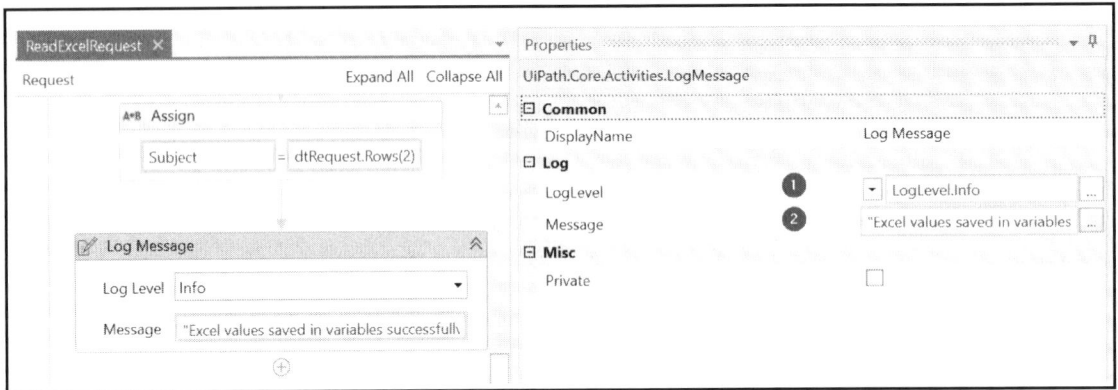

That completes our **Try** block sequence. We will now add exception handling to the **Catches** block.

Exception handling

Let's handle any exceptions for this Excel automation:

1. For this, click on **Add a new Catch** in the **Catches** block beneath the **Try** block.
2. Choose **exception** as `System.Exception` and click the box next to it.

3. Also, add a **Log Message** activity to the catch block and add the following:
   - **Error** as the **Log Level**
   - "Error in Excel read operation with following exception: "+exception.Message" as the **Message**:

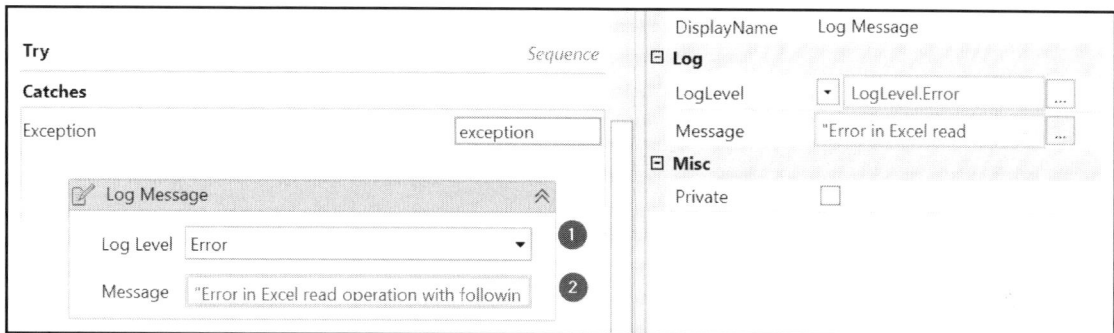

Try		Sequence
Catches		
Exception		exception

Log Message		⋀
Log Level	Error	▼ ❶
Message	"Error in Excel read operation with followin	❷

DisplayName	Log Message	
⊟ **Log**		
LogLevel	▼ LogLevel.Error	...
Message	"Error in Excel read	...
⊟ **Misc**		
Private	☐	

4. Finally, within the **Catches** block, add a **Terminate Workflow** activity to stop the automation if there are any exceptions:

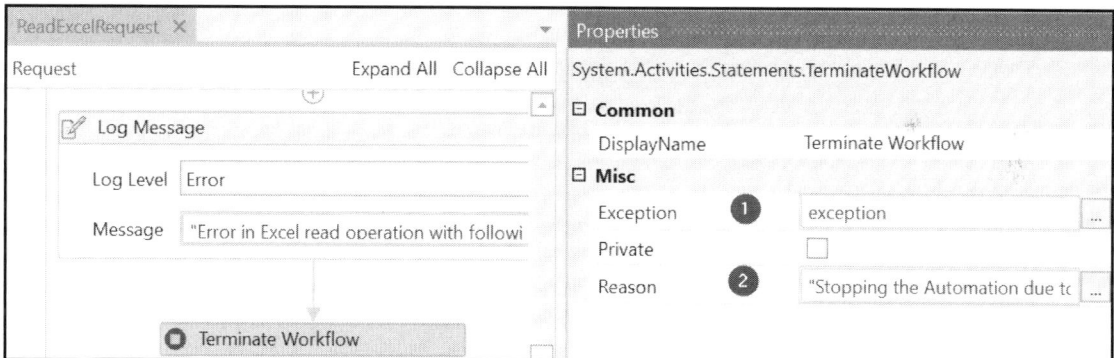

ReadExcelRequest ✕		▼
Request	Expand All	Collapse All
	⊕	▲
Log Message		
Log Level	Error	
Message	"Error in Excel read operation with followi	
	▼	
⦿ Terminate Workflow		

Properties		
System.Activities.Statements.TerminateWorkflow		
⊟ **Common**		
DisplayName	Terminate Workflow	
⊟ **Misc**		
Exception ❶	exception	...
Private	☐	
Reason ❷	"Stopping the Automation due to	...

Great! This completes the ReadExcelRequest workflow where we read the Excel and stored the request data as arguments. Now, we will invoke this from the main workflow.

Invoking the Excel workflow from Main

Let's now go back to the Main sequence to invoke this newly created `ReadExcelRequest` workflow. If you recall, we added a message within the main workflow if there are requests available to process. Let's invoke the read Excel workflow right after that:

1. Let's add the **Invoke Workflow File** UiPath activity in the **Then** block of the **If** control:

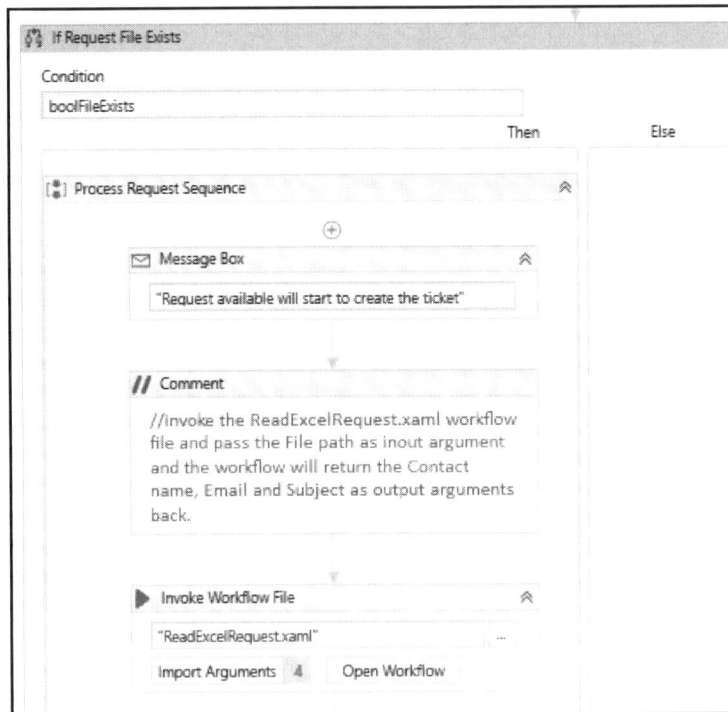

2. Let's populate this new activity with the `ReadExcelRequest` workflow path. To do that, click on the three dots on the right of the first parameter. Select the `ReadExcelRequest.xaml` file in your project folder:

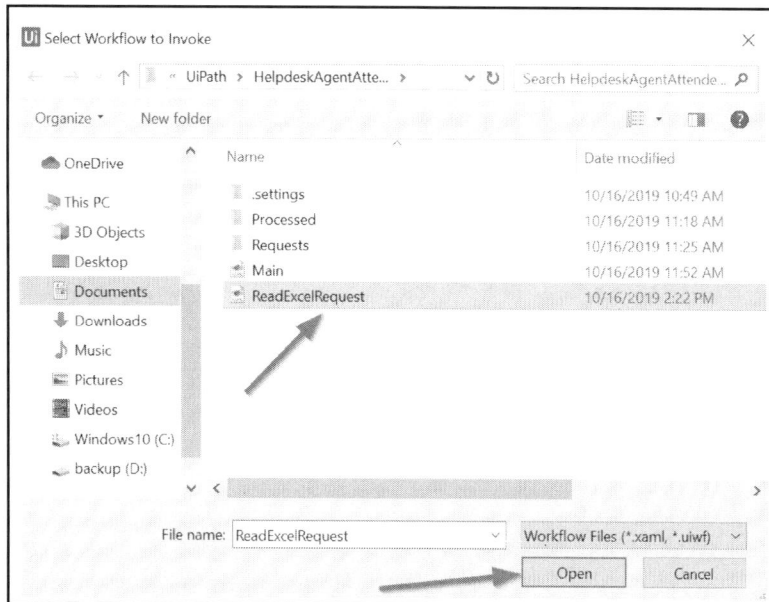

3. Now, let's create three new variables to store the data that we would get from the ReadExcelRequest workflow. Go to the **Variables** pane at the bottom of Studio and add variables for contact name, email, and subject, as shown in the following screenshot:

Name		Variable type	Scope
EditableText		UiElement	Event Handler
boolFileExists		Boolean	Event Handler
strContactName	①	String	Sequence
strEmail	②	String	Sequence
strSubject	③	String	Sequence

Note **Variable type** and **Scope** and ensure that you match what is shown.

> Naming convention: Please use descriptive names for variables and arguments to enable easy understanding. We recommend that variables follow camel case, with the standard prefixed with the type of variable, for example, boolFileExists. Arguments can follow Pascal case; for example, ContactName.

4. If you recall, we had a few arguments in the `ReadExcelRequest` workflow to pass data back to **Main**. Let's now pass data by clicking on **Import Arguments** and mapping the data. For that, within the **Invoked workflow's arguments** window, let's perform the following steps:
   - Populate `RequestFilePath` with the path to the file: `Environment.CurrentDirectory+"\Requests\Request.xlsx":`

Invoke Workflow File		"No Requests available to process."
"ReadExcelRequest.xaml"	...	
Import Argum		

Invoked workflow's arguments

Name	Direction	Type	Value
RequestFilePath	In	String	*Enter a VB expression*
ContactName	Out	String	*Enter a VB expression*
Email	Out	String	*Enter a VB expression*
Subject	Out	String	*Enter a VB expression*
Create Argument			

- Map the new variables we added previously to the respective argument value:

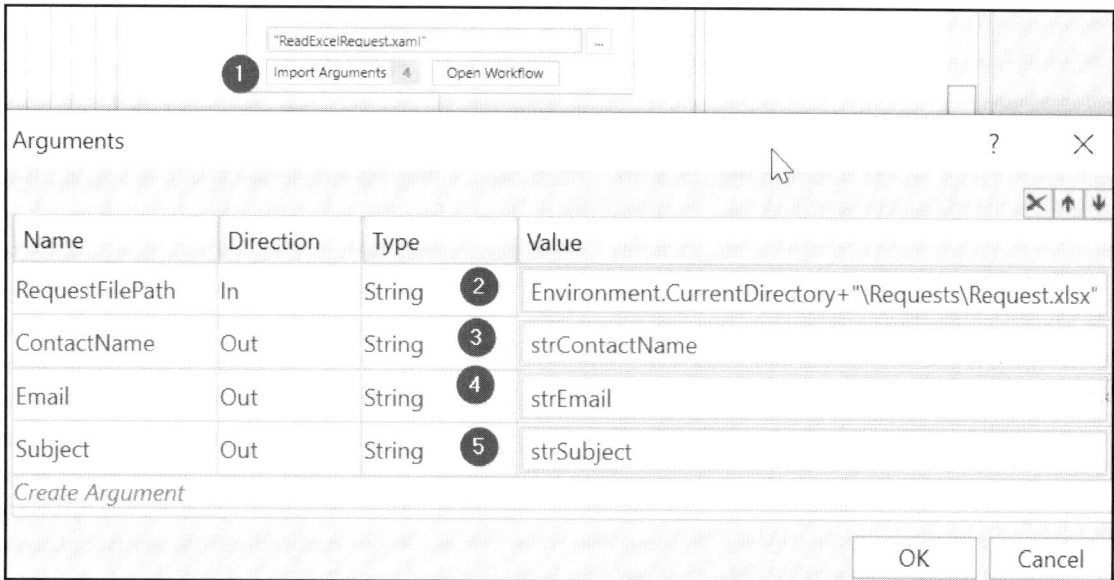

5. Since this is a learning exercise, let's add a message box to display **ContactName**, **Email**, and **Subject** for us to establish whether the bot got it right:

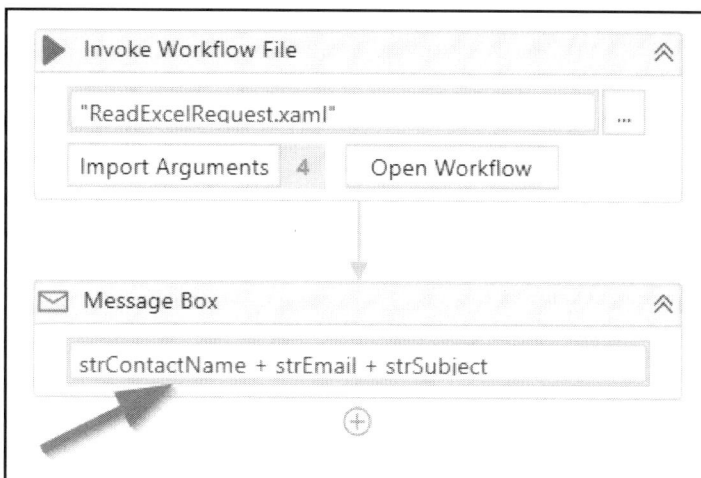

6. Let's now perform a quick test of the workflow so far. Click on **Run** to run this main workflow. Please ensure that your Excel file is closed before you run the workflow:

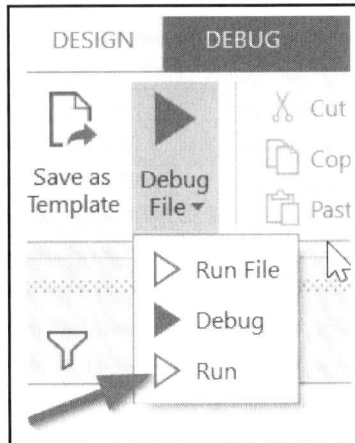

You should get the initial message that we added: `Agent Ready. Press` *`Alt + s`* `to` `trigger Automation.` Click **OK** on this message box to acknowledge and press *Alt + S* to start the bot. Next, you should get the second message that there is a `Request` file to process and so to proceed with ticket creation. Finally, when it runs successfully, we can expect the message box with the name, email, and subject content that we added in the steps we just completed.

Automation will always continue to run by default. Therefore, please click on the Studio **Stop** button to stop the bot.

We have now completed the part where we read the data from the Request spreadsheet and are now ready to take this data and create our support ticket. Let's go!

Creating a support ticket in the Zoho Desk ticketing system

In this final workflow that we will create for this project, we will use the data read from the `Requests` file to create the support ticket within Zoho Desk. This will help us understand how we can automatically input data into web applications through web application screens. Let's perform the following steps:

1. We'll start by creating another sequence for Zoho web app automation. You can call it `ZOHOAutomation`:

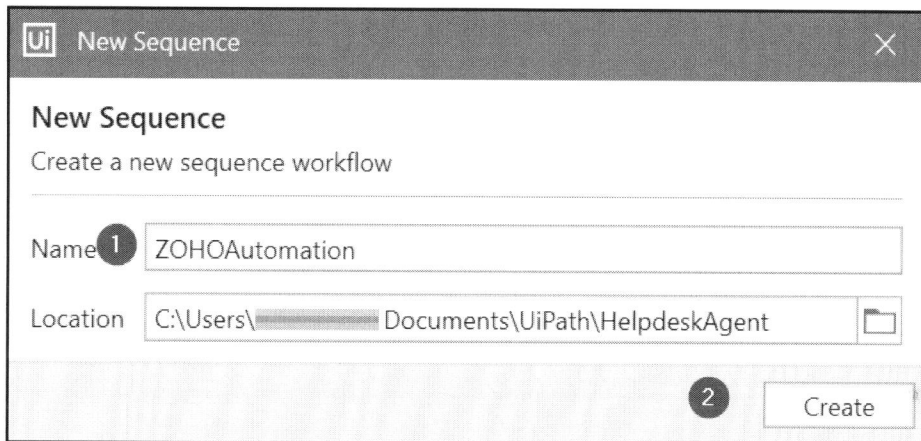

2. Within the UiPath default workflow, let's add a **Try Catch** activity. Let's also add four arguments, as shown in the following screenshot, to pass the data around:

Name		Direction	Argument type
ContactName	1	In	String
Email	2	In	String
Subject	3	In	String
Successful	4	Out	Boolean

Ensure that you match **Direction** and **Argument type**.

3. Next, we will use the UiPath web recorder to record the steps to enter the Ticket data in Zoho and create a new ticket. First, go to your Chrome browser and ensure that the Zoho Desk home page is open in one of the tabs. Also, ensure that you have installed the UiPath add-on for Chrome in your Chrome browser. It is available on the Chrome App store.

> UiPath has a recorder that allows you to record mouse clicks and keyboard sequences to automatically generate UiPath scripts. You can also add these activities by yourself, but the recorder is a much faster way to create these sequences. Hence, we like to show you how you can do it.

4. Click within the **Try** block and activate the web recorder by clicking on the **Web** recorder option within **Recording:**

5. UiPath opens a web recording panel to control the recording. Click on the **Record** button with the Zoho Desk browser tab open:

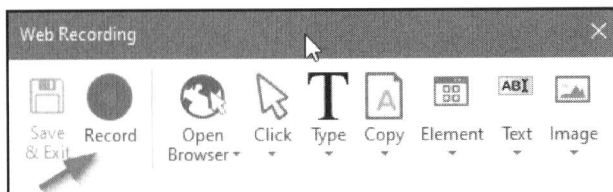

Now that we have the recording set up and ready, let's record the actions to create a ticket in Zoho.

Recording ticket creation activities

On the Zoho desk browser tab, perform the following actions to enable the UiPath recorder to record:

1. Click on the + symbol to create a new ticket (at the top right of the Zoho desk screen):

2. On the new **TICKETS** screen, type a contact name followed by the *Enter* key on your keyboard:

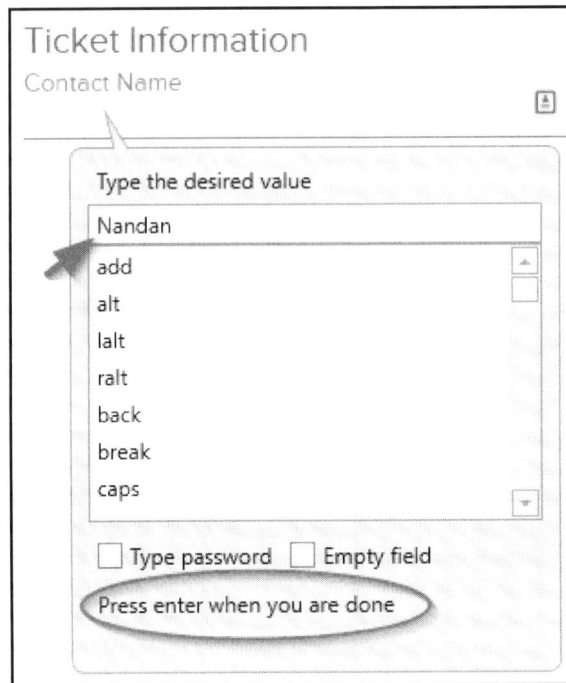

Ticket Information
Contact Name

Type the desired value

Nandan

add

alt

lalt

ralt

back

break

caps

☐ Type password   ☐ Empty field

Press enter when you are done

3. Similarly, type an email followed by the *Enter* key.
4. Type a subject followed by the *Enter* key.
5. Click on the **Submit** button on the Zoho **Add Ticket** screen.
6. Once you perform all the preceding steps, use the Windows *Esc* key to stop the recording. Then, click on **Save & Exit** on the UiPath web recording panel.

7. You may occasionally find the recorded steps outside the **Try** block. Move the recorded activity into the **Try** block if that is the case. Your workflow should look like the following:

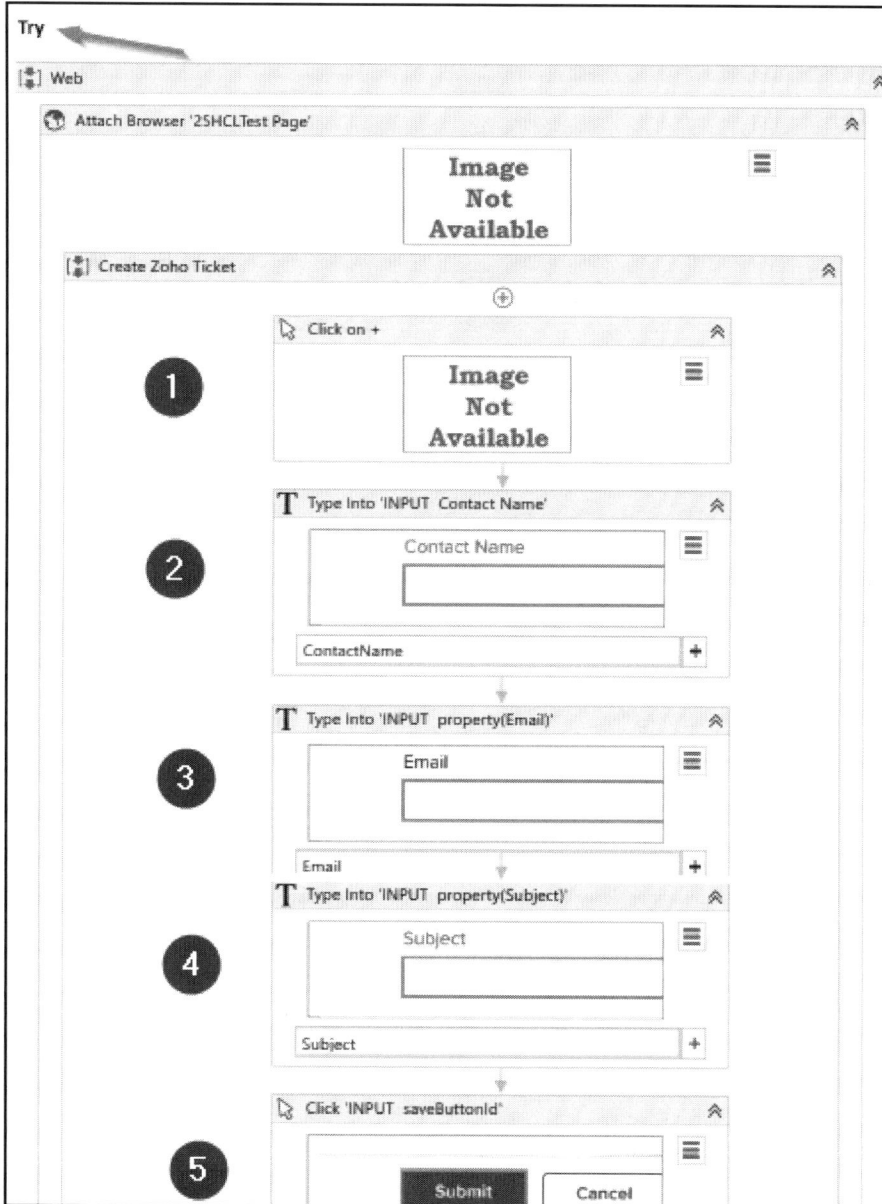

Now that we have the recorded activities, let's configure them for our automation.

Configuring the recorded activities

We will now update the recorded activities as required to complete the ticket data input. Let's start with the browser title name:

1. You can see that the recorder has created an **Attach Browser** activity. This uses the browser title to attach to the browser tab and perform the recorded actions.

    In our case here, the browser title is dynamic because there is a ticket number in it. So, we will need to use wildcards to attach to the browser tab. If your browser tab for the Zoho desk is "123zyx", we will just use "`*xyz*`" with wildcards on both sides.

    Wild characters: It is good practice to use wild characters such as `*` (one or more characters) or `?` (any single character) in the browser selectors if we know that the index, prefix, or postfix will dynamically change during execution.

    Since we may need the browser title in other activities, let's define a variable called `strBrowserTitle` and add this as a default value, as shown in the following screenshot:

Name	Variable type	Scope	Default
strBrowserTitle **1**	String **2**	ZOHOAutomation **3**	"*xyz*" **4**

2. Now, let's update the **Attach Browser** activity that the recorder added for us with the browser title variable. Click on the **Attach Browser** activity within the **Try** block. In the properties panel on the right, click on the option to update the **Selector**:

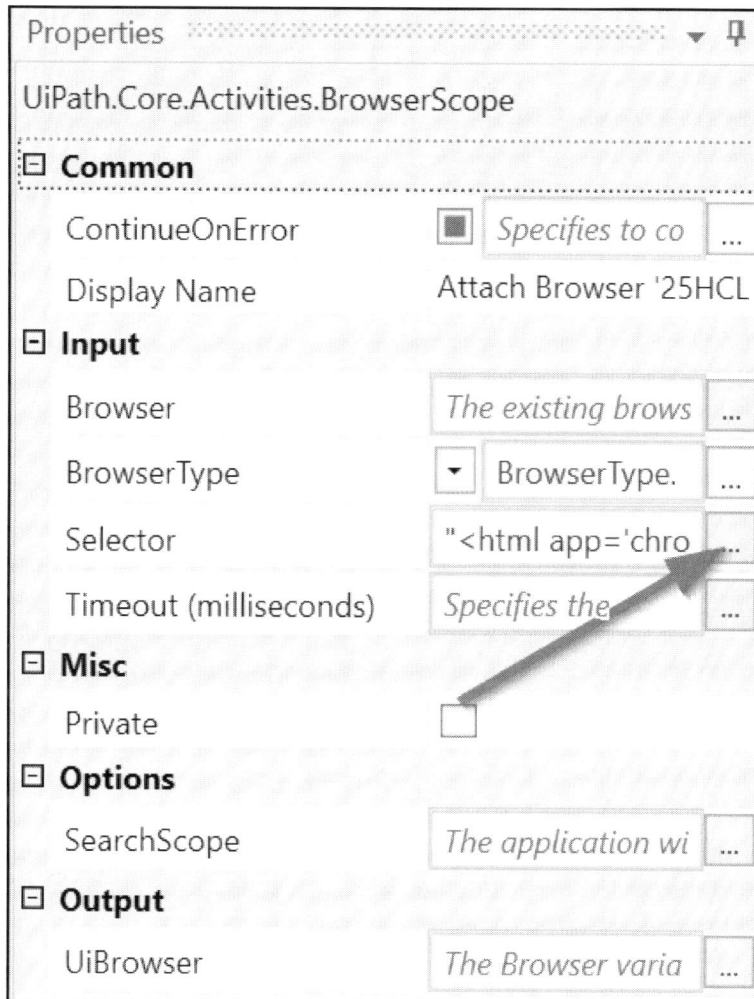

Properties		
UiPath.Core.Activities.BrowserScope		
Common		
ContinueOnError	☐ *Specifies to co*	...
Display Name	Attach Browser '25HCL	
Input		
Browser	*The existing brows*	...
BrowserType	▾ BrowserType.	...
Selector	"<html app='chro	...
Timeout (milliseconds)	*Specifies the*	...
Misc		
Private	☐	
Options		
SearchScope	*The application wi*	...
Output		
UiBrowser	*The Browser varia*	...

3. In the **Selector Editor** window that pops up, click on **title** to update with the newly created `strBrowserTitle` variable, as shown in the following screenshot:

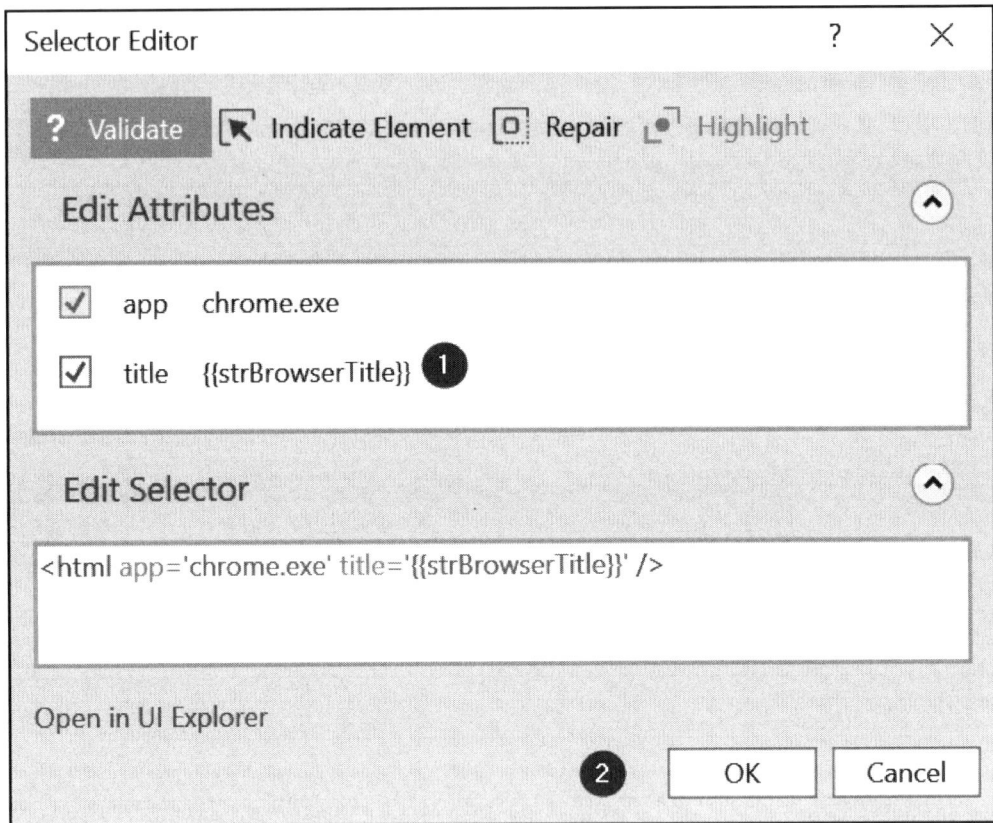

Selector Editor	? ✕
? Validate 🖈 Indicate Element ▣ Repair ⬚ Highlight	

Edit Attributes ⌃

☑ app   chrome.exe

☑ title   {{strBrowserTitle}} **❶**

Edit Selector ⌃

```
<html app='chrome.exe' title='{{strBrowserTitle}}' />
```

Open in UI Explorer

❷   OK   Cancel

4. Let's also add a new variable within the **UiBrowser** output property for the **Attach Browser** activity. We will call it `ZohoBrowser` and set its scope to **ZOHOAutomation**. We will use this variable to handle exceptions later in the workflow. You can use *Ctrl + K* to add the variable and set the scope, or you can add it directly to the variables pane in Studio:

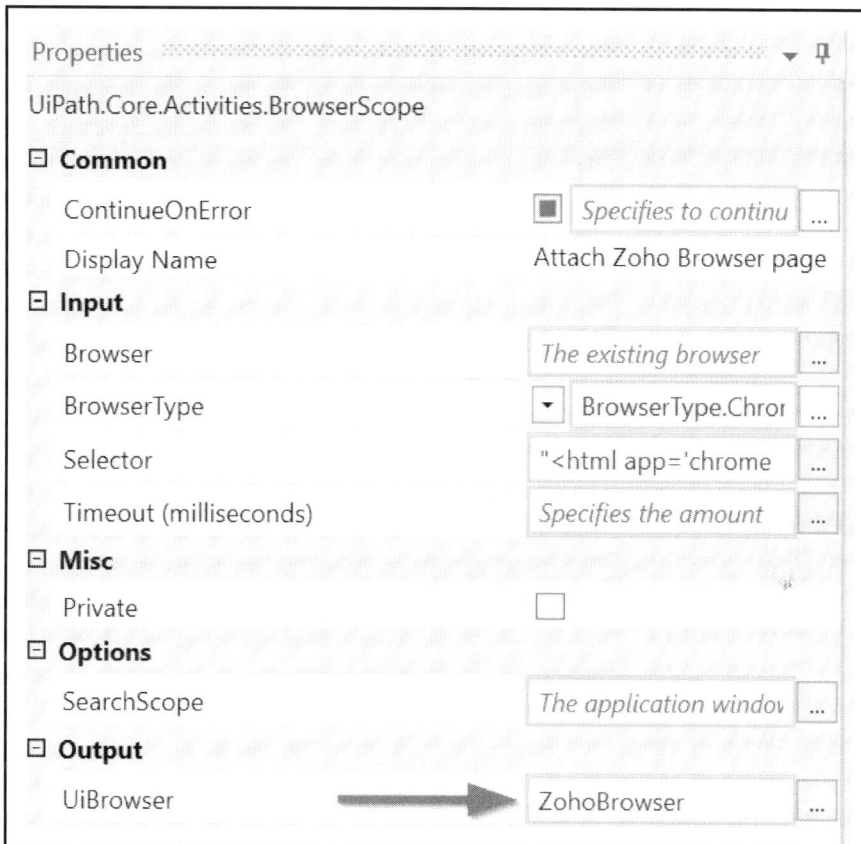

Properties	
UiPath.Core.Activities.BrowserScope	
⊟ **Common**	
ContinueOnError	■ *Specifies to continu* ...
Display Name	Attach Zoho Browser page
⊟ **Input**	
Browser	*The existing browser* ...
BrowserType	▾ BrowserType.Chror ...
Selector	"<html app='chrome ...
Timeout (milliseconds)	*Specifies the amount* ...
⊟ **Misc**	
Private	☐
⊟ **Options**	
SearchScope	*The application windov* ...
⊟ **Output**	
UiBrowser	⟶ ZohoBrowser ...

TIP

It is best practice to use a `Browser` variable when you attach the browser, so as to pass the control around during web automation. In our case, we will use this variable in the error handling sequence, as we will use the same browser session to perform error handling.

5. Next, let's activate the specific browser window by using the **Activate** UiPath activity. Add the **Activate** activity, click on **Indicate element inside browser**, and then click on the Chrome browser title. Let's also maximize the browser window if it's not already maximized. For that, let's use the **Maximize Window** UiPath activity:

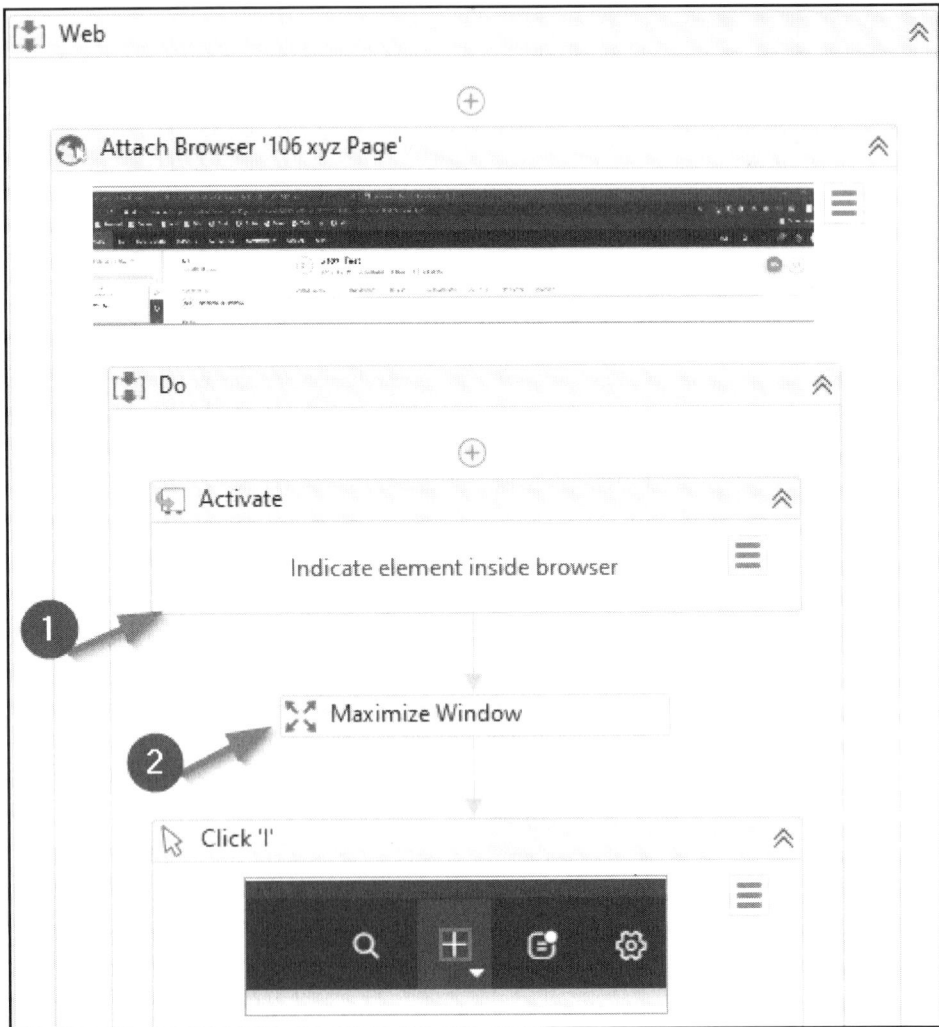

6. To pass the ticket data to the Zoho desk fields that we recorded, let's replace the recorded text here with argument variables for **Contact Name**, **Email**, and **Subject**:

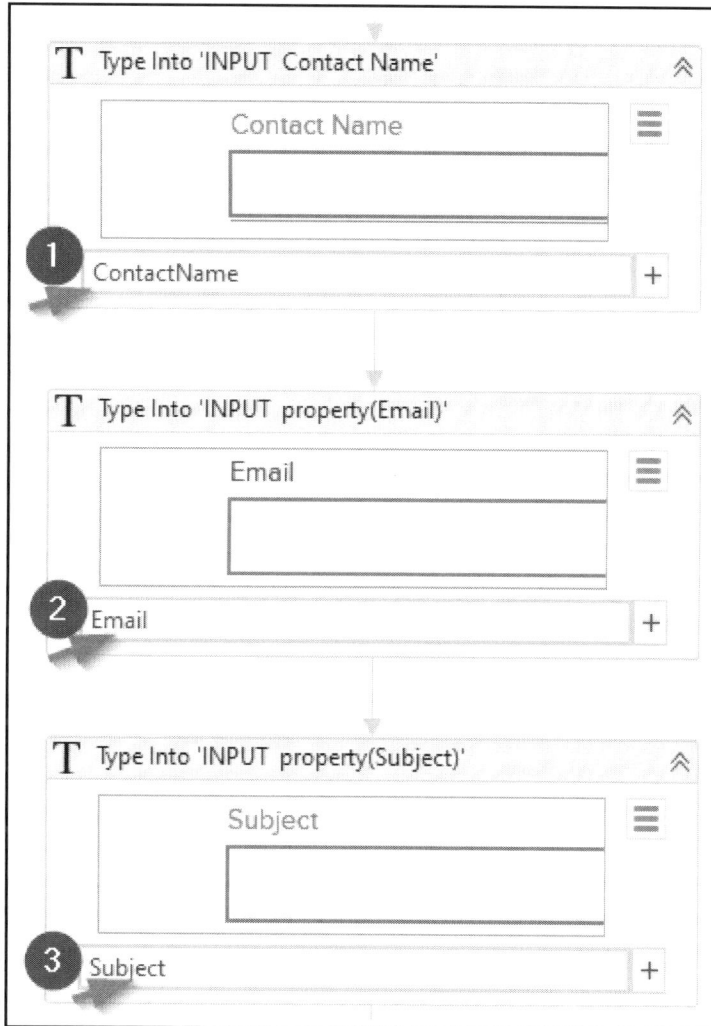

7. Let's also set the **ContinueOnError** flag to `False` in the **Properties** panel for these three activities so that we can stop execution and handle them if there are errors:

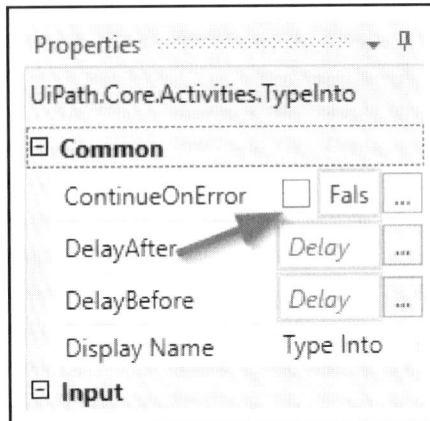

That is all the updates we require in order to make to the recording. Let's now check whether the ticket was created successfully.

Validating successful ticket creation

By way of a final step in this ticket creation automation, let's ensure that the ticket was added successfully:

1. To do this, let's check whether Zoho Desk moved to the next page by checking whether the **Close Ticket** option is on screen.

2. Since our ticket is already created (during our record sequence), go back to the Zoho ticket application in Chrome and click on the newly created ticket. You should now see the **Close Ticket** option at the bottom of the screen:

3. To check for the element, let's add an **Element Exists** activity within the ZohoAutomation workflow. Within the added activity, click on **Indicate element in the browser** and choose **Close Ticket** in the bottom-right corner of the Zoho ticket details screen:

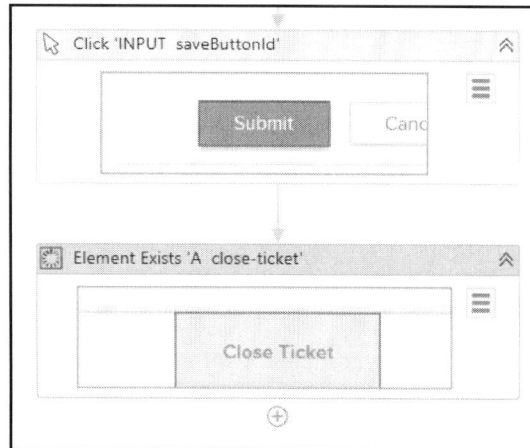

4. Also, go to the **Properties** window (on the right pane) of this **Element Exists** activity and add the `Successful` argument as output:

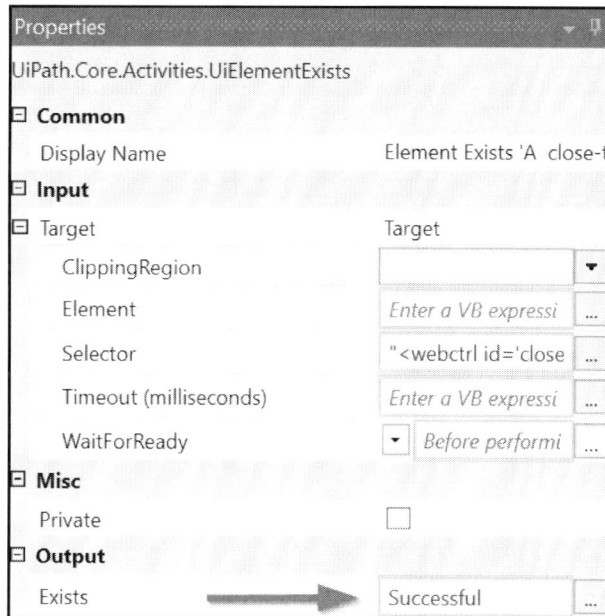

5. Let's now check whether the ticket was added successfully. Let's add an **If** activity to check for the **Close Ticket** element.

6. If the element exists, we will log a message to say `Ticket was created in Zoho desk`. Use the **Log Message** activity for that.

7. If the element does not exist, this means that we have a functional error (for example, there was no data in the sheet) and the ticket could not be created. In this scenario, let's log an error message indicating that the ticket could not be created. For that, add a new **Sequence** activity within the **Else** part. Within **Sequence**, add a **Log Message** activity with the **Log Level** Error and a **Message** box with a `"Ticket Not created in Zoho desk"` message:

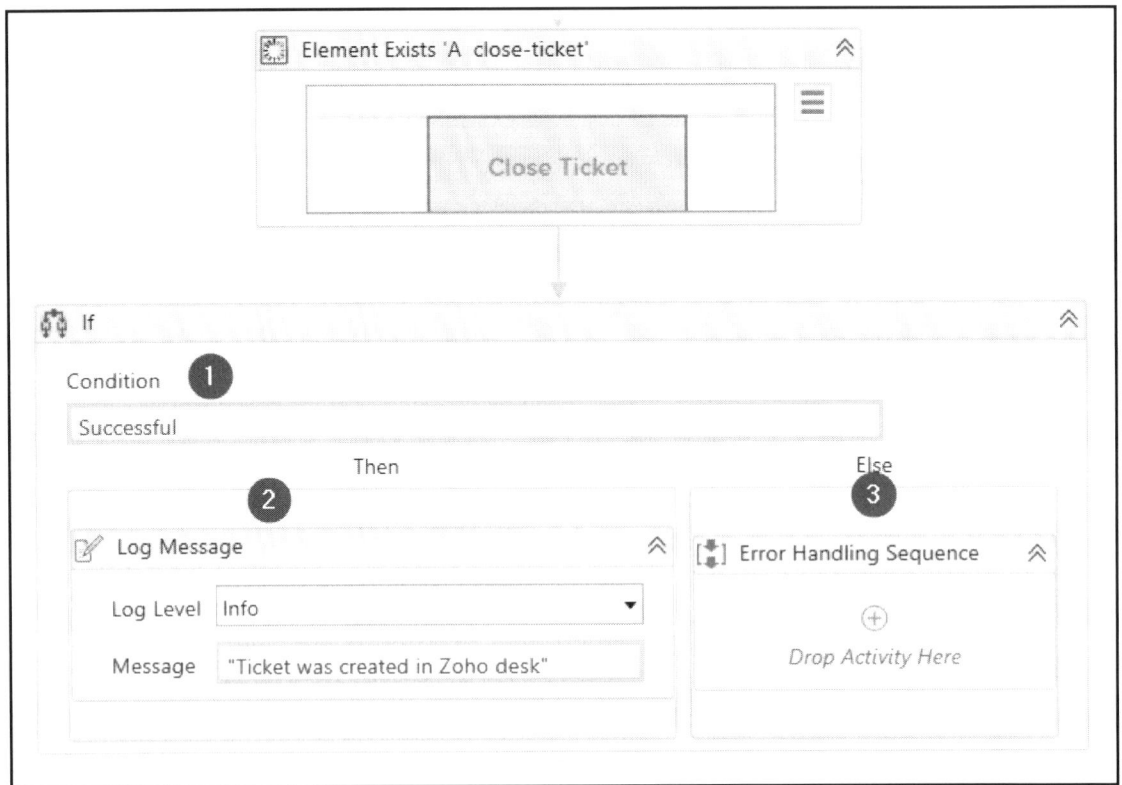

We checked for the successful creation of the ticket. Let's now handle any exception scenarios.

Handling exceptions

If there is an unexpected exception or error, then the bot should ensure that we bring the target application to a stable state where it can proceed with the next transactions. The following few steps guarantee this:

1. Within the **Else** block, to ensure that the target application is in a stable state, we will attach an element on the screen to the browser. Let's add a new **Attach Browser** activity to handle the error handling activity in the already opened Chrome browser:

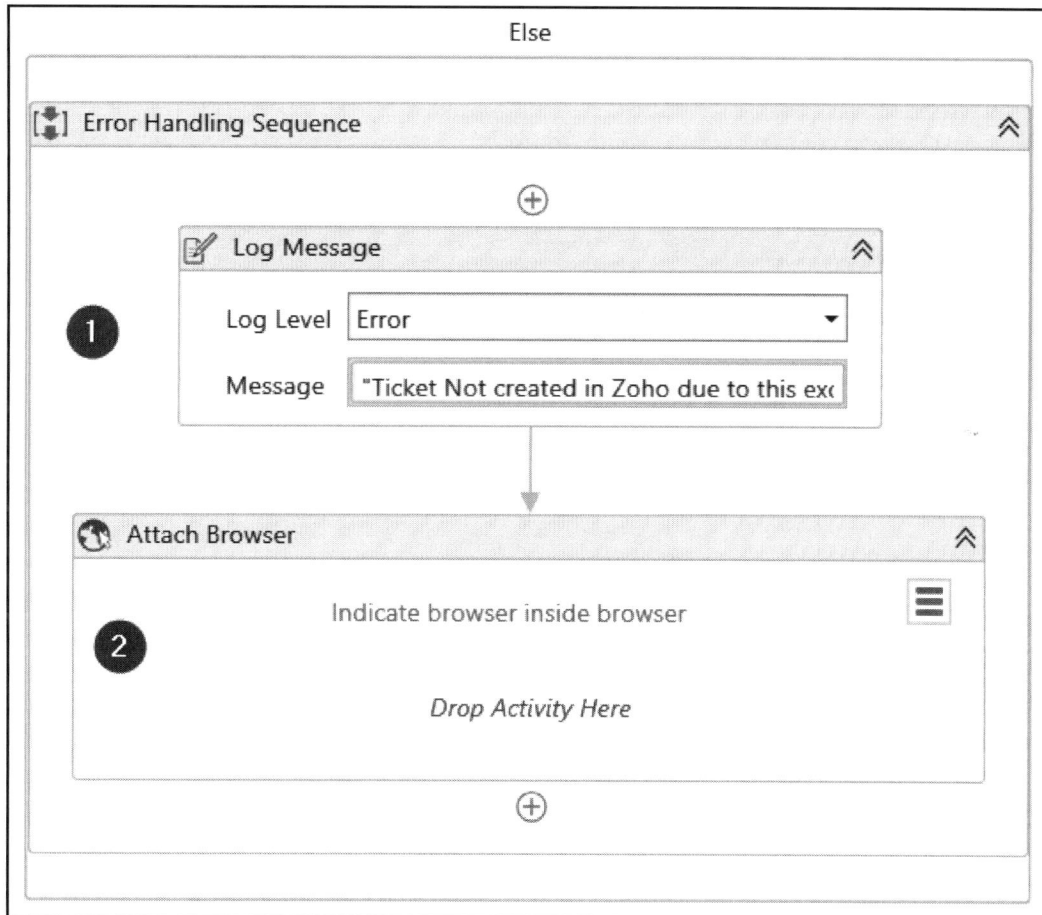

2. On the properties side of **Attach Browser**, update **Browser** with the
   `ZohoBrowser` variable and set the **BrowserType** as Chrome to continue to use
   the same browser session:

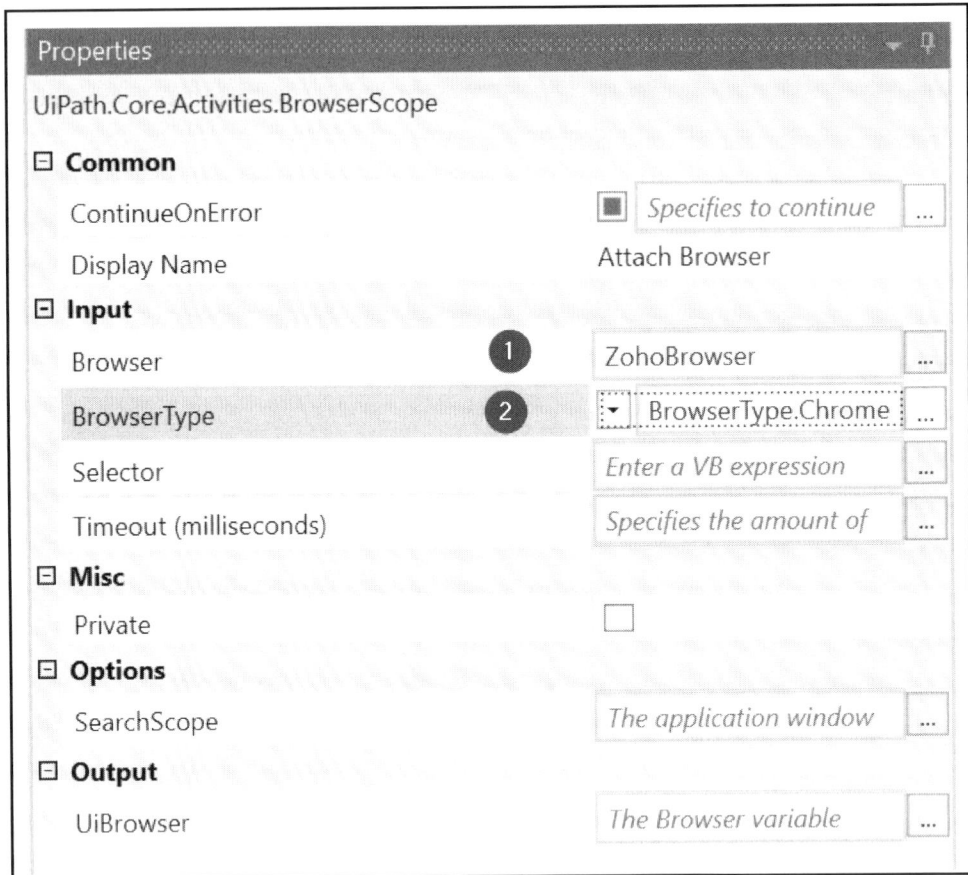

3. Add a **Mouse Click** activity to the newly created sequence and click on **Indicate element inside the browser**. Then, go to the browser, and click on the **TICKETS** menu option in the top left-hand corner of the Zoho desk screen:

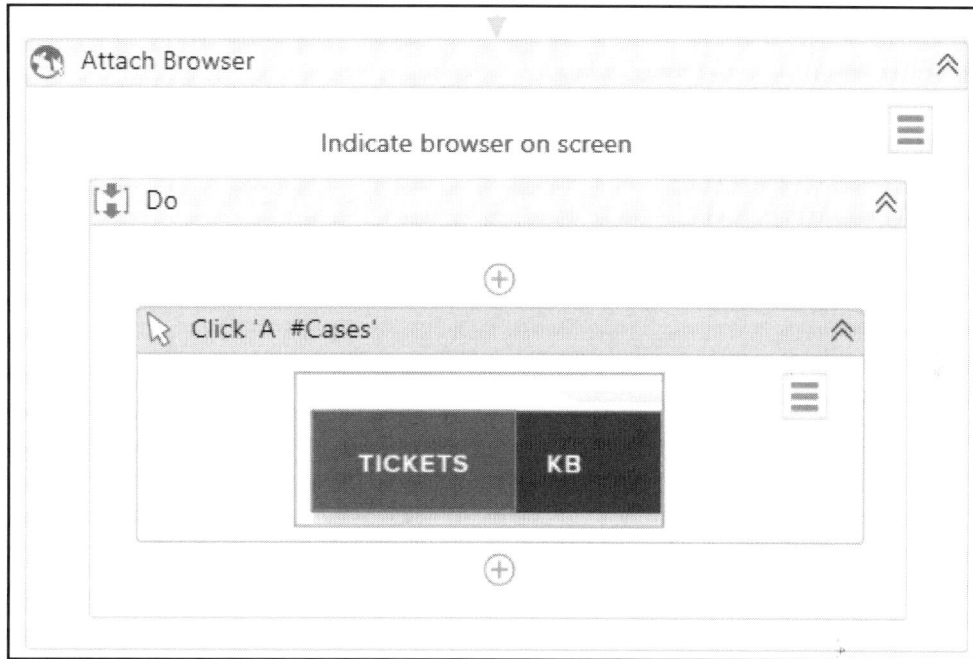

This step will enable automation to get control of the home page of the web application if a ticket has not been created.

This completes the **Try** block. Now, let's handle any system exceptions.

4. Moving out of the overall **Try** block, let's update the **Catches** block. Add a new catch of the `System.exception` type to the **Catches** block. Copy the error handling sequence that we added in the **Else** block and paste it into this **Catches** block:

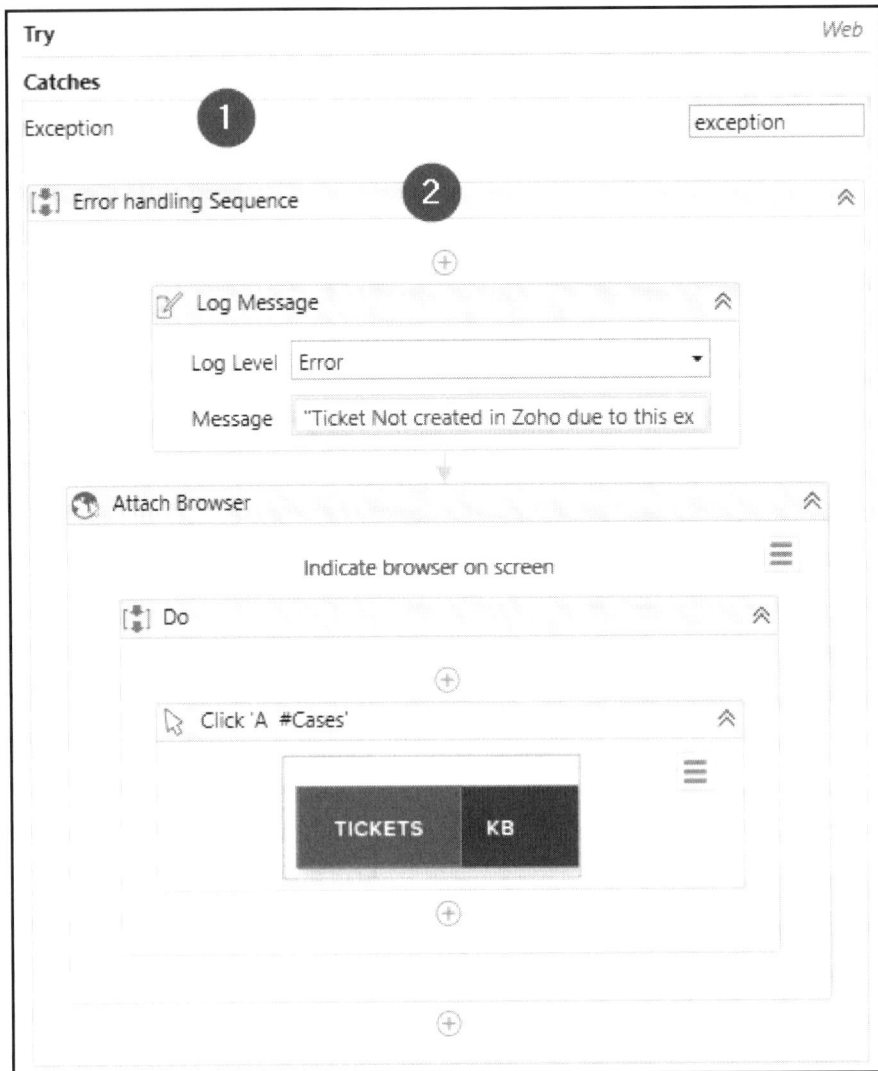

So we have now completed the web (Zoho Desk) automation as well. Here, we took the request data and incorporated it into Zoho Desk. Finally, we will go to the main workflow, invoke this workflow, and finalize the automation.

Putting it all together

It is time to finish up the main workflow so that it reads the requests, creates the tickets, and then moves the Request spreadsheet out once processed. In order to do this, perform the following steps:

1. Go back to Main.xaml, create a new variable called boolTicketCreated of the Boolean type, set the scope to **Event Handler** sequence, and set the default value as False:

Name	Variable type	Scope	Default
strEmail	String	Sequence	Enter
strSubject	String	Sequence	Enter
EditableText	UiElement	Event Handler	Enter
boolFileExists	Boolean	Event Handler	Enter
boolTicketCreated ①	Boolean ②	Event Handler ③	False ④

We will use this to check whether the ticket was created successfully.

2. To invoke the Zoho Desk workflow that we just added, let's add a new **Invoke Workflow File** activity and browse to the ZOHOAtuomation.xaml file:

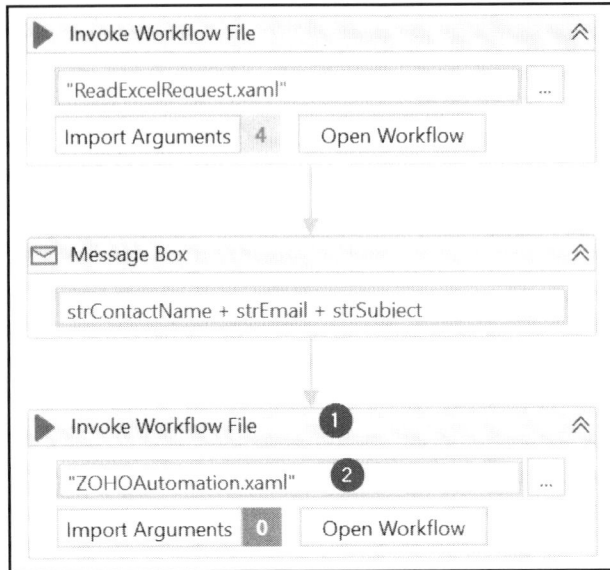

Note that we are adding this to the **Then** part of the **If** control we last added in **Main**.

3. Let's import the arguments by clicking on **Import Arguments** within the Invoke activity. On the popup, map the arguments to the strContactName, strEmail, strSubject, and boolTicketCreated variables:

4. Next, let's use this last variable, `boolTicketCreated`, and add an **If** control:

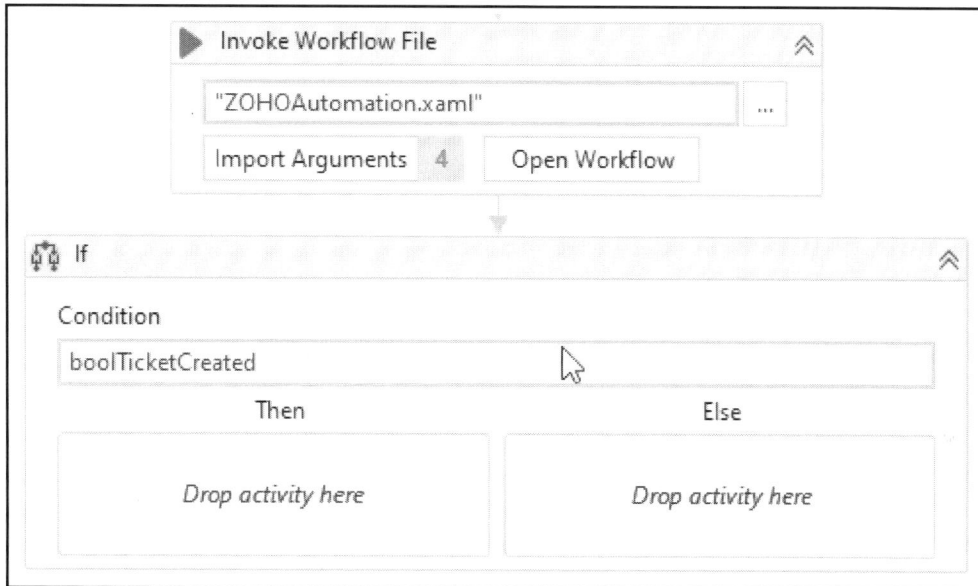

5. If the ticket was created, then we will move `Request.xlsx` from the `Requests` folder to the `Processed` folder. For that, let's add a **Move File** activity within the **Then** block with the following inputs:
    - **From**:
      `Environment.CurrentDirectory+"\Requests\Request.xlsx".`
    - **To**:
      `Environment.CurrentDirectory+"\Processed\Request.xlsx".`
    - Check the **Overwrite** checkbox.

6. Finally, add a **Message Box** with the message `"Zoho Ticket Created and File Moved to the Processed Folder. Use ALT+S to check for new requests to process."`. Also, add a **Log Message** activity with the same message and a **Log Level** of `Info`.

7. Next, in the **Else** branch, let's add a **Message Box** saying `"Zoho Ticket not created and file is not processed yet. Please check the input request file and Use ALT+s to reprocess the same request"`. Also, add a `Log Message` activity with the same message and a **Log Level** of `Error`:

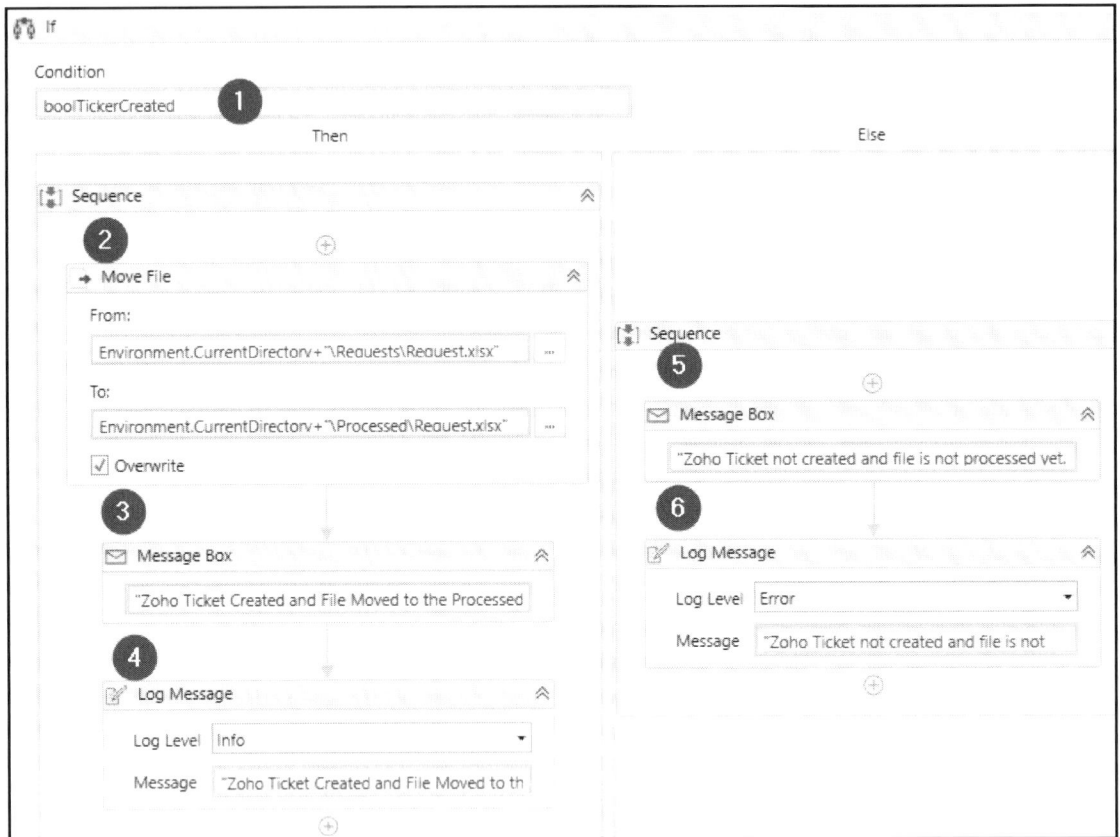

8. Let's save the project. Go to **Remove Unused Variables** in Studio and click on **Validate Project**:

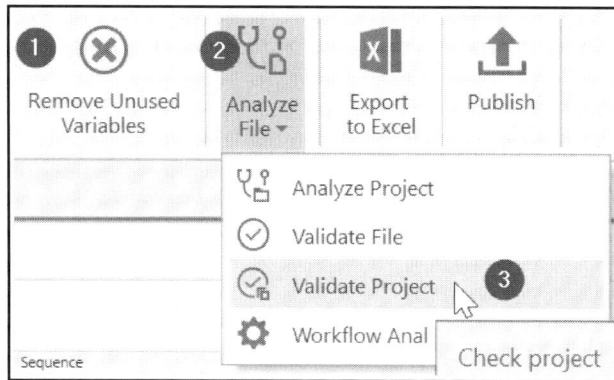

You should get a message from Studio saying **No errors found**. Now, we are ready to test the project.

Testing the automation

Let's now test the automation with all the workflows end to end:

1. Go to the main workflow and click on **Run**, as shown in the following screenshot:

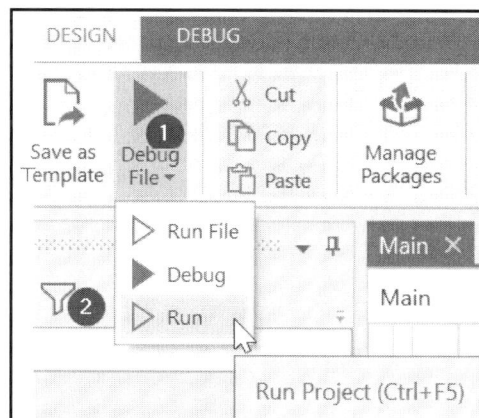

2. Once you get the first message box, click **OK** and then use *ALT + S* to trigger the automation. Click **OK** on the next few message box prompts. Remember that we added these message boxes to bring visibility to the workflow execution:

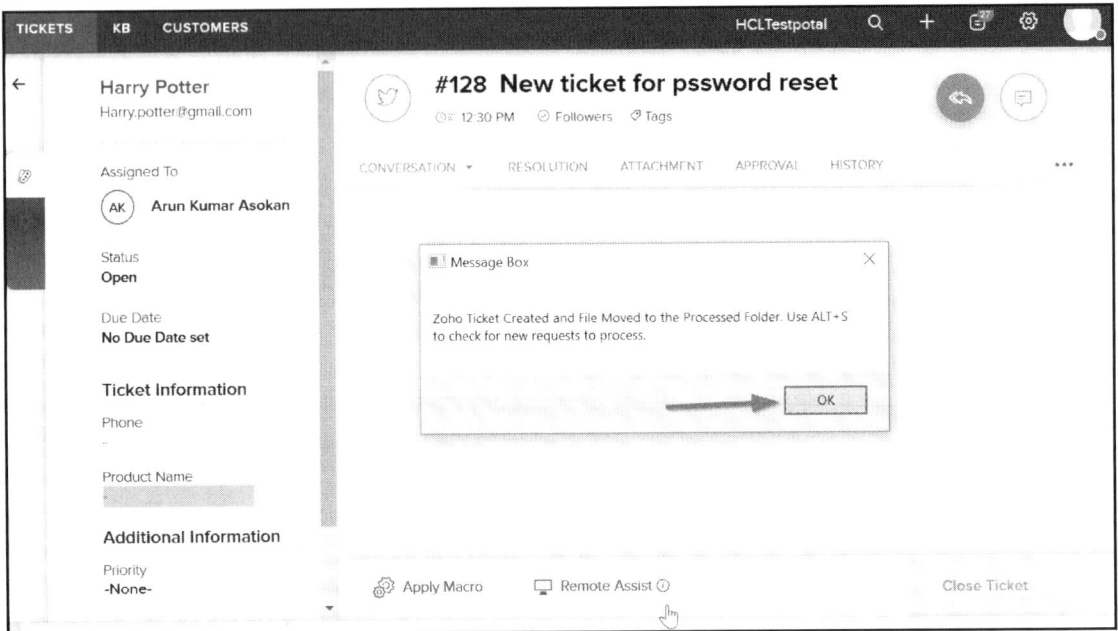

3. Go to the `Processed` folder and check whether the `Request.xlsx` file has been moved there:

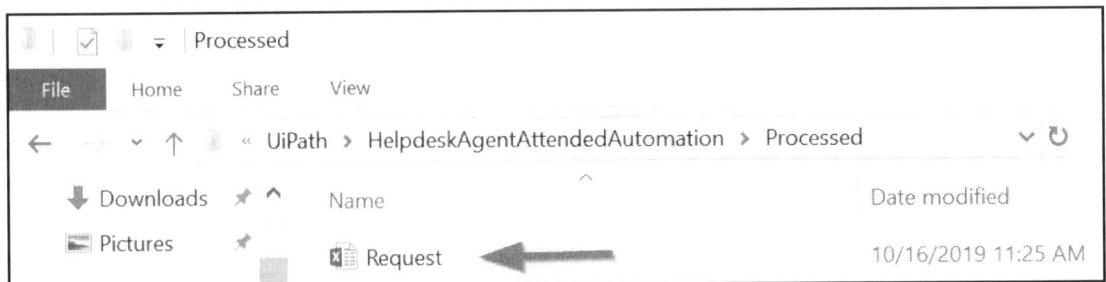

If you encounter issues, you can use the **Debug** option to run through the steps and ascertain where the issues are.

4. Before you go, do not forget to stop the automation by clicking on the **STOP** button on UiPath Studio.

That's it! We have completed our first project in UiPath that automated the process of creating a support ticket.

We can implement a few enhancements and make things a little more interesting by trying out the following suggested enhancements.

Project enhancements

Here are a few simple, but interesting, things you can try out to enhance the project and learn more:

1. After processing, try to rename the `Request` file as `Request + Date Timestamp` before moving it to the `Requests` folders.
2. Try to capture all the fields (not just the mandatory three) to create the ticket in Zoho.
3. Enhance attended automation to include the option to **Stop Automation** by using a hotkey.

Summary

We have completed an attended automation project with UiPath! We explored Excel and web app (Zoho Desk) automation. We broke the automation down into logical parts, including Excel, Zoho, and the main workflow, to keep it clean and separate.

We used arguments to pass data around and variables to store them within a workflow. You also got a sense of how you can use `Try-Catch` blocks to handle exceptions and the `If` control to handle true-false conditions.

While this project may have been a bit of an effort, this experience should give you a good foundation as we head into more complex projects. In the next chapter, we will automate customer data lookup and data entry in CRM applications. See you there!

CRM Automation 3

Have you ever had to look up data from one application and update another system?

There are many scenarios where people copy and move data between systems. Sometimes, "swivel chair activities" can occur, which can result in human errors. RPA can help us automate these activities to make them quicker while also eliminating any human errors.

In this project, we will automate one such swivel chair activity in customer services. We will look up customer information on an external website and update that information in our **Customer Relationship Management (CRM)** system.

This project will help you understand the following:

- Using RPA for swivel chair activities
- Looking up data on a third-party website
- CRM application Automation
- Data scrapping in UiPath
- Updating DataTable using UiPath
- Exception handling in UiPath
- Unit testing UiPath bots

Technical requirements

We will need the following hardware and software for this project:

- A PC with UiPath Community edition version 19.10.0 installed.
- Chrome browser with the UiPath add-on.
- The Apptivo Saas ERP application with the CRM module. You can sign up for free at `https://www.apptivo.com`.
- Crunchbase. Go to `https://www.crunchbase.com/register`, enter the required details, and register for an account.

- Check out the following video to see the Code in Action: `https://bit.ly/3cTPjcK`.

You can find the code files present in this chapter on GitHub at `https://github.com/PacktPublishing/Robotic-Process-Automation-Projects/tree/master/CRMAutomation`.

Project overview

Organizations add customers all the time, and we can do this and update their information within the **Customer Relationship Management (CRM)** system. Customer information such as key contacts, email, phone, address, website, and social media information is looked up using websites such as Hoover, D&B, and so on and kept updated. Here is a high-level workflow for the project:

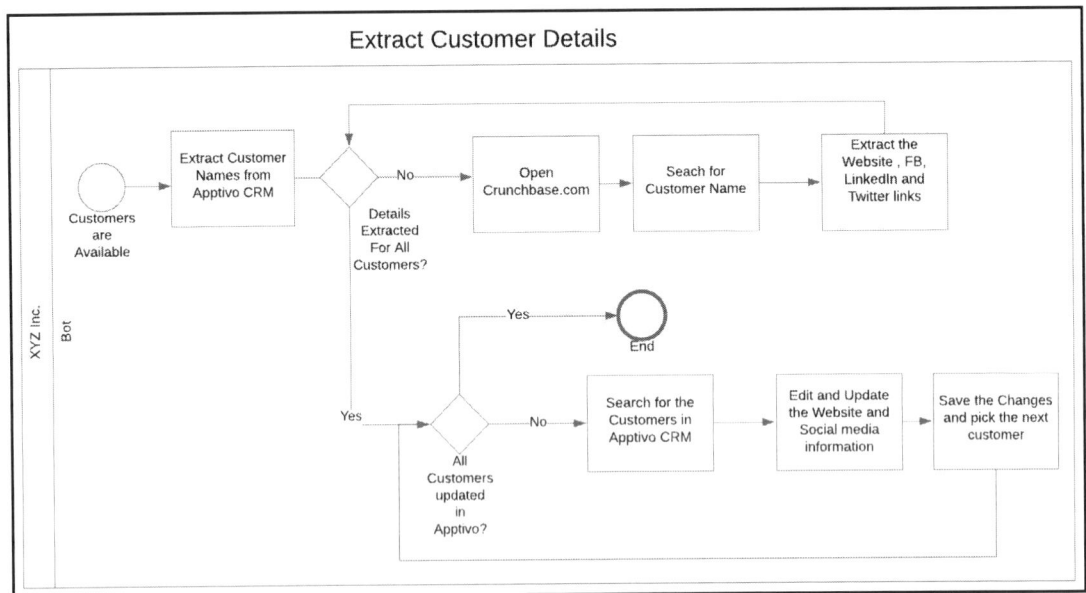

In this CRM project, we will extract the list of customers to be updated from the CRM application known as Apptivo. Automation will then open up Crunchbase, a third-party site that provides company information. It will search and capture the website and social media data for each customer. This data will then be used to search and update the customer record in Apptivo.

Now, let's look at the project's components and walk through the creation of Automation.

Project details

As we did in `Chapter 2`, *Help Desk Ticket Generation*, we will divide our Automation into logical workflows to come up with our Automation. Let's have a look at the technical components we will be building for this project.

We will have a main workflow called `Main.xaml` where we will extract the customers using `Get Customer List Sequence`. Once we have the customer list, we will invoke `RequestCustomerDetails.xaml` so that we can search `Crunchbase.com` and capture the customer details. We will pass the customer details back to `Main.xaml`, where we will then use `Update Customer details Sequence` to update the customer data in Apptivo CRM.

The following is a high-level sequence diagram depicting this:

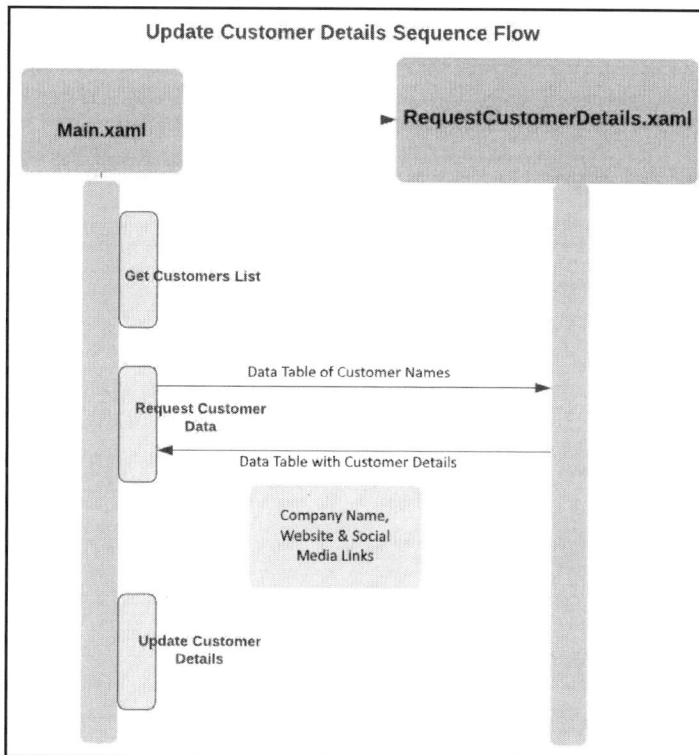

Now that we've had this overview, let's create these technical components and test them. Before we do that, however, we need to prepare our CRM application – Apptivo.

CRM preparation

As shown in the preceding diagram, we will be updating the customer information in the Apptivo CRM application. So, let's add a few customers so that we can update their information:

1. Log into Apptivo (`apptivo.com`). If this is your first time on the site, please sign up using the appropriate option.
2. Once you've logged in, go to the **CRM** menu option and select **Customers**.
3. Within the **CUSTOMERS** tab, use the **Create** option to create our customers, as shown in the following screenshot:

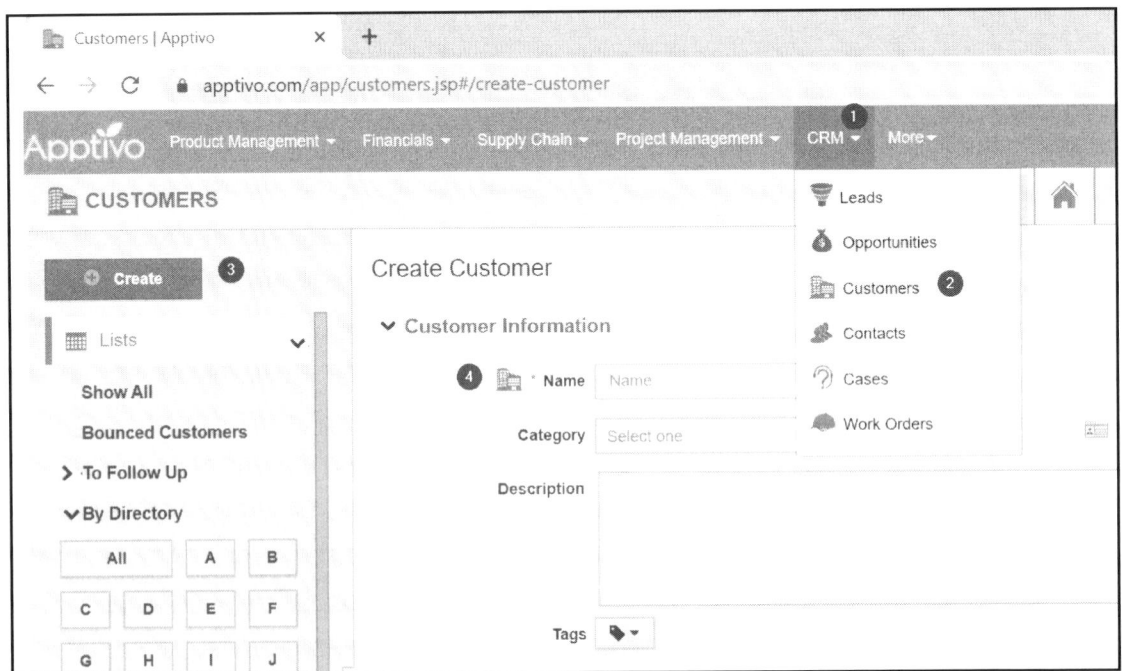

For now, we will only enter the names of the customers. We will update their information from a lookup site.

Let's add three customers called `Amazon`, `Salesforce`, and `Uber`. You can play around with other companies as well, but I suggest that you stick to these company names so that it's easier for you to step through the project creation process. It is important to have customer names that exist on our lookup site, that is, `Crunchbase.com`.

> Please ensure that Apptivo is open in one of your browser tabs and that you are logged in. This project assumes that you are logged in to Apptivo and ready to work on the application.

Now that we have got the preparation out of the way, let's go ahead and create our project with UiPath Studio.

Setting up the project

For this project, we will start with a blank project and design Automation within that. Let's get started:

1. Launch UiPath Studio and choose **Process** under the **New Project** group, as shown in the following screenshot:

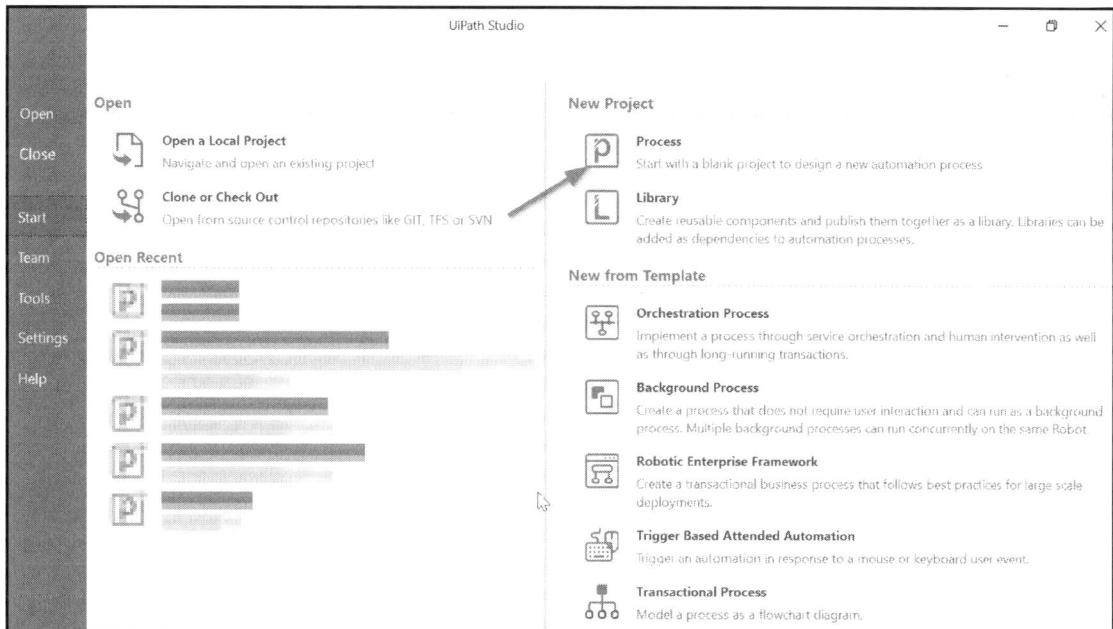

2. On the popup for **New Process**, go ahead and provide a name and description for the project and click on **Create**. On the Studio screen, choose **Open Main Workflow**, as we did in the previous chapter, to get to the initial screen.

3. We'll choose to start with a blank process, which means we have to build everything from scratch. Let's start by adding a **Sequence** UiPath activity and renaming it `Main Sequence`. You can just click on the name on the Activity box and add the name `Main Sequence`. This is optional but recommended as it gives better readability to your workflows. You can see this Sequence in the following screenshot (in the next section), along with the other Sequences.

Within this `Main Sequence`, we will have three subSequences. We will start by creating a Sequence to get the customer list.

Extracting the customer list from CRM

First, let's get the list of customers in the Apptivo CRM that we need to update. For that, we'll need to create a new Sequence and prepare the browser to record our customer's web activities.

We will start by adding a new Sequence within the `Main Sequence`. We will call this `Get Customer List Sequence`. Within this, we'll add a **Try-Catch** block activity for exception handling. Your Main workflow should now look like this:

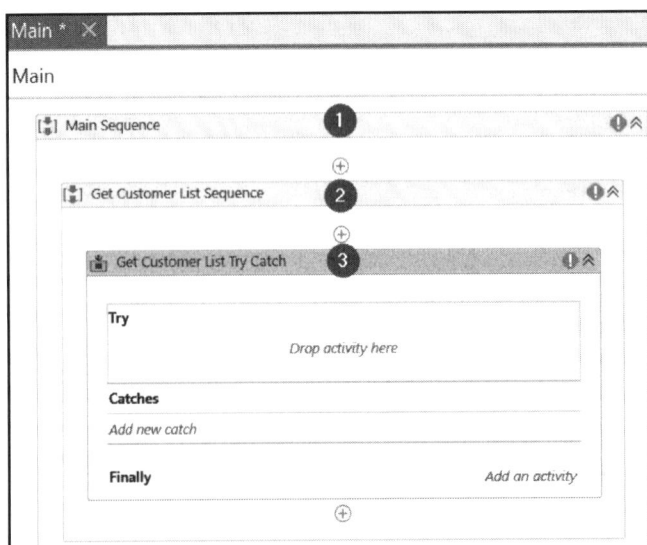

Now, we are ready to add our Automation activities to the workflow.

Preparing the browser

Let's identify the Apptivo application tab for Automation:

1. Start by adding the **Attach Browser** activity and attaching it to the browser tab. After that, perform the necessary extraction steps.

2. If you don't have Apptivo open in your Chrome browser, ensure that you have it open and are logged in. Now, click on **Indicate browser on-screen** within the **Attach Browser** activity and point to the Apptivo home tab in the browser, as shown in the following screenshot:

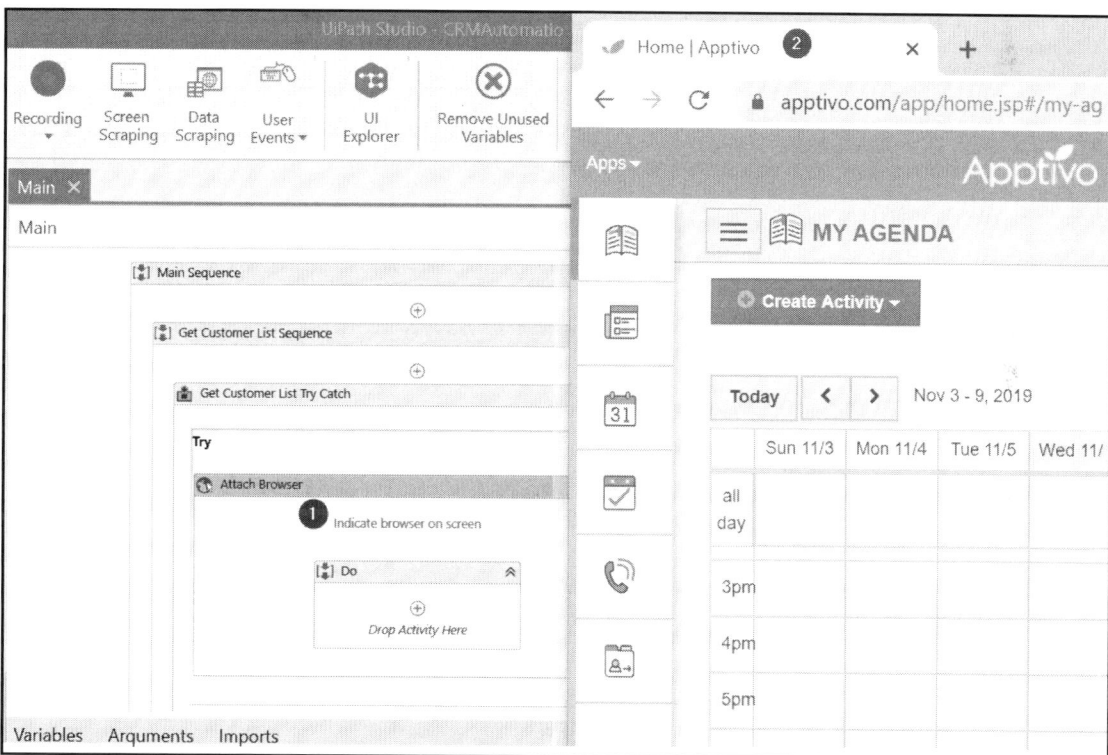

3. On the properties panel for the **Attach Browser** activity, do the following:
   - Make sure that the **BrowserType** is Chrome.
   - Add a new variable for the **UiBrowser** property under output using *Ctrl + K*, type in browserApptivo, and press *Enter*.
   - In the same properties panel, update the **Selector** property. We will update the **title** with wild characters to make it generic across all the web pages in the Apptivo application. Click on the option to edit the selector and update the **title** to *Apptivo*, as shown in the following screenshot:

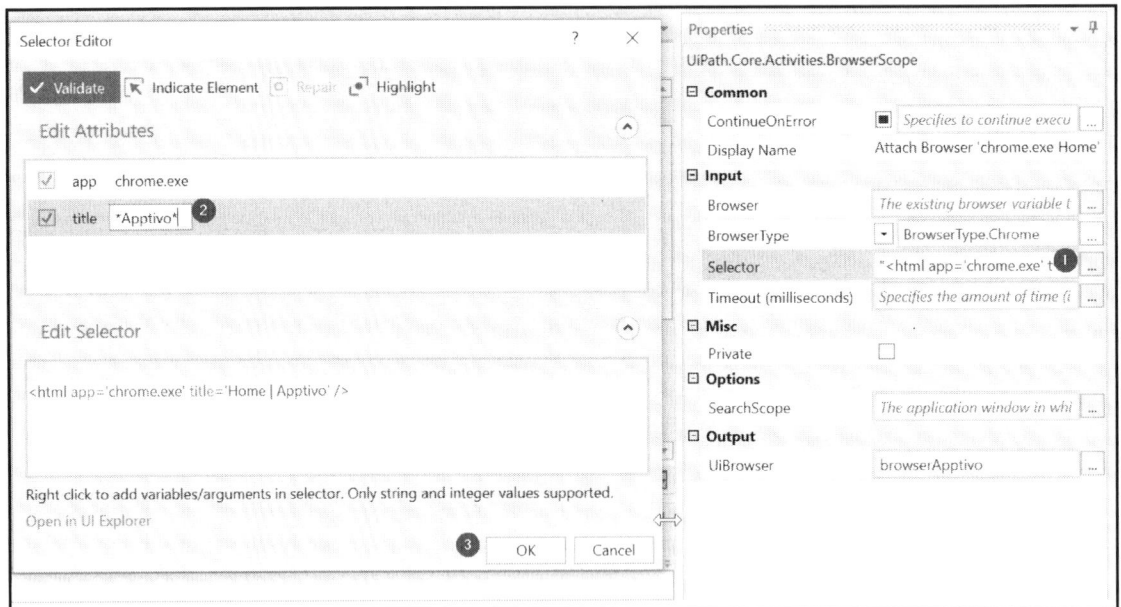

We are using a browser variable called browserApptivo so that we can reuse this variable wherever we need to perform any Automation steps on the Apptivo web application.

4. Next up, we will use the **Activate UiPath** activity to bring our window to the foreground and to maximize this window using the **Maximize window** activity. Add these within the **Do** Sequence.

One of the best practices in web Automation is to check that the browser is maximized and that the zoom is set to 100%. Use the **Maximize window** activity to always maximize the browser in case it isn't.

Now that we have the browser ready, we can add the necessary activities so that we can get to the customer list on Apptivo and retrieve that data. We will use UiPath's web recording feature to do so.

Web recording

Follow these steps to get to the customer's details from the Apptivo application:

1. Ensure that you have the Apptivo web application open in your browser. Then, within UiPath Studio, click on **Recording** and choose the **Web** option. Click on the **Record** button in the **Web Recording** dialog to start recording:

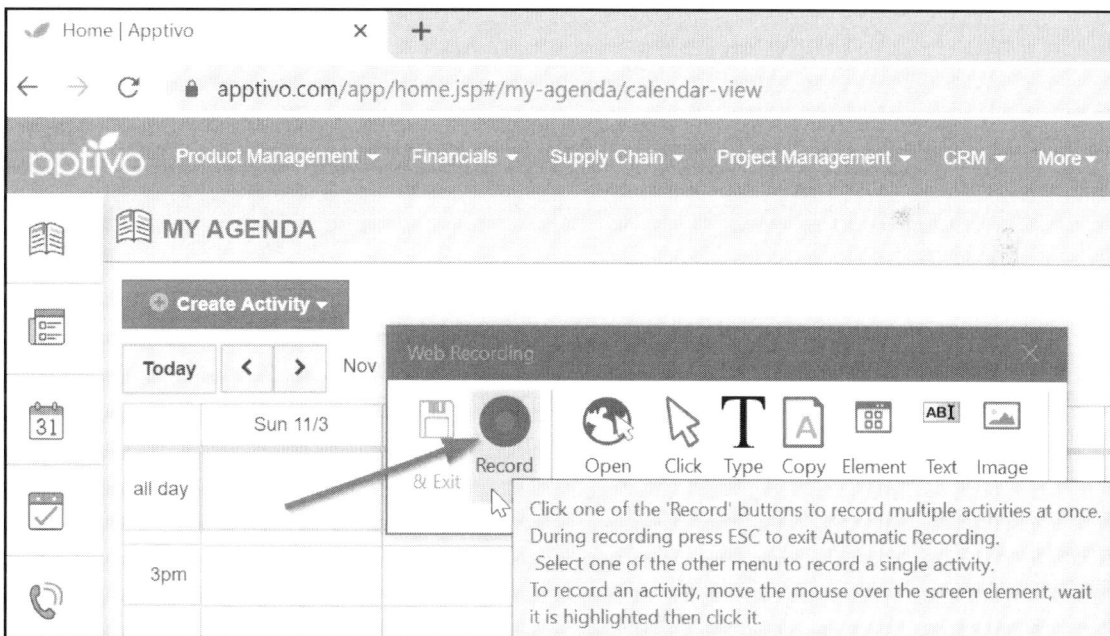

2. With the recorder on, click on **CRM** and then **Customers**, as shown in the following screenshot:

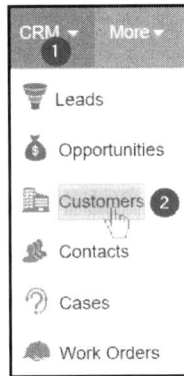

3. In the popup that opens, click on **Indicate Anchor** and point to the icon next to the **Customers** option, as shown in the following screenshot:

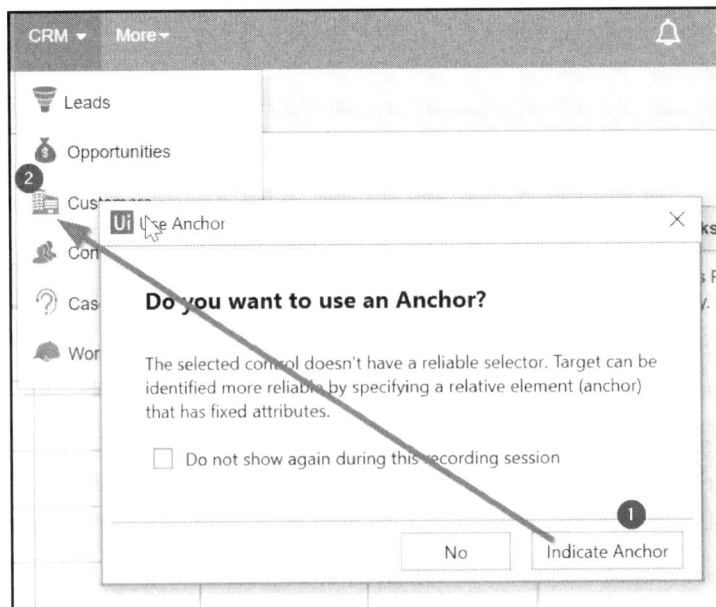

Doing this records the steps that we need to follow to navigate to the page with the customer listings. You will end up on the customers page in Apptivo. Press the *Esc* key to stop the recording and click **Save & Exit** on the recording panel to end the web recording.

4. You will find that the recorded steps are listed as a new Sequence at the end of the project. We only want a part of those activities and we need them in our **Try** block. So, copy the activities called **Click A** and **Anchor Base** and paste them under the **Maximize Window** activity, as shown in the following screenshot:

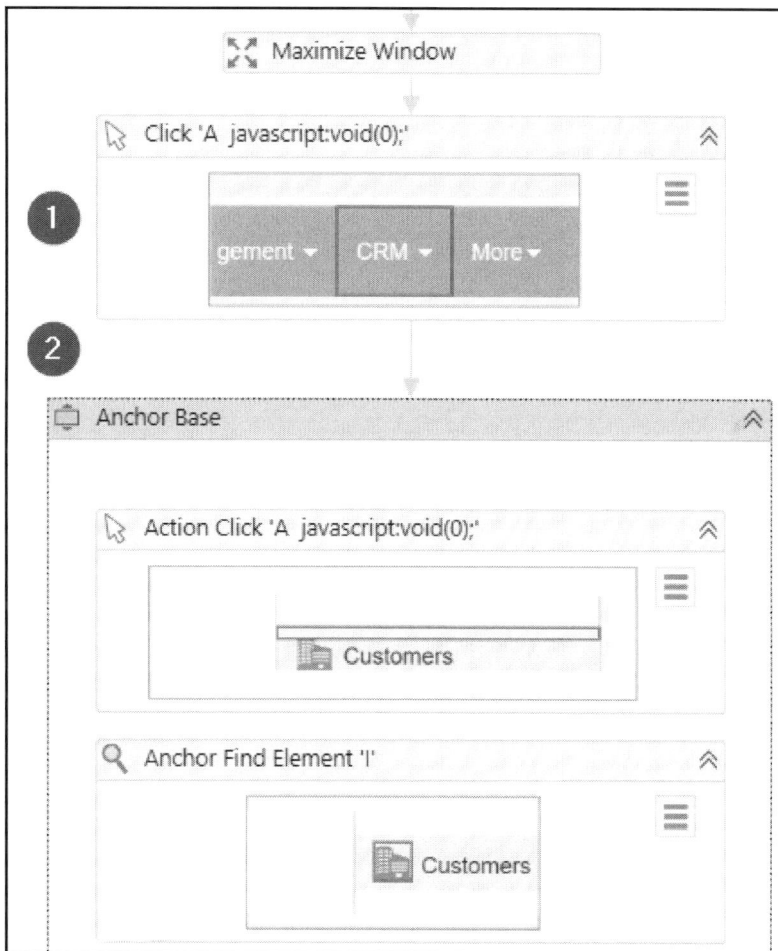

5. Ensure that you *delete* the Sequence that was automatically created by the web recording after you've copied the required activities (the Sequence named **Web** at the bottom).

Following these steps takes us to the **Customers** page. We will stay on the Apptivo **Customers** page and get all the customer names from this page using data scraping.

Data scraping

Now, we will extract the customer names from the displayed customer details using the **Data Scraping** feature in UiPath. Follow these steps:

1. Click on **Data Scraping** in the top ribbon:

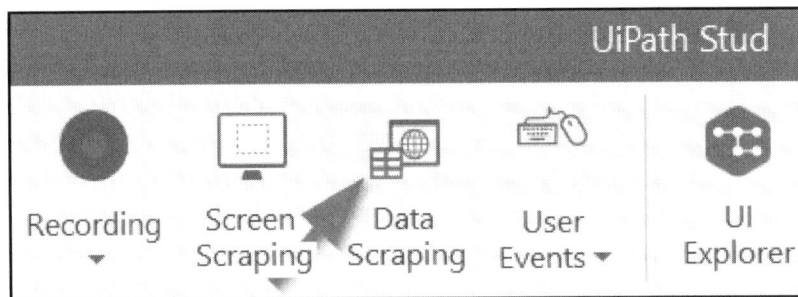

2. In the **Extract Wizard** that pops up, click on **Next**. Choose the first customer on the list (for example, **Amazon**). The wizard will prompt you with an option to extract the whole table. We'll choose **No** as we only need the customer names for this project.
3. Click **Next** and select another element for the **Data Scraping** wizard to be able to identify the table. Point to the last customer on the list (for example, **Salesforce**). Click **Next**.
4. On the next screen, provide a column name for the data we are extracting. Let's call it Name since the data is customer names. Click **Next**:

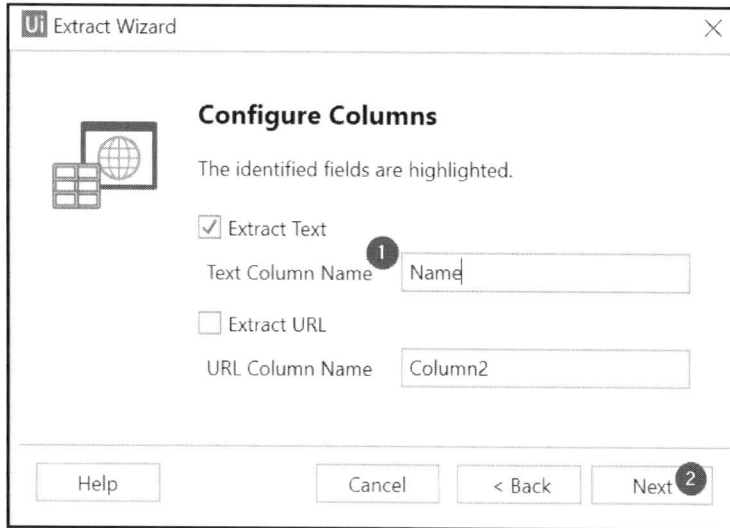

5. Now, you'll be shown a preview of the data that you extracted. Check the data and click on **Finish**, as shown in the following screenshot:

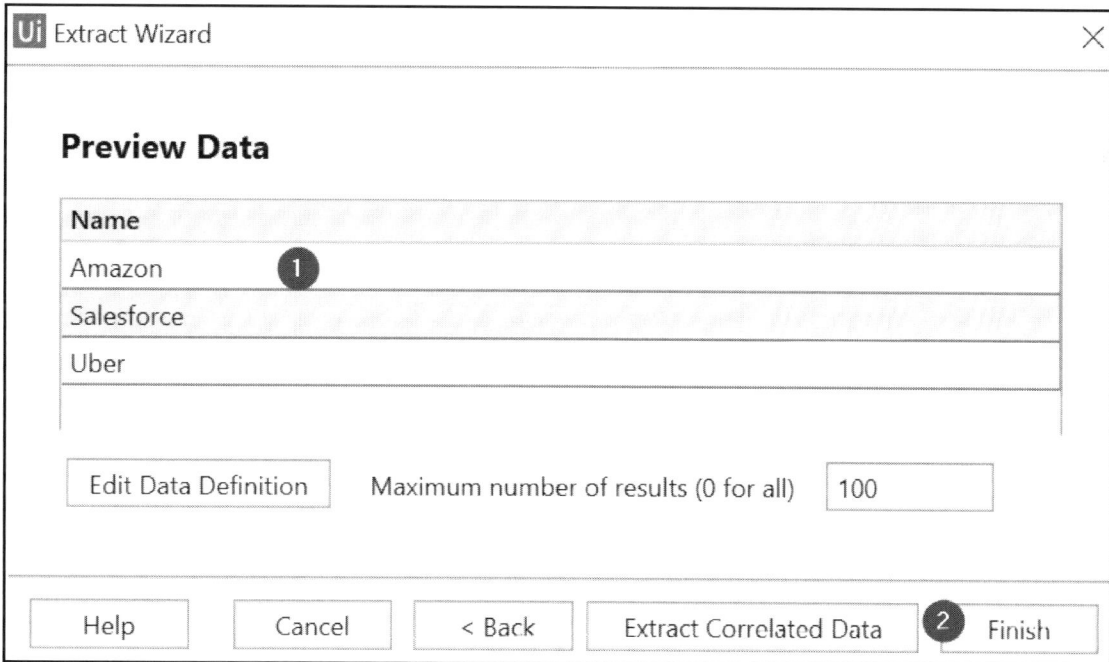

6. Choose **No** in the dialog that asks whether the data is spanning multiple pages. You will find the **Extract structured Data** activity within the **Data Scraping** Sequence that was created and appended at the bottom of the workflow.

7. Go ahead and copy this activity before pasting it within the **Try** block under **Anchor Find**. In the properties for the **Extract** activity, remove the **ExtractDataTable** variable. We will add a new variable in its place in the next step:

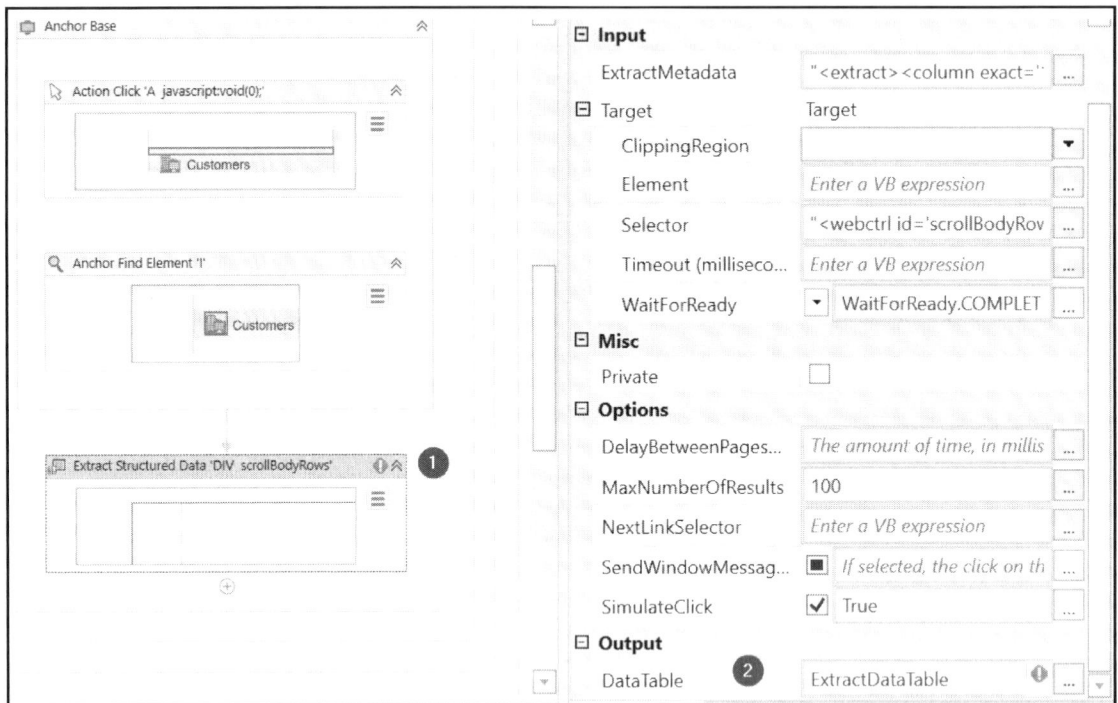

8. Create a new **DataTable** variable called `dtCompanyList` to store the customer list that contains the names of companies that will be passed as input to `Crunchbase.com`. We'll add this as the output for the **Extract Structured Data** activity. In the **Variable** pane, set its scope to `Main Sequence`.

9. Once we have copied what is needed, make sure to *delete* the **Data Scraping** Sequence that was created automatically.

That's all for the **Try** block. Next, we'll handle the exceptions in the **Catch** block.

Using a Catch block for the Get Customer List Sequence

Let's handle any exceptions within the **Catch** block:

1. In the **Catch** block, we will handle system exceptions. So, let's choose **Exception** as `System.Exception`. Click on **Add Activity** in the **Finally** part and add a **Log Message** of **Log Level** set to `Error` with a message stating `"Not able to Extract Customer list. Due to this Error: "+exception.Message`.

2. If there is an exception while we extract the customer list from CRM, then Automation won't be able to proceed. Let's add a **Terminate Workflow** activity to handle this. Within the properties for the **Terminate** activity, set **Exception** to `exception` (start typing and the list should pop up) and add `"Cannot Extract Customer list from CRM, so terminating the Automation."` as a reason, as shown in the following screenshot:

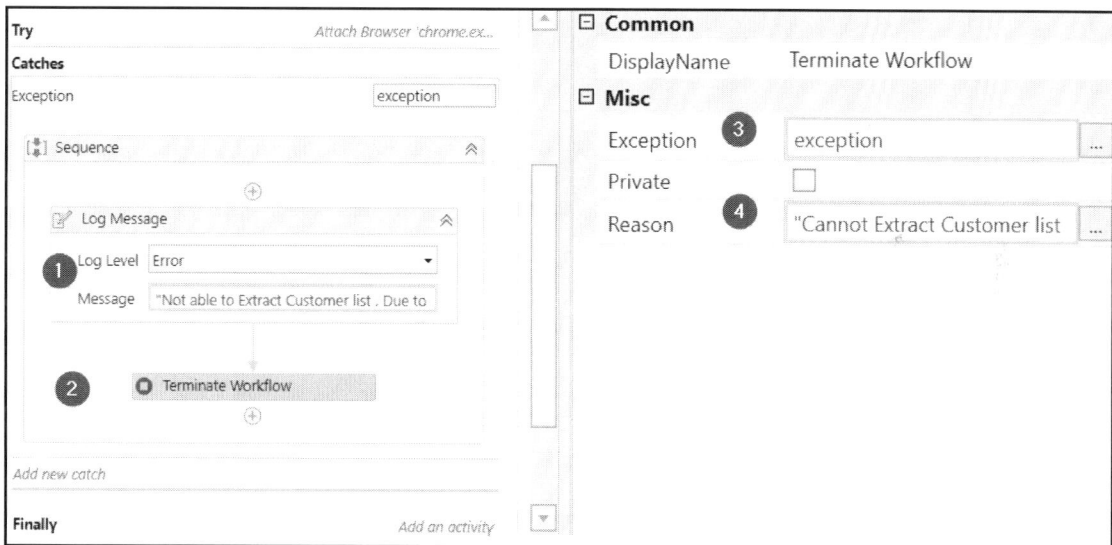

3. Now, we have completed the first part of extracting the customer list from CRM. To test this Sequence, let's add a **Message box** activity with the message `dtCompanyList.Rows.Count` at the end of the **Try** block, after the **Extract Structure Data** activity.

4. Let's run and test the Automation we have so far. Ensure that Apptivo is open in Chrome. Go ahead and click the **Run** button on the Studio ribbon. If the message box returns your number of customers (3, in our case), then we have successfully completed this part of the main workflow.

5. Please ensure you remove the message box after the unit test has completed.

Next, we will use the customer's names to look up their information from the Crunchbase website.

Looking up customer information

We will use the Crunchbase.com website to look up the company information for our customers. This information will be used to update the customer information in our Apptivo:

1. If you haven't done so already, go to Crunchbase.com in Chrome and create an account by providing the necessary details. You can also use social authentication. Just ensure you are in a logged in for the Automation process.

2. With the lookup site ready, let's create the Automation to get the customer information. We will create a new Sequence by clicking on **New** and then choosing **Sequence** from the Studio ribbon on top. Name it RequestCustomerDetails in the Sequence box that pops up and click **Create**.

3. To pass the customer data around, we'll need to create two arguments. Select the RequestCustomerDetails.xaml Sequence and click on **Arguments** to create two **DataTable** arguments called CompanyList and CompanyData:

Now that we have completed the groundwork for the lookup, let's create a data table that we will be passing back to the main workflow, complete with customer (company) data.

Creating a data table

Follow these steps to create the data table:

1. Let's use the **Build Data Table** activity to build a data table for CompanyData, as shown in the following screenshot:

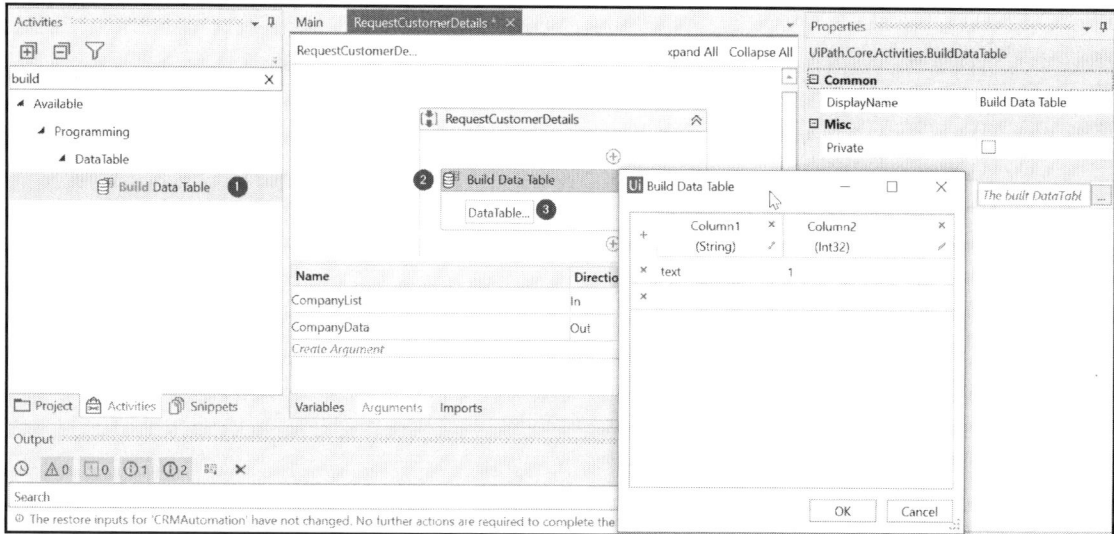

2. We will be looking up the customer's name and gathering their website and social media information to update our CRM. Let's create five columns for the data table so that we can gather this information. Click on **DataTable** in the activity and within the popup, edit and rename the existing column names. Then, use the **Add column** option (the plus (+) sign on left) to create the rest of the columns (Company name, Website, Facebook, LinkedIn, and Twitter):

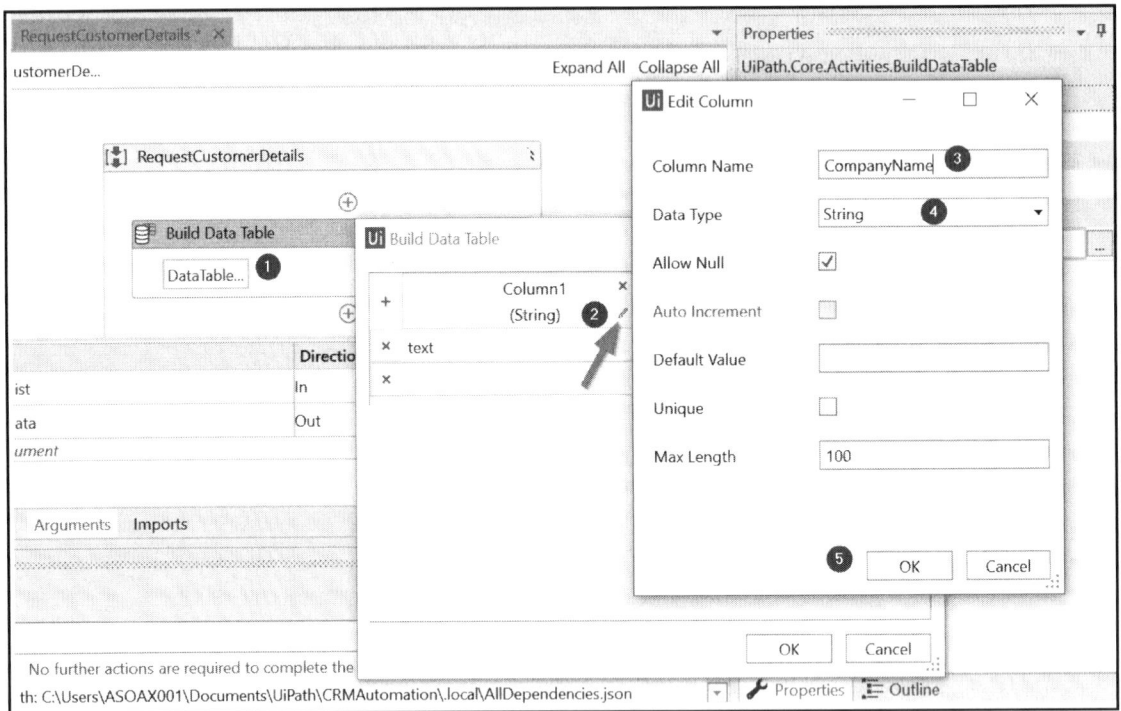

3. Once added, your **Data Table** will look as follows. Click on **OK** to continue:

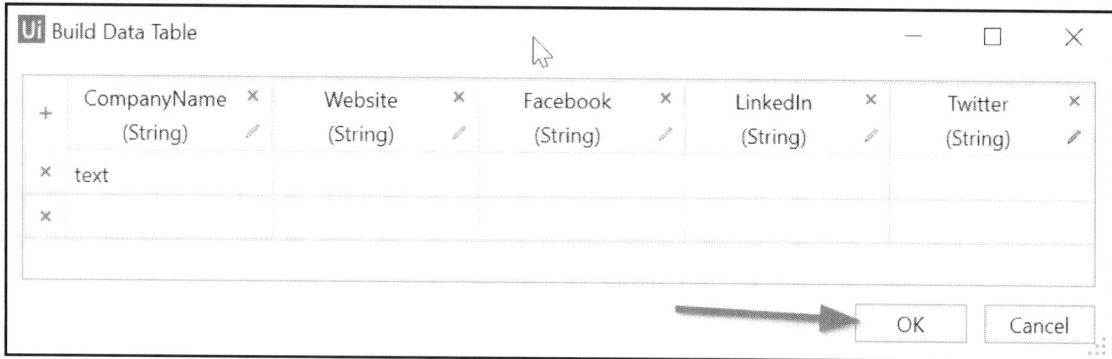

+	CompanyName ✕ (String) ✎	Website ✕ (String) ✎	Facebook ✕ (String) ✎	LinkedIn ✕ (String) ✎	Twitter ✕ (String) ✎
✕	text				
✕					

OK   Cancel

> **TIP**
> Make sure that you delete the default rows in the table. There is usually a row with the first column set to **text** as shown in the preceding screenshot. Also, ensure that all five columns are of the **String** type.

4. In the properties for the **Build Data Table** activity, update **Output | DataTable** to the `CompanyData` argument that we created earlier:

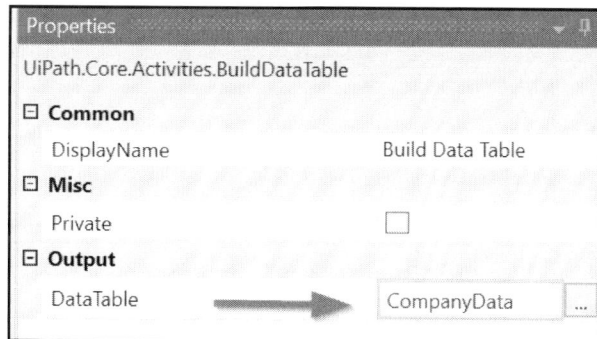

Properties

UiPath.Core.Activities.BuildDataTable

⊟ **Common**
  DisplayName   Build Data Table
⊟ **Misc**
  Private   ☐
⊟ **Output**
  DataTable   CompanyData   ...

Now that we have the data table, let's access the Crunchbase site.

Looping and creating company URLs

Now, we will construct company URLs so that we can look up the data for each company on the Crunchbase.com website:

1. Open Chrome and navigate to the lookup site:
    1. Use the **Open Browser** activity and configure the URL so that it's https://www.crunchbase.com/.
    2. Ensure that **Input | BrowserType** is Chrome.
    3. Create an output UiBrowser variable for this activity called browserCrunchBase.

   Your **Open Browser** activity will look like this:

2. As always, we will use a **Try-Catch** block to handle any exceptions. In the **Try** block, we will loop through the customer list and get the details of the company from this site.

3. Let's add the **For Each Row** activity in order to loop through the company names (customer names from CRM). Let's add the `CompanyList` argument we created previously as our input:

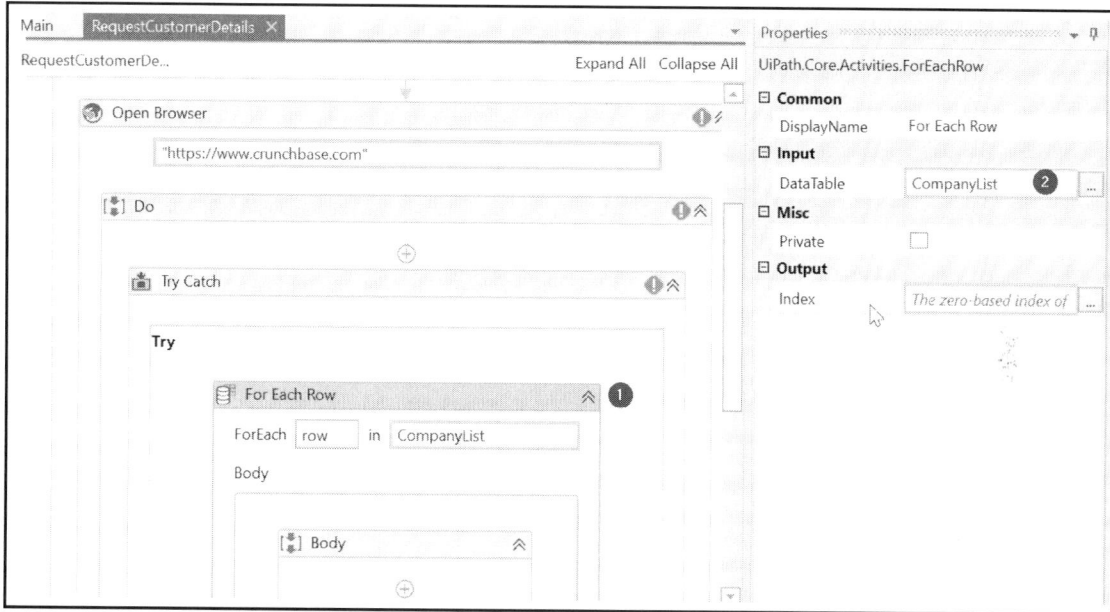

4. Next, we'll add variables for each piece of data we'd like to read from the Crunchbase website. As you may recall, this data is the customer's website and social media information. Let's add the respective variables, as shown in the following screenshot:

> strCrunchBaseURL has to be populated with the default, that
> is, "https://www.crunchbase.com/organization/".

5. We will use this URL to append company names and open the browser to a specific company detail view.

6. Now, we will go directly to the company page on Crunchbase.com and capture the company details. The first step is to construct the URL that contains the details for the specific company. The URL's format is www.crunchbase.com/organization/<company name>. We will use the strCrunchBaseURL variable that we created previously and append the company name to it. This needs to be in lowercase.

> At the time of writing this book, this is the current format of the
> Crunchbase.com company URL. If this changes, you may have to change
> the strCrunchBaseURL default value to the appropriate one.

7. Let's use the **Assign** activity to populate the strCompanyName variable with the lowercase name of the company from the CompanyList data table. To read and convert the company value from the data table into lowercase, we need to use row(0).ToString.ToLower. Then, we need to use the **Navigate To** activity and pass this parameter, which constructs the URL for the specific company, that is, strCrunchBaseURL+strCompanyName:

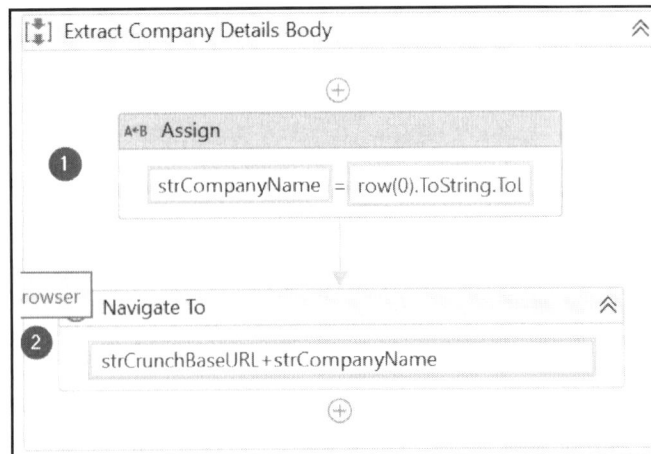

With the company URLs created, we are ready to extract the website and social media information for the company.

Extracting company details from Crunchbase.com

Now, let's use the UiPath recorder function to add the activities so that we can extract data from the Crunchbase website:

1. On your Chrome browser, go ahead and open `https://www.crunchbase.com/organization/uber` and scroll down to the place where **Website**, **Facebook**, **LinkedIn**, and **Twitter** information is visible:

2. Now, let's extract the website address and save it as the variable we created. To do this, open the UiPath web recorder and click on **Copy Text** on the **Recorder** panel. Then, point to the text on the website that says `www.uber.com`. Once you've done that, click on **Save and Exit** on the **Recorder** panel:

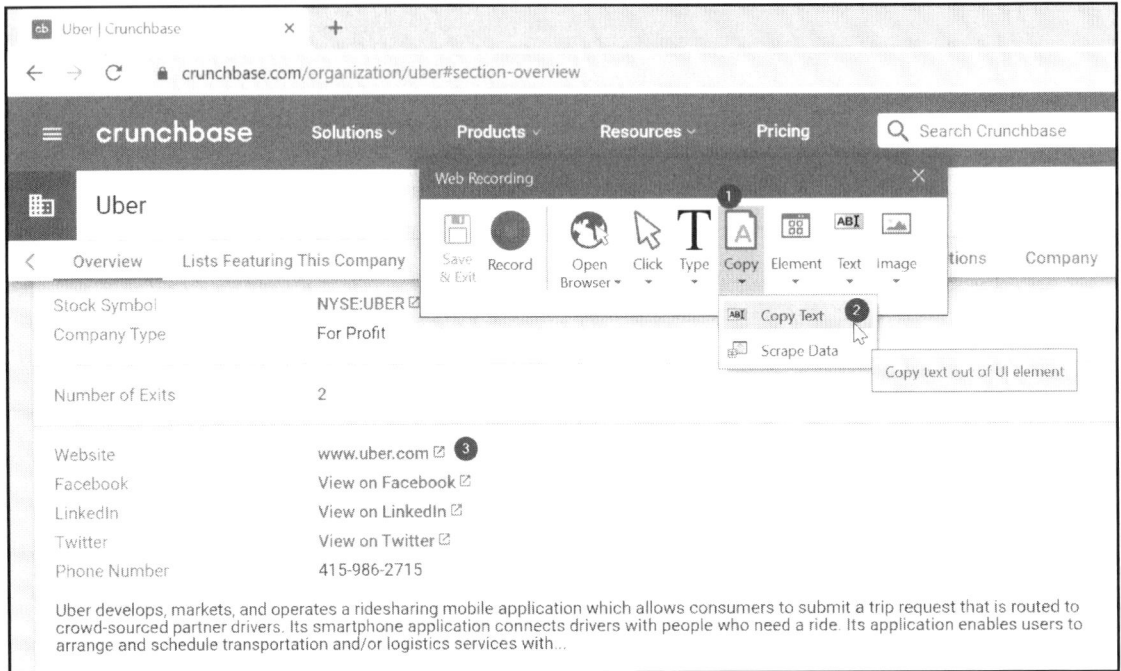

The recorder will add a new Web Sequence with the recorded action. Cut and move this Sequence to the **Try** block below the **Navigate to** activity.

3. Within the activities we just moved, click on the **Attach Browser** activity, update the **Browser** property to `browserCrunchBase`, and remove the existing values in the **Selector** parameter:

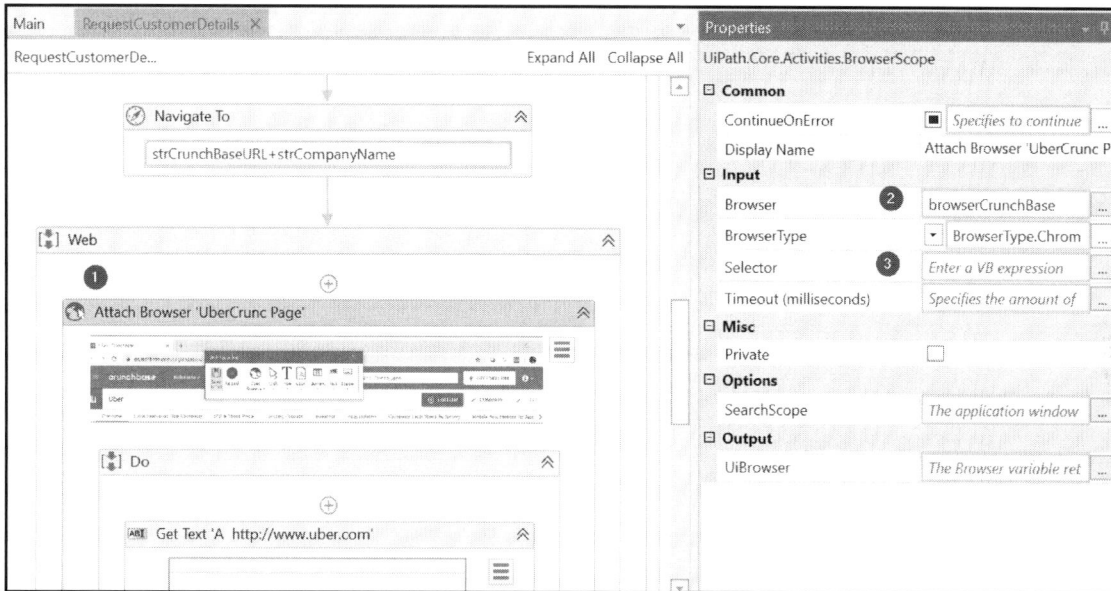

4. As we have been doing with our web Automations, let's add the **Activate** and **Maximize Window** activities before the **Get Text** activity within the **Do** Sequence.

We have to use *PgDn* key to get to the required information on the page. So, let's use the **Send HotKey** activity with the **pgdn** key and point to an object on the web page frame that contains the company information. Point to an object in the frame below the menus – one such label is **Overview** heading, which can be found on the default information tab:

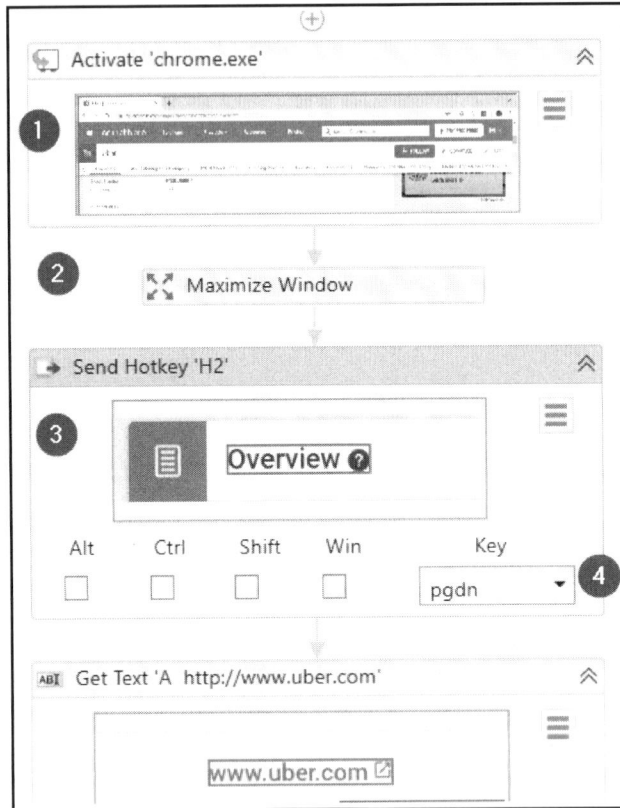

When working with web Automation, use **DelayAfter** and **DelayBefore** in the **Activities** properties panel to provide some wait time in milliseconds based on the performance of the system.

5. Now, let's assign this website data to the variable we created. Let's go to the **Get Text** activity properties and assign the output to the `strWebsite` variable that we created.

6. Let's also update the target selector so that it can work for any website data. To do this, click on the **Selector** and update the `aaname` from `www.uber.com` to `*com*`:

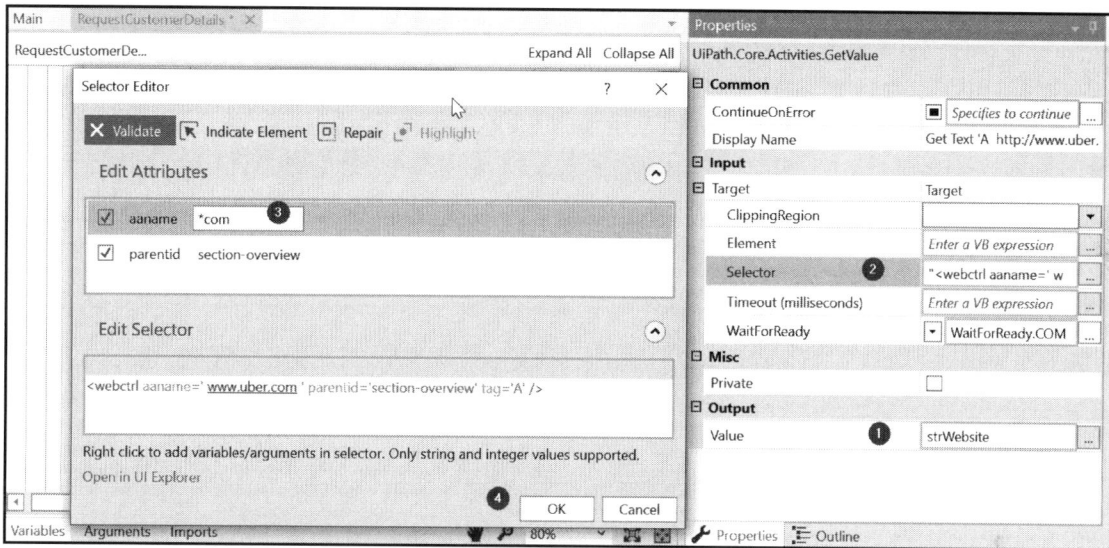

7. Next, let's extract the social media information, starting with the Facebook link. To do that, we will right-click and copy the Facebook link address. The shortcut key for this is *E*.

8. We will use the **Click** activity and point to the **View on Facebook** link on the web page. In the properties for this activity, let's update the properties of **MouseButton** to **BTN_RIGHT**:

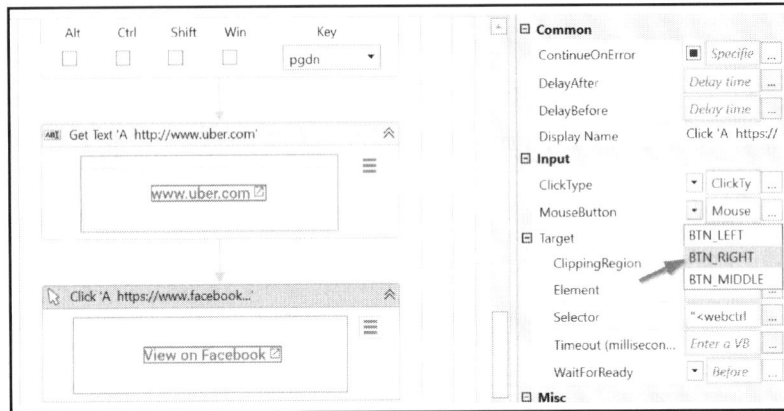

9. To copy the Facebook link address, we need to add a **Send HotKey** activity. Click on **View on Facebook** on the web page and press the *E* key. This will copy the Facebook link to the clipboard. We will then use **Get From Clipboard** to output the result to the `strFacebook` variable. Please use **DelayBefore** and **DelayAfter** in activity properties as necessary:

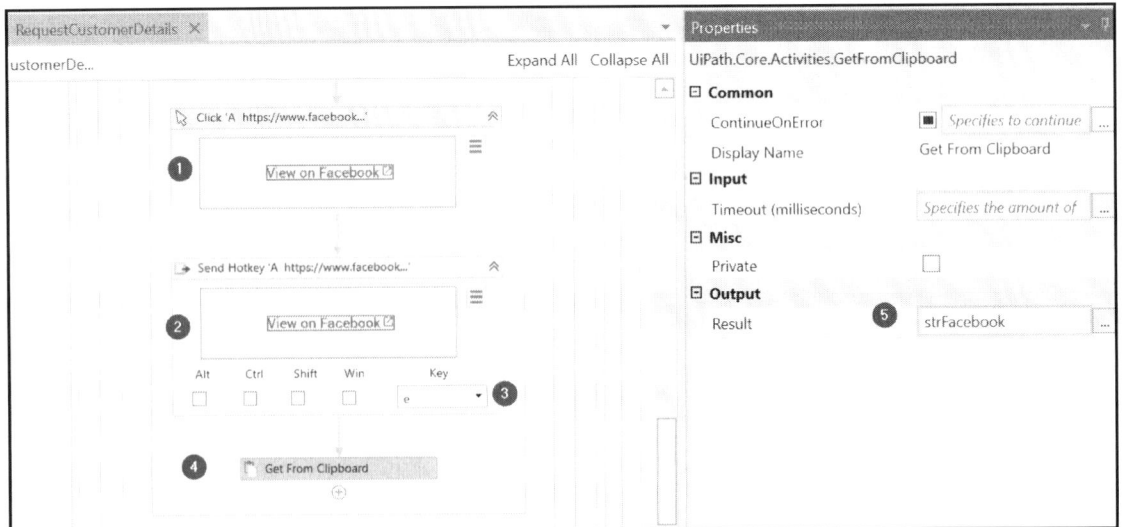

10. Repeat the **Click**, **Send HotKey**, and **Get From Clipboard** activities to capture the links for LinkedIn and Twitter. Then, store them in the `strLinkedIn` and `strTiwtter` variables.

> **TIP**
>
> You can find the recently used activities in the **Recent** section of the **Activities** panel on the left. So, all three activities can be easily dragged and dropped from the **Recent** section.

11. Now that we have extracted all the company data from `CrunchBase.com`, let's build the output data table so that we can pass it back to the **Main** workflow.

12. Let's use the **Add Data Row** activity to update the **ArrayRow** property to `{strCompanyName, strWebsite, strFacebook, strLinkedIn, strTwitter}` and the **DataTable** property to `CompanyData`. We will pass this **DataTable** argument back to `Main.xaml` once we've finished extracting:

13. Finally, let's add a **Log Message** activity to ensure extraction is successful. Set the **Level** to `Info` and add `"Customer details Extracted Successfully for: "+ strCompanyName` as the log message.

That's it for the **Try** block. Now, let's handle any exceptions within the **Catch** block. After doing this, we will test this Sequence once by invoking it from the **Main** workflow.

14. In web Automation, most exceptions occur because the selector of a web element hasn't been found. So, within the **Catch** block, let's add an exception called `SelectorNotFoundException`. In **Finally**, we'll add a **Log Message** activity with **Level** set to **Error** with the following message: `"Not able to get the information for Customer: "+strCompanyName + "Due to this Exception: "+exception.Message`.

> We can add multiple exceptions of different types based on the project's requirements. Here, we are only checking for and handling one exception.

15. Finally, add a **Close Tab** activity outside the **Try-Catch** block and pass `browserCruchbase` for the **Browser** parameter. This will ensure that we close the `Crunchbase.com` website after the data has been extracted:

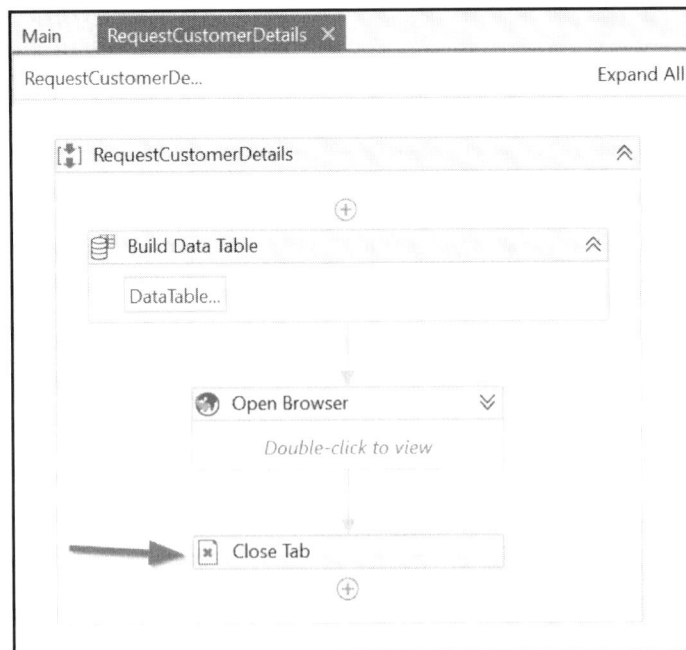

Now that we have a workflow set up so that we can capture the company data for our customers, let's use this workflow to get the customer details that we need to update CRM. With this, we have completed the `RequestCustomerDetails.xaml` workflow.

Invoking the RequestCustomerDetails workflow from the Main workflow

Now, we will go back to the **Main** workflow and invoke the customer information lookup workflow that we created in the previous section. Let's start by creating a variable that we'll use to store the company data:

1. In the `Main.xaml` file, create a new data table variable, call it `dtCompanyData`, and set its scope to `Main Sequence`. Let's also set the default values for both `dtCompanyList` and `dtCompanyData` to `New System.Data.DataTable`, as shown in the following screenshot:

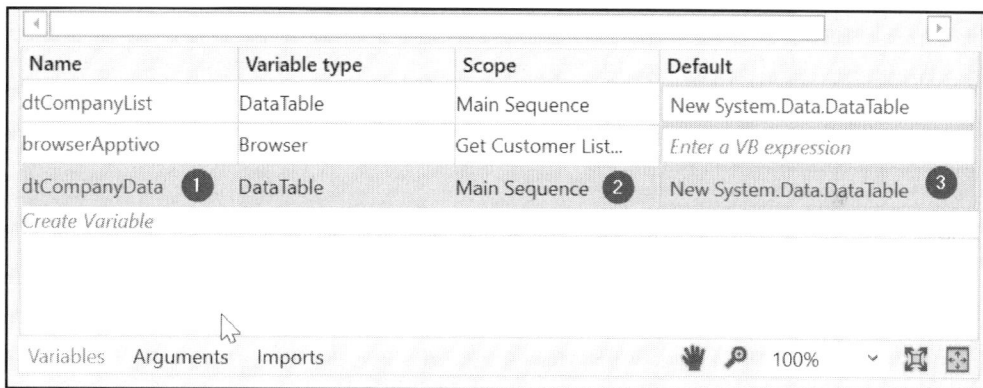

2. Now that we have the variable, let's add a new Sequence below the `Customer List Sequence` called `Request Customer details Sequence` and add the **Invoke Workflow file** activity. Point the activity to `RequestCustomerDetails.xaml`, click on **Import arguments**, and map the arguments to the respective input and output data table variables, as shown in the following screenshot:

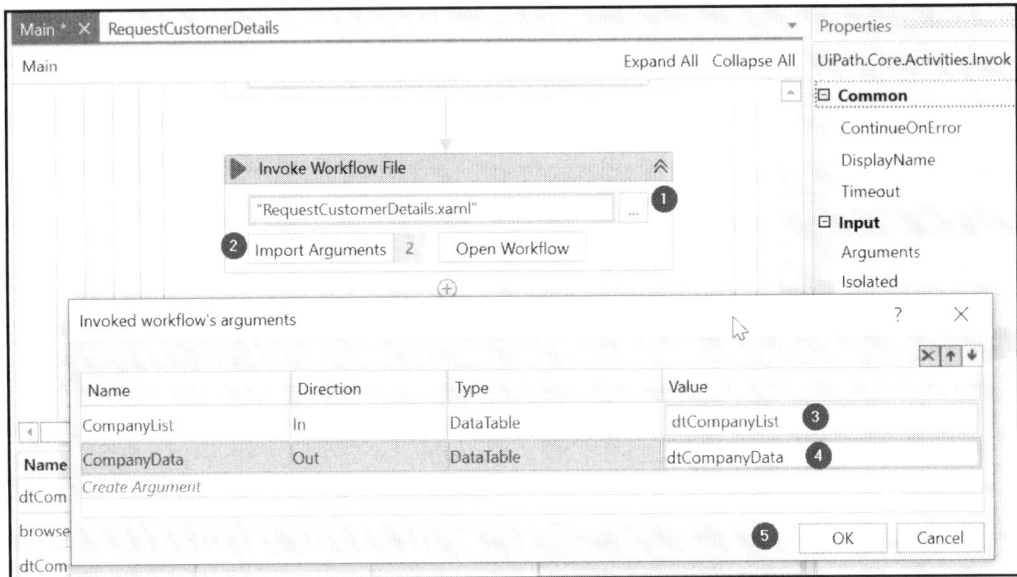

3. To test what we have so far, let's add a message box under **Invoke Workflow** and add `dtCompanyData.Rows.Count` as our message, as shown in the following screenshot:

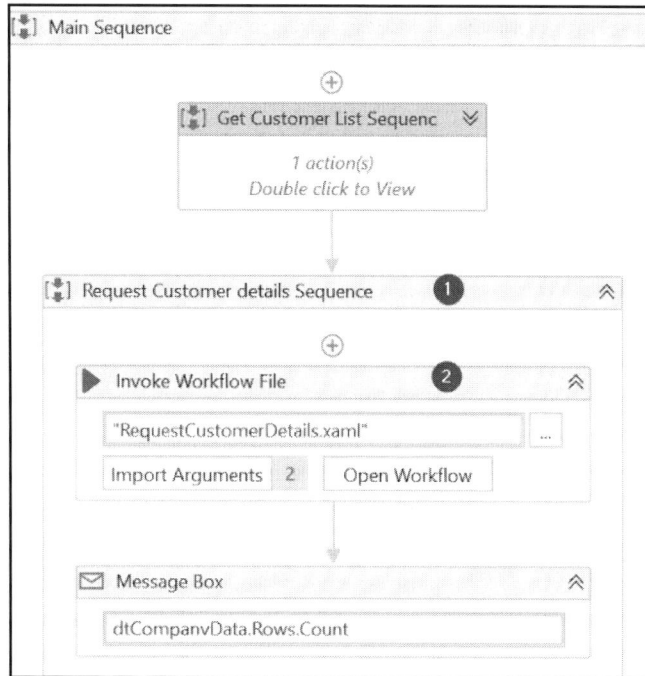

This will help us understand whether the output data tables have been populated and how many rows there are.

Now, let's run a test for the Automation we have so far. From the `Main.xaml` file, go ahead and run the Automation. You should receive a message with the count set to 3. This means the company details for all three companies have been extracted.

Now that we have the company information within the **Main** workflow, let's use that data and update the CRM.

Updating the CRM with customer information

In this final Sequence for `Main.xaml`, we will update the Apptivo CRM with the customer details we got from `Crunchbase.com`. Follow these steps to do so:

1. Let's create a new **Sequence** called `Update Customer Details Sequence`. We will continue to add this part of the Automation to the **Main** workflow. Add this Sequence under the **Invoke Workflow** from the previous section:

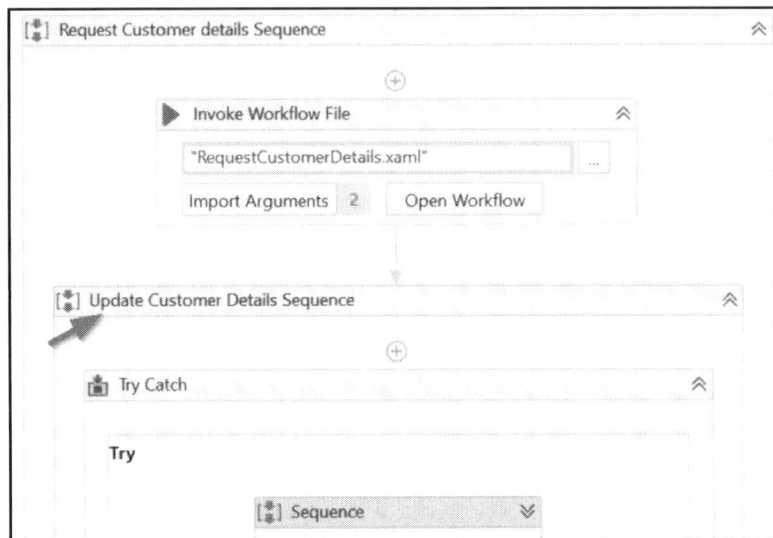

2. Let's add a **Try-Catch** block to the Sequence so that we can handle any exceptions that occur during the update operation in the CRM. In the **Try** block, we'll need to create some variables so that we can store the company name, website, Facebook, LinkedIn, and Twitter details:

Name		Variable type	Scope
strCompanyName	1	String	Try Catch
strWebsite	2	String	Try Catch
strFacebook	3	String	Try Catch
strLinkedIn	4	String	Try Catch
strTwitter	5	String	Try Catch

With the Sequence and variables added, let's loop through each customer's details and make the updates in Apptivo.

Looping through the data table and updating the CRM

Now, we will loop through the data table of extracted company details and update the CRM:

1. Let's add the **For Each Row** UiPath activity, which you can find under **DataTable**. Let's loop through the `dtCompanyData` data table.

2. Within this loop, we will use the **Assign** activity to assign values to all the variables we created previously. We will extract each row from the data table and convert them into strings using the `row(columnname or ColumnIndex).ToString` syntax; for example, `strCompanyName = row("CompanyName").ToString`. Your looping part of the Sequence will look as follows:

Note that we have to assign data to all five variables we defined previously.

3. With the data assigned to our variables, we can update the Apptivo CRM application. We will search for our customer in Apptivo and then go to that specific customer record and update the same.

4. To automate the search, we will use the UiPath web recorder to record the search steps. For that, manually open the customer page in Apptivo by going to the **CRM** menu option and then choosing **Customers**. Then, go to the UiPath web recorder option. From the **Recorder** panel, choose **Type** and input a customer name (say, `Amazon`) in the Apptivo search box, as shown in the following screenshot:

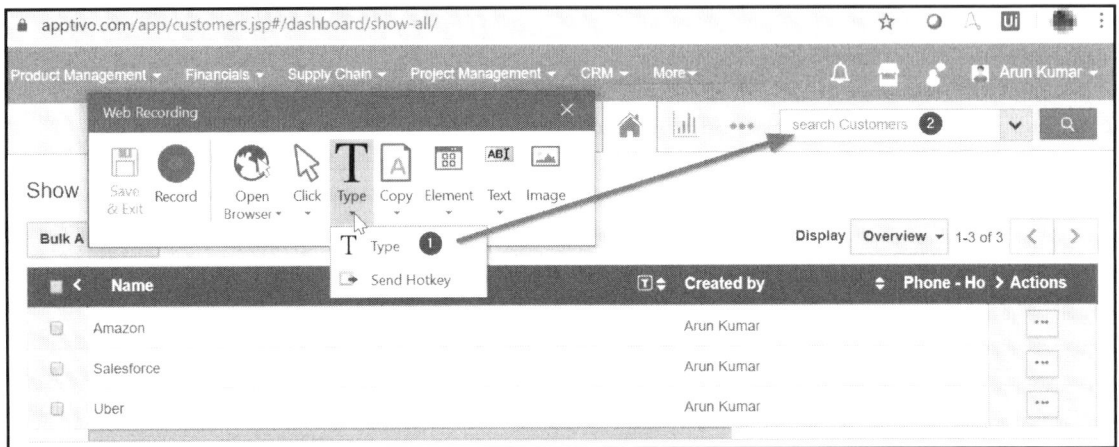

Once you've done that, **Save and Exit** the recording.

5. Now that we've got to the customer record, we will start the web Automation process so that we can enter the data into Apptivo. For that, we'll need to add the **Attach Browser** activity to the **Try** block, just below the set of Assign activities. Within the properties for this activity, update the browser attribute to `browserApptivo`. As you may recall, this is the browser variable we created during the first part of the Automation process.

> 💡 **TIP**
>
> If you are not able to reuse this browser variable, go back to the variable and ensure the scope of the variable is set to `Main Sequence`.

6. Now, let's copy the **Type Into** activity that was created by the web recorder into the **Attach Browser** activity. In the properties for this activity, let's update the **Target Text** value from **Amazon** to `strCompanyName`. Ensure you delete the web recorder's **Web** Sequence from the bottom, after copying the **Type** into the activity.

7. Next, we will use the **Send HotKey** activity, point to the same search box in Apptivo, and use the *Enter* key:

When we use the **Type Into** activity, in the properties panel, please use **DelayAfter**, **DelayBefore** to generate any necessary delays. Also, set the **EmptyFields** property to **True** to remove any existing input from the text boxes.

8. Apptivo displays the search results in a table with an action button so that we can edit the customer record. We will use the UI Automation `Click` activity and point that to the **More details** action button (**...**).

9. Clicking the action button takes you the customer details page in Apptivo. We have to click on any one of the text boxes – say, **Name** – to go to Edit mode. Let's use a **Click** activity again and point to the text next to the **Name** label:

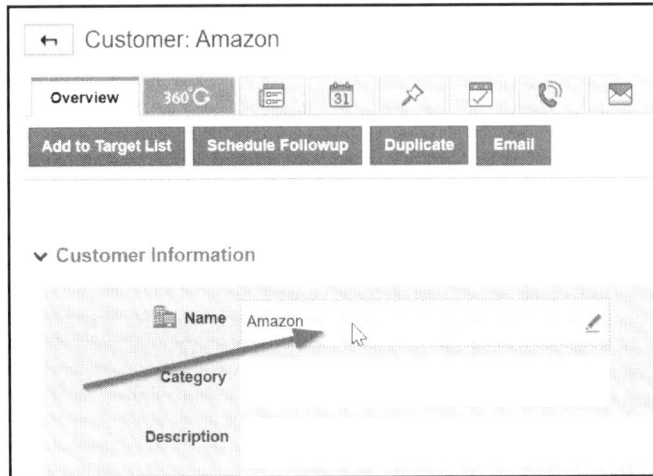

You will see the **Save** and **Cancel** buttons on the customer record, which means that you are in Edit mode.

10. In Edit mode, we can update the customer details. First, let's update the website's information. To do this, we have to scroll down to the **Website** text box. Let's use the **Send HotKey** activity and point to the name text box and **pgdn**. Copy this activity again to page down twice. You should be able to find **Website** in the **Additional Information** section.

11. Now, we will use the keyboard **Type Into** activity and point to the text box next to the **Website** label. Use the `strWebsite` variable to input the necessary value:

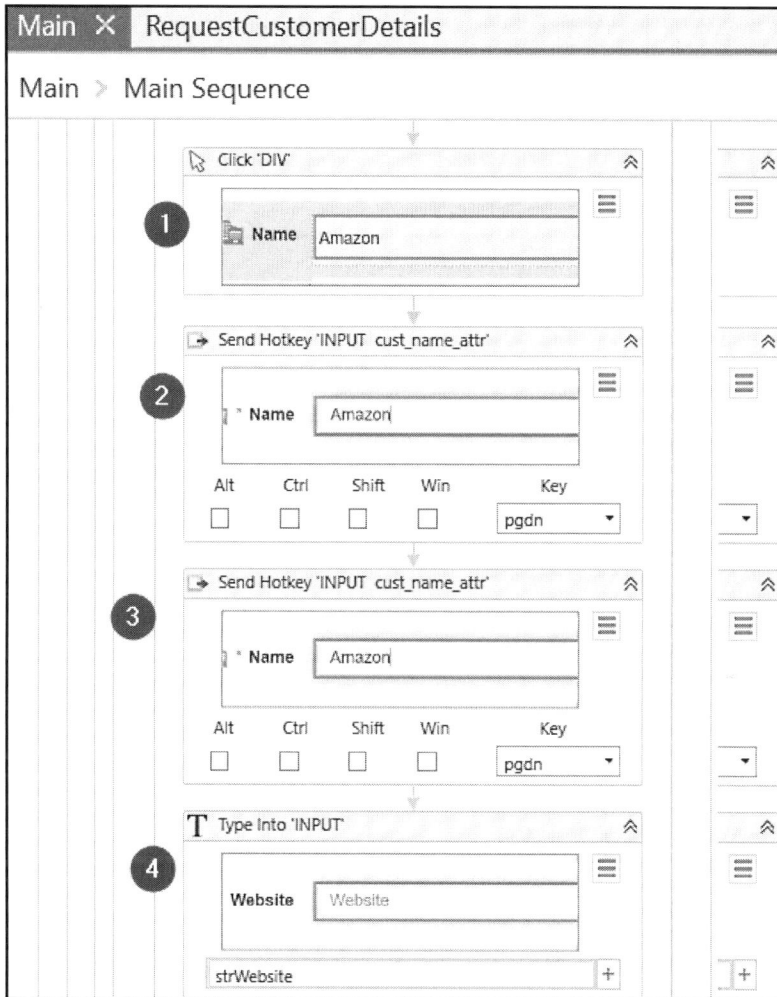

12. Next, we will find the social media fields on the page and update them as well. Let's use the page down twice more by using the **Hot Key** activity. You should be able to find the **Facebook**, **LinkedIn** and **Twitter** fields under the **Social Information** section.

13. Similar to the previous step, we will use the **Type Into** activity and perform the same steps to get the values of **Facebook**, **LinkedIn**, and **Twitter** into the `strFacebook`, `strLinkedIn`, and `strTwitter` variables.

14. Now that we have updated all the information, let's click on the **Save** button. Let's use the **Click** activity and point to the **Save** button at the top of the page:

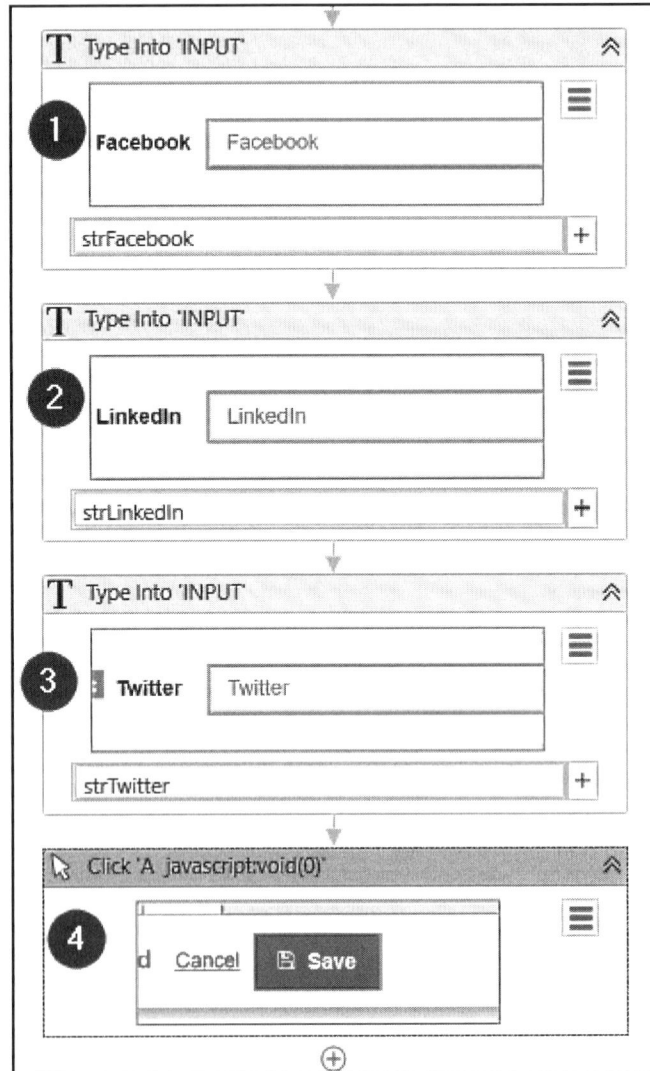

15. To make the Automation generic, let's edit the selector property in **Save** so that it only includes **aaname**. Go ahead and uncheck the **parentId** as the selector may change every time the Automation runs:

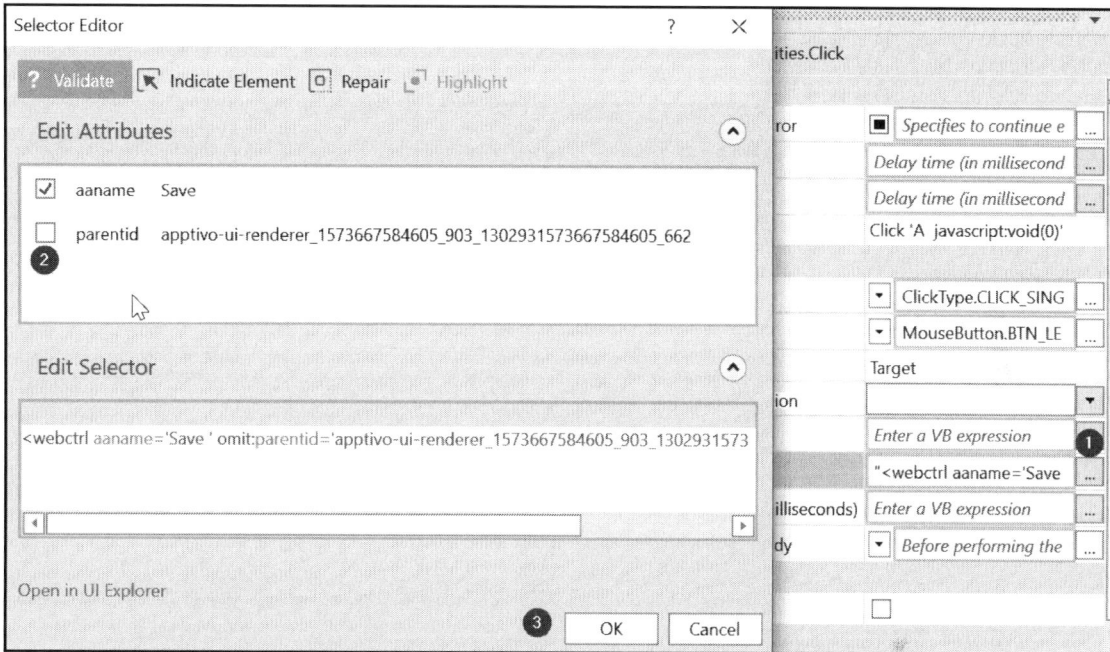

16. Finally, let's add a **Log Message** within the **Try** block that states, "Successfully Updated the Customer details for :"+ strCompanyName.
17. In the **Catch** block for Update Customer details Sequence, let's handle any exceptions that may arise. Let's add a new exception called SelectorNotFoundException. Within that, add a **Log Message** with the log **Level** set to **Error** and a message stating, "Cannot Update Customer details for :"+ strCompanyName+ " Due to this Error :" + exception.Message.
18. Please add a **Message box** activity stating that the **Automation is Completed** in the Finally block.

To test the complete Automation, make sure the Crunchbase.com web page is closed but ensure you're still logged in to your Apptivo page in your Chrome browser. Then, click on **Run**. The Automation process should take a few minutes to run and update the Apptivo CRM application.

Summary

In the chapter, we looked at a real-world project in order to learn how to keep the **Customer Relationship System (CRM)** updated. We captured information for the customers from a third-party website called `Crunchbase.com` and updated our CRM application, that is, Apptivo.

This project added a little more complexity in terms of data scraping, passing data tables containing customer information, and using that data to update our CRM application. We are steadily exploring more and more advanced features of UiPath.

In the next chapter, we will step things up a bit more and use AI computer vision to moderate social media posts.

Moderating Social Media Using 4 AI

So far, we've covered a few projects by completing basic UiPath activities such as web automation and Excel automation. In this chapter, we will cover further ground by invoking libraries from the UiPath marketplace, UiPath Go!, and creating our first **artificial intelligence** (**AI**)-based automation!

We will learn how to automatically moderate images that are uploaded to social media sites. This type of automation will process images using the Google Cloud Vision API and send the administrator a spreadsheet with its recommendations.

This project will help you understand the following:

- The basics of the Google Cloud Vision API using the Detect Explicit content or SafeSearch feature
- Using the UiPath Go! marketplace
- Using configuration files to avoid hardcoding
- UiPath Excel operations
- Using advanced Try-Catch blocks to handle exceptions in individual sequences

Technical requirements

You will need the following hardware and software to complete this project:

- A PC with UiPath Community Edition version 19+ installed.
- UiPath Go! registration. Go to `https://go.uipath.com` to sign up.

- Microsoft Excel 2007 or later.
- The Google Cloud Vision API. This allows developers to easily integrate vision detection features within applications, including image labeling, face and landmark detection, **optical character recognition** (**OCR**), and explicitly tagging content. More information can be found at `https://cloud.google.com/vision/`.
- Check out the following video to see the Code in Action: `https://bit.ly/2ZpArim`.

The code for this chapter can be found on GitHub at `https://github.com/PacktPublishing/Robotic-Process-automation-Projects/tree/master/SocialMediaSafeSearch`. Please follow it throughout.

Project overview

In this project, we will use the image recognition cloud service (SafeSearch in the Google Cloud Vision API) to detect whether any images being uploaded to a website contains any explicit content.

The administrators of social media sites have scripts running, as per a pre-defined schedule, to check any new images that are uploaded. If there are new uploads, the script copies those images to another folder for the bot to process. The administrator does not want the bot to be working directly on the social media website folder.

Once the bot detects that new files have been uploaded, it reads each file and creates an Excel log to pass to the administrator. It then loops through all the image entries in the spreadsheet and invokes SafeSearch in the Google Cloud Vision API to check the images. The API returns an output that indicates whether the image contains adult, medical, violent, or racy content. We add this output to Excel and send this to the administrator for him/her to take the appropriate action.

In this chapter, we will be building out the automation process performed by the bot. Here is a high-level workflow for the project:

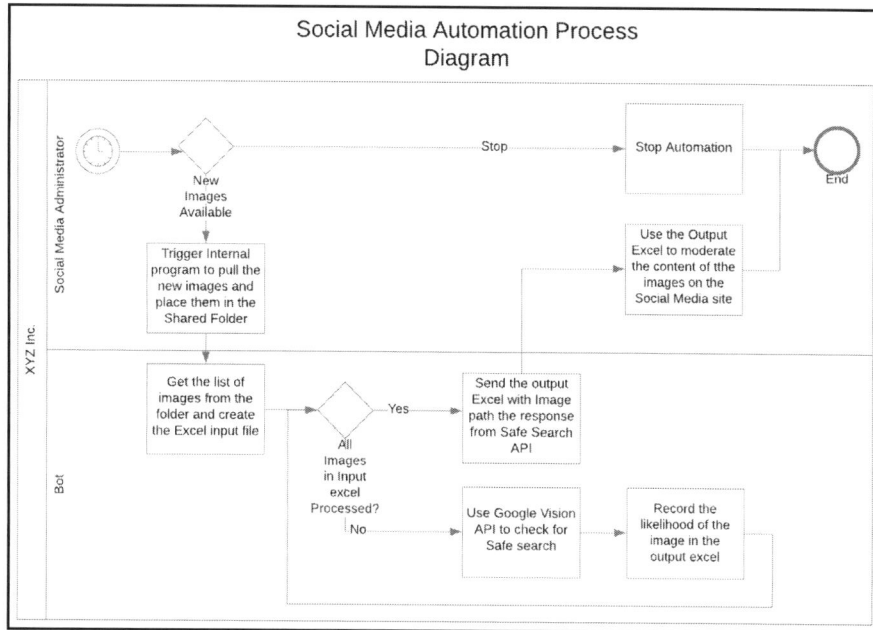

Social Media Automation Process Diagram

The SafeSearch API is an alias of Detect Explicit Content in the Google Cloud Vision API and might be used interchangeably in this chapter.

Now, let's look at the technical details for this project.

Project detail

In this section, we'll look at the overall flow for this project in terms of the UiPath project components we will be building and their interaction.

We will have a main workflow called `Main.xaml` that will invoke other workflows and orchestrate the automation. From this workflow, we will invoke the `ReadConfig.xaml` file to read the configuration parameters – the input and output file paths and Google Authentication.

The reason we have a configuration file is to avoid hardcoding values in the automation process. This also gives users the option to update the parameters without making any code changes.

With the configuration parameters, we will invoke the `BuildExcelList.xaml` file in order to read the images placed in the `Input` folder and create a list of images that we'd like to pass to the Google Vision SafeSearch API. We will create this image list, which includes the image's filename, and their path, which will be placed in another Excel file called `ImageDetails.xlsx`.

Next, we will retrieve the Google API's credentials and pass those along with the Excel file we built to `SafeSearch.xaml`. Within this SafeSearch workflow, we will loop through and invoke the Google Vision SafeSearch API for each image in the list. The SafeSearch Google Vision API returns the likelihood of the images being adult, medical, violent, or racy. This is populated in the `ImageDetails.xlsx` Excel file and placed in the `Output` folder for the administrator to review and moderate. Here is the sequence diagram for this automation process:

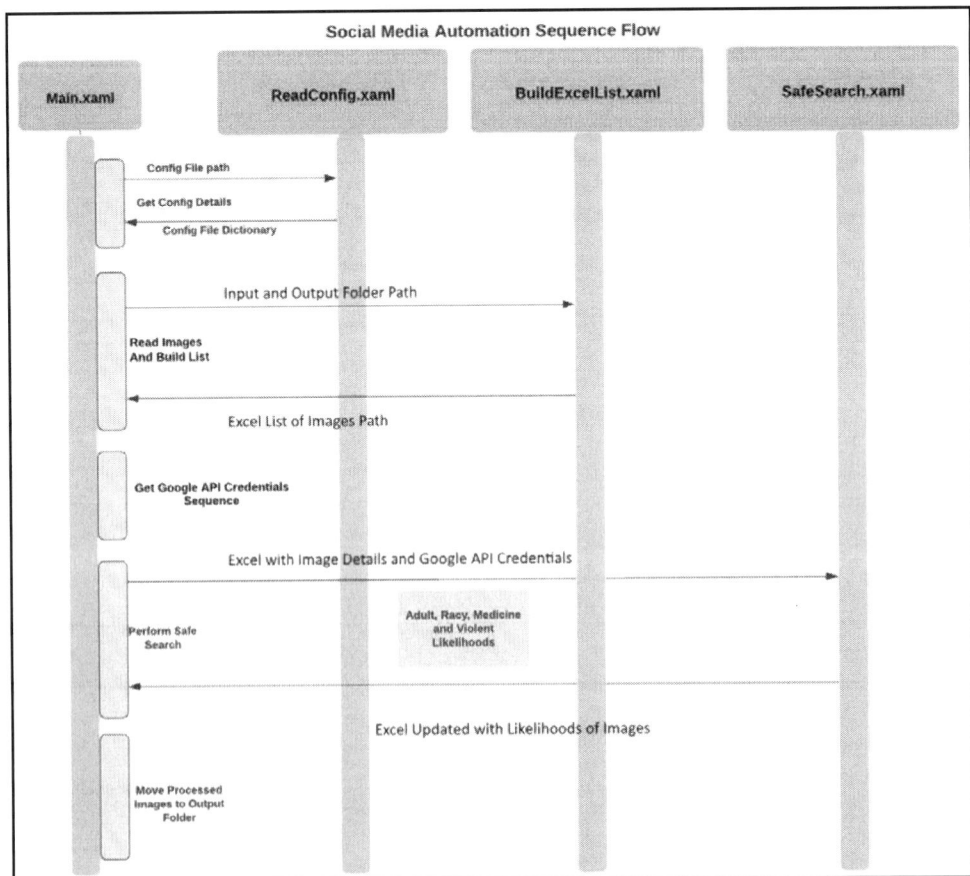

Now, let's start stepping through each of the workflows in detail, starting with the main workflow.

Getting started with the project

As with any UiPath project, we will start by opening UiPath Studio and creating a new project. Perform the following steps:

1. Open UiPath Studio and choose the **New Blank Process** option on the initial screen.
2. In the main workflow, let's start by adding a sequence called `Main Sequence`.
3. Next, we'll add a **Try-Catch** block to manage exceptions.
4. Within the **Try** block, add a new sequence called **Config Sequence**. This is where we will add the activities related to reading in values from the configuration file.
5. Within this sequence, we need to add a **Log Message** that says `Open Config.xls and store the values`. So far, your main workflow should look like this:

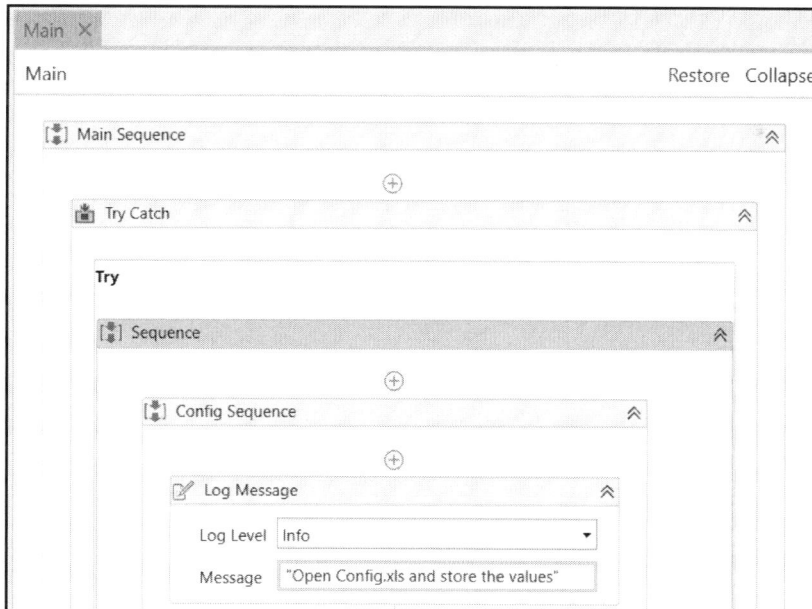

Before we configure our main workflow further, let's do some groundwork that's required for the project.

Project groundwork

We will create the image folders for the bot to pick up and place the processed images. We will also create an Excel configuration file that the administrator can use to specify the parameters to be used by the bot. Let's get started:

1. First, we need to create two folders in the UiPath project folder:
   - `Input`: This folder will hold social media images to be moderated. Place a few image files here that you would like to detect explicit content for.
   - `Output`: The bot will place the file with the image likelihood results in this folder. Create an Excel file called `ImageDetails.xlsx` with five columns called `ImagePath`, `Adult`, `Violence`, `Racy`, and `Medical`, as shown in the following screenshot:

2. Next, let's prepare the configuration file. To store the configuration parameters, we'll create an Excel file called `Config.xlsx`. We will place it in the same UiPath project folder we placed the `Input` and `Output` folders, as shown in the following screenshot:

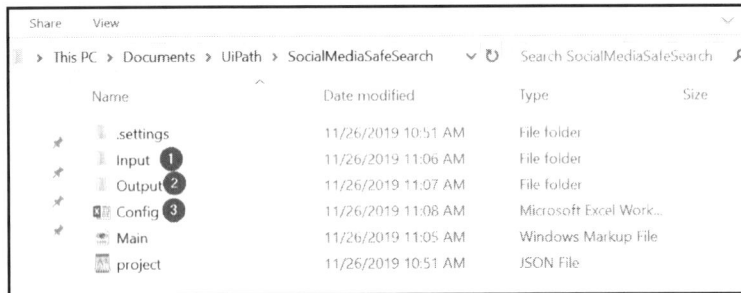

3. Open the `Config.xlsx` file and rename `Sheet1` to `Constants`. In the sheet, add the following content shown in the following table and save it:

Name	Value	Description
InputFolder	C:\Users▓▓▓▓▓▓▓ocialMediaSafeSearch\Input	Input Folder will hold the Social Media Images to be moderated
OutputFolder	C:\Users▓▓▓▓▓▓▓\SocialMediaSafeSearch\Output	Output Folder will have a ImageDetails.xlsx file with the result of the image safe content response.
GoogleAuthenticationName	GoogleAuthentication	Microsoft Credential Manager's credential's name for Google Authorization

The **Description** column values are optional.

> We are using a configuration file to avoid hardcoding values through automation. This also allows users to update the parameters without opening UiPath Studio.

Now that we have completed the groundwork, let's get back to the main sequence and read the configuration file we just added.

Reading parameters from the configuration file

We will use a separate workflow to read the configuration parameters and pass them to the main workflow. So, let's create the new sequence file by clicking on **New** on the UiPath Studio ribbon and choosing the **Sequence** option. Name the new sequence ReadConfig.xaml and click on **Create**.

In this sequence file, we will open the Config.xlsx file that we created in the previous section, read the values, and store them as Dictionary arguments. Then, we will pass this Dictionary variable with the populated key-value pairs back to **Main** for the automation process to use.

> The UiPath Dictionary variable or argument type is used to store key-value pairs.

Let's open the ReadConfig.xaml sequence and step through how to create the workflow:

1. Add an input **String** argument called in_ConfigFile with a default value of Config.xlsx. Add an **Output** argument of the **Dictionary** type called out_Config.

2. Add the following variables. Ensure that the direction and type of argument match:

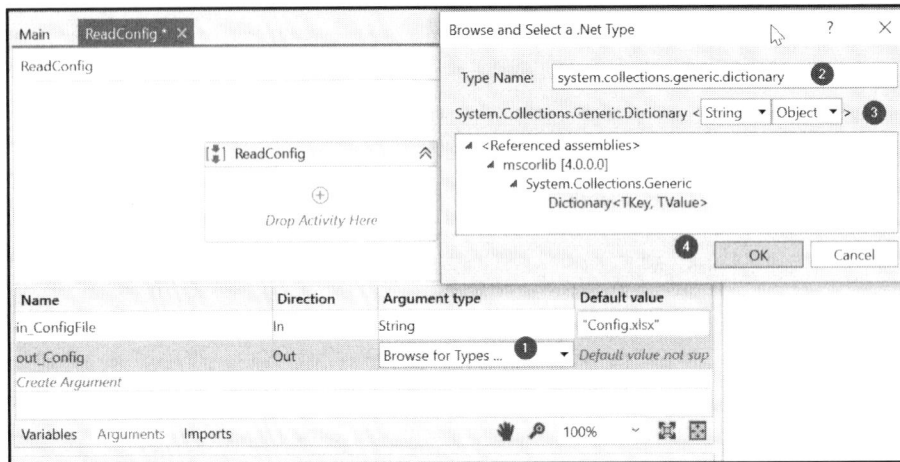

3. We will start the workflow by adding the **Try-Catch** block for exception handling. In the **Try** block, let's initialize the Dictionary argument before we use it.

4. Let's use the **Assign** activity and set `out_Config` to `new Dictionary(of String, object)`.

5. Next, let's use the **Read Range** activity under the workbook to read the `config.xlsx` file's content. Your workflow should look as follows:

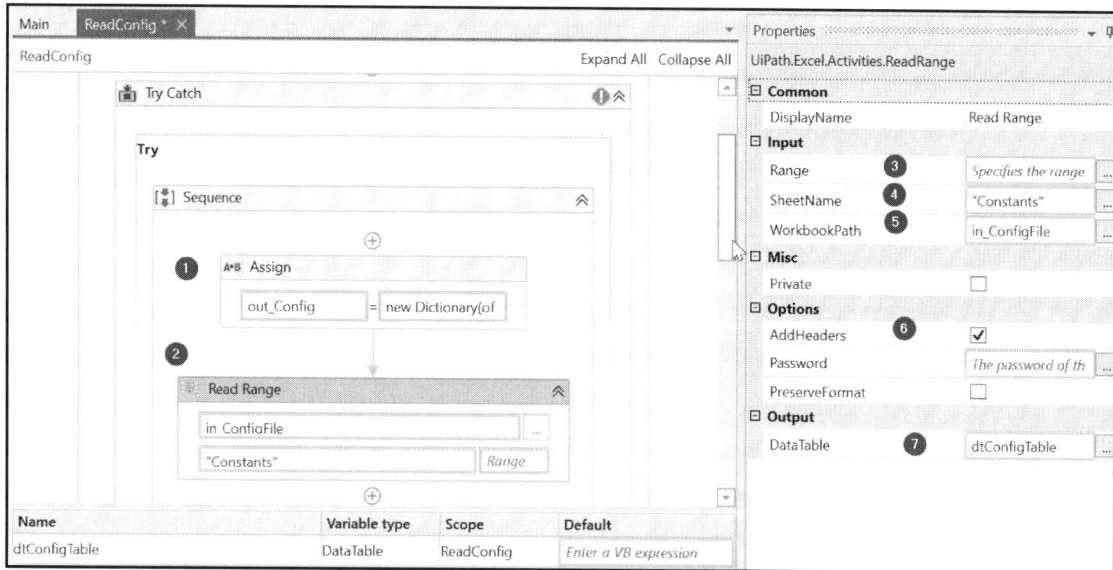

6. Set the properties of the **Read Range** activity as follows:
   - Leave the **Range** property blank as we want to read all the content in the sheet.
   - Add the **SheetName** – we named it "Constants".
   - In the **WorkbookPath**, add the in_ConfigFile input argument.
   - Check **AddHeaders.**
   - For **Output | DataTable**, create a new variable called dtConfigTable (use *Ctrl + K*).

7. The **Read Range** activity helped us read the value of an Excel range and store it in the **DataTable** named dtConfigTable. Now, let's iterate the dtConfigTable and store it in the output Dictionary argument.

8. We will use the **For Each Row** activity to read each row from the **DataTable** and update the key-value pairs in the dtConfigTable Dictionary argument.

9. As we read each row, we'll omit the empty rows and only get values that are not null. To do that, we need to add an **If** control activity and add a condition stating `NOT string.IsNullOrEmpty(row("Name").ToString.Trim)`. Your workflow should now look like this:

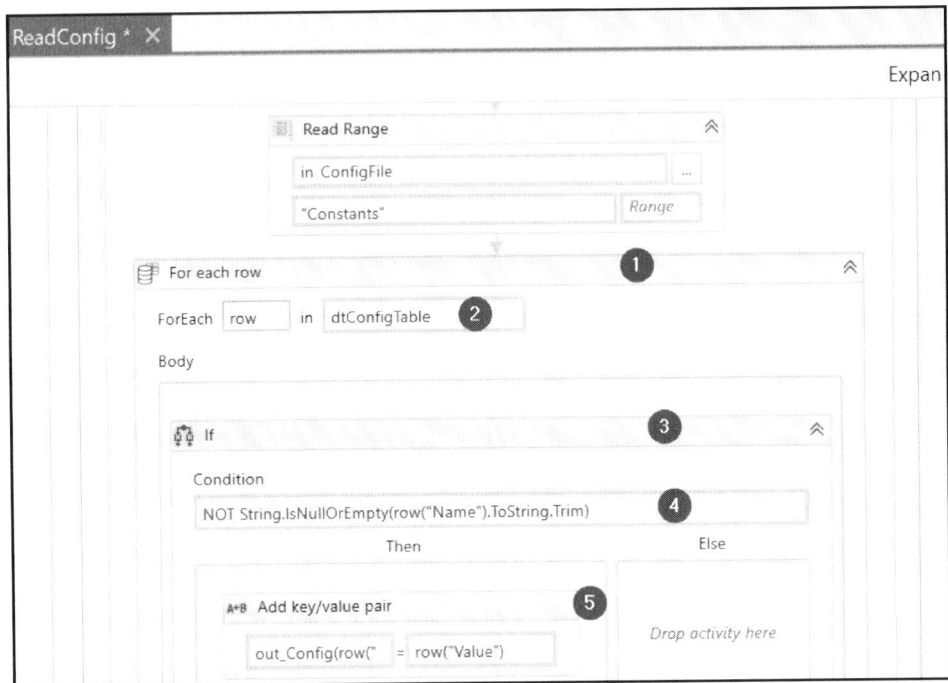

10. If the rows are not null, then you'll need to populate the Dictionary variable. We'll use the **Assign** activity to do so – let's name it `Add key/value pair`. In this activity, we will assign `out_Config(row("Name").ToString.Trim)` to `row("Value")`. This will take the row values from the DataTable and store them in the output Dictionary argument.

11. Finally, let's go to the **Catch** block and handle the system exception. For that, choose **System.exception** and add a log message at the **Trace** level stating `"No Constants defined for the process"`.

Now that we have a workflow that can be used to read the configuration file, let's invoke this sequence from Main and test whether the values are retrieved.

Passing the configuration parameters to the main workflow

Now, let's get back to the main workflow, `Main.xaml`, and continue from where we left off:

1. Add an **Invoke Workflow File** activity, right after the log message that we had added within the main sequence's **Try** block. Within the **Invoke** activity, set the workflow filename to `ReadConfig.xaml`.

2. To read in the arguments, we'll need to add a couple of variables. Create a new variable called `Config` of the Dictionary type (**Dictionary<String, Object>**) and set the scope to a **Try-Catch** block.

3. Add three more variables to store the config file values: `strInputFolder`, `strOutputFolder`, and `strGoogleAuthName`. All these variables are of the **String** type and the Sequence scope.

4. Click on **Import Arguments** within the activity and map the newly created variable to the output argument values, as shown in the following screenshot:

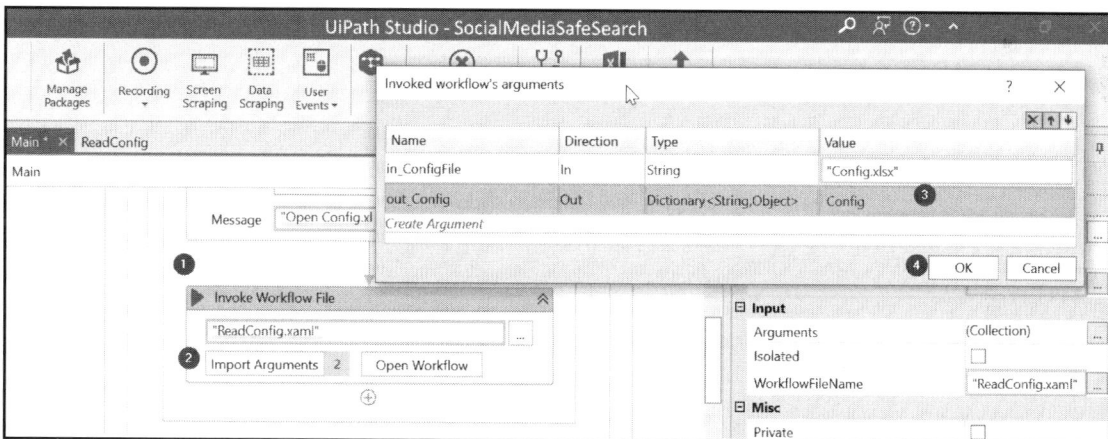

5. Next, let's use three **Assign** activities to store the outputs from the config file into the three **String** variables that we created previously. The **Assign** activities should have the following code:

   - `strInputFolder = Config("InputFolder").ToString`
   - `strOutputFolder = Config("OutputFolder").ToString`

- strGoogleAuthName =
  Config("GoogleAutheticationName").ToString

6. To test these, let's use a **Message Box** to display the values and test the automation so far. Add the following message to check whether the values have been populated: strInputFolder +" "+strOutputFolder+" "+strGoogleAuthName.

7. Staying within the main workflow, go ahead and run the project using the **Run** option in the UiPath Studio ribbon. Choose **Debug File** and then **Run**, just as we did in previous projects. Your output should look as follows:

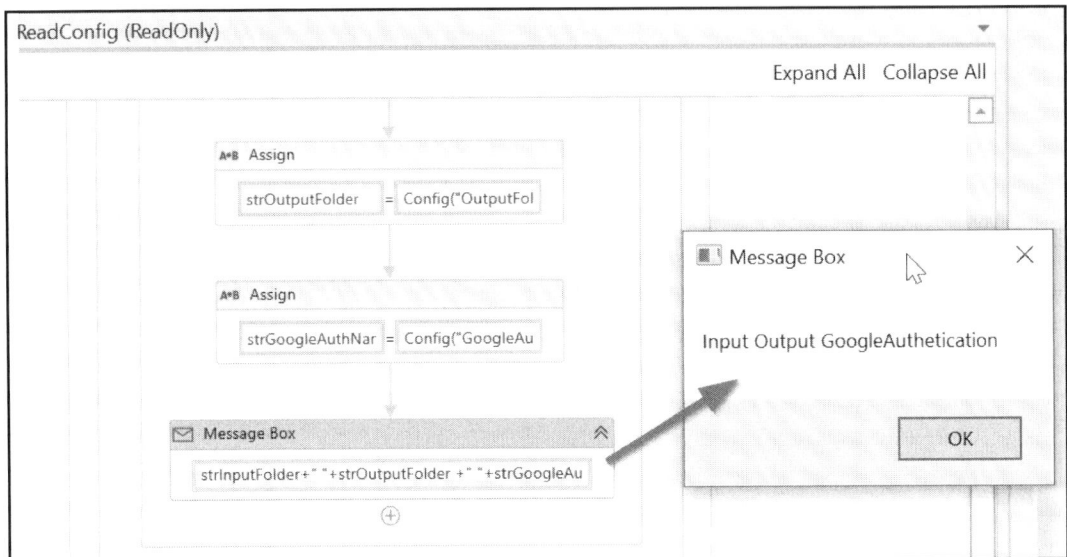

Please remove the message box after performing this test. Alternatively, you can use the **Write Line** activity to test and leave it in the workflow, even after testing.

8. Finally, let's add a **Log Message** of the **Log Level** set to **Info** and a **Message** stating "Config File content extracted successfully". This will help us with the debugging process, if required.

Now, we can invoke the configuration workflow and get the values we wish to use within the automation process.

Now, we can use these parameters to call the Google SafeSearch API. Before that, however, let's build an Excel list that we will pass to the API.

Reading image files from the input folder and creating a list

In this section, we will build an image details list in an Excel file called `ImageDetails.xlsx` in the `Output` folder. This file will be used to store the names (along with the file paths) of the images that will be submitted to the SafeSearch API for moderation. Once we get the results for the image back from the API, we will add them to the sheet. Let's start by reading the files in the `Input` folder.

Reading files in the input folder

Perform the following steps:

1. First, let's add a new sequence to the project. Click on **New** and choose **Sequence** from the UiPath ribbon. Name the sequence as `BuildExcelList` and click **Create**.
2. Before we configure the workflow, let's add the input arguments for the sequence `InputFolder` and `OutputFolder`, both of which are of the **String** type. Your workflow should look like this:

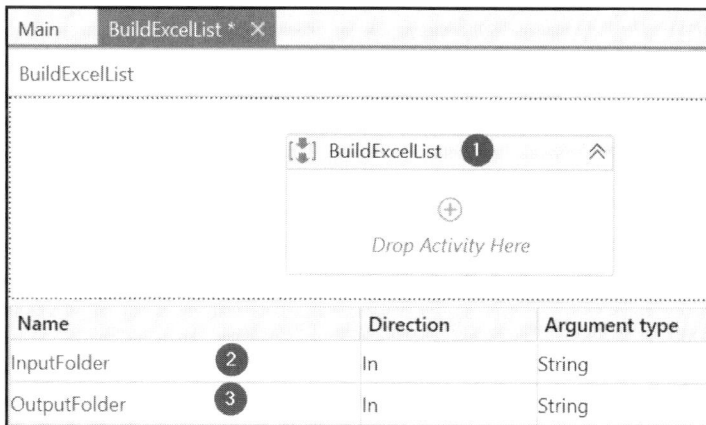

3. Now, let's add a **Try-Catch** block for exception handling.

4. Within the **Try** block, add the **Excel Application Scope** activity and set the workbook path to `OutputFolder+"\ImageDetails.xlsx"`. Within this scope, we will get the list of image paths from the input folder and write the image paths to the first column of the output file.

> The Excel application scope opens the Excel workbook for you. You can create your Excel activities within this block. When you've finished executing this activity, the workbook and the Excel application will be closed.

5. With the Excel scope set, use the value of the `InputFolder` argument to get all the files present in that folder path. To do that, add a **For Each** activity within the sequence and update the properties, as follows:
   - Set the **TypeArgument** property to **Object.**
   - Set the **Values** property to `Directory.GetFiles(InputFolder)`. This will help us get all the files present in the `InputFolder` path.

Your workflow should now look like this:

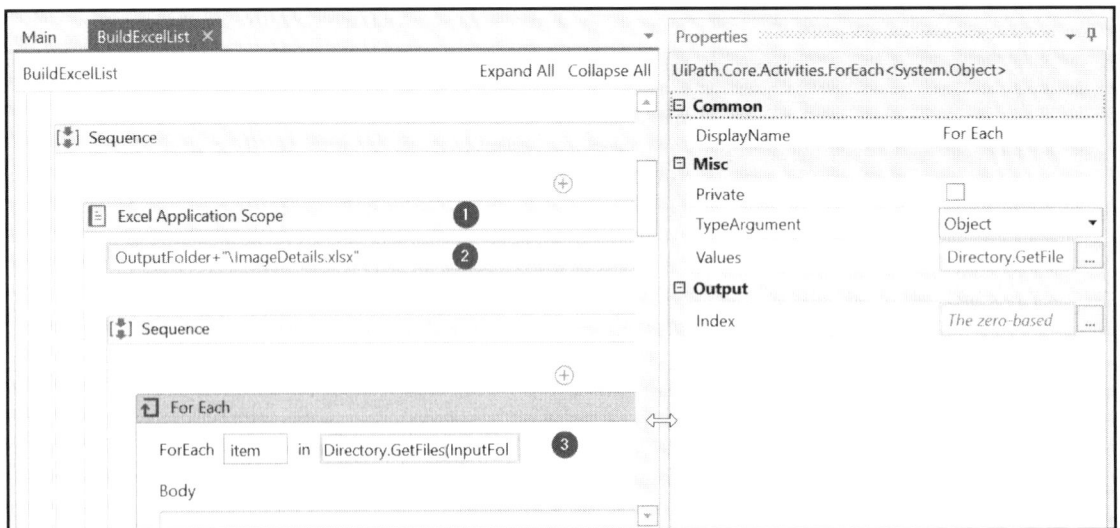

Next, let's get ready to read and write the image file paths in the `Input` folder.

Reading and writing the image path list to the ImageDetails Excel file

Perform the following steps:

1. Since we only need the image files, we need to check whether the files have a certain extension – we will only pass JPG or PNG images in this project. To inspect the file properties, create a new variable called `strFileInfo` of the **FileInfo type** and set the scope to the **Try-Catch** block.

2. Let's also add a counter variable called `intCounter` of the **Int32** type and set the scope to **Try-Catch** as well. We will be using this variable to loop through the Excel cells. Go ahead and set the default value for this variable to "**2**" since we want to start from the second row in Excel.

3. Now that we have the variables, let's use the **Assign** activity to pass the file information (`New FileInfo(item.ToString)`) value to the `strFileInfo` variable we just created. Now, we are ready to inspect the variable for file information. Here is what your **For Each** part of the workflow should look like:

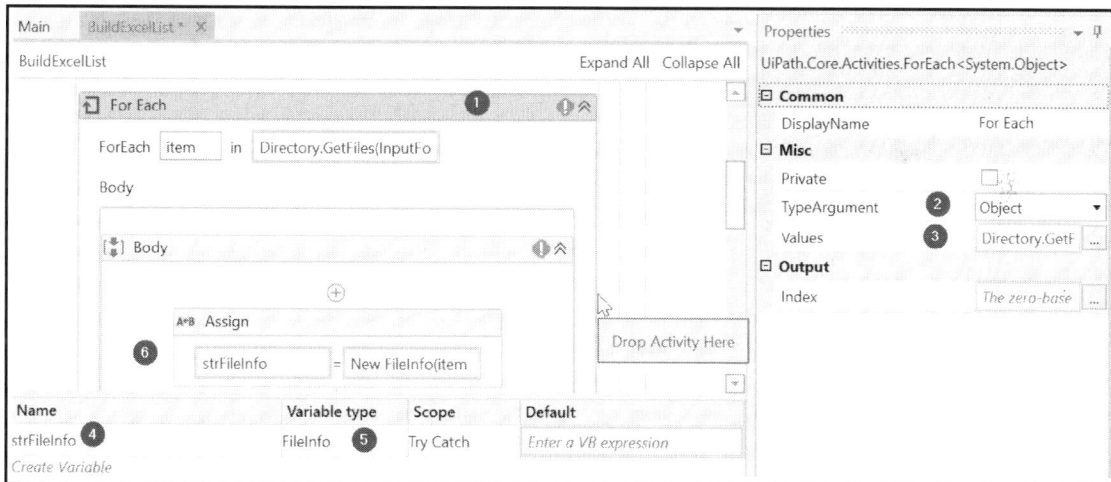

4. Let's add some conditions so that only image files are extracted. For that, we will add an **If** block with the condition set to `strFileInfo.Extension =".jpg" Or strFileInfo.Extension =".png"`.

The Google Cloud Vision API supports images of different types too. Please go ahead and try adding different image types, such as `.img`, `.tiff`, and so on, as you need to in order to test out this API.

5. In the **Then** part of the **If** block, write the file path to the Excel cells in column **A**. To do that, we will use the **Write Cell** activity (**App Integration** | **Excel** | **Write Cell**). For this activity, update the following properties:
   - Set the **Range** property to `"A"+intCounter.ToString`.
   - Set **Value** to `strFileInfo.FullName`.

As you can see, we set the range for **Column** with the incrementing counter for the rows. The **Value** would be the full file path of the image files.

6. Since we want to loop, let's add an **Assign** activity to increment `intCounter`. To do so, assign `intCounter` to `intCounter +1`. Your workflow should look like this:

7. Now that we have written the `ImageDetails.xlsx` file with the image file paths, we need to add a **Log message** with **Log Level** set to **Info** and a **Message** that states "`Image list was successfully retrieved`". Let's add this outside the Excel application scope and within the **Try** block, as shown in the following screenshot:

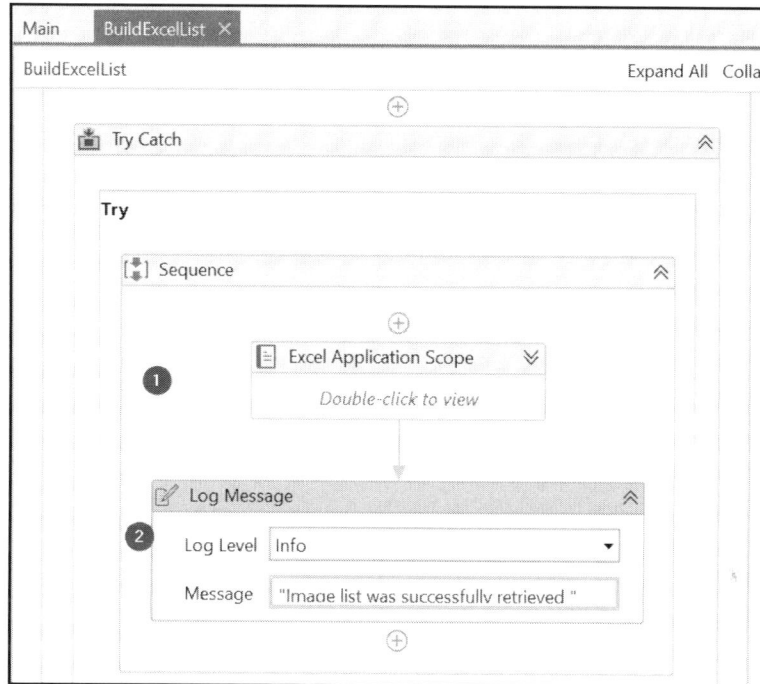

With that, we have completed our `BuildExcelList` sequence. Let's finish this by handling any exceptions using the **Catch** block.

Handling exceptions for the BuildExcelList workflow

Go to the **Catch** part of the `BuildExcelList` sequence and handle **System. Exception**. Select **System. Exception** and add a **Log Message** activity that states, "`Cannot read the images list from the Input Folder. Hence terminating the workflow.`".

Follow this up by adding a `Terminate Workflow` activity under the log message to stop the automation process. We're doing this since we cannot proceed further without the images list. Your workflow for the `BuildExcelList` workflow should look like this:

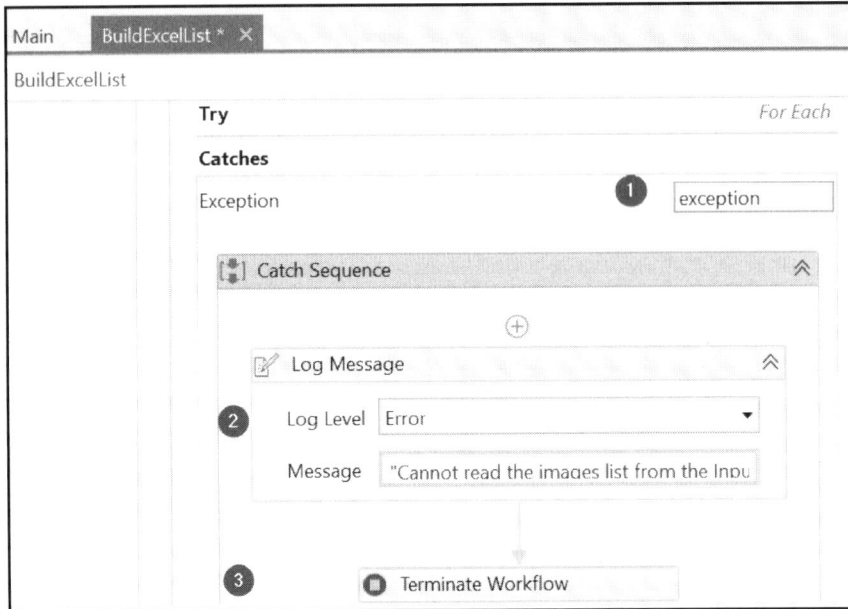

That completes our `BuildExcelList` workflow, where we read the image files and wrote their paths into an output Excel sheet. Now, we will perform a unit test for this workflow.

Testing the BuildExcelList workflow

In this section, we will invoke the `BuildExcelList` workflow from the main workflow and check whether the output Excel file has been updated with the image paths:

1. Go back to the main workflow and add a new sequence, just after the **Config Sequence**. Let's call this sequence **Read Images and Build List Sequence**.
2. Within this sequence, we'll add an **Invoke Workflow File** activity and point this activity to `BuildExcelList.xaml`.

3. Next, click on **Import Arguments** and map `InputFolder` and `OutputFolder` to the variables we created to store the values we retrieved from the configuration file, as shown in the following screenshot:

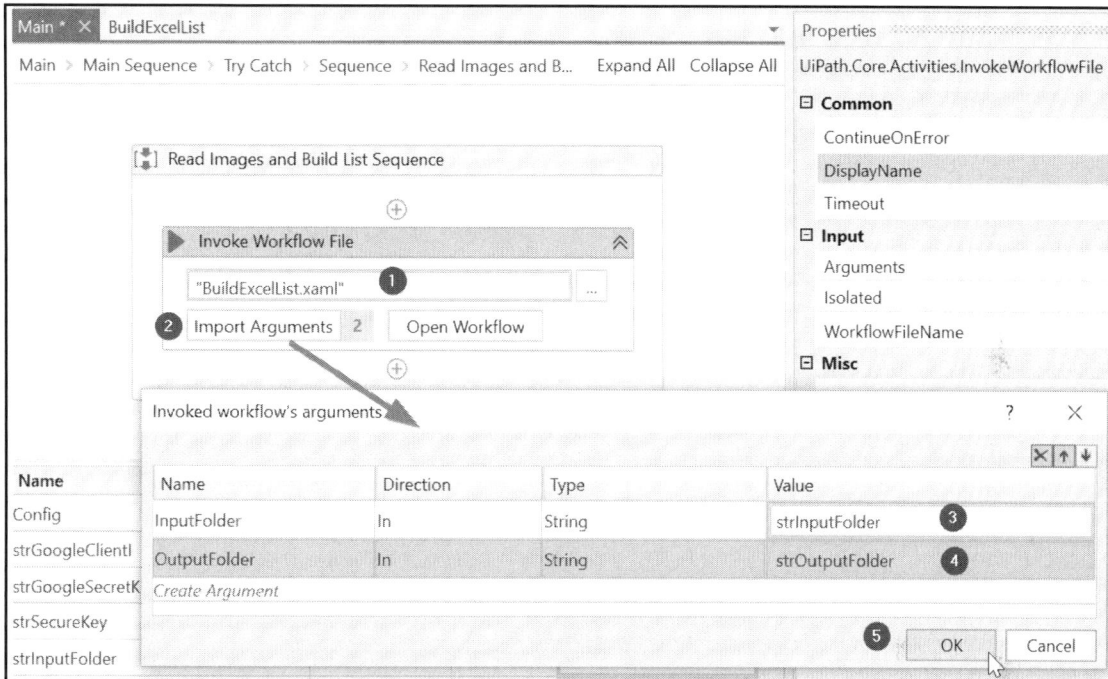

4. Once you have mapped the variables, it is time to unit test. Go ahead and click on **Run** from the UiPath Studio ribbon. Once the run is complete, open the `ImageDetails.xlsx` file in the output folder to check whether the correct image paths have been captured.

Now that we have the Excel `ImageDetails.xlsx` file, along with the image paths, we can pass these to the Google Cloud Vision API and get the image likelihood of having explicit content. Before we do that, let's do the groundwork to invoke the Google Cloud Vision API.

Setting up the Google Cloud Vision API's key and credentials

As we mentioned in the *Project overview* section, we will use the Google Cloud Vision API to detect explicit content. This feature is also called **SafeSearch**. It estimates the likelihood that any given image includes adult content, violence, and so on.

> The Google Cloud Vision API allows you to easily add machine learning-based vision detection to your applications. The vision detection features you can include are image labeling, face and landmark detection, **optical character recognition** (**OCR**), and tagging explicit content. We will be using the last feature, called SafeSearch, for moderation purposes here. Visit `https://cloud.google.com/vision/` for more details.

Let's set up the Google Cloud Vision API services so that we can use its explicit content detection (SafeSearch) feature.

Setting up the Google Cloud Vision API services

To use Google Vision services, we have to set up a Google API key. Perform the following steps to do so:

1. Go to the Google API console by going to this link: `https://console.developers.google.com/`.
2. Log in to your Google account or create a new one.
3. Create a new project or select one from the list of projects available.

4. The **APIs & Services** page should open. If not, go to the left-hand side menu and select **APIs & Services**.

5. On the left-hand side menu, go ahead and choose **Credentials**:

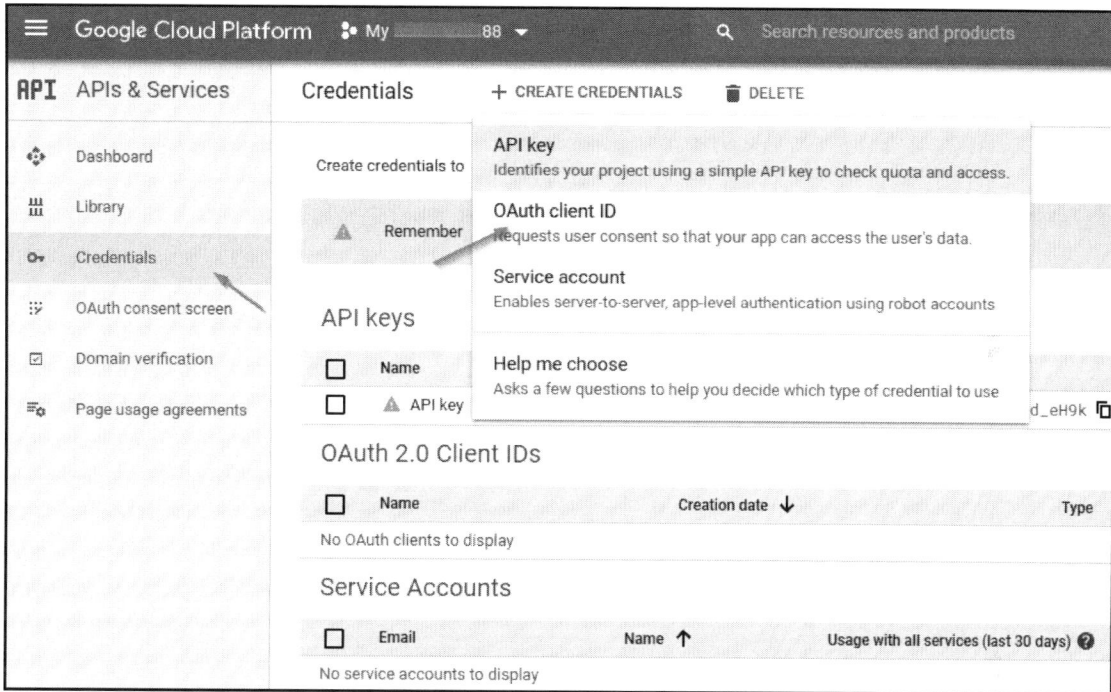

6. On the right-hand pane, click on **Create Credentials** and choose **OAuth client ID**.

7. On the next page, you should have a message stating **To create an OAuth client ID, you must first set a product name on the consent screen**. Click on **Configure consent screen**.

8. On the next screen, provide a name for the application. Any name will do. Go ahead and click **Save**.

9. On the next page, choose **Others** as the application type and provide a name, for example, `GoogleAPIclientID`, and click on **Create**.

10. Your client ID and client secret should be displayed. Copy them to a secure place:

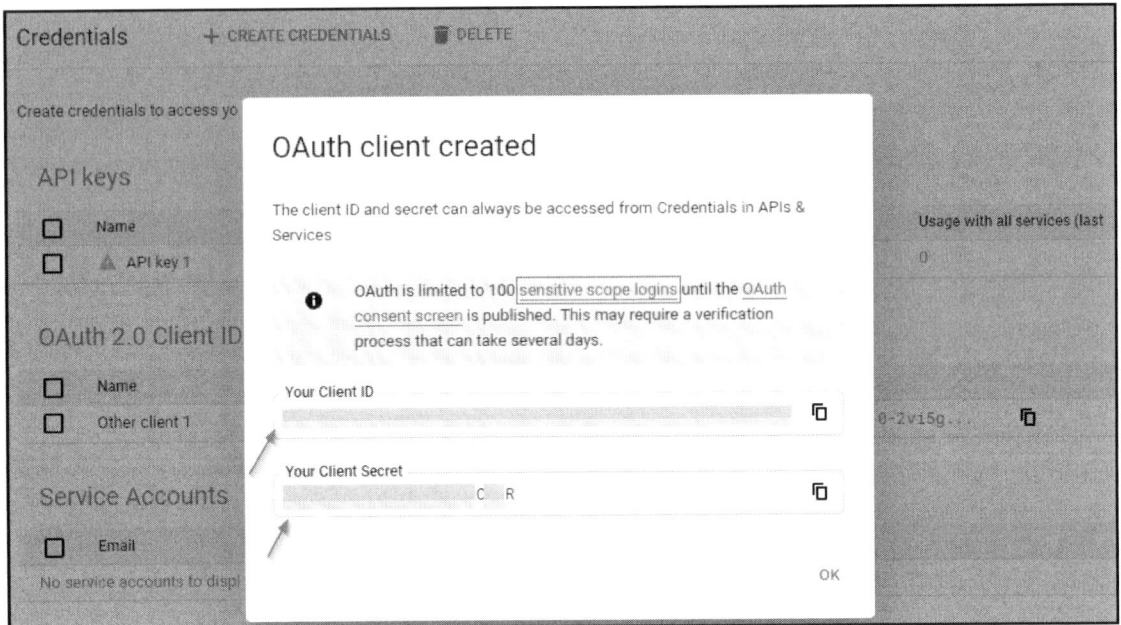

We will be using this key to invoke Google Vision from automation.

Next, let's enable the Google Cloud Vision API services. Perform the following steps to do so:

1. Click on the **Google** logo at the top of the page to get to the home page and go to **APIs & Services**.
2. Click **Enable APIS and services**.
3. On the next screen, that is, the API Library screen, search for Cloud Vision API:

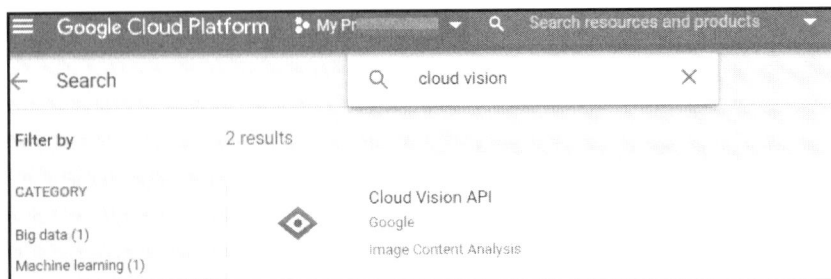

4. Doing this will open the page for the API. Click on **Enable**.

This enables the Google Cloud Vision API. We also got the credentials to invoke this API. Note that this process may change from time to time. Therefore, search for `Create Google API` and follow the steps provided if the ones given here aren't working for you.

Note that you may need to follow some steps to set up billing, depending on your account. Carefully review those terms before you sign up. Usually, there is a trial period that you can use to test these APIs.

So, now that we have the Google Cloud Vision API set up, let's place the credentials retrieved so that automation can read them.

Setting up a credential manager

It is always good practice to store and retrieve all your credentials in/from a credential manager. Let's learn how to do this for the Google Vision credentials we just got. We will use Windows Credential Manager in this project.

> Windows Credential Manager is like a "locker" where you can store usernames, passwords, and other sensitive information. These credentials can be used by Windows itself or by other applications, such as UiPath in this case.

UiPath has integration with Windows Credential Manager, which means you can create, query, or delete credentials using UiPath activities. Perform the following steps to store the Google API credentials we retrieved earlier in Windows Credential Manager:

1. Go to the **Windows Control Panel** and search for **Credential Manager**. Click on the **Credential Manager** application. On the window that pops up, go to the **Windows Credentials** tab. Then, look for **Generic Credentials** and click on **Add a generic credential**, as shown in the following screenshot:

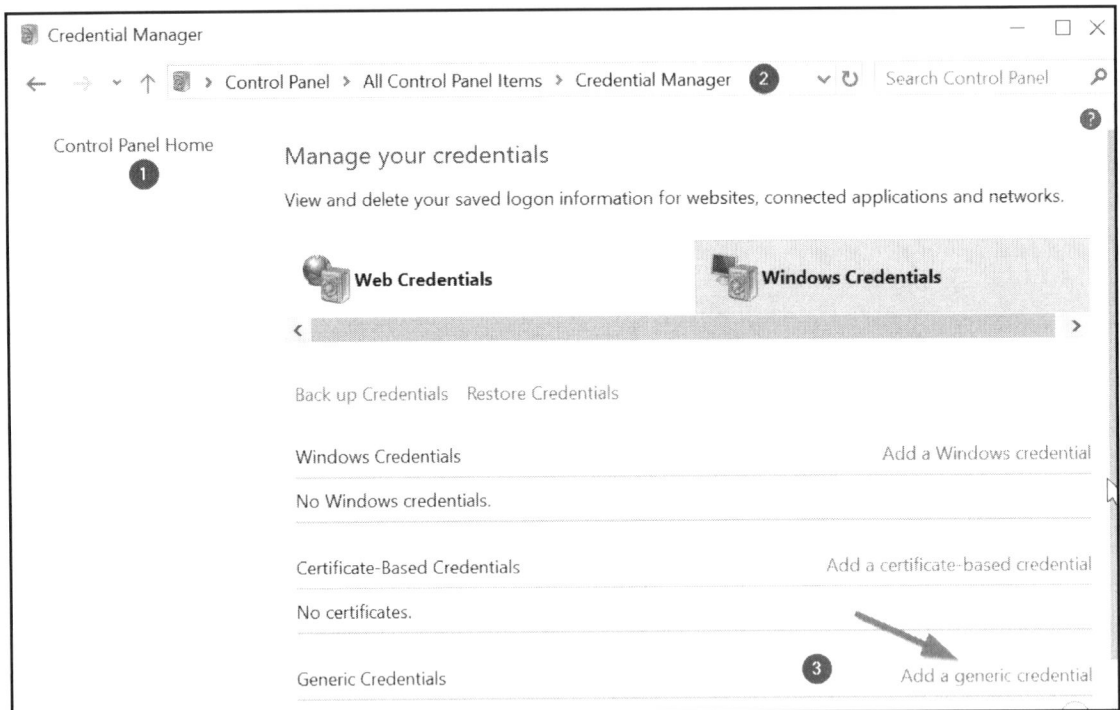

2. On the next screen, provide the same **Name** that we used in the configuration file, that is, `GoogleAutheticationName`. In place of the **User name**, provide the client ID, and in the **Password** field, use the client secret we got for the Google API key:

Now that we have the Google API credentials stored in Credential Manager, let's get ready to use in our automation workflow.

Reading credentials from Windows Credential Manager

Now, let's read the credentials and store them in local variables for automation:

1. To work with the credentials we stored, we have to use certain activities in UiPath. These activities are part of a package called `Uipath.Credentials.Activities package`. Let's add that first. Go ahead and click on **Manage Packages** in UiPath Studio. Then, within **Official** packages, look for this package. Once found, click on **Install** on the right-hand pane to install the package:

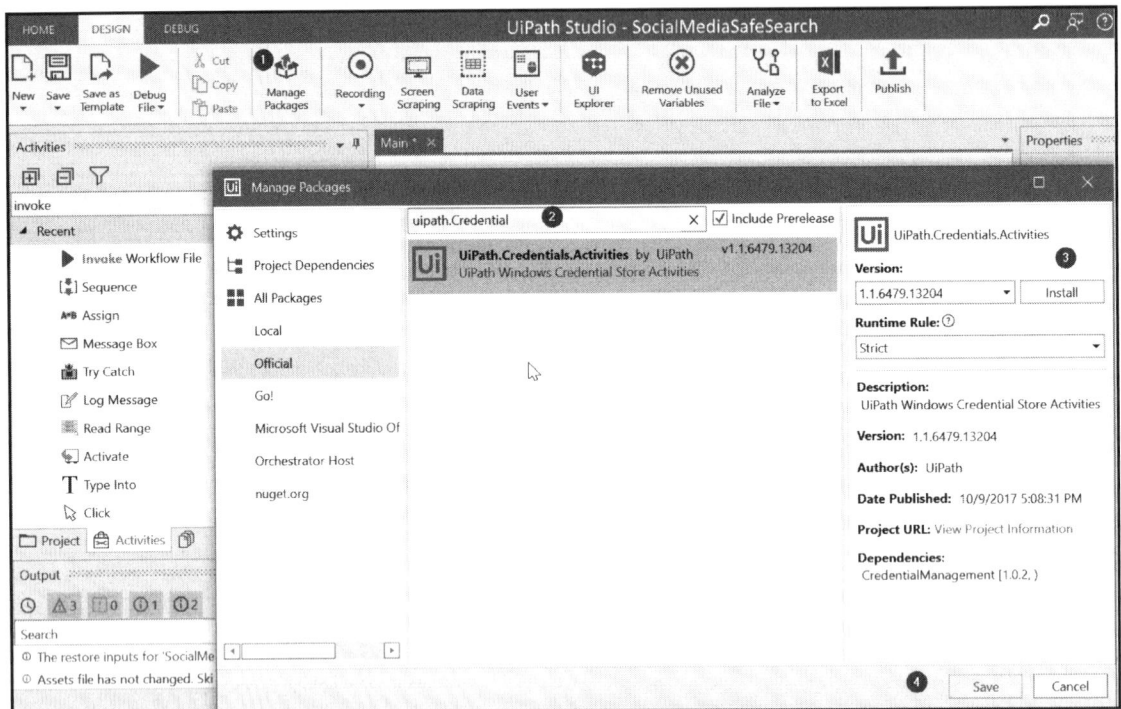

2. To make the main workflow readable, we'll add a sequence within the **Try** block and call it `Get Google API Credentials Sequence`.

3. Now, let's add two variables so that we can store the credentials. Call these `strGoogleClientID`, of the **String** type, and `strGoogleSecretKey`, of the **SecureString** type (`System.Security.SecureString`). Set the scope to a **Try-Catch** block.

4. Next, we will use the `Get Secure Credential` UiPath activity to read the credentials and store them in the variables. So, set the properties for this activity as follows:

- Set **Target** (credential name) to `strGoogleAuthName`.
- For **Result**, create a new variable (use *Ctrl + K*) called `boolIsValidCredentials`.
- Set **Password** to `strGoogleSecretKey` and **Username** to `strGoogleClientID`:

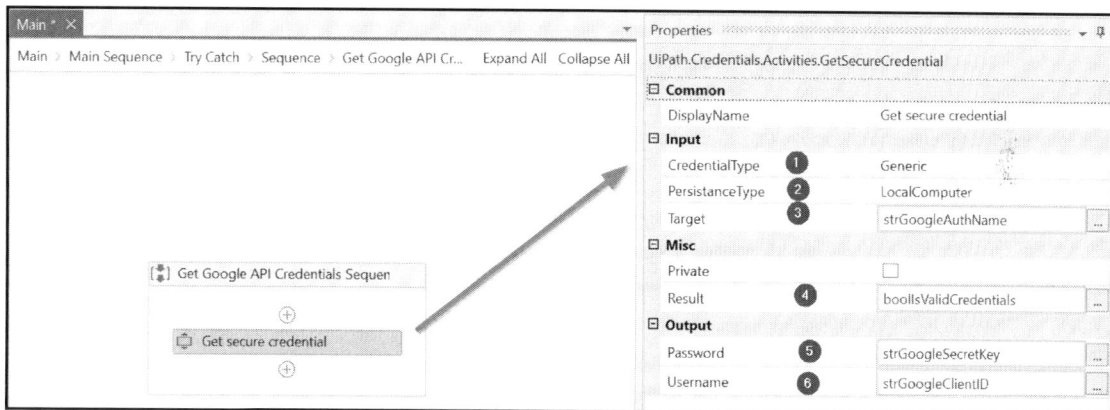

5. Now, let's convert `strGoogleSecretKey` of the **SecureString** type into a normal **String** for use in automation. To do that, create a new variable of the **String** type called `strSecureKey`. Now, use an **Assign** activity and set its value to `New System.Net.NetworkCredential(string.Empty, strGoogleSecretKey).Password`.

6. Finally, let's check whether the credentials were successfully retrieved from Windows Credential Manager. If not, we would like to log an error and terminate the workflow. The automation process cannot continue without the Google API authentication variables set.

7. Let's add an **If** control and within the **Then** block, check
   if `boolIsValidCredentials` is set to `True`. Add a log message if the condition
   passes; otherwise, log an error message and terminate the workflow, as shown in
   the following screenshot:

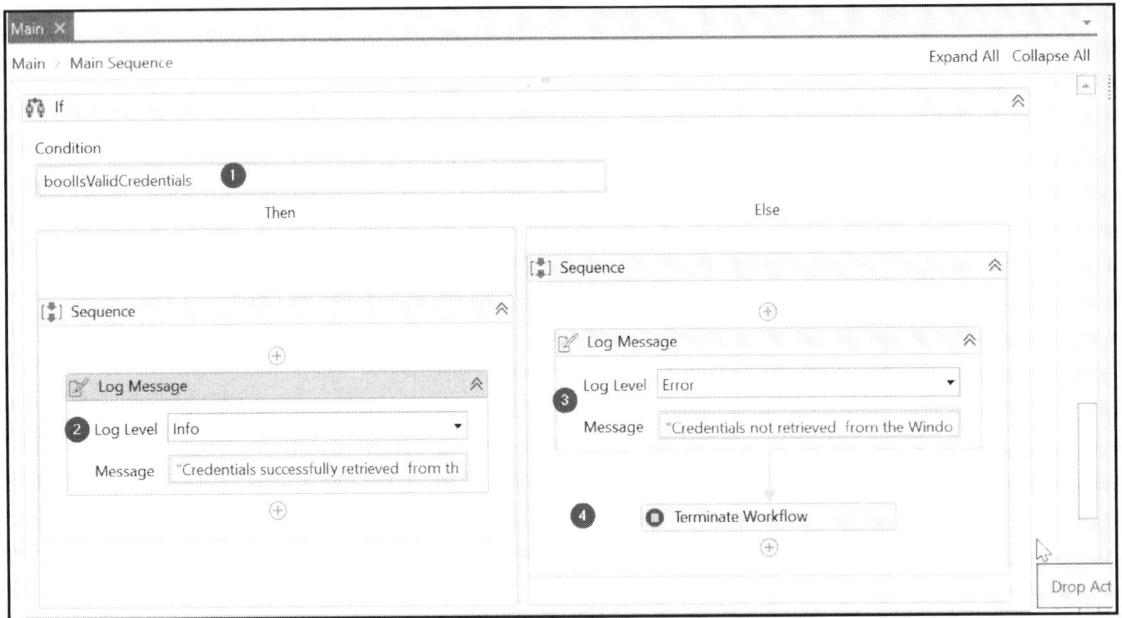

Now that we have the credentials, let's go ahead and invoke the Google Cloud Vision API
with the list of images from the `ImageDetails.xlsx` file and update the results in the
same sheet.

Looping through images and invoking the Google Cloud Vision API

As we mentioned earlier, we will be using the Google Cloud Vision API to detect and
moderate explicit content. We will invoke this feature of Google Vision, which Google calls
SafeSearch.

Installing the UiPath GoogleVision package from UiPath Go!

To invoke this feature, we need to install a package called **Google Vision Activities** from the UiPath marketplace:

> UiPath Go! is an RPA marketplace where users or organizations can upload custom packages that we can use in automation. Here, we are using one of the custom activities developed and provided by UiPath on the marketplace.

1. On your UiPath Studio ribbon, go to **Manage Packages** and choose **Go!** from the left pane.
2. In the search box above the middle pane, search for **Google Vision**.
3. From the results, choose `UiPath.GoogleVision.Activities` and click on **Install** on the right. These steps can be seen in the following screenshot:

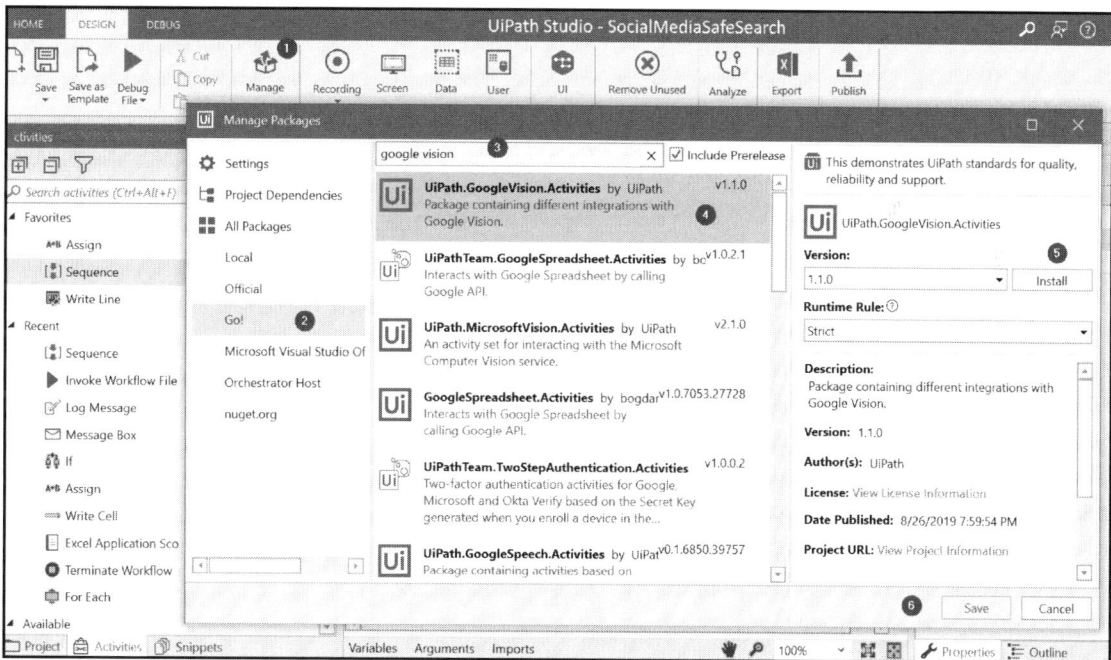

Now that the package has been installed, let's create a new workflow to carry out the SafeSearch process.

Adding SafeSearch to the main workflow

Now, we are ready to invoke the Google Cloud Vision SafeSearch API and get the likelihood estimate that any given image includes adult content, violence, and so on. This is the core component of this project.

To do this, we will create a new sequence file called `SafeSearch.xaml` for the project. Use the **New | Sequence** option from UiPath Studio. Now, within the sequence, do the following:

1. We will start by adding two arguments called `ClientID` and `ClientSecret`, both with the **In** direction. We will use these arguments to pass the Google client ID and secret from Main to this workflow.

2. Now, let's start configuring the workflow by adding a **Try-Catch** block for exception handling. Within that block, we'll add a sequence and call it `Try Sequence`. Your workflow should look like this:

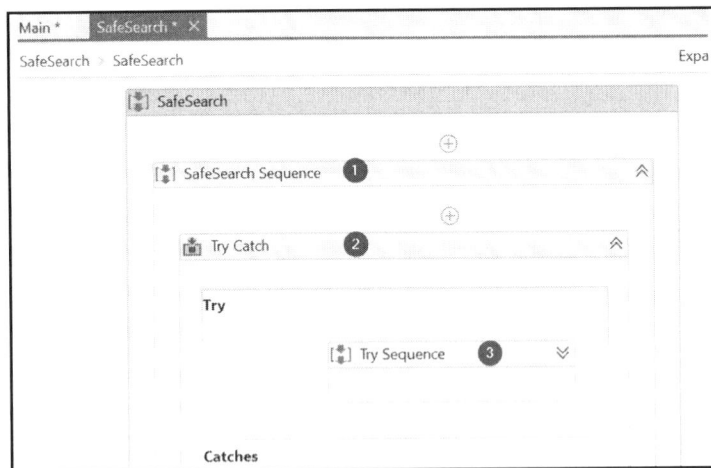

3. Next, we will get a list of all the images, one by one, as well as their paths, from the `ImageDetails.xlsx` file that we populated earlier. We will pass this image list to the Google Vision activity to check for explicit content.

4. In the **Try Sequence**, add an `Excel Application Scope` activity to open the Excel file. Within the activity, point to the `ImageDetails.xlsx` file in the `Output` folder (as this is the `Output` folder name from the configuration file).

5. In the **Do** sequence within this Excel activity, add an **Excel Read Range** activity to read the **Sheet 1** data into a new **DataTable** variable called dtImageDetails, as shown in the following screenshot:

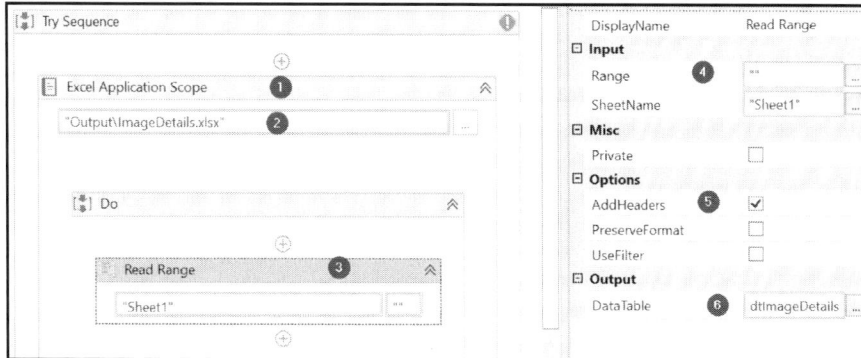

6. We will now iterate on the rows that we read from the sheet using this **DataTable** variable. For that, let's add a **For Each Row** activity that loops through the **DataTable** called dtImageDetails. To loop through, add a new **Integer** variable called intCounter and set the default value to 2 (as we will need to start from A2).

7. Next, we will use the Excel **Read Cell** activity to get the value of the file path. To do this, in the properties of Read Cell, set **Cell** to "A"+intCounter.ToString and result in a new variable called strImagePath (Use *Ctrl + K*). This populates the strImagePath variable with the first image path:

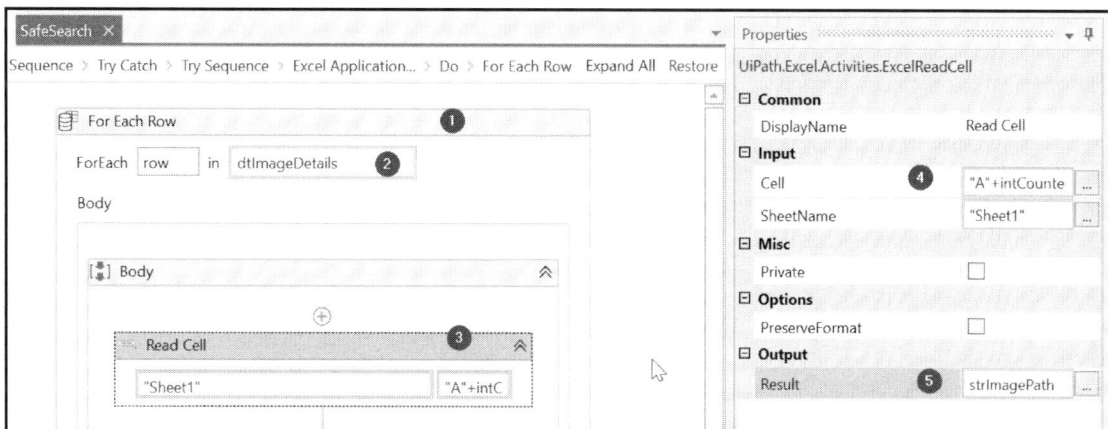

8. Now that we have the file path, let's add the `Google Vision Scope` activity right below the **Read Cell**. In the properties for this activity, update the properties' **ClientID** with the `ClientID` argument and **ClientSecret** with the `ClientSecret` argument, both of which we created earlier.

9. Next, add the **Safe Search** activity into this scope. This activity will return the likelihood values of `Adult`, `Medical`, `Racy,` and `Violent` based on the image. Here is how you need to add the Google Vision activities and configure them:

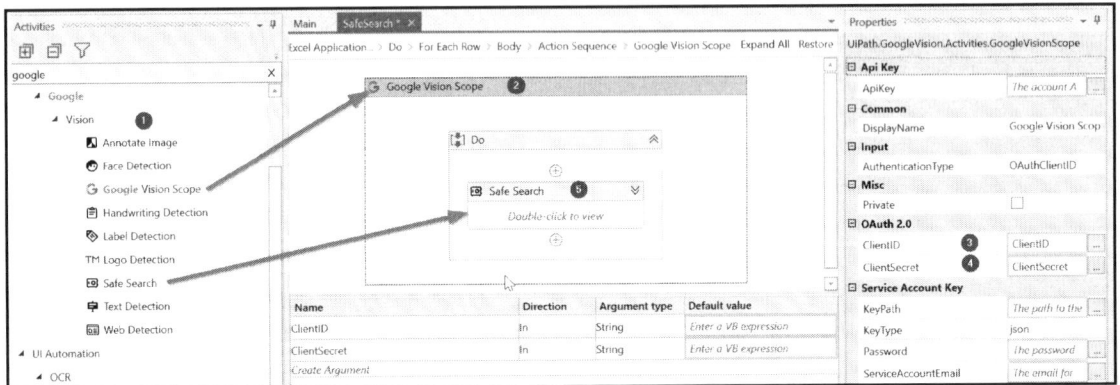

10. For the Safe Search activity, let's update the properties, as follows:

- **ImagePath** needs to be a `strImagepath` variable. This passes the path of the image we want likelihood for.
- Create four new **String** variables with the scope set to **SafeSearch** in order to capture the output from `Adult` (`strAdult`), `Medical` (`strMedical`), `Racy` (`strRacy`), and `Violent` (`strViolent`), as shown in the following screenshot:

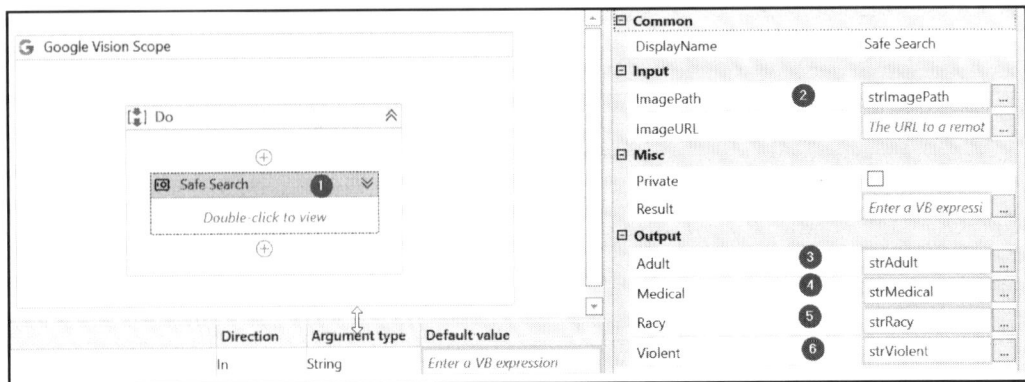

Now that we have the likelihood of the images being any of the aforementioned types captured in these variables, let's create an Output report for the images that were passed.

Updating the image sheet with the API results

Now, we will update the likelihood values we got from Google Cloud Vision SafeSearch API in Excel, within the `Output` folder. To do so, we will use a series of **Write Cell** activities to update the `ImageDetails.xlsx` file. We will update each of the respective columns with the likelihood:

1. First, we will write the likelihood in `strAdult` to the B column. For that, let's add the first **Write Cell** activity (under Workbook) and update the **Range** property, `"B"+intCounter.ToString`, by setting its value to `strAdult`, as shown in the following screenshot:

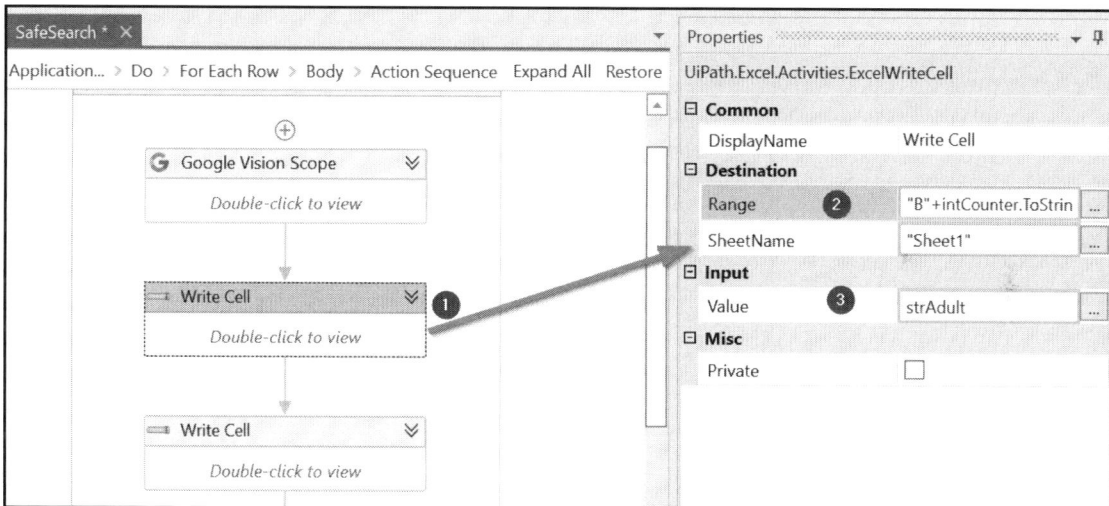

2. Similar to the previous step, let's add three more **Write Cell** activities for `strViolent`, `strRacy`, and `strMedical` and write them to columns C, D, and E, respectively.

3. Next, add an **Assign** activity to increment the counter by 1 in order to pick the next row within the Excel scope, as follows:

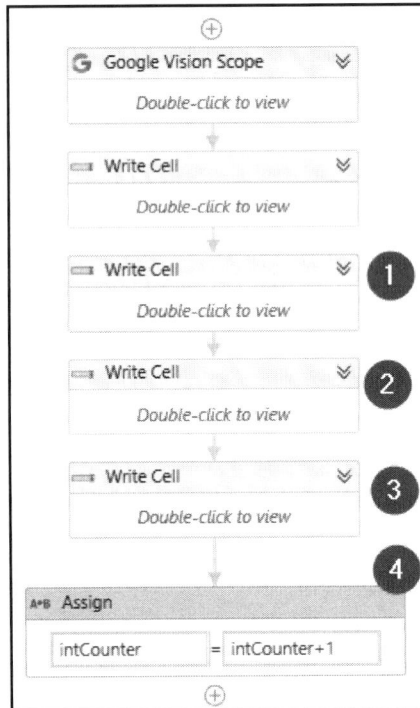

This completes the Excel application scope block, which reads each image path, invokes the Google Cloud Vision API, and writes the likelihood to the respective columns in the output Excel file.

Now, let's add a log message after the Excel scope:

1. Add an information log message that states, "`Safe search output updated successfully in the output Excel file.`". This completes the **Try** block of SafeSearch.
2. Finally, in the **Catch** block, add a new system exception with an error log message that states, "`Cannot update the Safe search results in the output Excel file.`".

That completes the SafeSearch workflow. Now, let's invoke it from Main.

Passing the parameters and invoking SafeSearch

Now, we will call the SafeSearch workflow from Main using the configured parameters to get the updated Excel file. This file can then be used by our administrator to review and moderate the files within it:

1. Let's go back to the main workflow and add a new sequence called `Perform Safe Search Sequence`, right after `Get Google API Credentials Sequence`.

2. Within that new sequence, add an **Invoke Workflow File** activity and point it to `SafeSearch.xaml`.

3. Click on **Import Arguments** and map the `strGoogleClientID` and `strSecureKey` variables to the input arguments, as shown in the following screenshot:

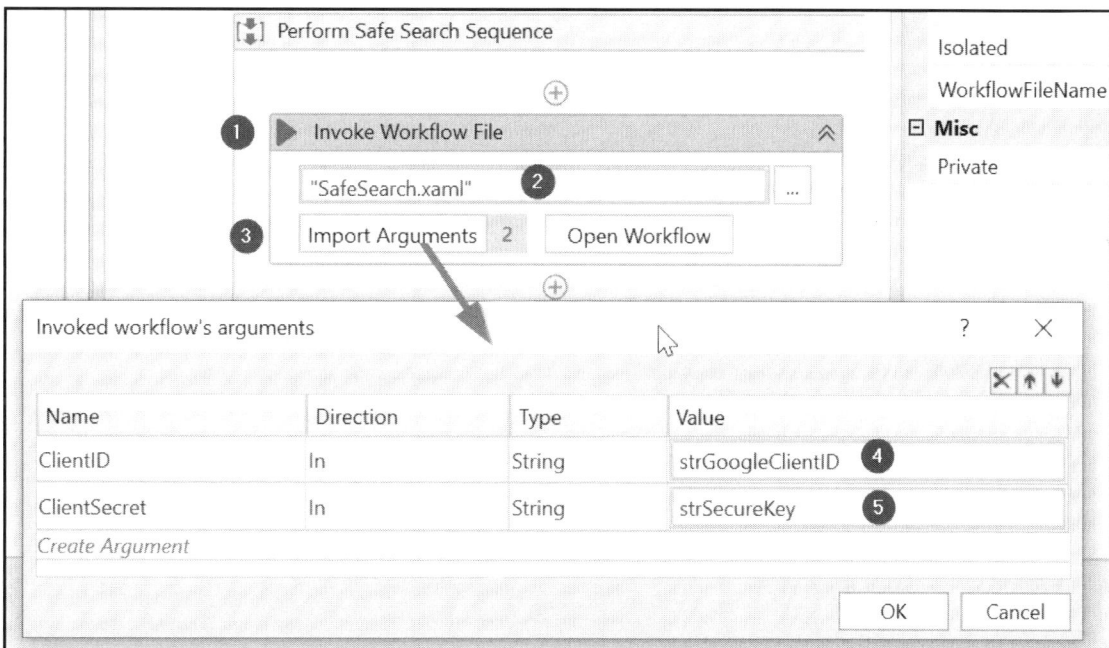

This completes the **Perform Safe Search Sequence** part of the main workflow.

Now that the bot has processed the images, let's move the completed the files to another folder. The administrator can then add new images for processing.

Moving processed images to the Output folder

The last step in this project is to move the processed images to the output folder. We will use a similar method to the one we used in the `BuildExcelList` workflow to read the files in the input folder and move them to the output folder:

1. We'll start by adding a new sequence in Main that we will call `Move Processed Images to Output Folder Sequence`.

2. Next, we'll add two variables to read in the information for the files in the input folder:
   - A `strFilename` variable of the **String** type. Set the scope to **Try-Catch.**
   - A `strFileInfo` variable of the **FileInfo** type. Set the scope to **Try-Catch.**

3. Let's add a **For Each** activity to step through the files. We will iterate for each item in `Directory.GetFiles(strInputFolder)`. This will iterate through all the files in the input folder.

4. Next, add two **Assign** activities to get the file information and filename from the object. Assign `strFileInfo` to `New FileInfo(item.ToString)` and assign `strFileName` to `strFileInfo.Name`:

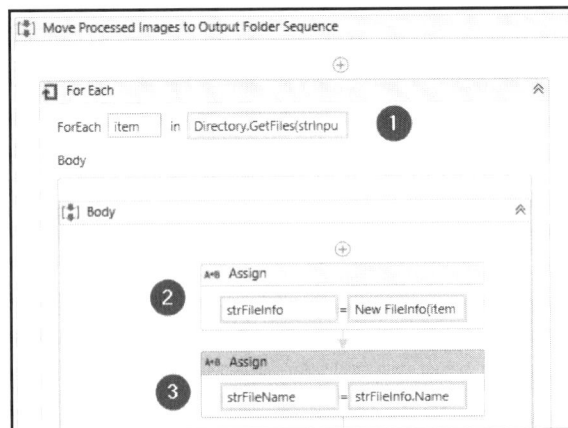

5. As we did previously, we will choose only JPG and PNG images to move out. Use an **If** control with the condition set to `strFileInfo.Extension ="".jpg"` Or `strFileInfo.Extension ="".png"`.

6. If the condition is met, we'll use a **Move File** activity to move the file from `strFileInfo.FullName` to `"Output\"+strFileName"`. Your later part of Main will look as follows:

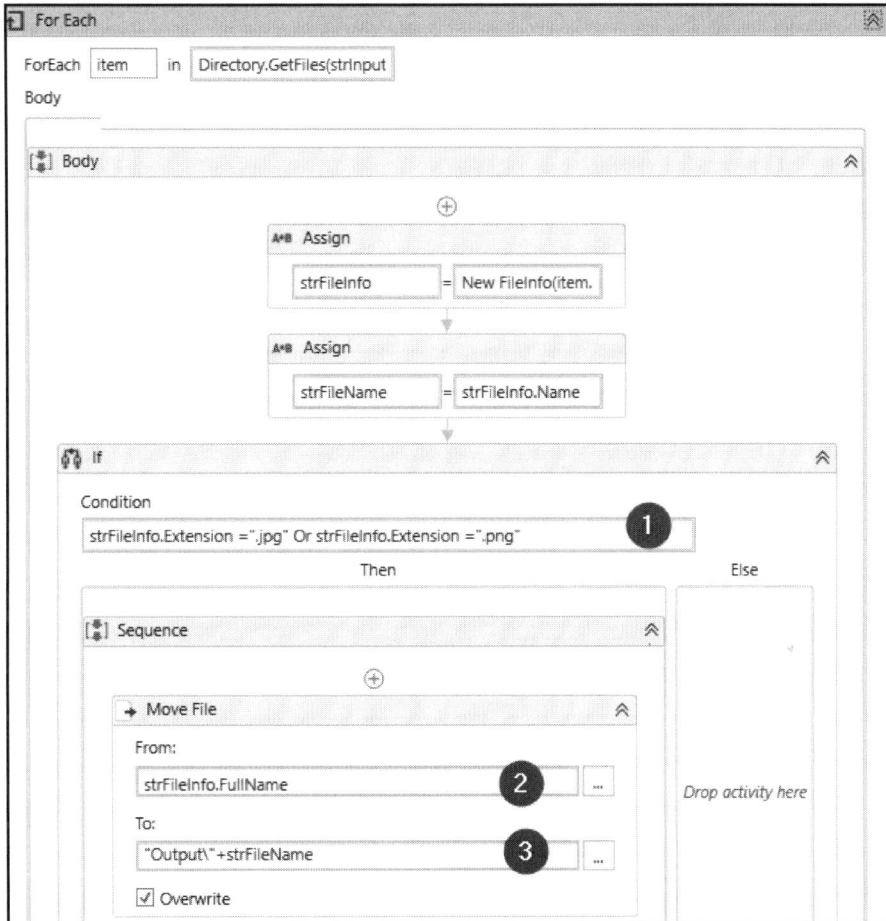

7. Outside the **For Each** activity, add an information log message stating, `"Processed Image Files moved to Output Folder."`. This completes the **Try** block for the main sequence:

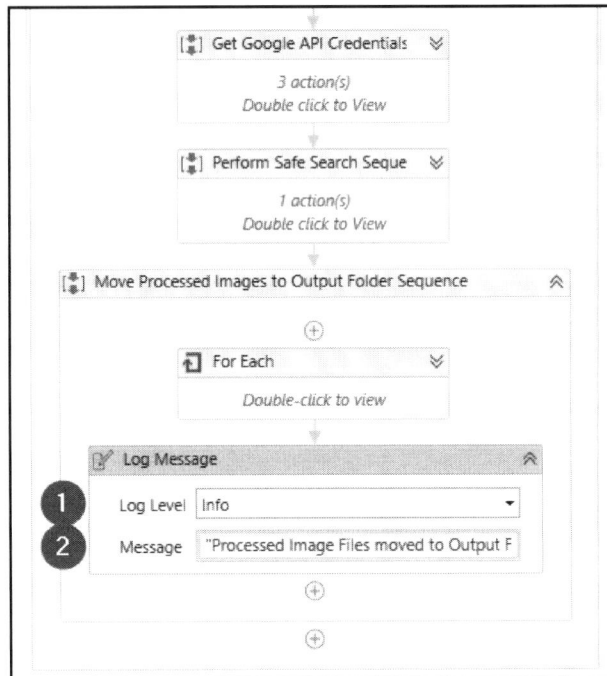

8. Finally, let's handle any exception in the **Catch** block. Add a new system exception and add a log message with an **Error** log level and a message stating, `"Automation run Failed. Error Occurred during automation run."`:

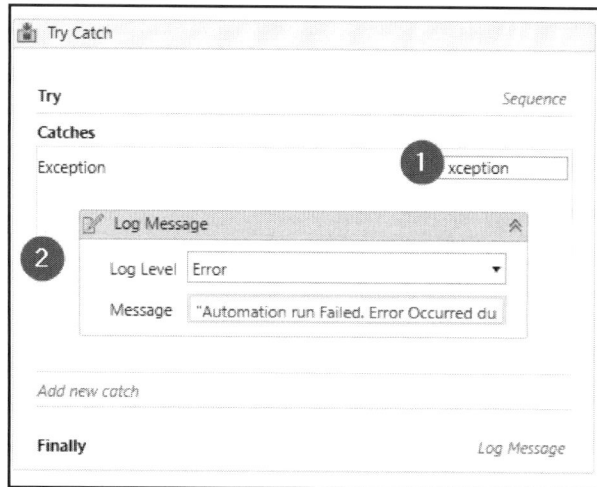

This step of moving the processed files to the output folder is also optional, but it's good practice to know how to do this.

That concludes how to configure the main workflow and automation. Now, let's test the automation.

Testing the automation

Now, we can perform an end-to-end test to check whether the automation process works fine:

1. Make sure the input folder contains the images to be checked for explicit content and that the ImageDetail.xlsx file is in the output folder with only header information.

2. From UiPath Studio, run the automation process from the `Main.xaml` file. After the automation process completes, the `ImageDetail.xlsx` file will contain updated likelihoods and the images will have been moved to the `Output` folder:

Once the integration test passes, we can move the package to the orchestrator and schedule the job to run periodically for the administrator. Refer to *Appendix B*, which details how you can run and schedule bots from an orchestrator.

Summary

In this project, we covered quite a bit of ground. We read the configurations from a file and used that information, along with images, to invoke the Google Cloud Vision API to detect explicit content. Then, we updated that information in Excel to enable the moderation of those images.

In the next project, we will explore how we can use an advanced concept known as UiPath ReFramework to process purchase orders in bulk.

5
Purchase Order Processing with UiPath ReFramework

In this chapter, we will create our automation using the UiPath Robotic Enterprise Framework (or ReFramework for short). ReFramework is a template for building robust UiPath automations quickly. It can be used as the starting point for all your UiPath projects.

The templates take care of most of your core needs in any automation – reading and storing data in a configuration file, robust exception handling, and event logging. We will dive into the details of the framework as we work through the project.

In this project, we will use the **UiPath Robotic Enterprise Framework** (**ReFramework**) to process **purchase orders** (**POs**). We will read the POs from a spreadsheet, input them into a PO application, and write the generated PO number back into the spreadsheet.

As we configure these tasks, we will cover the following:

- Basics of UiPath ReFramework
- Using different ReFramework states
- Using a Dispatcher and Performer for parallel processing
- Using Orchestrator queues
- UiPath Excel operations
- UiPath web application automation

Technical requirements

Let's look at the hardware and software we will require for this project:

- A PC with UiPath Community edition version 19+ installed.
- Google Chrome with the UiPath extension installed.
- Access to UiPath Orchestrator.
- The Apptivo SaaS ERP application with the PO application. You can sign up for free at https://www.apptivo.com.
- Microsoft Excel 2007 or later.
- Check out the following video to see the Code in Action: https://bit.ly/2LOd4Xw.

You can find the code files used in this chapter on Github at https://github.com/PacktPublishing/Robotic-Process-Automation-Projects/tree/master/PurchaseOrderRoboticEnterpriseFramework.

Project overview

Organizations create POs to procure items from suppliers. Usually, there are lots of POs generated depending on the size of the organization.

For this project, we are assuming that we are working with a high volume of POs. The list of POs gets updates frequently in an Excel spreadsheet – say, hundreds of new purchase requests every hour. The automation reads the POs from the spreadsheet and loads them into an UiPath Orchestrator queue.

Once transactions are available, the automation reads those transactions and writes them to the PO application. The PO application auto-generates a PO number, which is updated in the spreadsheet for the corresponding PO by the bot.

The automation continues to pick and process the transactions from the queue until there are no further transactions to process. Here is the project workflow:

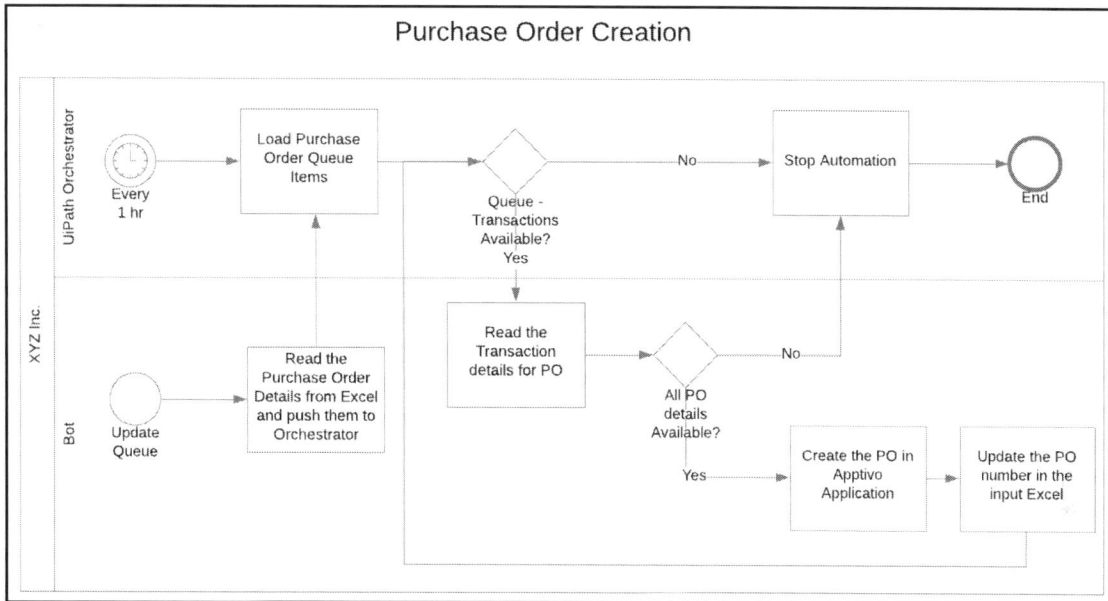

That was an overview of what the automation will do. As we mentioned in the introduction, we will be using the UiPath ReFramework for this project. Let's see what it is.

Robotic Enterprise Framework (ReFramework)

ReFramework is a UiPath template that you can build upon to create your automation. The framework offers a way to handle common project tasks. Here are some advantages of using ReFramework:

- Easily store, read, and modify configuration data
- Handle exceptions and retry failed transactions
- Extensive event logging for all exceptions
- Automate complex processes using defined states

The framework is recommended for creating scalable and robust automation with UiPath.

Here is an overview of ReFramework and its states:

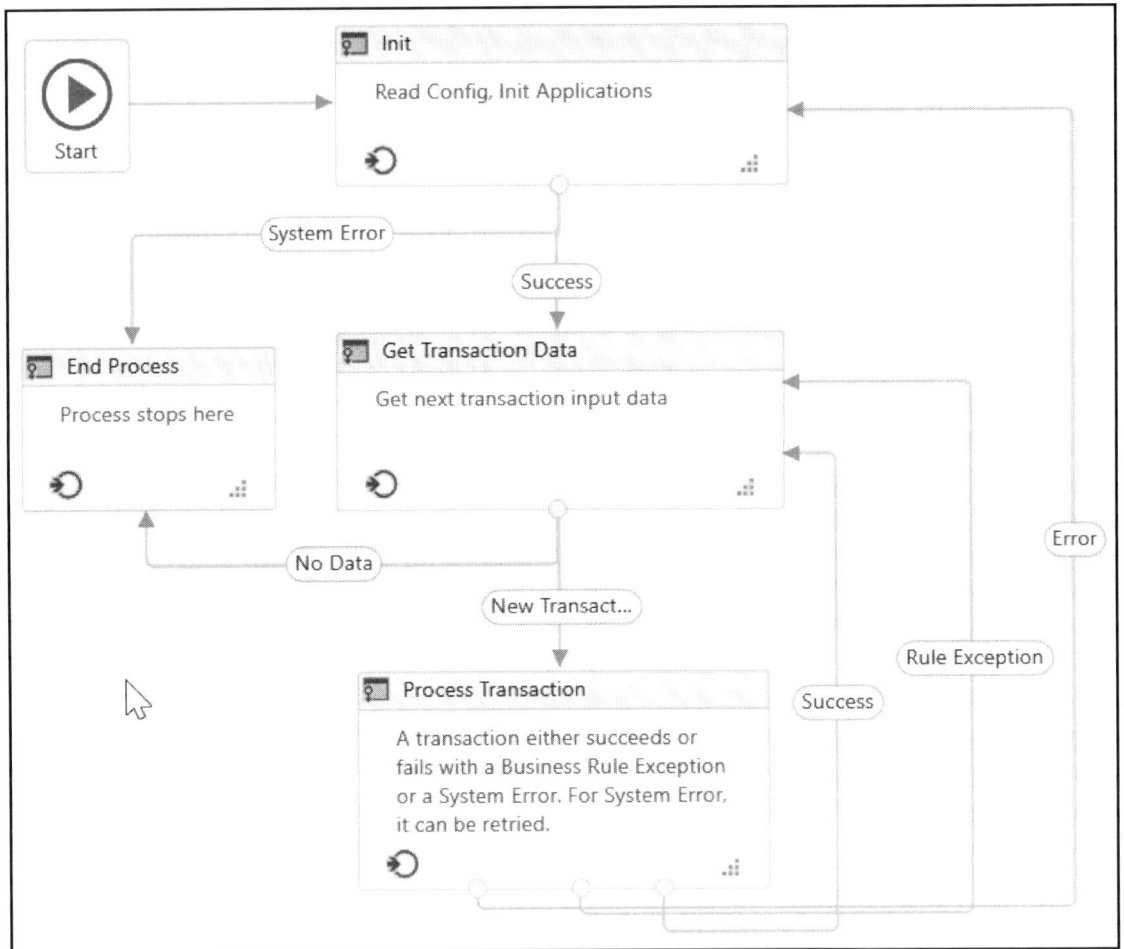

ReFramework uses the concept of state machines. It has four states to build robust automations. These states are as follows:

1. **Init State**: In this state, we initialize the automation. This includes the following:
   - Initializing the settings; for example, the loading of configuration data from the config file
   - Initializing the applications; for example, logging in to applications using credentials
   - Killing all working processes; for example, killing open applications
2. **Get Transaction Data State**: Used to get data from spreadsheets, databases, emails, web APIs, or Orchestrator queues. It has two possible outcomes:
   - **New Transaction**: If `TransactionItem` contains data, process it.
   - **No Data**: If `TransactionItem` is `Nothing`, go to **End Process**.
3. **Process Transaction State**: This where all the processing work for transactions takes place. It results in three conditions:
   - **Success**: In the case of a business rule exception, we log it and go to the next transaction.
   - **Rule Exception**: If we have a business rule exception, we log it and move to the next transaction.
   - **Error**: If we have an application exception, we close all programs.
4. **End Process State**: We will close all the applications and processes here.
   - Close All Applications: This will soft close all working applications.
   - `KillAllProcesses.xaml` workflow: This kills all the working processes.

The complete documentation of ReFramework and its components are available at `https:/` `/github.com/UiPath/ReFrameWork/blob/master/Documentation/` `REFramework%20documentation.pdf`.

Project detail

Let's now look at the overall flow for this project in terms of the UiPath project components we will be building and their interactions.

As we said, one of the distinguishing characteristics of this project is that we will be processing a lot of POs. So we need a strategy to handle the high workload.

For this, we will design the bots in a manner where we can use multiple bots to process POs in parallel. This is best accomplished with the UiPath Orchestrator queues and by splitting the workload. We will split the workload between two components:

- **Dispatcher**: This component will read from the Excel file and upload PO transactions to the queue.
- **Performer**: This component will process the uploaded queue items. We will use ReFramework to build this component.

As we step through the project, we will be customizing the various components and states of ReFramework for our project. We will start with some groundwork for the project.

Project groundwork

We need a spreadsheet for the POs, and then to set up the Apptivo application to input these POs. Let's create them.

Creating the PO spreadsheet

We will create an Excel spreadsheet with a few sample POs for our automation to process. The PO will have the following columns: **Supplier**, **Address**, **City**, **State**, **Zip**, and **ItemName**.

Add three sample rows to the sheet, as shown here:

Supplier	Address	City	State	Zip	ItemName	PO
Lenovo	1009 Think Pl	Morrisville	North Carolina	27560	Laptop	
Cisco	2300 E President George Bush Hwy	Richardson	Texas	75082	Routers	
Avaya	4851 Regent Blvd	Irving	Texas	75063	Phones	
HP	1501 Page Mill Rd	Palo Alto	California	94304	Monitors	

We will place this folder within the `Project` folder once we create it in the next section. For now, you can save it to any place where you can retrieve it quickly. Make sure to name it `PurchaseOrders.xlsx`. The sample input file is also available on the GitHub repo for the project.

Setting up Apptivo

As we did in `Chapter 3`, *CRM Automation*, we will be using the Apptivo Business Management Software here.

Since this is a cloud-based application, all you need to do is sign up on the website specified previously in the *Technical requirements* section. Once you log in, the **Purchase Orders** module is accessible in the **Supply Chain** drop-down menu:

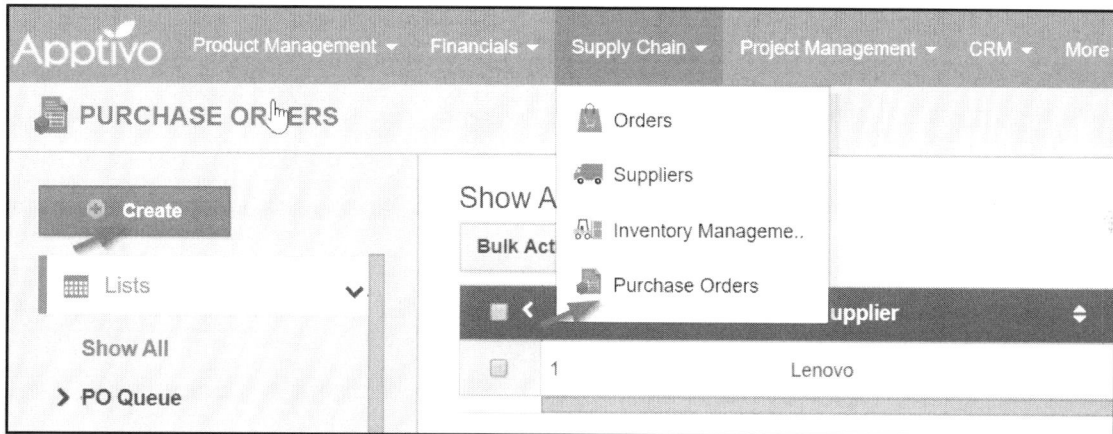

Let's start by creating a few new suppliers and items in Apptivo:

1. Within the **POs** option, click on the **Create** button on the left panel (highlighted in the preceding screenshot).

2. In the new PO form that shows up on the right, scroll over to the **Supplier Information** section. On the **Suppliers** text box, use the **+** button to create new suppliers. For this project, let's add four new suppliers:
   - Lenovo
   - Cisco
   - Avaya
   - HP

> **Name** is the only mandatory field needed to create the suppliers and items in the Apptivo application.

3. Similarly, scroll over to the **Items** section and add the following four item names by clicking on the + sign:

- Laptop
- Phone
- Monitor
- Router

Now that we have done the groundwork, let's start with the automation using UiPath.

Getting started with the project

It is time to start on our first ReFramework project. Let's go:

1. Open UiPath Studio.
2. On the **New Project** options on the initial screen, choose the **Robotic Enterprise Framework** option:

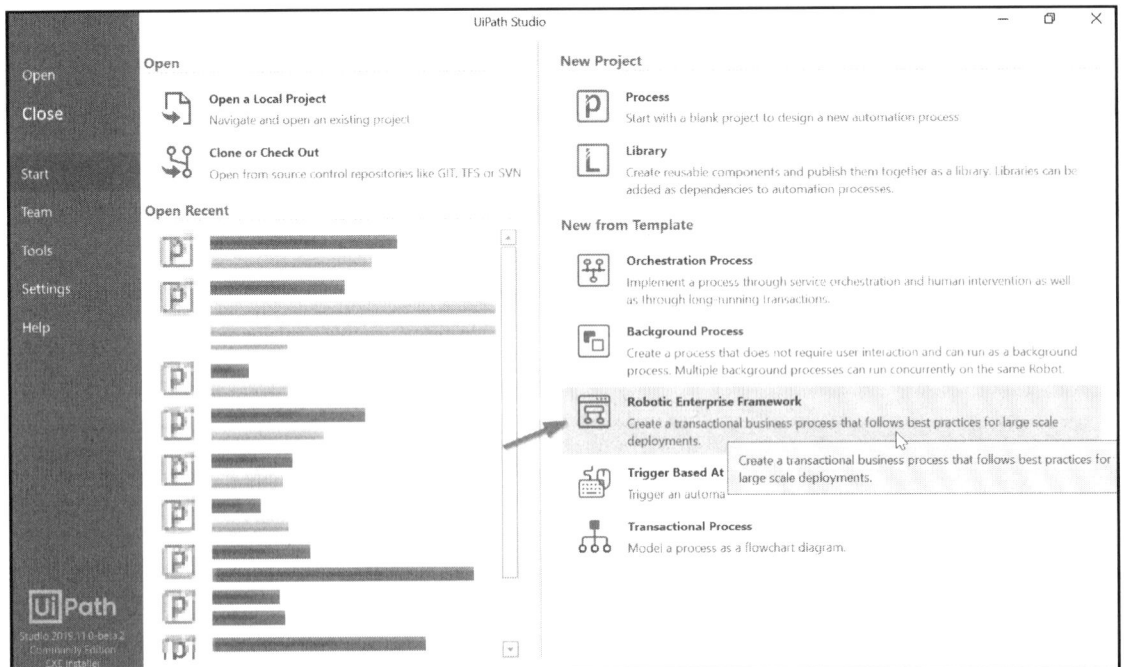

3. Choose an appropriate name for your project on the popup and click on **Create**.

This will take you to the project screen. When you go to the main workflow, you should see it pre-populated with the ReFramework template.

You can go to the UiPath project folder to see the files created as part of the framework template. Let's now add and customize this framework by adding a Dispatcher.

Purchase order Dispatcher

Create a new sequence called `PurchaseOrderDispatcher` in UiPath Studio. Within the Dispatcher, we will read the Excel file we created earlier and upload each row as a queue item. Before we do that, go ahead and put the `PurchaseOrders.xlsx` file we created earlier in the **Data** folder of the project:

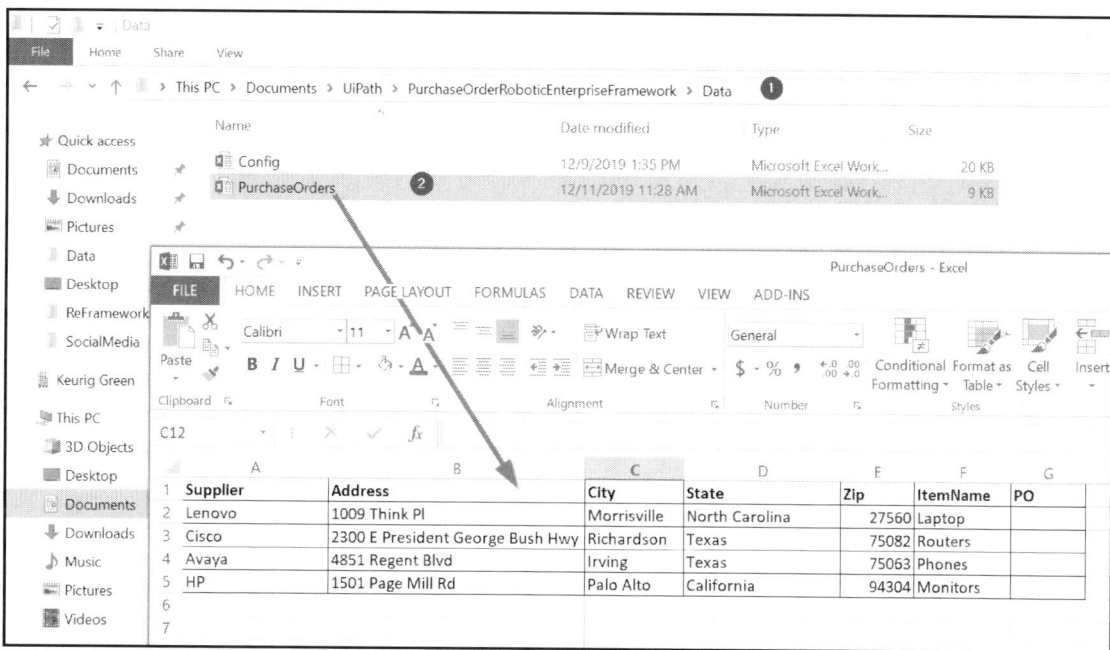

Let's now read each of the Excel rows to upload them to the queue:

1. We'll start by adding an `Excel Application scope` activity within the sequence that we just created. For this activity, go ahead and update the Workbook path to point to the `PurchaseOrders.xlsx` file.

2. Within the **Do** sequence of the Excel scope, let's add an Excel **Read Range** activity to read the content to a new DataTable variable called dtPurchaseOrders, as shown in the following screenshot:

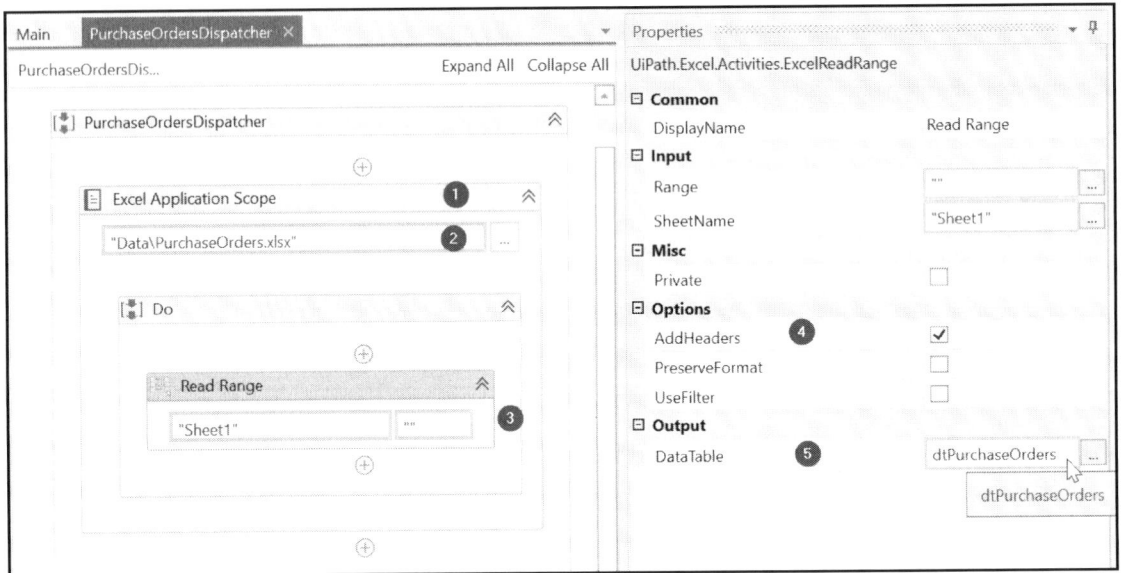

3. We will now use the **DataTable** we created as the input for the Dispatcher to create the queue items. We will iterate each DataTable row and add them to the queue. To do that, let's use the **For Each Row** activity and update the **DataTable** value to dtPurchaseOrders.

4. In the **Body** sequence, add an **Add Queue Item** activity and name the queue "PurchaseOrders", as shown in the following screenshot:

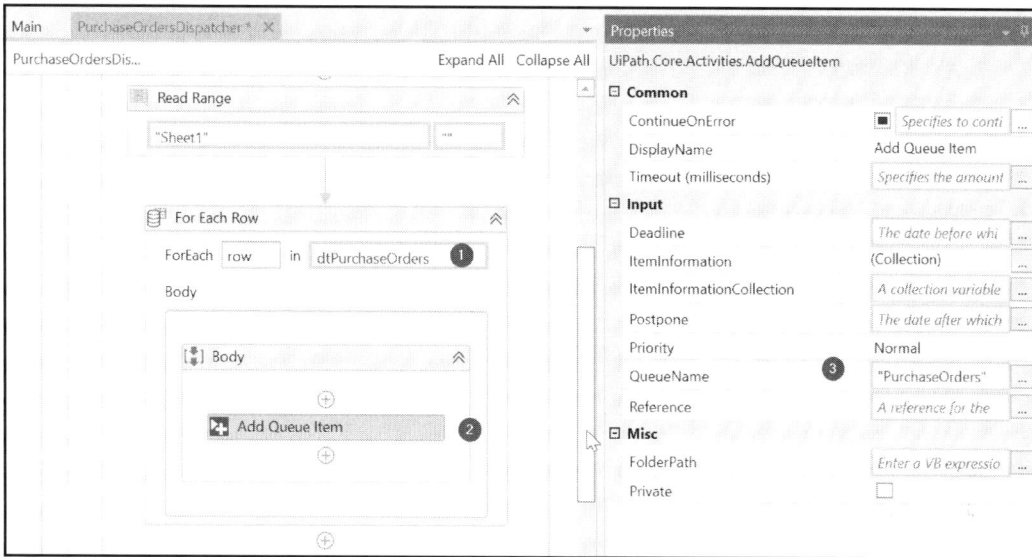

5. We'll now map the DataTable columns to the queue items. To do that, we will update the **ItemInformation** property of the **Add Queue Item** activity. Let's map the column value of **Name** to **Supplier** and set the **Value** as `row.Item("Supplier").ToString`, and so on for the rest of the columns – **Address**, **City**, **State**, **Zip**, and **ItemName**, as shown in the following screenshot:

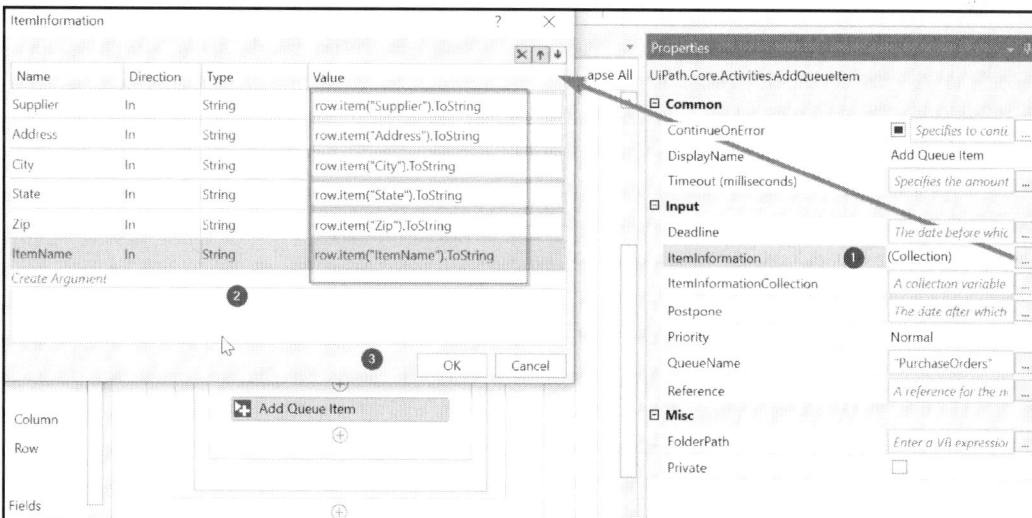

6. So, we now have the Dispatcher that uploads the Excel rows to the queue. We'll do a quick unit test to see whether the Dispatcher is working as expected. For that, let's go to the UiPath Orchestrator and add a new queue called `PurchaseOrders`:

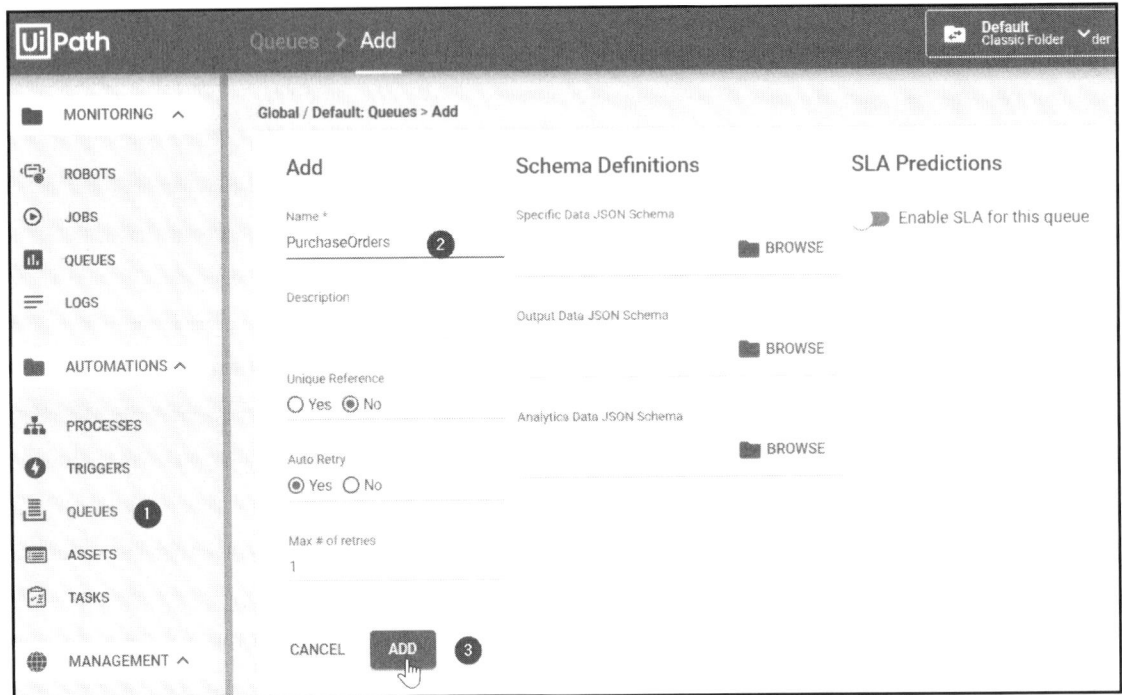

7. Make sure UiPath Studio is connected to the Orchestrator. To do that, go to **Robots** in the Orchestrator and check if your **Robot** shows its status as **Available**.
8. On UiPath Studio, use **Run File** to run the Dispatcher sequence. Once the execution ends, go to the Orchestrator and check if the queue items were added. To do that, go to the newly added queue and click **View Transactions**:

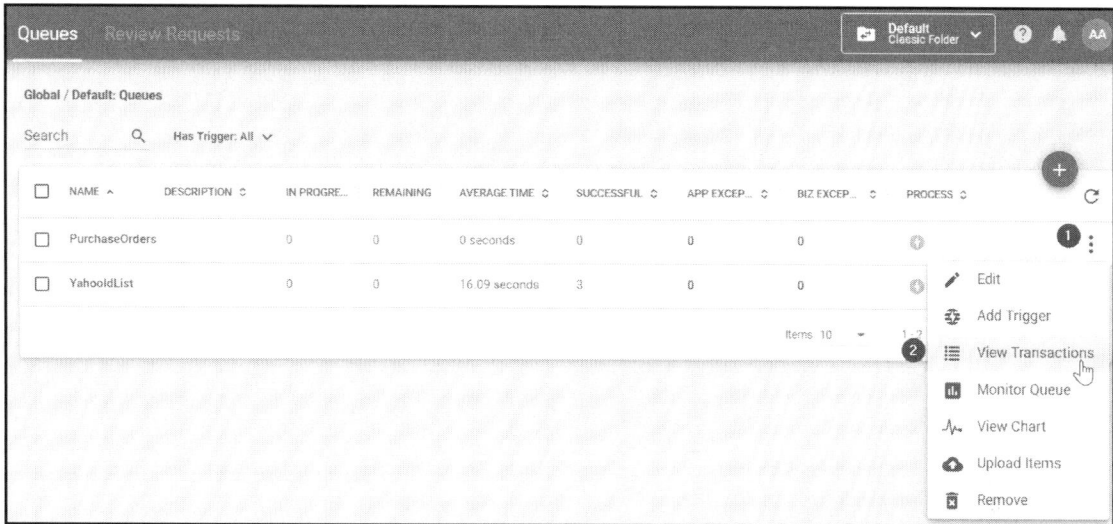

9. On the transactions that show up, you can view the details and ensure that the details match with the Excel input:

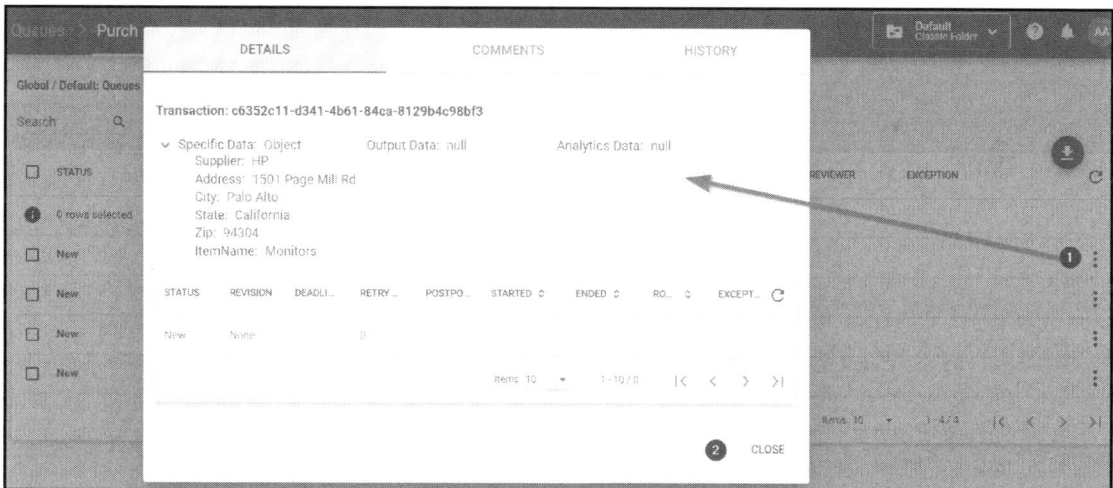

As we are introducing the ReFramework, we have kept a few aspects simple to reduce the project complexity. First, the Dispatcher in this section only runs once. In a complete implementation, the automation would run in a loop reading all new PO data as it's added. Also, in the next section, the Performer can be scheduled to run periodically (say, every hour) to process new transactions. We have covered how to schedule the process in UiPath Orchestrator in *Appendix B*.

Now that we have verified we have all the four POs in the queue, let's move to process these transactions within the next component – the Performer.

Purchase order Performer

We will use ReFramework as the Performer. It will take the transactions in the queue and input them into the Apptivo PO application.

Let's update the ReFramework config file with the inputs to the Performer. Open the `Config.xlsx` file in the **Data** folder in your project. Update the values for **QueueName** and **BusinessProcessName**, as shown in the following screenshot:

A		B
Name		**Value**
OrchestratorQueueName	①	PurchaseOrders
logF_BusinessProcessName	②	PurchaseOrderRoboticEnterpriseFramework

Now that we have the inputs, let's initialize the automation.

Init state changes

As we said earlier, ReFramework starts with the Init state, where we initialize the settings and applications. There are three workflows here. All of these files can be found in the **Framework** folder of the project:

- **InitAllSettings**: This workflow initializes the config dictionary variable. We will not make any changes to this workflow for this project.
- **KillAllProcesses**: This workflow is used to close the working processes. We will not make any changes to this either.
- **InitAllApplications**: This is where we open and initialize applications. For this project, we will open the PO application where we will input the POs.

Let's initialize the PO application within the InitAllApplications workflow.

Updating the InitAllApplications workflow

Let's open the Apptivo application and initialize it for the project by implementing the following steps:

1. Double-click and get into the **Init** state in `Main.xaml` and scroll down a bit to open the workflow from **Invoke InitiAllApplications workflow**, as shown in the following screenshot:

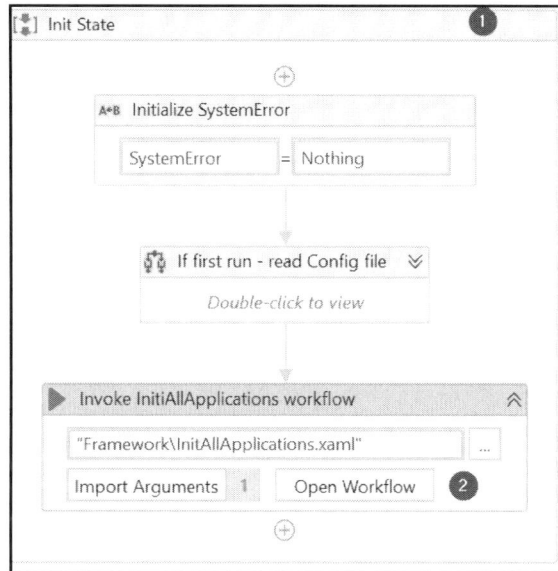

2. Next, we'll define the argument to pass around between the states. In the `InitAllApplications.XAML` file, let's add a new output argument called `out_Browser` with direction **Out** and type **Browser** (`UiPath.Core.Browser`). Note that you can get to `InitAllApplications.xaml` from the **Framework** folder in the **Project** tab.

3. Add an **Open Browser** activity within `InitAllApplications.xaml`. In the **Properties** for this activity, update the following:
    - Update the **BrowserType** to **Chrome**.
    - Input the following URL into the Apptivo PO app:
      `"https://www.apptivo.com/app/purchaseorders.jsp#/dashbo ard/show-all/"`

In ReFramework, the URL can be added as an *asset* in UiPath Orchestrator and referred to here. We have added the URL directly here to keep things simple for your first ReFramework project. Also, note that the Apptivo URL could change in future (as Apptivo upgrades their website)– so ensure you input the URL into the PO option in Apptivo.

4. Add a `Delay` activity with a duration of 10 seconds (00:00:10) to ensure that the web application opens completely before we proceed.
5. Add a new web sequence to keep our automation organized. Within that, add an **Attach Browser** activity, click on **Indicate Browser**, and point to the Apptivo PO application in the Chrome browser:

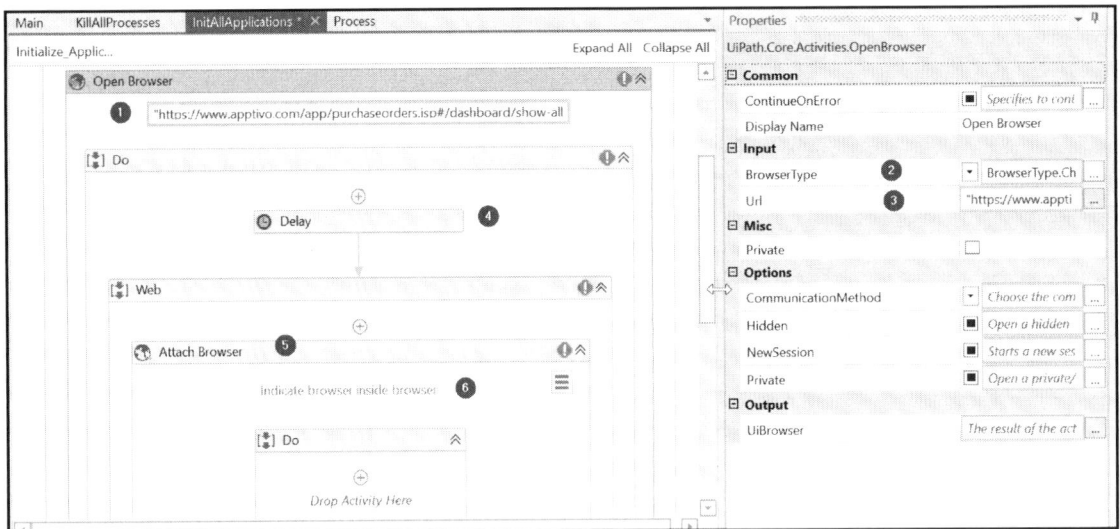

6. In the **Attach Browser** properties, update the Selector **title** to `*Apptivo*` and the output UiBrowser argument to `out_Browser`, as shown in the following screenshot:

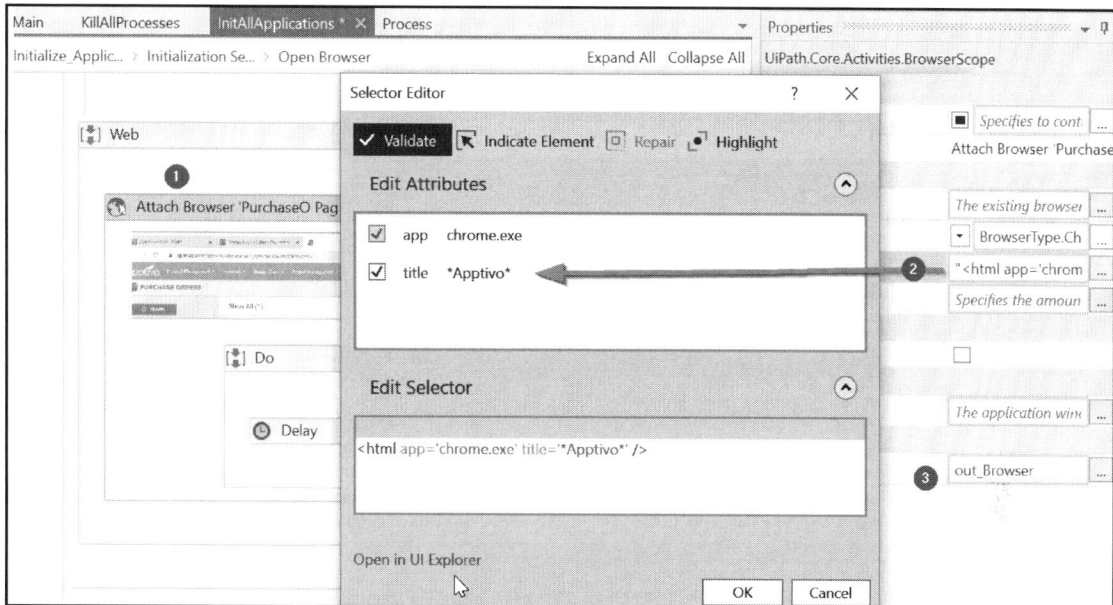

The `out_Browser` argument will be used in the `Process.xaml` file when we create POs in this opened browser. Updating the selector with wildcards ensures that we can attach the automation to Apptivo browser tabs to carry out the activities.

7. Finally, within the **Do** sequence for the **Attach Browser** activity, let's add a **Delay** activity for 10 seconds. This will give the Apptivo PO application some time to load completely.

Now that we have completed the `InitAllApplications` workflow update, let's invoke it from the Main workflow.

Invoking the InitAllApplications workflow

Let's go back to Main workflow and invoke the `InitAllApplication` that we just created:

1. In the `Main.xaml` file, we'll create a variable called `Browser` of type **Browser** (UiPath.Core.Browser) and set its scope to **General Business Process**. We will use this variable to pass the `out_Browser` argument in `InitAllApplication.xaml`.

2. In the `Main.xaml` file, double-click on the **Init** state block. Go to the **Invoke InitiAllApplications workflow**, click on **Import Arguments**, and add the newly created `Browser` variable to store the value of the `out_Browser` argument:

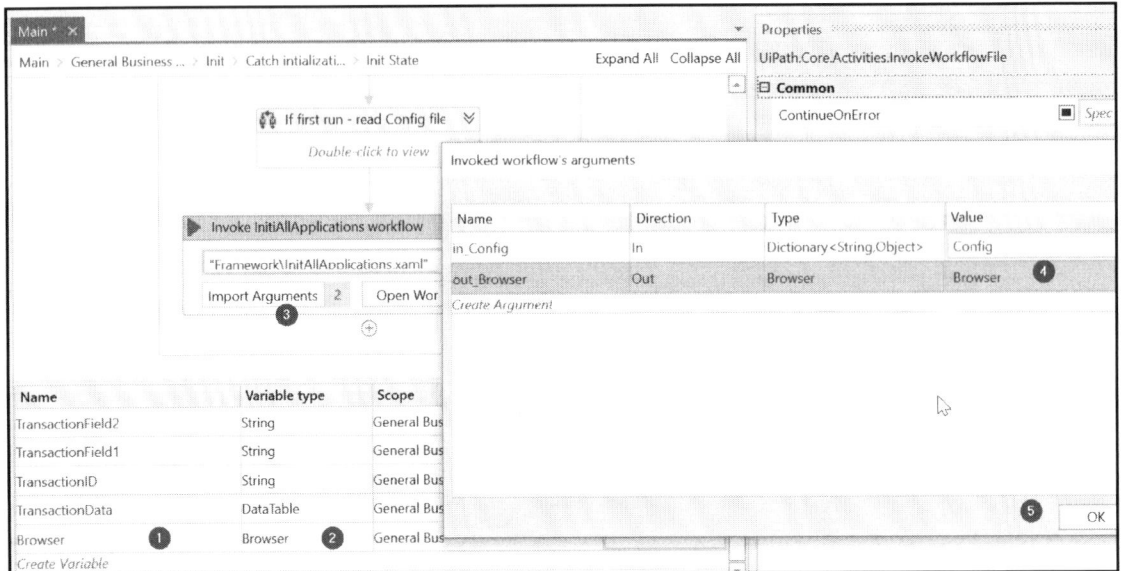

That is all for the updates to the **Init** state for this project.

The next state in ReFramework is the **GetTransactionData** state. This state processes the items in the Orchestrator queue one by one. You can also get the automation to process data from spreadsheets, databases, emails, or Web APIs. Since we have added our PO entries to the Orchestrator queue itself, we can skip any changes to **GetTransactionData**.

The next step is to process the transactions within the **Process Transaction** state.

Process state changes

Let's open the `Process.xaml` file in the project. We will create the POs within this workflow.

Attaching and activating the PO application

Let's work through the steps to activate the Apptivo application in order for us to input the POs:

1. We will start by adding a new argument called `in_Browser` of type **Browser** in `Process.xaml`.

2. Within the **ProcessTransaction** sequence generated by the template, let's add a new sequence called **Purchase Order Creation Sequence**.

3. Within the **Purchase Order Creation Sequence**, add a **Try Catch** block for exception handling.

4. Within the **Try** block, add an `Attach Browser` activity and point to the Apptivo PO tab. Update its **Browser** property to the `in_Browser` argument. Delete the content in the **Selector** property, as we are now using the `in_Browser` argument. The value of this argument will be passed by the `Main.xaml` file, which will hold the already existing opened URL:

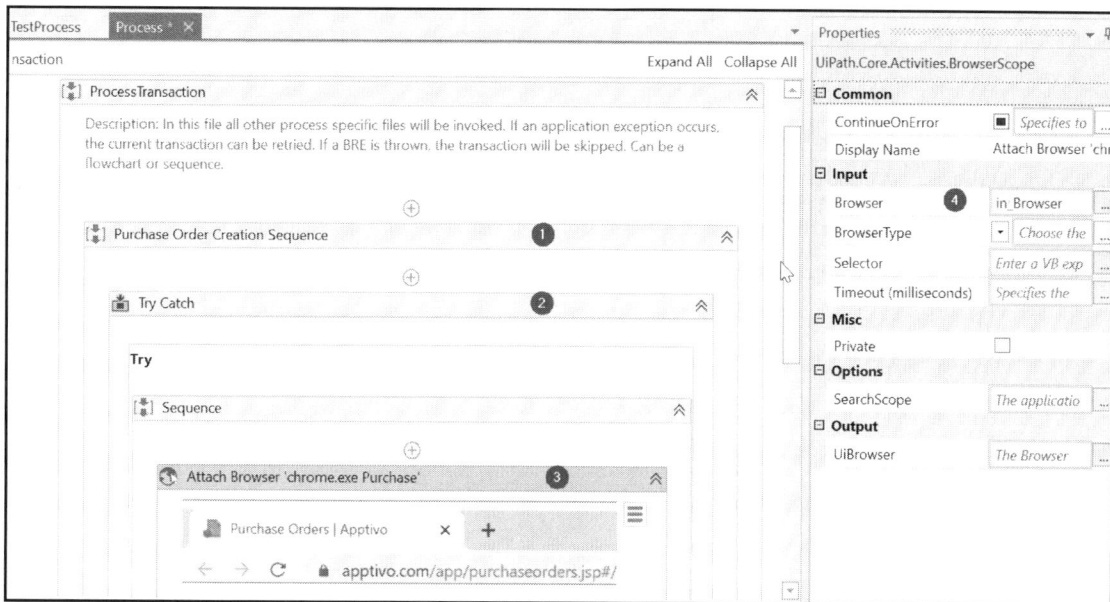

5. Let's create the variables that we will be using to store the PO details. So, add the variables `strSupplier`, `strAddress`, `strCity`, `strState`, `strZip`, `strItemName`, and `strPO` of type **String** and **Scope** to **Try Catch**, as shown in the following screenshot:

6. Finally, let's add a **Maximize Window** activity to maximize the browser, followed by an **Activate** activity to activate the PO application. So, within the **Activate** activity, indicate any element in the Apptivo PO application open in your Chrome Browser.

Now that the PO application is activated, let's go ahead and create the POs.

Creating the POs

We will create the POs now in the Apptivo PO application. Let's start by doing some prep work.

Preparing to input PO data

Before we input the POs, let's initiate the PO creation and assign and validate the data:

1. To create a new PO, we start by clicking the **Create** button in Apptivo. Within `Process.xaml`, and under the **Activate** activity we added in the last section, let's add a mouse **Click** activity. Within this activity, highlight the **Create** button on the Apptivo PO application.

2. Next, we'll check if the **Supplier** input field is available for input. So, use a **Find Element** activity and point to the input box next to the **Supplier** label. For this activity, ensure that you check the **WaitVisible** and **WaitActive** options so that the activity waits for the **Supplier** input box to become visible and active. Your workflow for this part will look like this:

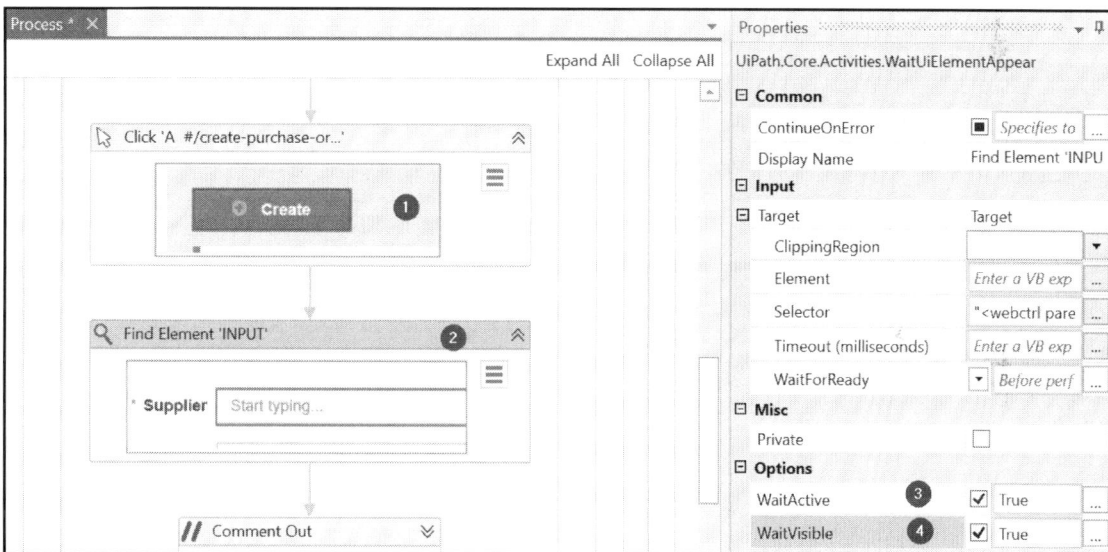

3. Now, let's assign the values we have in the queue to the PO variables. To do this, we will use the **Assign** activity. Add six **Assign** activities as follows:

- Assign `strSupplier` to `in_TransactionItem.SpecificContent("Supplier").ToString`
- Assign `strAddress` to `in_TransactionItem.SpecificContent("Address").ToString`
- Assign `strCity` to `in_TransactionItem.SpecificContent("City").ToString`
- Assign `strState` to `in_TransactionItem.SpecificContent("State").ToString`
- Assign `strZip` to `in_TransactionItem.SpecificContent("Zip").ToString`
- Assign `strItemName` to `in_TransactionItem.SpecificContent("ItemName").ToString ng`

4. The Apptivo PO application requires a few mandatory fields before it can create the PO. So let's check if we have values for these mandatory fields. If not, we will skip and input the next PO.

5. Here, we need to check if we have values for the **Supplier** and **Item Name**. For that, let's add an **If** control with the appropriate condition: `NOT String.IsNullOrEmpty(strSupplier.Trim)` and `NOT String.IsNullOrEmpty(strItemName.Trim)`, respectively.

Our workflow with the **Assign** activity and **If** control added should look like this:

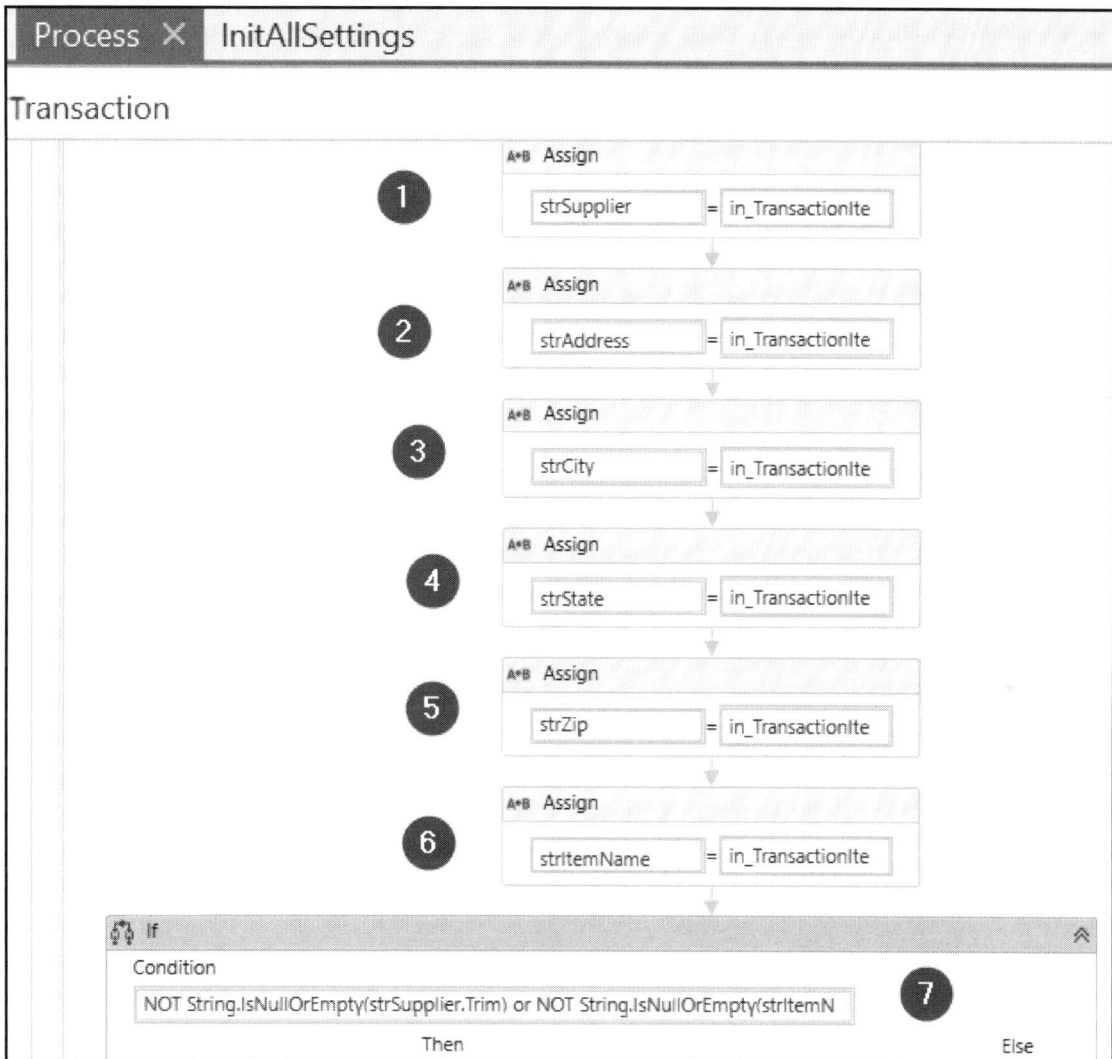

6. Let's start with the **Else** block, where we handle the exception scenario. We'll add a **Log message** activity with the **Log Level** set to **Error**. Add the following message: `"Purchase order cannot be created as mandatory items are not available in the transaction details."`

Now that we have the groundwork complete, let's input all the PO data.

Inputting the PO data

Let's input the data into the PO application form within the **If** control, as follows:

1. In the **Then** block of the **If** control, we are ready to input the data. We will start by inputting the **Supplier** data. For that, we'll add a **Type Into** activity and indicate the **Supplier** input box and update the value as `strSupplier`. To confirm the input, add a **Send HotKey** activity, indicate the **Supplier** input box and set **enter** under **Key**, as shown in the following screenshot:

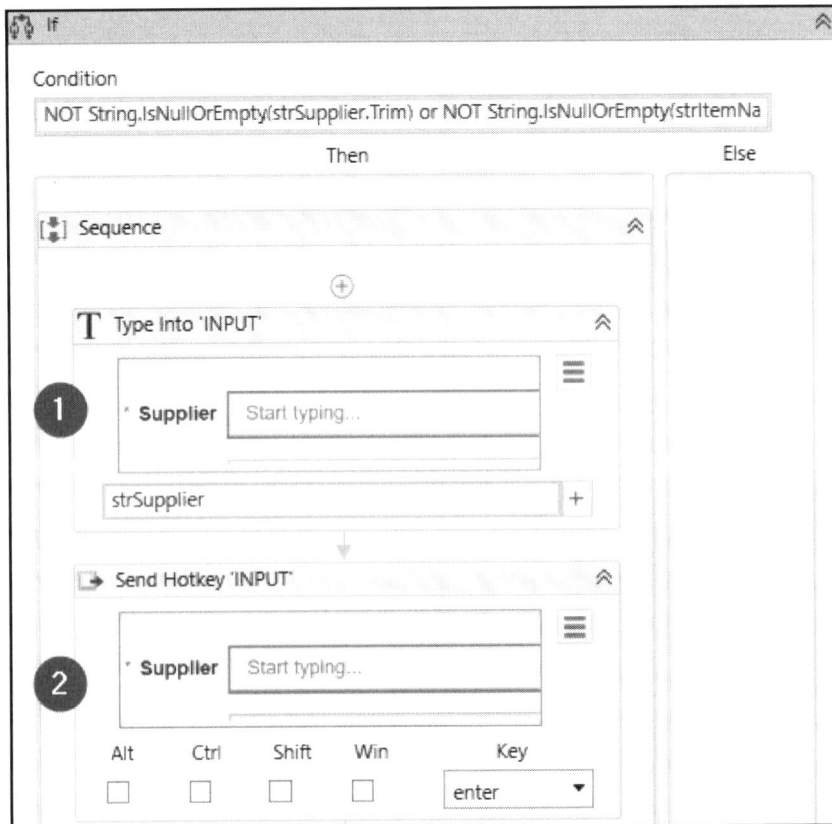

2. Next, we will fill in the supplier's address information. Since this is the next section in the form, we will use a page-down keypress to get to those fields. Add a **Send Hot Key** activity, indicate the **PO** label at the top-left section of the page, and send a **pgdn Key**.

3. To give the automation some context to identify our address fields faster, let's use a mouse **Click Image** activity and indicate the **Address Line 1** label by dragging to it:

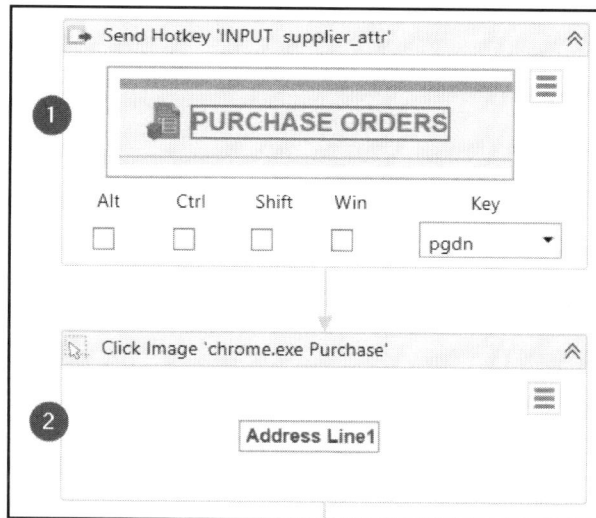

4. Now we can just use the **Type Into** activity to enter the address. Let's add the activity and indicate the **Address Line 1** input box in the browser. For the activity, update the properties as follows:
   - Set **Text** to strAddress.
   - Make sure that **Activate** and **ClickBeforeTyping** are checked and set to **True.**
   - Provide a **DelayBetweenKeys** of **100** milliseconds.
   - In **Selector**, within **Target**, make sure **parentId** is unselected (**parentId** will dynamically change for each order, so it's better to exclude this parameter of the selector).

5. Perform the same steps as previously and use another **Type into** activity to input **City** information into the **Address Information** section. Your workflow for this part will look as follows:

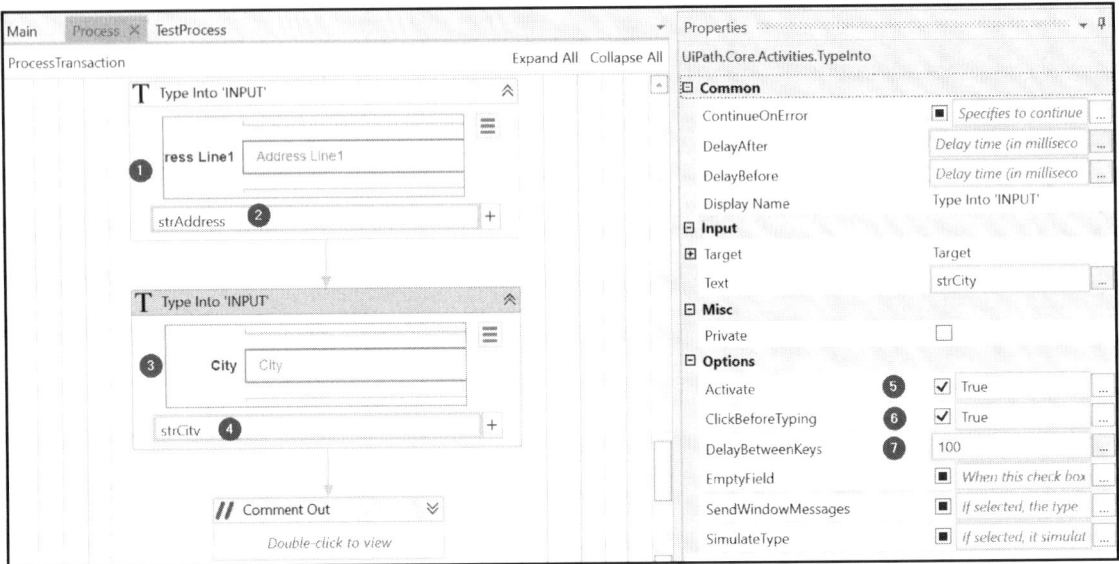

6. Since the state is a dropdown that accepts user input, we need to click before typing in the value. To do that, let's use the **Click Image** activity and drag to the **Select one** text in the **State** field. We do this because the selector of this element was not captured by the UiPath recorder.

> The use of `Click Image` is not a recommended practice, but we can use it in places where the normal `Click` is not able to perform the required function due to bad selectors and where we've tried all possible options with the other selectors.

7. Use the **Type Into** activity to enter the state value and then use a **Send Hotkey** to send an **Enter** key to the **State** field and complete the selection:

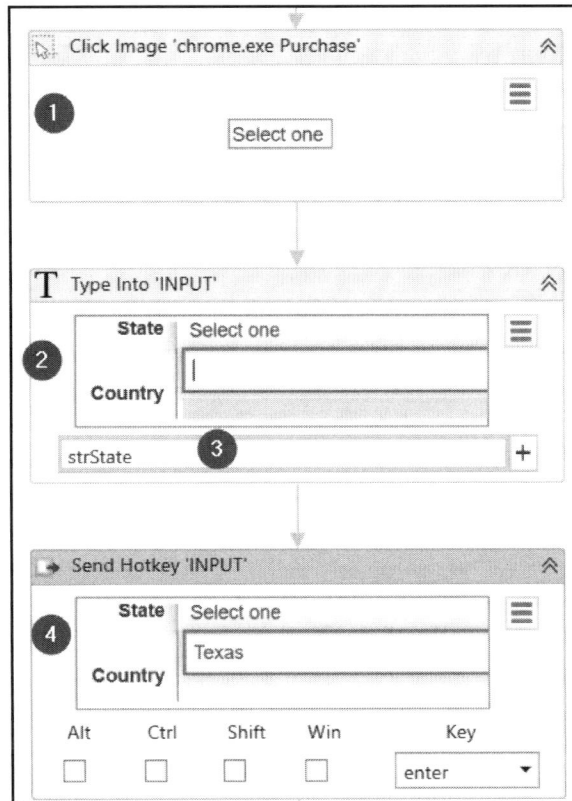

8. Similar to the preceding, add another **Type Into** activity to enter the zip code. In the properties for this activity, ensure that the **Selector** within **Target** has the **parentId** unselected.

Those were the **Supplier** and **Address** fields. Now, let's enter the item details and create the PO:

1. We will again use another **Type Into** activity and indicate the **Item Name** text field in the browser. Follow that with a **Send Hotkey** activity for the *Enter* key to complete the selection.
2. We will leave the rest of the item details blank. Let's go ahead and create the PO by clicking on the **Create** button at the bottom of the screen. For that, add a **Send Hotkey** activity to send the *PgDn* key. Highlight the **Purchase Order** label at the top left-hand section of the page to scroll to the end of the page.

3. Finally, use the mouse **Click** activity to click on the **Create** button at the bottom of the screen to create the PO:

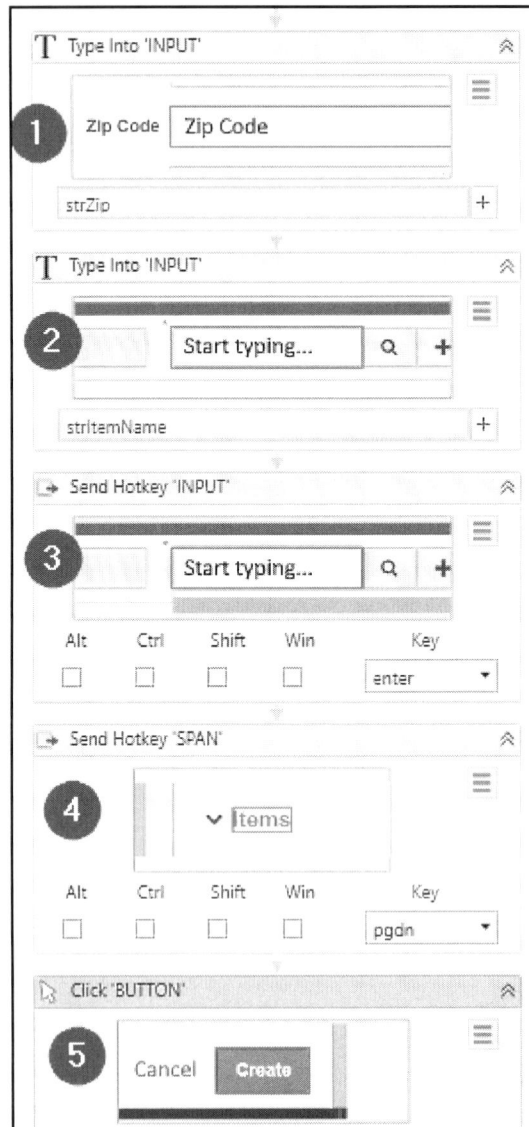

> Web automation may need some trial and error to find the correct selectors and interact with the form elements. Here, we are looking to populate the data we extracted from the input file (the supplier name, address, item, and so on) into the PO form in Apptivo.

Now that we have completed inputting the PO, let's handle any errors that may come up.

Handling PO entry errors

There are times when the PO application will throw error messages. This could happen when the automation has issues entering data into the mandatory fields. Let's handle such a scenario so that we can continue to the next transaction:

1. Let's generate an error message in our PO application. Go to the Apptivo PO application and create the PO without filling out any details. The application will throw an error as follows:

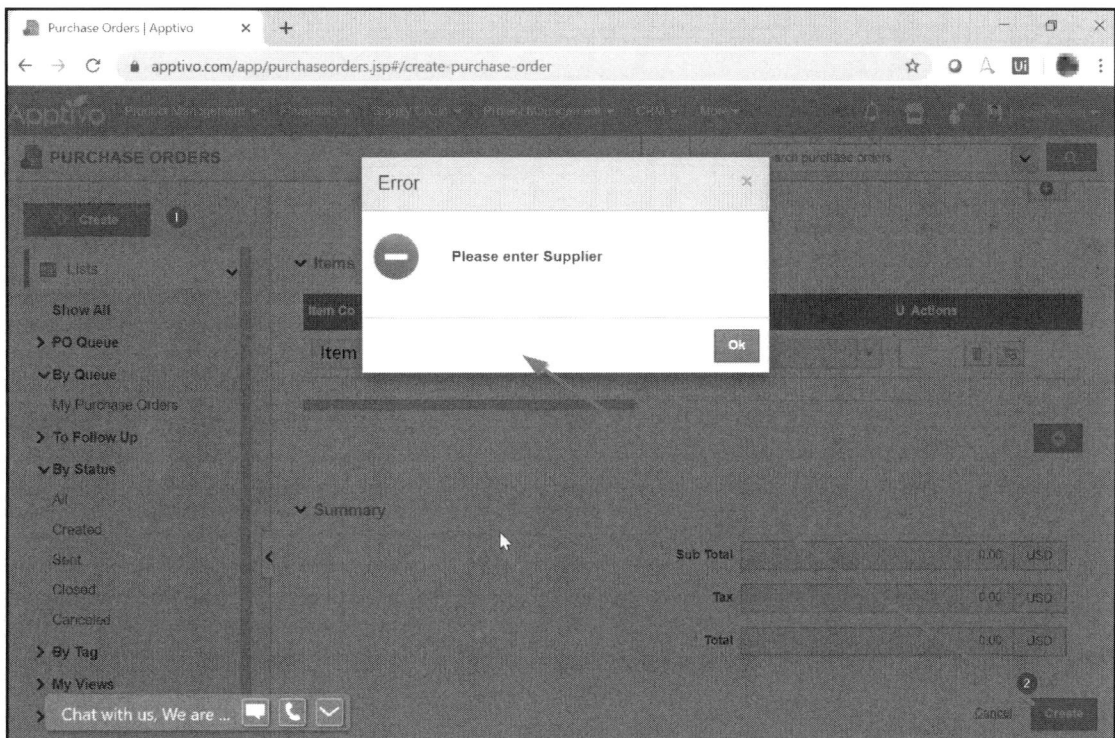

2. Now that we have the error message, let's handle it by pressing **Ok** to continue.

3. Let's go to UiPath Studio and add an **Element Exists** activity right after the **Create Click** activity. Indicate the **Error** dialog header in the browser and update the properties as follows:
   - **WaitForReady** within **Target**: `WaitForReady.COMPLETE`
   - For **Exists within Output**, create a new variable called `boolError`:

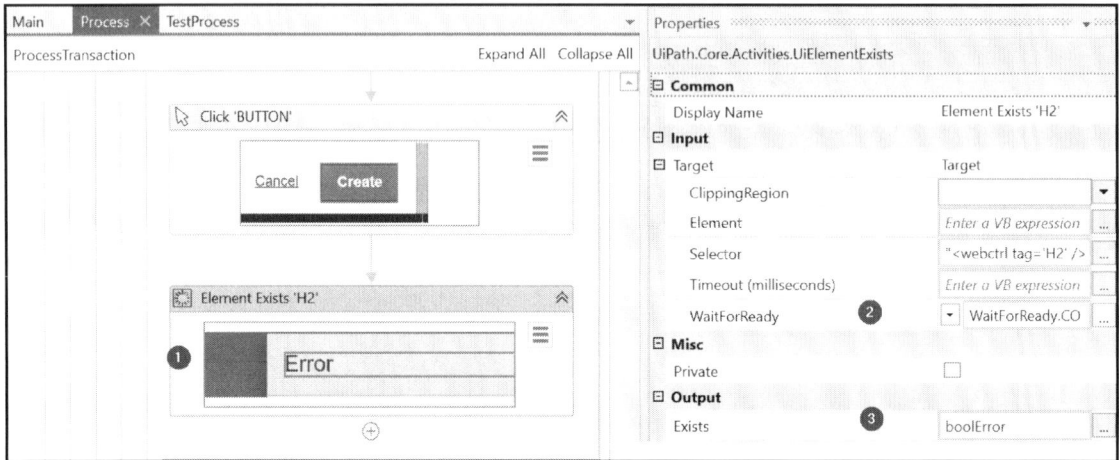

4. Let's add an **If** control activity with the `Not boolError` condition to check if the error dialog does not exist.
5. In the **Else** block, we will click **Ok** on the error dialog and log an error message. To do that, add a mouse **Click** activity and indicate the **Ok** button of the error dialog. Let's also add a **Log Message** with the **Log Level** set to **Error** and the message `"Purchase Order not created"`:

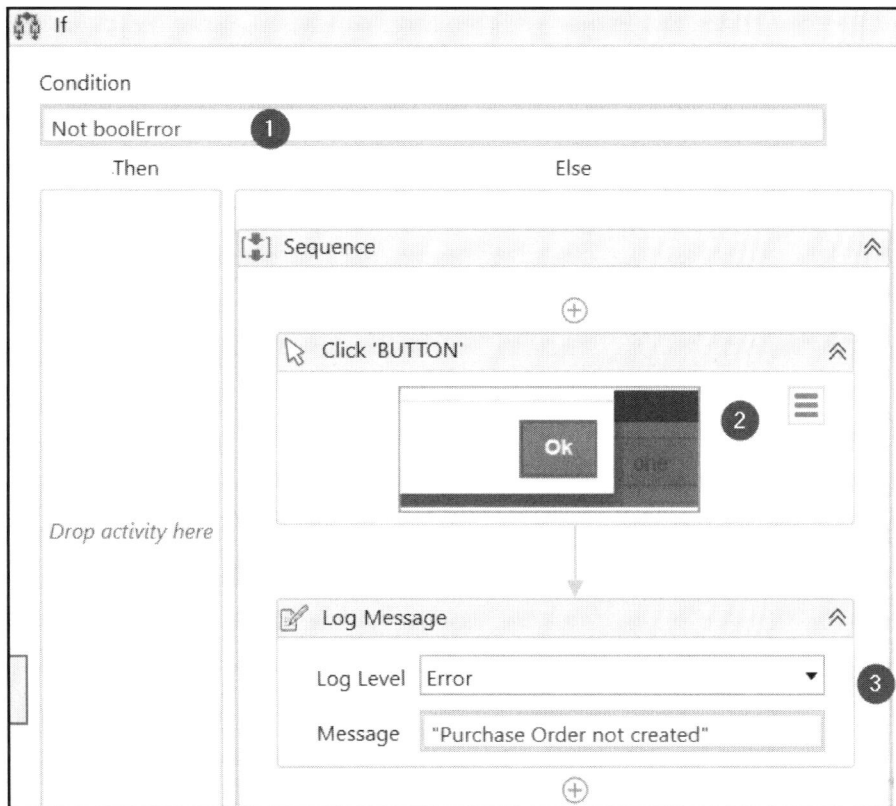

Now that the error scenario is handled, let's go ahead and capture the PO number from the Apptivo application and add it to the spreadsheet.

Capturing the PO

As a final step, we will update the PO number generated by Apptivo to the Excel spreadsheet:

1. Let's first open an already created PO in the Apptivo PO management application. If you do not have one already, create a new one by filling in the mandatory PO fields and clicking on **Create**. Then go to **My POs** on the left pane and open the new PO.

2. Go back to UiPath Studio and within the **Then** block, add a `Find Element` activity and indicate the PO number element, as shown in the following screenshot:

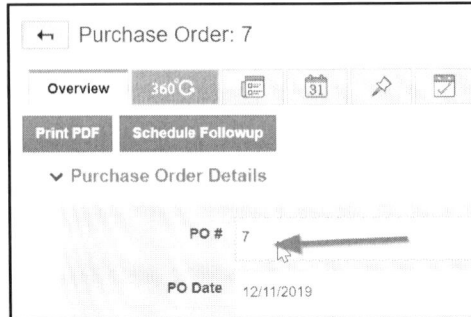

3. For the `Find Element` activity, update the selector **aaname** field with a wildcard character * so that any value is accepted. Check the **WaitActive** and **WaitVisible** options in the properties panel:

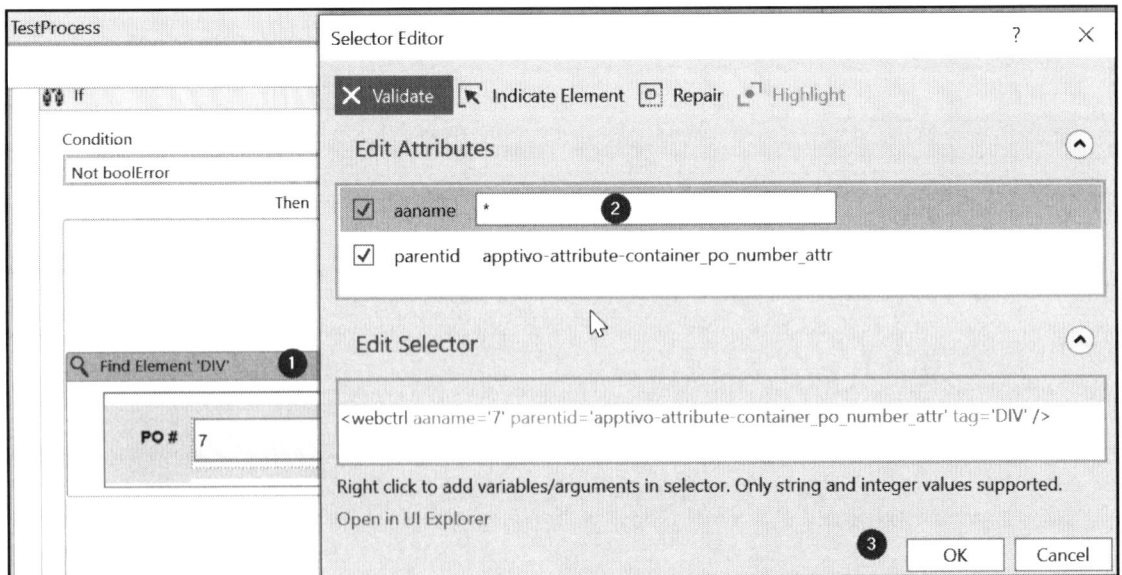

4. Let's also add a log message with the level set to **Info** and the message `"PO Created Successfully"`.

5. Now that the PO is created, let's extract the PO number and store it in a variable. Add a **Get Text** activity within the **Then** block and indicate the PO number. For this activity, update the properties as follows:

    1. Fill the **aaname** selector field with *, as shown in the following screenshot. (The wildcard character * can be substituted for any characters that can go in this field, for example, 1, 12, and 103, and so on.)

    2. Update **WaitForReady** with WaitForReady.COMPLETE.

    3. Set the **Output Value** as strPO. This is the variable where we will store the extracted value:

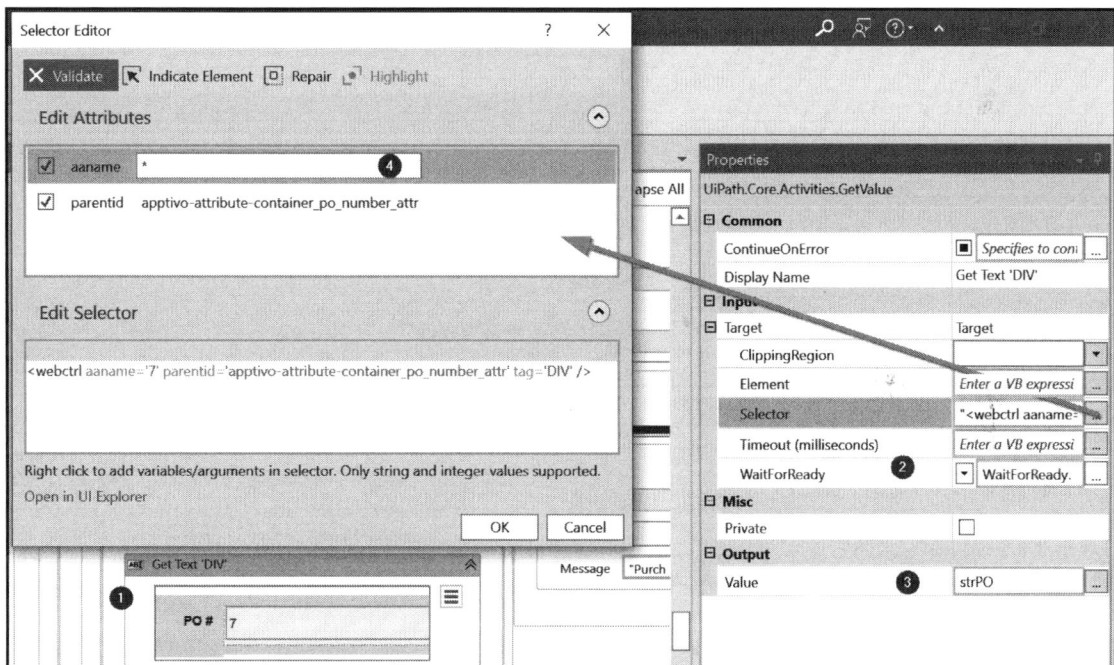

Now that we have extracted and stored the PO number, let's update the spreadsheet.

Updating the PO in the spreadsheet

We will now write the PO number we captured from Apptivo to Excel. To update the Excel sheet, we will look up the row based on a combination of supplier details and the item name, and update the last column, **PO**. To keep things simple for this learning project, we are assuming that each supplier only orders an item once:

1. First, let's first check that the PO number is not empty. Add an **If** control activity with the following condition: NOT string.IsNullOrEmpty(strPO.Trim).

2. If the PO number is empty, let's handle the error in the Else block. Add a **Log Message** with the **Log Level** set to **Error** and a **Message** reading "Cannot Retrieve the PO for this Item Name: "+ strItemName:

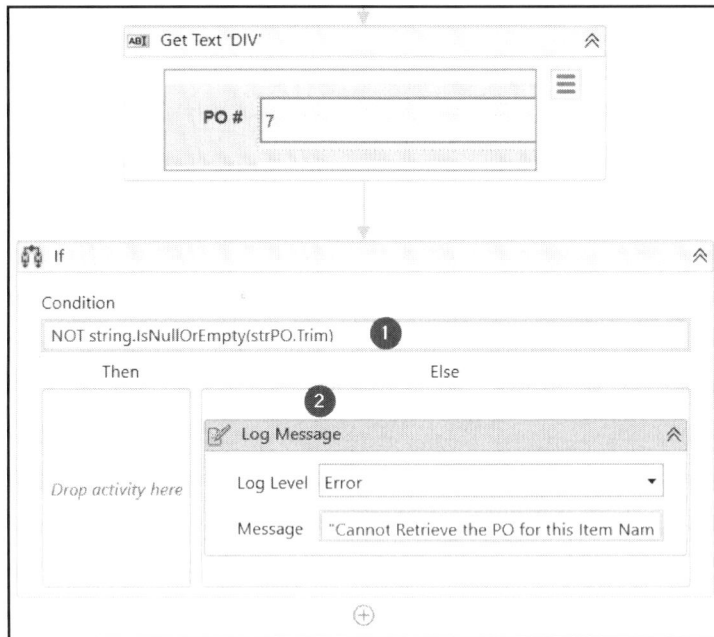

3. In the **Then** block, let's open the Data\PurchaseOrder.xlsx Excel file, find the corresponding row based on a combination of **ItemName** and **Supplier** and update the **PO** column. To do that, add the Excel Application Scope activity and update the workbook path to "Data\PurchaseOrders.xlsx".

4. Next, let's use the Excel **Read Range** activity to read the table into a new DataTable variable, dtPO. Ensure that the **AddHeaders** property is checked, as shown in the following screenshot:

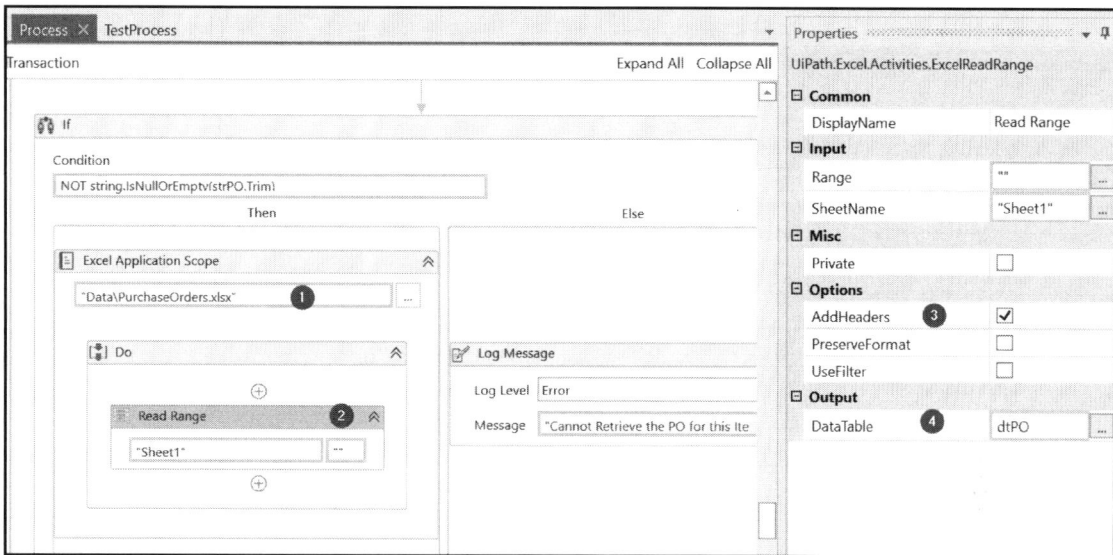

5. Now, iterate the DataTable `dtPO` and find the respective row in the Excel sheet based on the combination. Add a **For Each Row** activity and within that, add an **If** control activity with the following condition:

```
row("ItemName").ToString+row("Supplier").ToString =
strItemName+strSupplier:
```

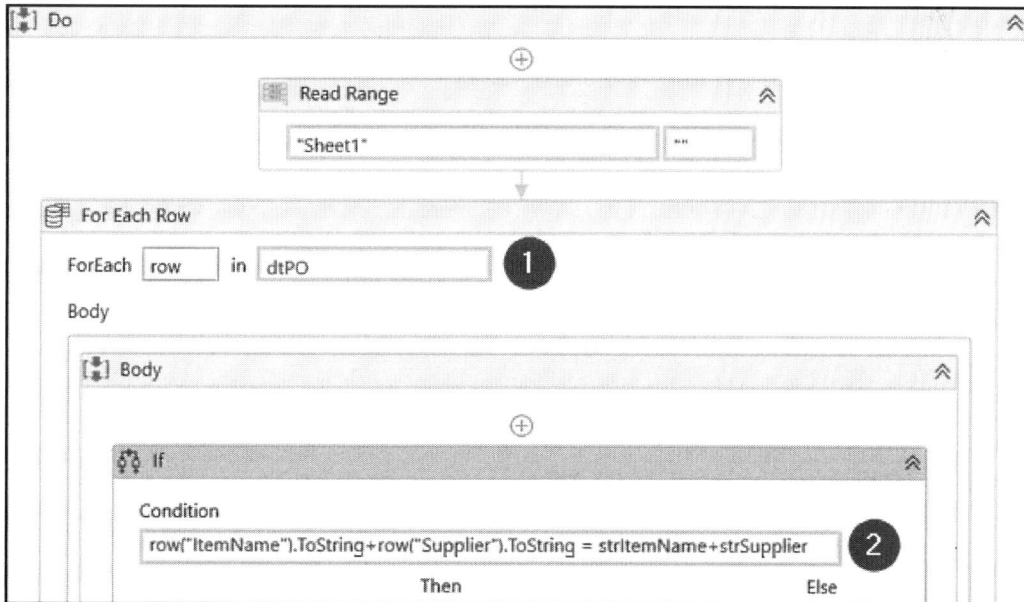

6. Create a new `intCounter` variable of type `Number` (**Int32**) and set the default value to **2**.
7. Add the **Assign** activity `intCounter = intCounter+1` to increment the counter outside the **If** control scope.
8. Use a **Write Cell** activity to write each of the PO numbers in the **G** column with the correct index. To do that, update the **Range** property with `"G"+intCounter.ToString` and set the value to `strPO`. This increments the counter and writes to rows G1, G2, G3, and so on, as it reads from the DataTable:

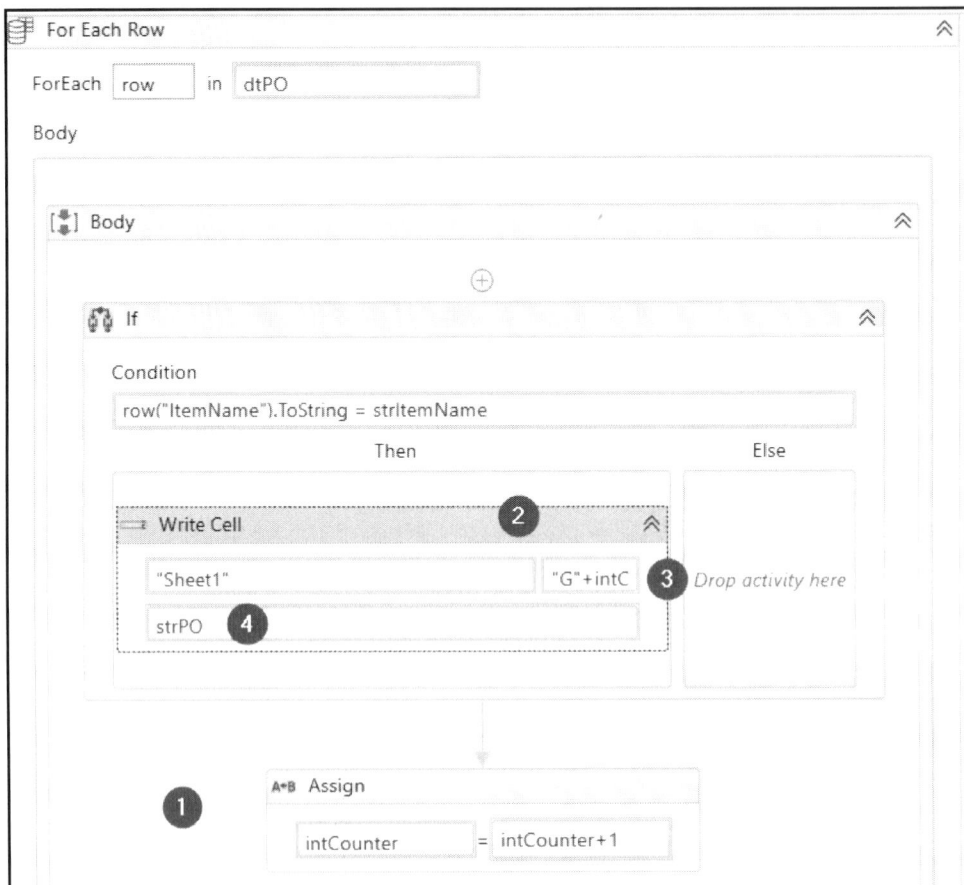

9. Add a **Log Message** with a level of **Info** and set the message to read `"PO`
    `Number: "+strPO+ " Successfully update in PurchaseOrder.xlsx".`

    This completes the **Try** block. Let's now handle any exceptions in the **Catch** block:

10. In the **Catch** block, add a **SelectorNotFoundException** and add a **Log Message**
    with the **Log Level** set to **Error** and the message as `"PO was not created for`
    `this Transaction due to this Error: " + exception.ToString:`

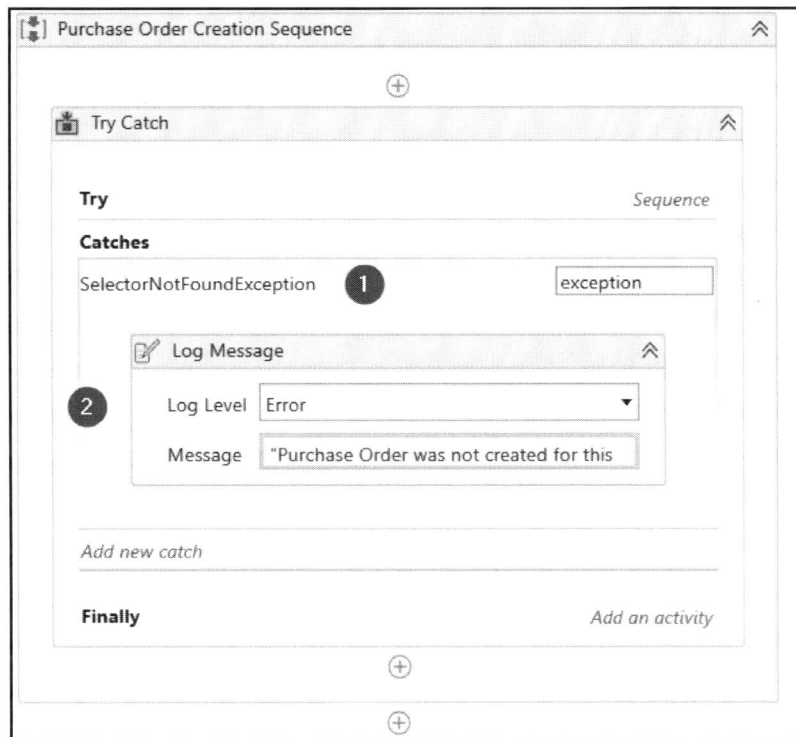

That completes our updates to `Process.xaml` for this project. As you saw, most of the
logic goes into this workflow. All the other workflows support the execution of logic in
the `Process.xaml` file.

To ensure `Process.xaml` gets the **Browser** variable, it is important to add it to the invoking activity. Go to the `Main.xaml` file and double-click on the **Process Transaction** state. Scroll over to the **Invoke ProcessTransaction workflow** and click on **Import Arguments**. Add the `in_Browser` argument with **Direction** as `In` and **Value** as `Browser`:

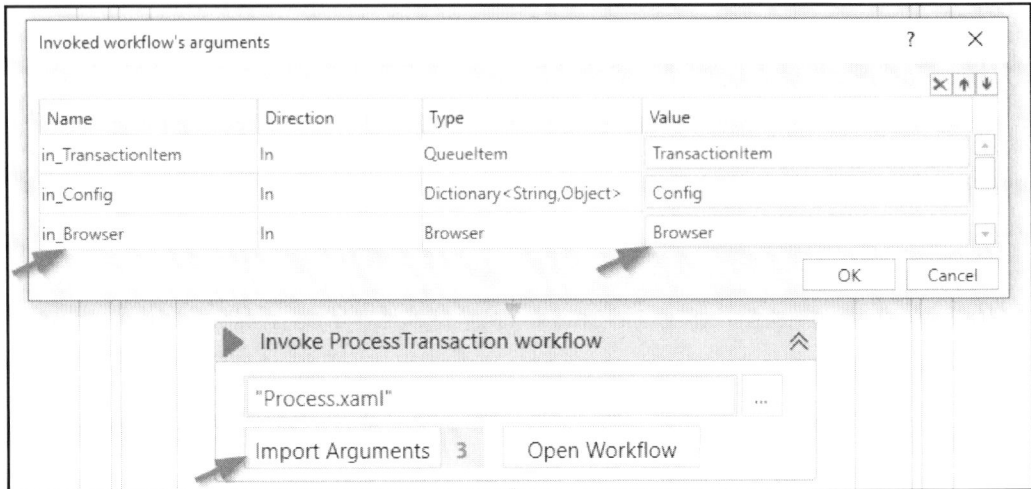

Next up, as part of the ReFramework, we have come to the transaction status. The framework handles all we need here and so we do not need to make any changes to the template.

Finally, we have to update the **CloseAllApplications** workflow. We can look to close the Apptivo application here. This is optional – we will leave it out here and go straight to testing the automation!

Before we test, we will update the **End Process State** in `Main.xaml`. Double-click on the state and add a **Message Box** right after **Invoke CloseAllApplications workflow** stating `All Transactions Processed`. Let's now test our automation.

Testing the Automation

We have completed our first ReFramework project! Let's go ahead and test it:

1. Go to UiPath Orchestrator and confirm that the four queue items that we had are available. If not, please run the `PurchaseOrderDispatcher.xaml` file (use **Run File** for this):

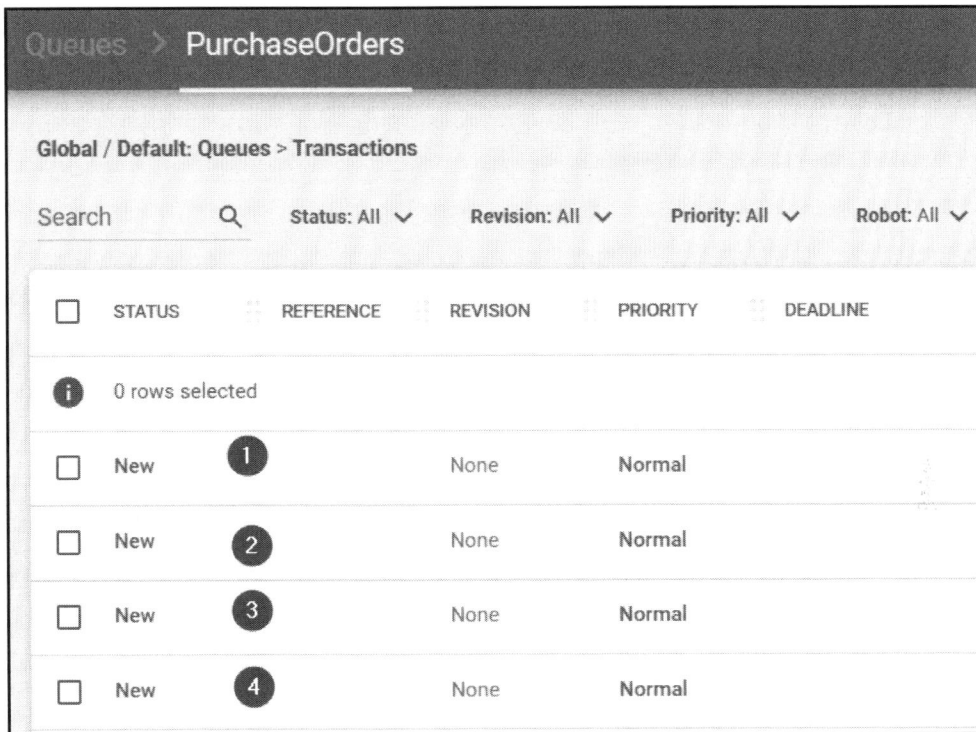

2. Ensure that the `PurchaseOrders.xlsx` file and Apptivo application in the Chrome browser are both closed (we need an active session, that is, you should have already logged in to Apptivo before closing the browser).
3. Go to the `Main.xaml` file in UiPath Studio and run the automation.
4. Once the automation runs through, we should get a message reading **All Transactions Processed.**
5. Open your `Data\PurchaseOrder.xlsx` file and check whether all four PO numbers were updated in the **PO** column:

Supplier	Address	City	State	Zip	ItemName	PO
Lenovo	1009 Think Pl	Morrisville	North Carolina	27560	Laptop	10
Cisco	2300 E President George Bush Hwy	Richardson	Texas	75082	Router	11
Avaya	4851 Regent Blvd	Irving	Texas	75063	Phones	12
HP	1501 Page Mill Rd	Palo Alto	California	94304	Monitor	13

That completes a quick test of our ReFramework automation.

Summary

In this chapter, we used the advanced UiPath ReFramework to build our automation. We used a Dispatcher to load PO transactions from a spreadsheet into an Orchestrator queue. We processed those transactions via a Performer that used the UiPath ReFramework.

The framework picked up the transactions from the queue, input them into the PO system, and updated the spreadsheet with the generated PO number. That completes our UiPath ReFramework project.

In the next chapter, we will take up and complete an RPA challenge!

6
Completing an RPA Challenge

We have come to our last UiPath project for this book—the RPA challenge. This project is also the beginning of our Automation Anywhere project, as we will carry out the RPA challenge with A2019 as well.

This RPA challenge chapter will introduce you to the concept of handling dynamic elements in a form. This challenge, with dynamically changing fields, is a fun way of trying out your newly acquired UiPath web automation skills. We will also begin our journey with Automation Anywhere A2019 using this challenge. You can, therefore, see how the same challenge can be approached on the new platform, which we will explore further in the next few chapters.

We will be taking on the challenge at `rpachallenge.com`. The website has a few challenges that can be completed using any RPA tool. We will take up the Input Forms challenge. The challenge is to create an automation that will take data from a spreadsheet and input the data into a set of 10 dynamic forms on the website. As this is a learning exercise, we will cover a basic version of completing the challenge here. We will first complete the challenge with UiPath and then with Automation Anywhere.

Here is what we will cover as part of this project:

- UiPath web automation
- Automation Anywhere A2019 web automation
- Inputting data into dynamic fields
- UiPath Excel operations
- Automation Anywhere A2019 Excel operations

Technical requirements

Let's understand the hardware and software requirements for this project:

- The RPA challenge website (`http://rpachallenge.com/`).
- Download the RPA challenge Excel file.
- Microsoft Excel 2007 and later.
- A PC with the UiPath community edition version 19.10.0 installed.
- Google Chrome with the UiPath extension installed.
- The Automation Anywhere A2019 community edition. Sign up at `https://www.automationanywhere.com/products/community-edition`.
- The A2019 bot agent installed. Make sure the **My Devices** tab has an "active" green status for the client machine.
- The UiPath code from GitHub (`https://github.com/PacktPublishing/Robotic-Process-Automation-Projects/tree/master/rpachallenge`).
- Check out the following video to see the Code in Action: `https://bit.ly/36hqIfn`.

Project details

We will be reading data from an Excel file, provided by the RPA challenge website, and entering that data into input forms on the website.

The input data fields on the form change position on the screen after every submission. That's what makes this data entry challenging compared to the projects we have carried out so far. There are a total of 10 rounds of input before the challenge completes and shows you your results. The objective is to complete the challenge accurately in the shortest time possible.

We will do some groundwork and then complete the challenge with both UiPath and Automation Anywhere, as mentioned earlier.

Project groundwork

As with any project, we'll start with some groundwork. Go to `rpachallenge.com` and download the Excel form from the website by clicking on the **DOWNLOAD EXCEL** button. This is at the bottom of the left pane, after the description of the challenge. Once downloaded, check the Excel form and move it to your project folder for easy access. The file should look like this:

First Name	Last Name	Company Name	Role in Company	Address	Email	Phone Number
John	Smith	IT Solutions	Analyst	98 North Road	jsmith@itsolutions.co.	40716543298
Jane	Dorsey	MediCare	Medical Engineer	11 Crown Street	jdorsey@mc.com	40791345621
Albert	Kipling	Waterfront	Accountant	22 Guild Street	kipling@waterfront.co	40735416854
Michael	Robertson	MediCare	IT Specialist	17 Farburn Terrace	mrobertson@mc.com	40733652145
Doug	Derrick	Timepath Inc.	Analyst	99 Shire Oak Road	dderrick@timepath.co.	40799885412
Jessie	Marlowe	Aperture Inc.	Scientist	27 Cheshire Street	jmarlowe@aperture.us	40733154268
Stan	Hamm	Sugarwell	Advisor	10 Dam Road	shamm@sugarwell.org	40712462257
Michelle	Norton	Aperture Inc.	Scientist	13 White Rabbit Stree	mnorton@aperture.us	40731254562
Stacy	Shelby	TechDev	HR Manager	19 Pineapple Bouleva	sshelby@techdev.com	40741785214
Lara	Palmer	Timepath Inc.	Programmer	87 Orange Street	lpalmer@timepath.co.	40731653845

Now that we have the Excel file, let's create the automation with UiPath.

Completing the challenge with UiPath

Let's start by building the RPA challenge automation with UiPath.

Getting started with the UiPath project

As with all UiPath projects, we will start by creating the project:

1. Create a new UiPath project in Studio, called `rpachallenge`, and open the **Main** workflow.
2. Within the **Main** sequence, let's add a **Try Catch** activity to handle any exceptions. We will add the automation to the **Try** block in the next section.
3. For now, let's handle any exceptions in the **Catches** block. Go ahead and add a new catch for **Exception**. This will handle any system exceptions. Add a **Message box** activity with the `"RPA Challenge Failed due to this Error:"+ exception.Message` text.

Your workflow so far should look like this:

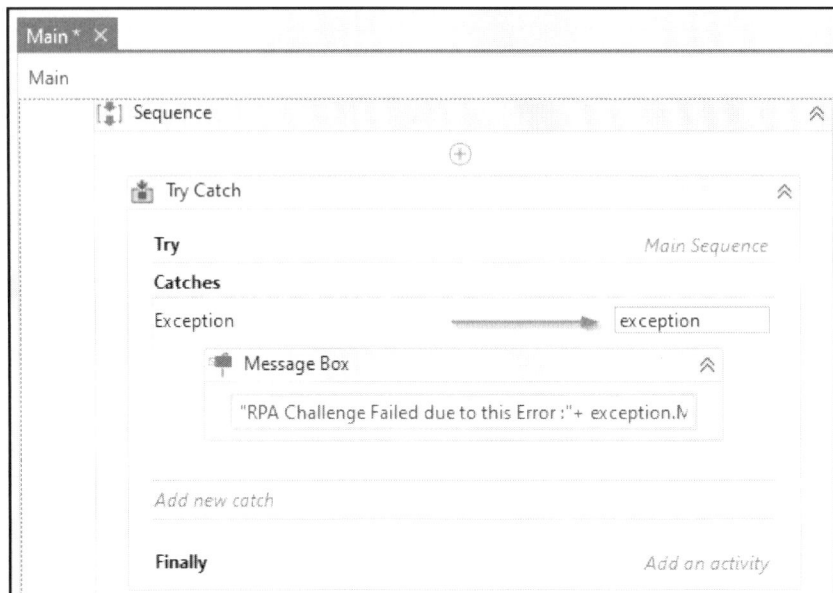

Now that we have handled the exception, let's get into the meat of the automation.

Creating the challenge automation

We will add all the elements for this challenge automation in the **Main** workflow itself. Let's start by reading the Excel file and storing the input data used when filling in the dynamic forms in the Data Table.

Reading the RPA challenge Excel data

We will use the **Read Range** activity to read the Excel content. Here are the steps for creating the UiPath automation:

1. In the **Try** block, add a new sequence called `Main Sequence`.
2. We will now read the input Excel file data into the `dataTable` variable that we just created. Add the **Read Range** activity and update the properties of the activity:
    1. Click and point on the RPA challenge Excel workbook location.
    2. Add the range to read on the workbook.
    3. Make sure **AddHeaders** is checked.

4. Set **Output** to a new `dataTable` variable.

Here is what our workflow looks like so far:

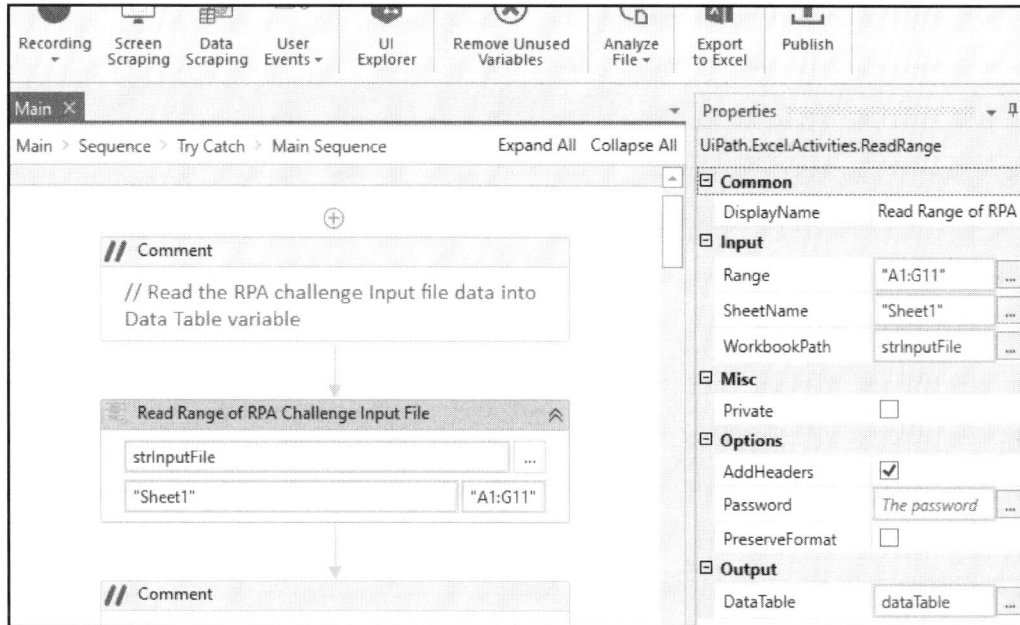

We now have the Excel data stored in the `dataTable` variable. Let's now iterate on each row and input the data into the forms on the website.

Inputting data into the RPA challenge forms

We will be using the UiPath **Anchorbase** activity here to find the form labels. We are using this activity since the fields can move and we do not have a reliable selector:

1. Let's make the automation open the Google Chrome browser and go to `rpachallenge.com`. To do that, add an **Open Browser** activity, specify the browser type as **Chrome,** and specify the URL to the RPA challenge website.

2. Next, add a **Click** activity and point to the **START** button on the RPA challenge page in the Chrome browser.

3. We will now iterate through all the rows of the Data Table and use that data to fill in the forms. To do that, let's add a `row` in the **ForEach** activity and update the Data Table value to the `dataTable` variable, as shown:

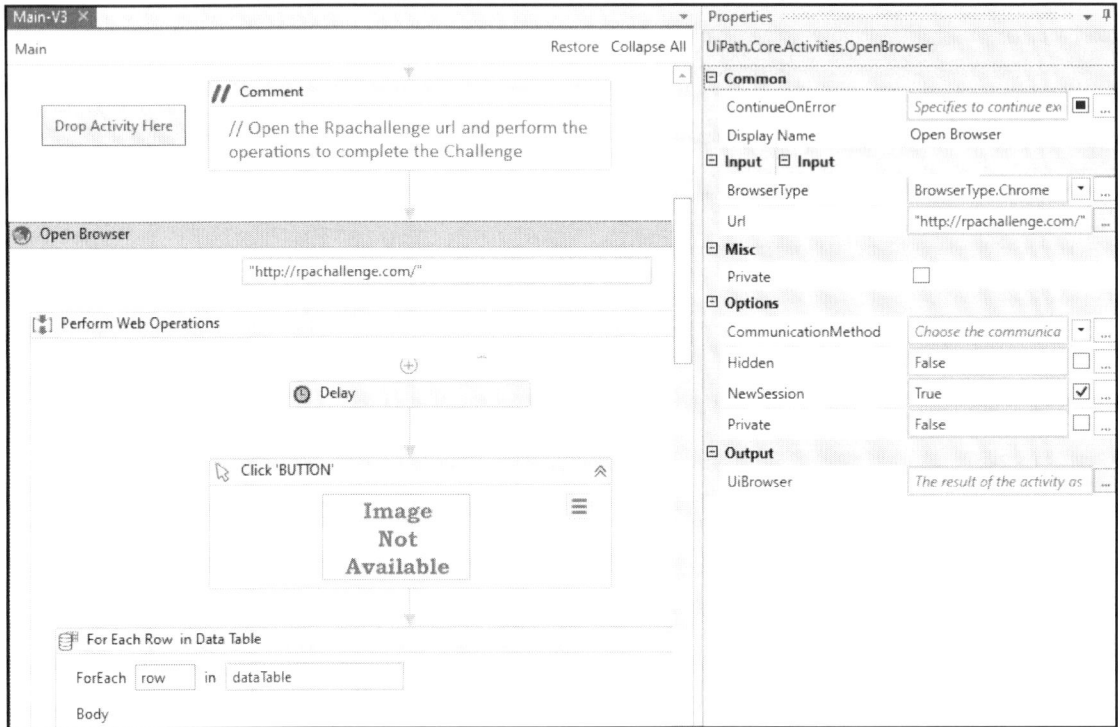

4. Let's now add a new sequence to the body called `Update the Form Sequence` to organize the input activities. Within this sequence, add an **Anchor Base** activity. For this activity's properties, set **ContinueOnError** to **False** and set **AnchorPosition** to **Auto**.

> UiPath's **Anchorbase** activity is a container that uses other UI elements as anchors to search for UI elements when a reliable selector is not available. The **AnchorPosition** property specifies which edge of the container the UI element is anchored to. When **Auto** is selected, it searches for the UI element to the left, right, or bottom of the container. The closest one is selected.

5. We will use the first **Anchor Base** activity that we added to fill in the value of the first name in the form. To do that, add a **Find Element** activity within **Anchor Base**. For this activity, indicate the label for **First Name** in the form. Then, go to the **Selector** property under **Target** and ensure that it has `aaname` set as `First Name` (as well as other parameters), as shown:

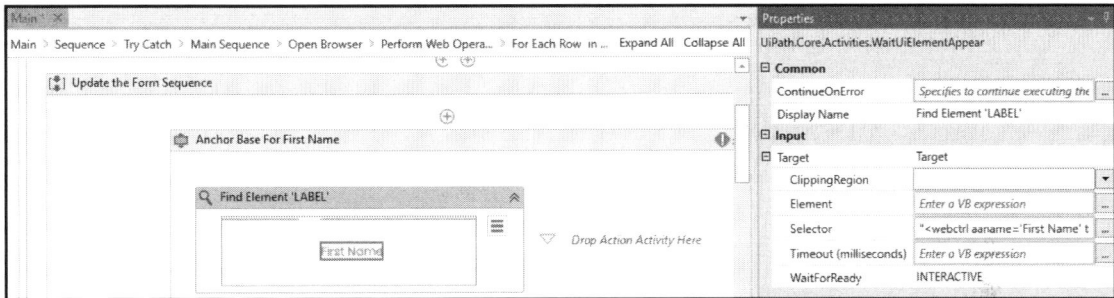

6. Now that the anchor is defined, let's add the **Type into** activity to fill in the value of **First Name**. To do this, mark the textbox next to the **First Name** label. Within the properties, under **Input**, update the property value to `Convert.ToString(row( "First Name"))`. This will fill in the value for the first name of the first row of the data table:

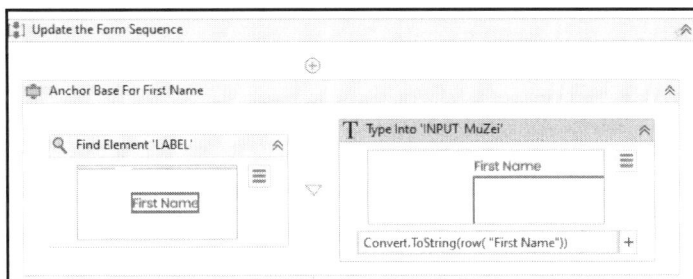

7. Let's now enter the data for the rest of the six fields—`Last Name`, `Company`, `Role in Company`, `Address`, `Email`, and `Phone Number`. Add six more **Anchor Base** activities and, within them, repeat the preceding steps to find the label and type it into the respective fields.

8. Finally, let's submit the form on the `rpachallenge.com` website. Add a **Click** activity and press the **SUBMIT** button.

That's it! We have completed the UiPath automation for the RPA challenge. Let's go ahead and test it.

Testing the UiPath challenge automation

To test the UiPath automation, go ahead and run the automation from the studio:

1. Click on **Run**. You can also use *Ctrl + F5*. The `rpachallenge.com` website should open in the Chrome browser.
2. The UiPath automation will fill in each of the 10 forms by locating the right elements.

If there are any issues, an exception message box will pop up explaining the exception. The challenge should complete with a 100% success rate in around 2 minutes or less. You will get a success message with the time taken by the automation to complete the challenge.

Congratulations! You have completed a basic version of the RPA challenge with UiPath. Let's now undertake quick recap of the UiPath projects we carried out before we move on to Automation Anywhere.

Recapping the UiPath projects

We completed five different projects in this book, which are as follows:

- We covered attended automation and unattended automation.
- We looked at projects that included basic to advanced Excel and web automation.
- The social media moderation project covered automation with the Google Cloud API using A.
- We were introduced to ReFramework and learned how to interact with UiPath orchestrator queues.
- In this chapter, with the RPA challenge, we learned how to handle dynamic elements on a web page.

Next, let's try to understand the Automation Anywhere cloud A2019 platform and see how we can complete the same challenge with Automation Anywhere.

Automation Anywhere A2019

As we learned in `Chapter 1`, *Getting Started with RPA*, Automation Anywhere is another RPA tool that is widely used. We will use the Automation Anywhere A2019 community edition for our projects in this book.

A2019 has a web-based control room to develop and deploy bots, as mentioned earlier. So, we will mostly be working out of a browser, unlike the local windows client we used with UiPath.

We covered the control room and its features in Chapter 1, *Getting Started with RPA*. We also showed you how to register and set up A2019. If you have not set up A2019 yet, now is a good time to do so before we start the RPA challenge with Automation Anywhere.

Once you are all set up, we can get started with some Automation Anywhere A2019 projects.

Completing the challenge with Automation Anywhere

Since this is our first Automation Anywhere project, let's start by checking the A2019 setup.

Getting started with the Automation Anywhere control room

Since A2019 uses a cloud version, we will mostly work through a web browser. Let's follow these steps to get started:

1. Log in to the A2019 community version in your browser, at https://community.cloud.automationanywhere.digital/#/login.

> If you have not yet signed up to the A2019 community edition, go to the link in the *Technical requirements* section of this chapter and sign up. You will receive an email with the control room URL and your credentials to log in to the community edition of A2019. When you log in for the first time, A2019 will prompt you to create your first bot in three steps. Go through the prompts to build your first bot and also install the bot agent, which allows the controller to connect to your PC, and then run automation.

2. Once you log in, you are directed to the A2019 web-based control room. This is where you will build, deploy, and manage your bots. You are greeted with the **Control Room** dashboard:

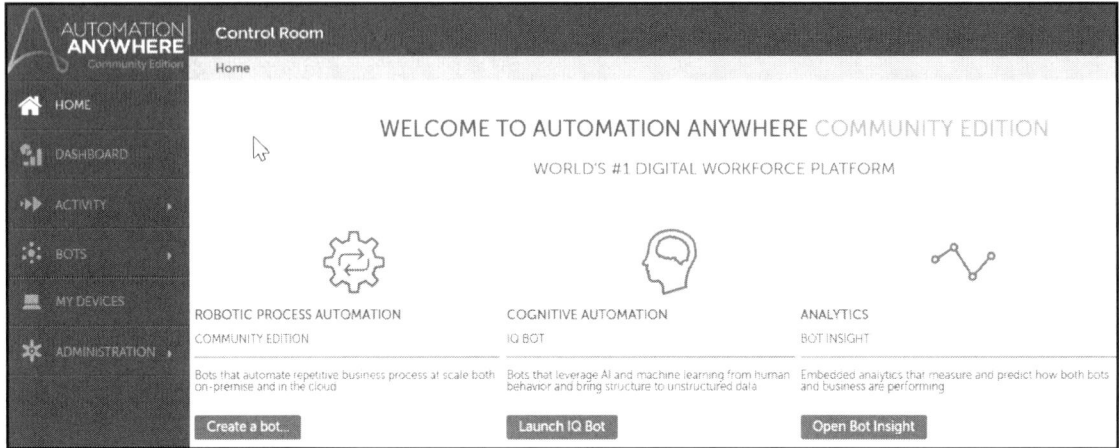

3. Let's first check whether your computer is connected to the control room. We will assume that you went through the first bot run, as stated in the preceding information box—otherwise, do that first. Go to the **MY DEVICES** option in the left-hand side pane and check whether your computer is in the green **Connected** state, as shown:

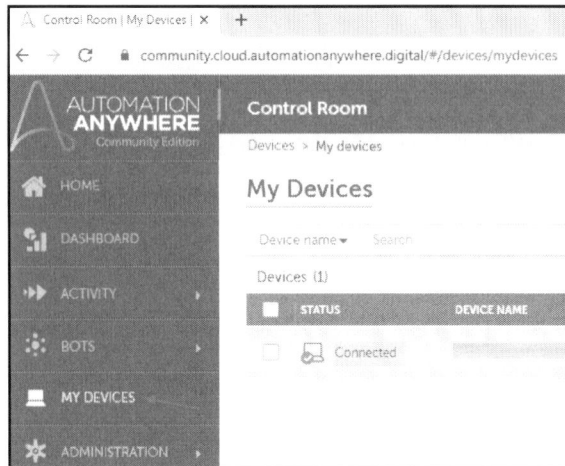

> If the device is not connected, rerun the Automation Anywhere bot agent service in Windows. If that does not solve the issue, try to reinstall the bot agent.

Now that we have the A2019 control room set up, let's create our RPA challenge bot.

Creating the RPA challenge automation bot

We will create the bot in the **Control Room** interface on our browser. To create the bot, let's follow these steps:

1. In the A2019 control room, go to the **Home** option in the left-hand side pane.
2. Once there, click on **Create a bot...**, as shown:

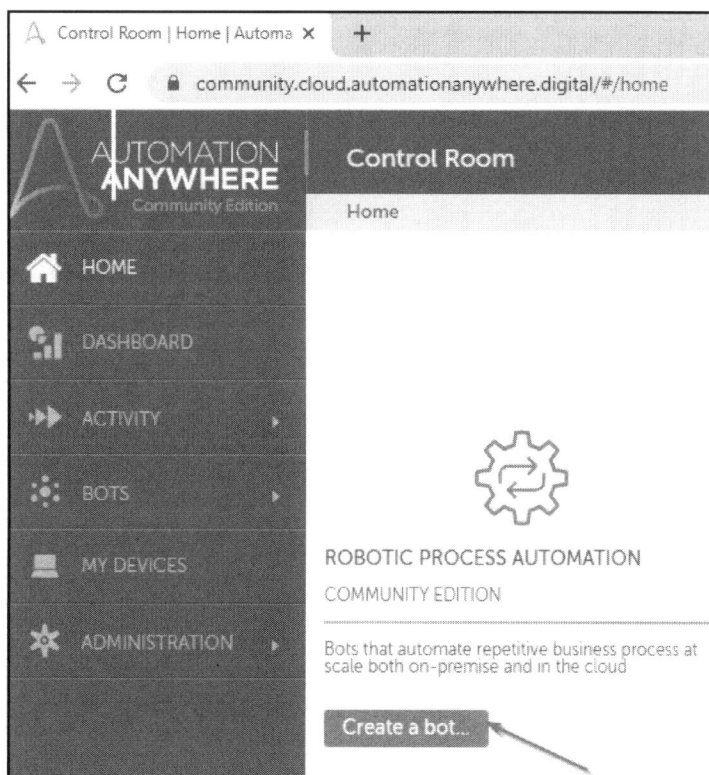

3. Provide a name for your bot and click on **Create a bot...** This will take you to the **Edit Task Bot** interface, where you can configure the automation.

4. We'll first check whether the connection to the controller is working okay by adding a message box and running the bot. To do that, search for `Message box` in the **Actions** pane. Drag and drop it into the workflow and configure its properties. Let's set **Enter the message to display** as `A2019 Bot is Attempting RPA Challenge` and check **Close message box after** to close the message box automatically after 5 seconds:

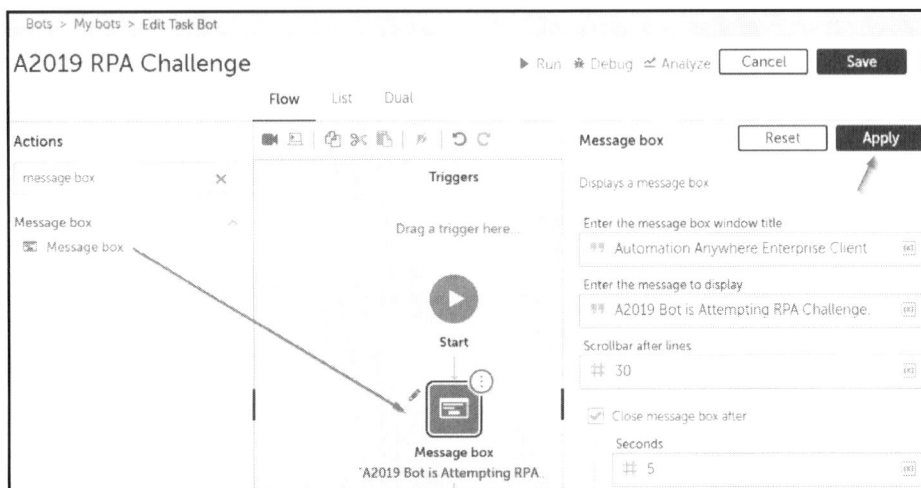

5. Click on **Save** to save your bot so far. Go ahead and click on **Run** to execute the bot. The controller will download the packages to the bot agent and display the message you added:

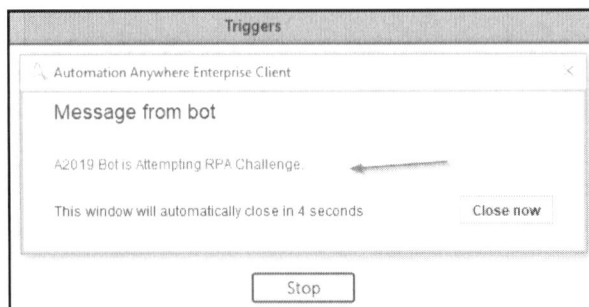

6. Let's now switch to the **List** view on the bot creation canvas. We will mostly use this view to create our automation:

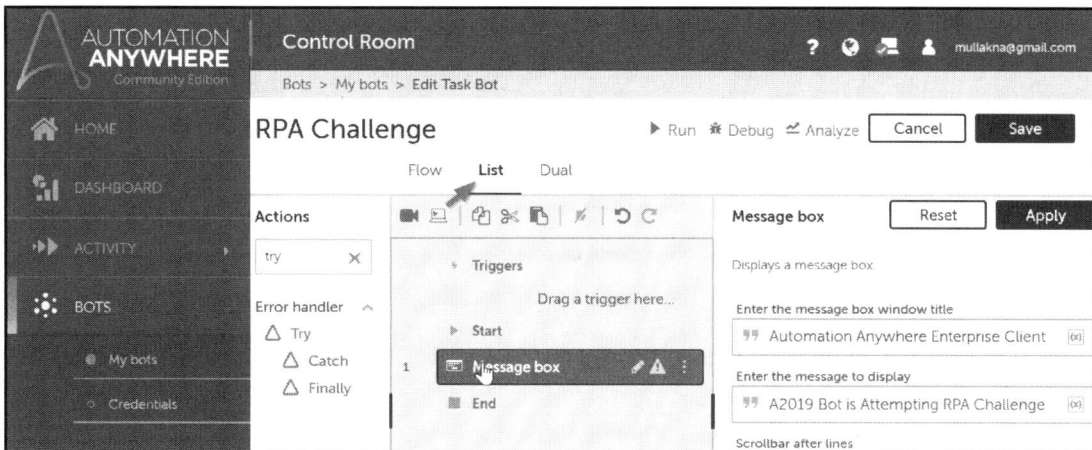

A2019 has the **Flow**, **List**, and **Dual** views available. You can switch your view and check the flows as you progress through the project. We will show you both the **List** and **Flow** views as we progress through the project so that you can get familiar with both modes.

7. We will now handle any exceptions before we add any automation logic. Search for and add the `Try` action. Let's move our existing message box to the **Error Handler: Try** block. We will add all our logic for the automation there.

8. Next, add the `Catch` action underneath **Try**. In the `Catch` properties, make sure the exception type is **All Errors.** Create a variable called `errorMesage` to store the error message. Click on the wizard icon to the right of the input box to create new variables. Click on **Apply** to apply the properties.

9. Add a message box to the **Error Handler: Catch** block with a `Following Error Happened $errorMessage$` message. Your automation so far will look like this:

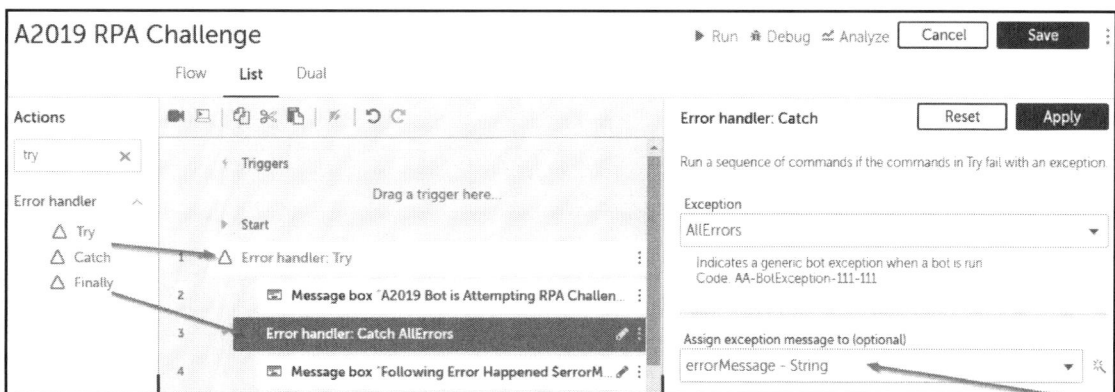

Now, we have completed the initial steps for the bot, so let's get to building the automation itself. We will start by reading the RPA challenge Excel file.

Reading the RPA challenge Excel data

In this section, we will read the input data from the RPA challenge Excel file and store it in a data table. We will use the data in the data table to iterate and input the data into the RPA challenge website. Let's start by opening the Excel file:

1. Search for `Excel Basic` in the **Action** panel to look up the Excel actions. Add the `Open Excel` action to open the input Excel file. Let's add the following properties:
   1. Set **Session name** as `S1`.
   2. Browse and select your RPA challenge Excel file.
   3. Select the option to open it in **Read-only mode**.
   4. Check the **Sheet contains a header** option:

2. Add the `Get multiple Cell` action to capture the Excel data into a `Data Table` variable. For this action, set **Session name** as `S1` and **Loop through** as **Specific rows** (inputting `1` for **From row** and `11` for **to row**) and create a `Table` variable called `excelTable` in the **Assign value to the variable (optional)** field, as shown:

3. Finally, close the Excel file by adding a `Close` action under the `Excel basic`
   action. Update the **Session name** property to `S1`:

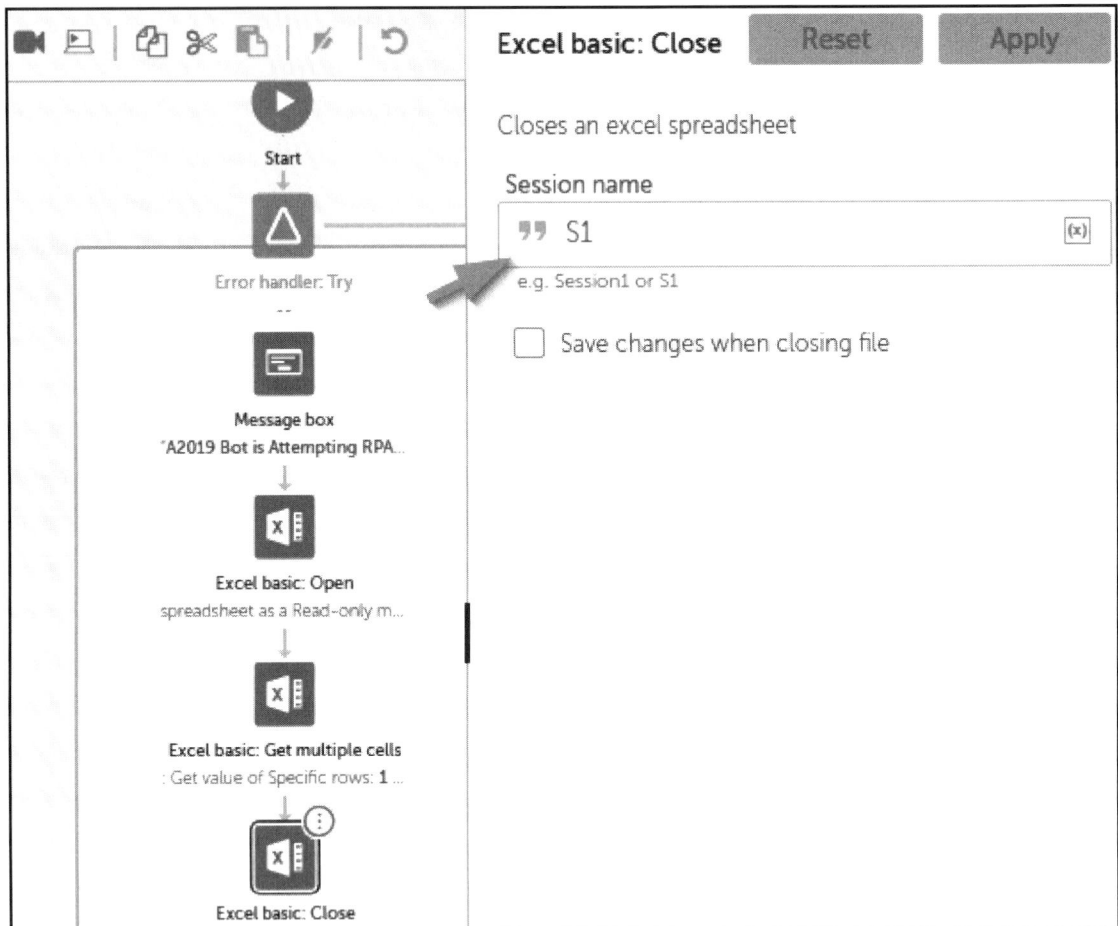

Now that we have the Excel data stored in the `excelTable` variable, let's open the browser
and perform the challenge.

Preparing the RPA challenge website for input

We will now iterate through the RPA challenge data in the `excelTable` variable and enter it into its respective input fields in the RPA challenge website. Before we do that, let's launch the RPA challenge website and click on the **START** button:

1. Add the `Launch Website` action and add `http://www.rpachallenge.com/` to the **URL** property. Also, choose **Internet Explorer** as your browser:

We will be using the Internet Explorer browser for web automation in this project. A2019 also works with Chrome. We will also be using Chrome for our other A2019 projects.

2. Open Internet Explorer and go to `rpachallenge.com`. We will start by clicking the **START** button on the website. Let's add the `Recorder Capture` action to do that. In the properties for `Capture`, choose **Window** for the **Object detail** property. Then, refresh the input box by clicking on the icon on the right. Choose the **Rpa Challenge - Internet Explorer** window from the dropdown. Finally, click on **Capture Object** and point to the **Start** button on the RPA challenge website in Internet Explorer:

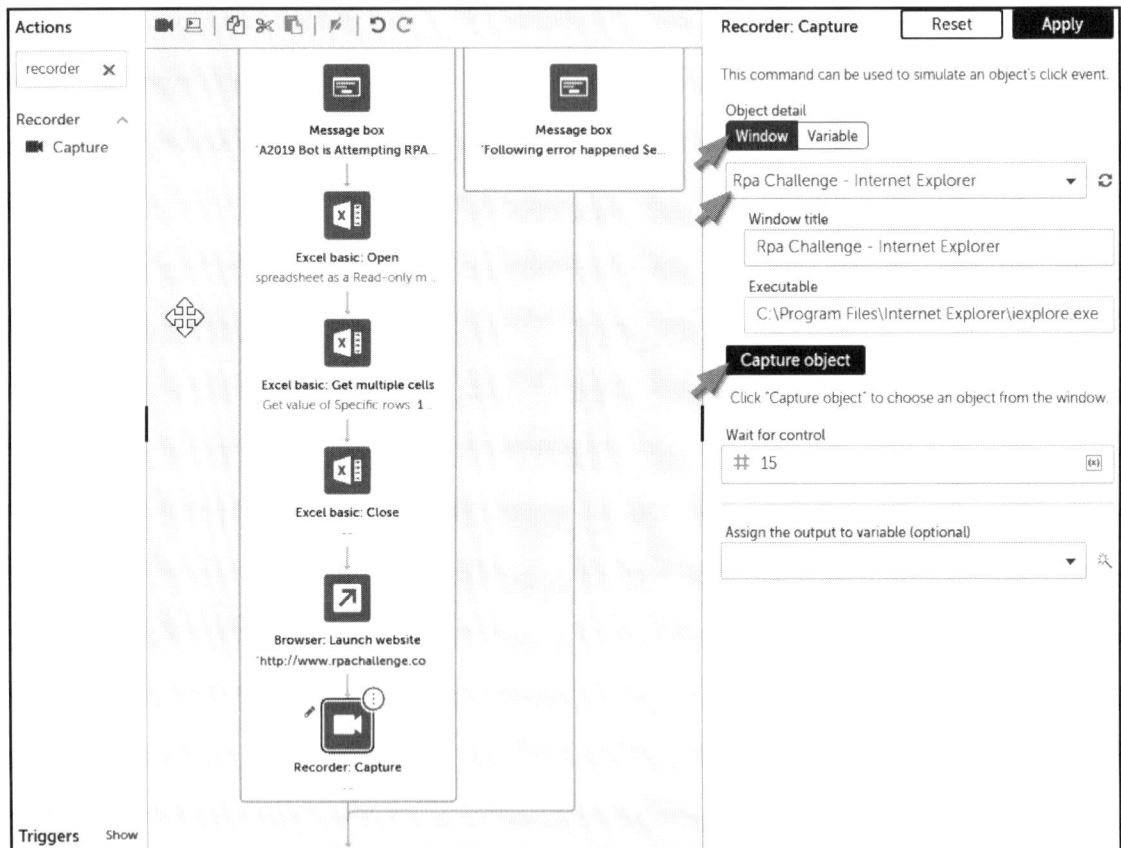

3. To perform the challenge, click on the **START** button. Let's update the selector properties for the captured object. Check the **HTML Tag** and **HTML InnerText** properties and choose **Click** for the **Action** property:

Recorder: Capture   Reset   Apply

Recapture object

Preview

DOWNLOAD EXCEL

START

Object properties (4 of 21)

Name	Value
Control Type	BUTTON
Technology Type	HTML
HTML Tag	🙶 BUTTON {x}
HTML InnerText	🙶 Start {x}

Action

Click ▼

A2019 automatically creates an **Object detail** variable called `Window-n` ("n" is an incremented number). We can use this same variable for all the browser operations.

Now that the website has been launched and is ready for input, let's iterate and read the data that needs to be inputted into the challenge forms.

Looping through each row and column

Let's now loop through the entire data table variable to input the Excel data to the RPA challenge website:

1. Add a `Loop` action. Choose **For each row in table** for the **Iterator** property and `excelTable –Table` for **Table variable**, and then create a new **Record** variable called `currentrow`:

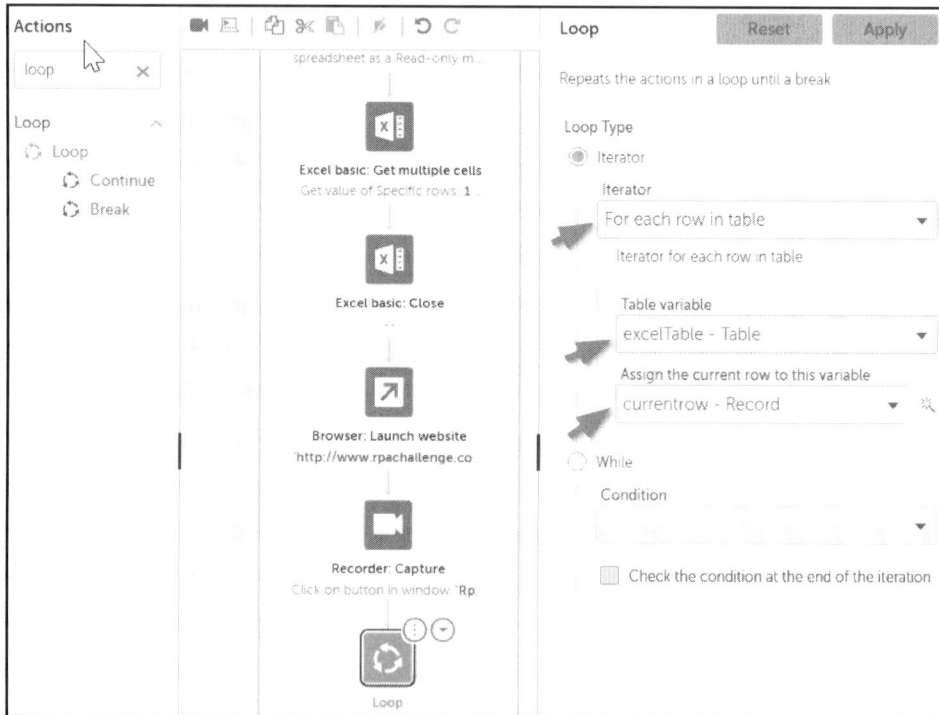

2. Let's now add the variables we will use in automation. Both of these variables will be used as a counter in our loops.
   1. Create a variable called `currentIteration` with a **Number** type. Check both **Use as input** and **Use as output** as the variable will be used for both input and output.
   2. Add another variable called `counterstring` with a **String** type, which will also be used for both input and output. `counterstring` will hold the same value as `currentIteration`, just with a different type:

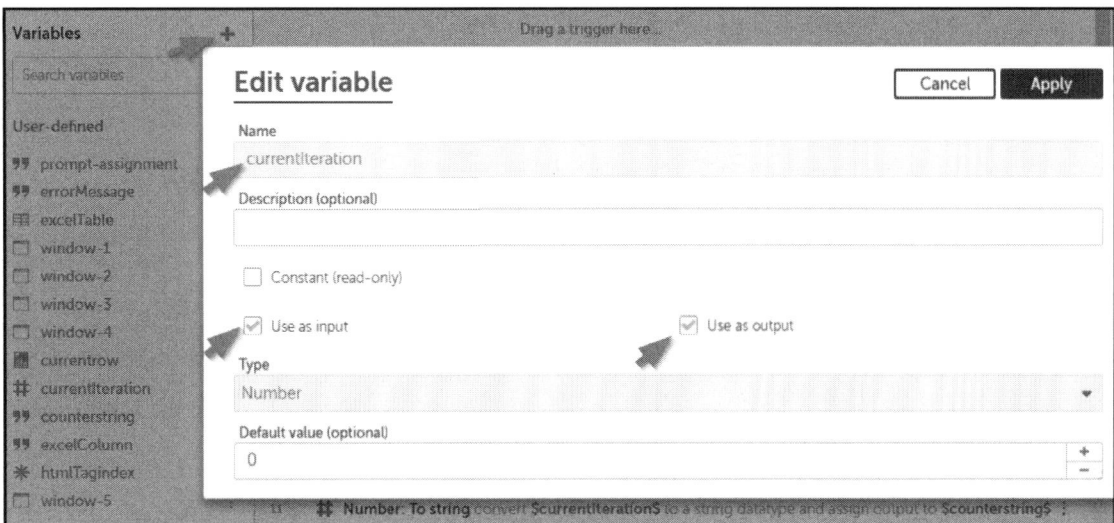

3. Within the loop, we will start by initializing the counter we just created. we'll shift to **List** view and code there for some time to see how it is progressing. Then add an `Assign` action to the `Number` action and assign a value of `1` for the `currentIteration` variable by updating the properties, as shown:

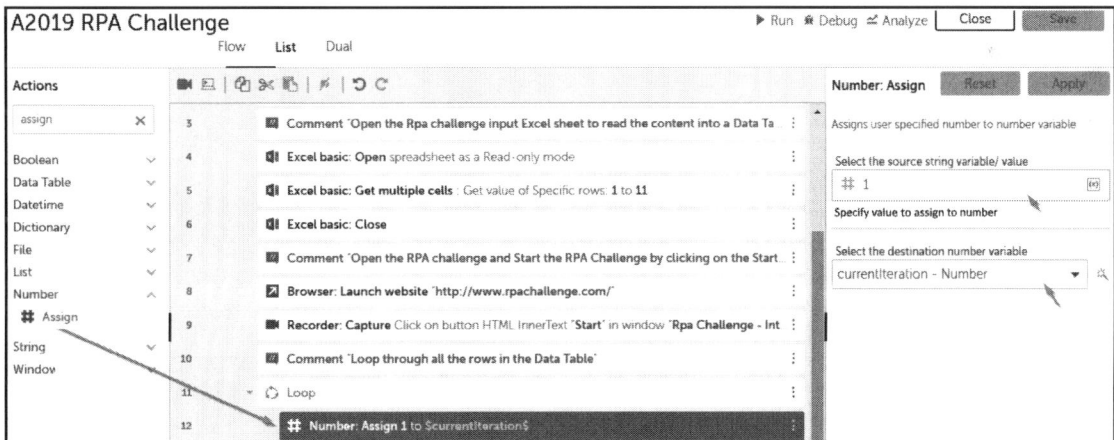

4. Next, let's loop through each column within each of the rows in the **Table** variable. To do that, add another **Loop** action and set **Iterator** as **For each value in record**, set **Record variable** as `currentrow` and create a new variable called `excelColumn` to store the value of the variable:

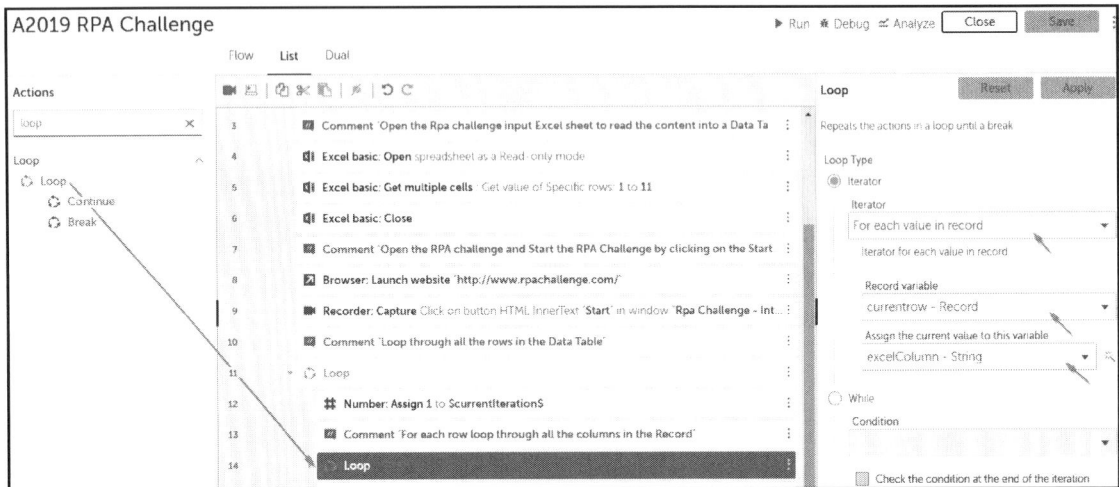

5. We also need a string version of the **Iteration** counter to use within our `If` conditions. So, let's add a **Number: To string** action to convert the `CurrentIteration` number to a `counterstring` string. Configure as shown:

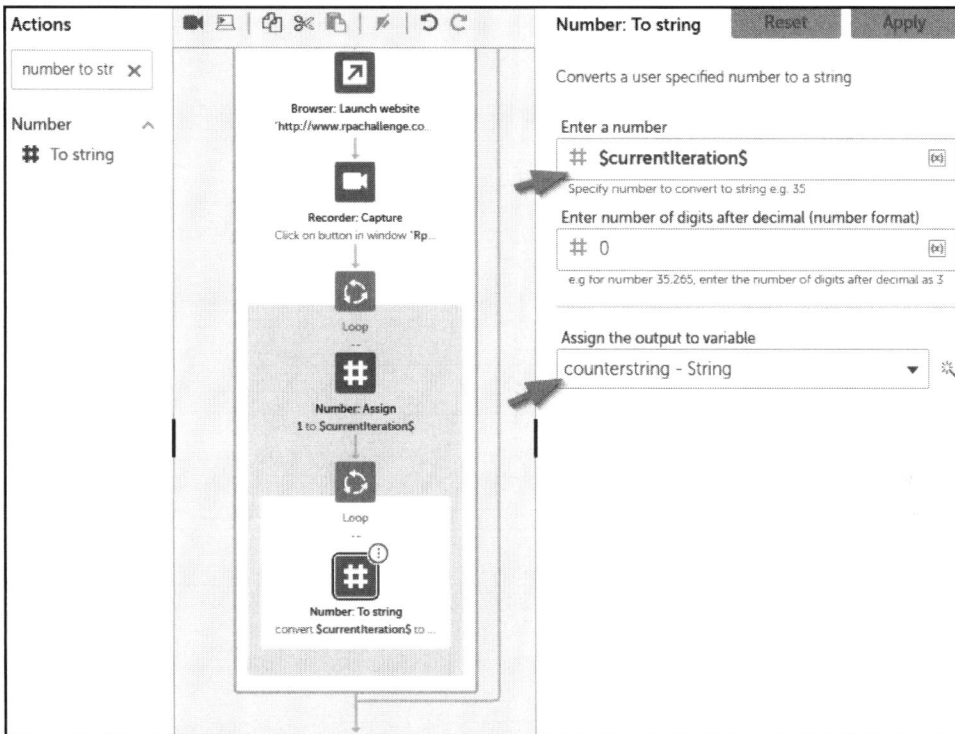

6. Finally, add a new variable called `CurrentColumnName` of the **Any** type to store the column names in the **Table** variable. We will use this `Column Names` variable later in the project to map column names to labels on the RPA challenge website.

Now that we have the loops set up, let's add the logic to read and map the columns.

Iterating through each column and reading headers

Let's now iterate through each of the columns in the row. We will associate each column with the corresponding header in Excel. These columns will then be mapped to the input fields on the RPA challenge website.

We will use the **If** condition and a series of **Else If** conditions to map the iteration counter to the headers, for example, `Counter#1` to **First Name**, and `Counter#2` to **Last Name**. Let's follow these steps to do that:

1. We will start by adding the **If** action. We will check whether it is the first column that has `counterstring` as 1. To indicate that, let's set the properties as follows:
   - **Condition**: `String condition`
   - **Source value**: `counterstring`
   - **Operator**: `=`
   - **Target value**: `1`

   This should look like the following screenshot:

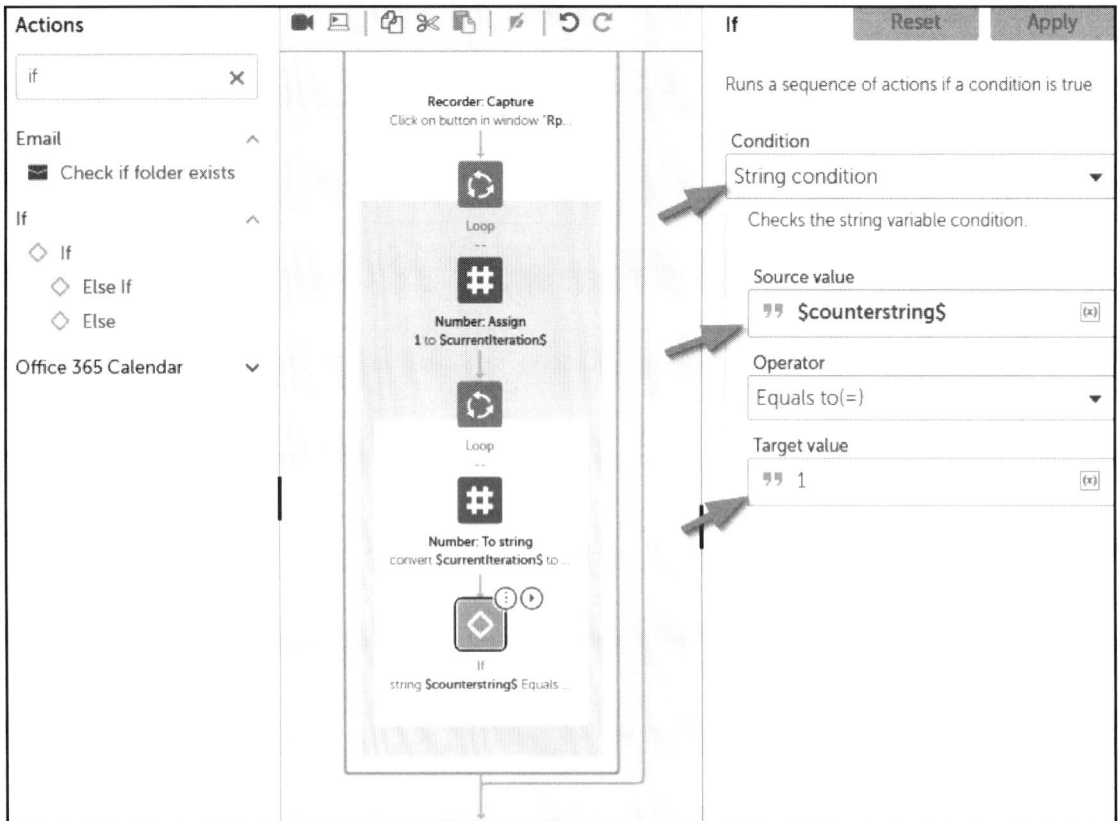

2. Next, let's indicate that the first column at position 1 is First Name. To do that, add a **String Assign** action under the **If** condition and set CurrentColumnName as First Name:

3. Now that we have indicated the first column in the row, let's do the same for the other columns. We will use the **Else If** condition to do that. For the second column, let's add an **Else If** action and set the properties as follows:
    - **Condition**: `String condition`
    - **Source value**: `counterstring`
    - **Operator**: `=`
    - **Target value**: `2`

4. Just below the **Else If** condition, let's add another `String Assign` operation and set `CurrentColumnName` as `Last Name`:

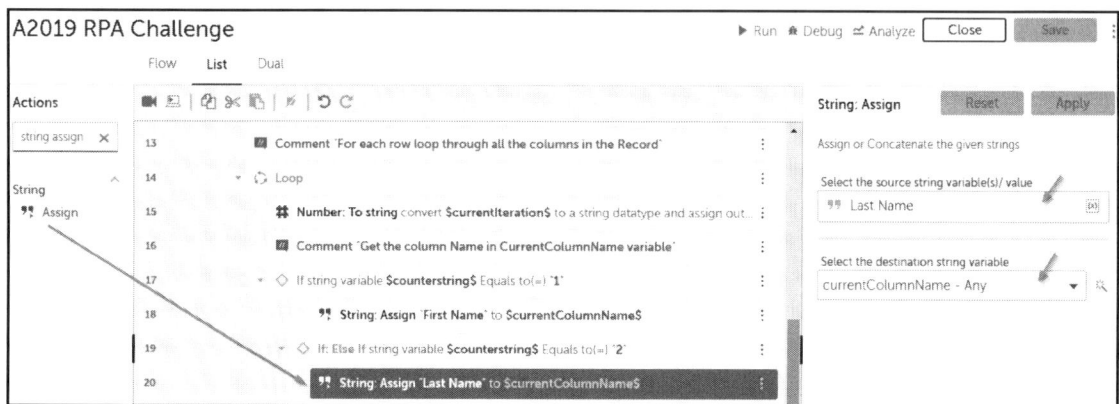

5. Do you get the drift? Go ahead and add **Else If** for the rest of the five columns. Add the `String Assign` operation for `Company Name`, `Role in Company`, `Address`, `Email`, and `Phone Number`, as shown:

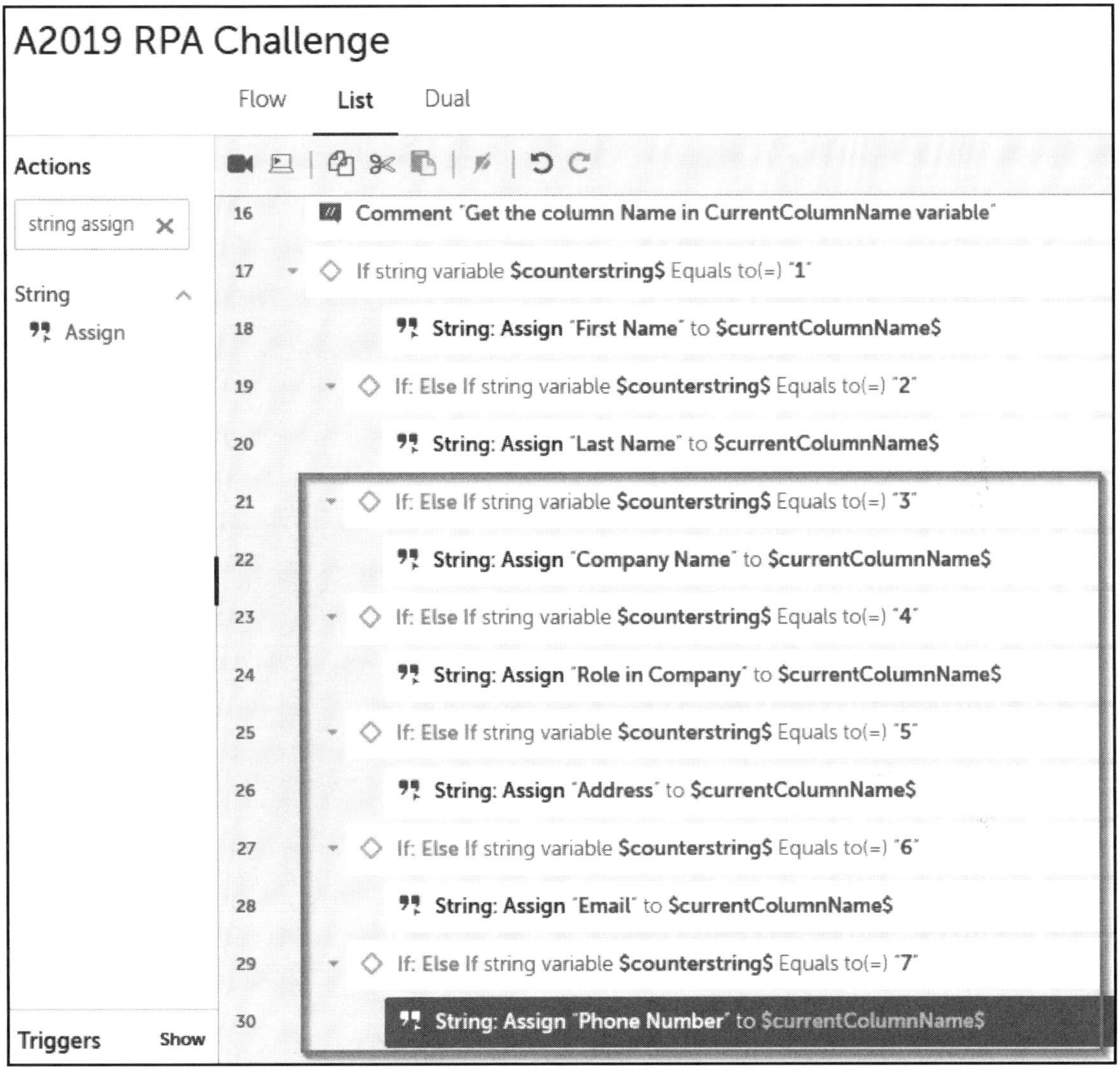
A2019 RPA Challenge
Flow
List
Dual
Actions
string assign
String
Assign
Triggers
Show
16 Comment "Get the column Name in CurrentColumnName variable"
17 If string variable $counterstring$ Equals to(=) "1"
18 String: Assign "First Name" to $currentColumnName$
19 If: Else If string variable $counterstring$ Equals to(=) "2"
20 String: Assign "Last Name" to $currentColumnName$
21 If: Else If string variable $counterstring$ Equals to(=) "3"
22 String: Assign "Company Name" to $currentColumnName$
23 If: Else If string variable $counterstring$ Equals to(=) "4"
24 String: Assign "Role in Company" to $currentColumnName$
25 If: Else If string variable $counterstring$ Equals to(=) "5"
26 String: Assign "Address" to $currentColumnName$
27 If: Else If string variable $counterstring$ Equals to(=) "6"
28 String: Assign "Email" to $currentColumnName$
29 If: Else If string variable $counterstring$ Equals to(=) "7"
30 String: Assign "Phone Number" to $currentColumnName$

We now have the current column name for the iteration stored in the `CurrentColumn Name` variable. We will use that name of the column to check for the corresponding RPA challenge field to enter the column data. For example, if the current column that is being iterated is `Last Name`, we will identify the `Last Name` field on the RPA challenge website.

Mapping and inputting the challenge data to the website

Let's now map the screen input fields to the column data that we need to populate with. We will use the HTML Tagindex property to locate the input fields and map them to their respective columns:

1. To capture the tag index for a field, let's add the **Capture** action and indicate the label name for the Last Name field. In the **Capture** properties, choose **Rpa Challenge - Internet Explorer** for **Window.** Click on **Capture** and point to the Last Name label (note that we are indicating the label, not the input box):

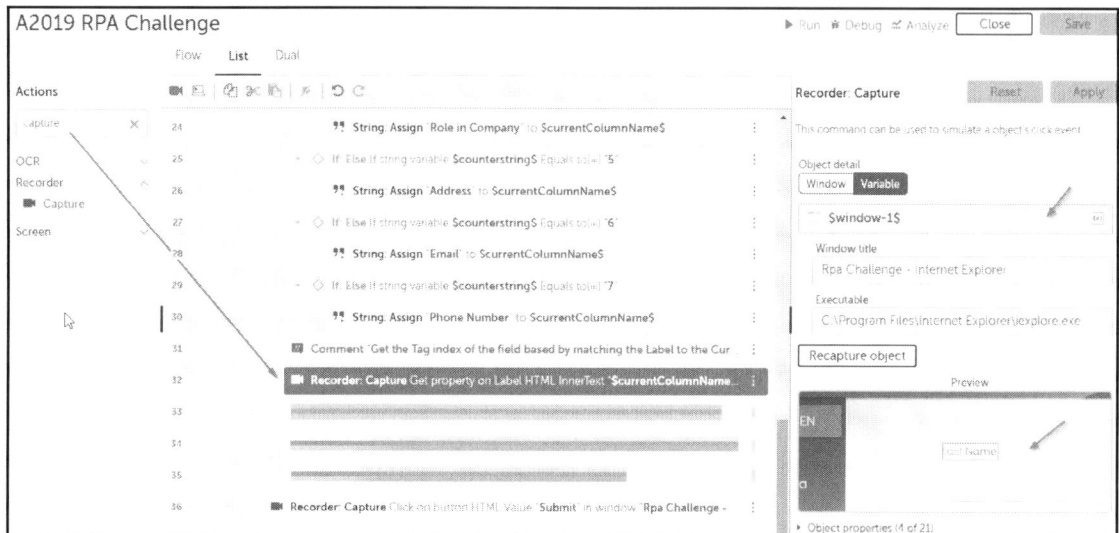

2. Within the **Recorder** properties, let's generalize the automation to work with the current column by setting HTML InnerText as currentColumnName. Let's also create a variable to store the HTML Tagindex value for the field. Let's call it htmlTagindex with an **Any** type. Finally, select the **Get Property** action for HTML TagIndex and assign it to the output htmlTagIndex variable. Ensure that only the four properties shown in the following screenshot are checked:

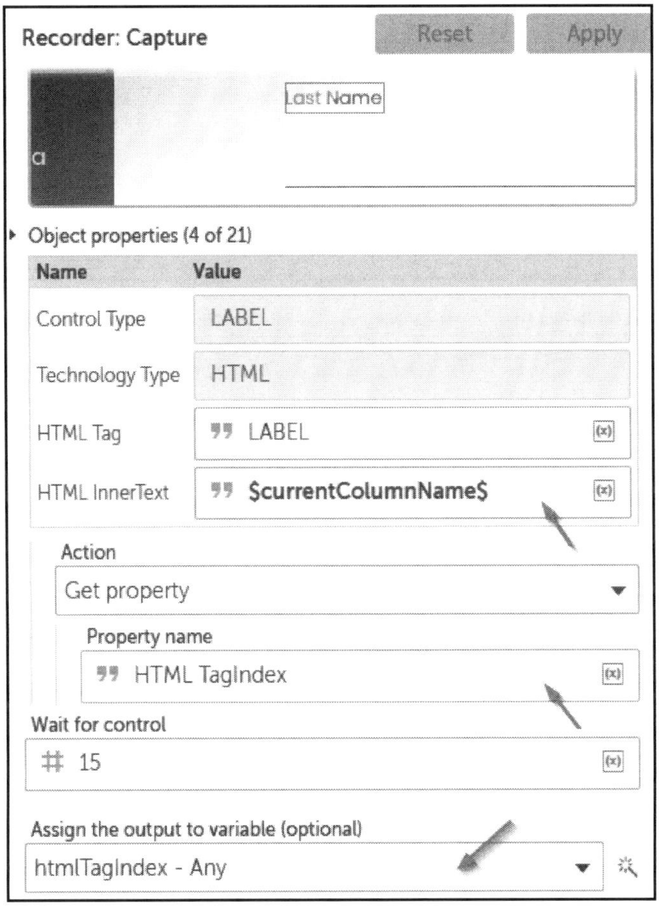

3. Now that we have `HTML Tagindex` for the field labels, it is time to map the Excel column headers to the input boxes. Let's add another `Capture` action for that. Go to the input box next to `Last Name`. Your **Recorder** properties will look like this:

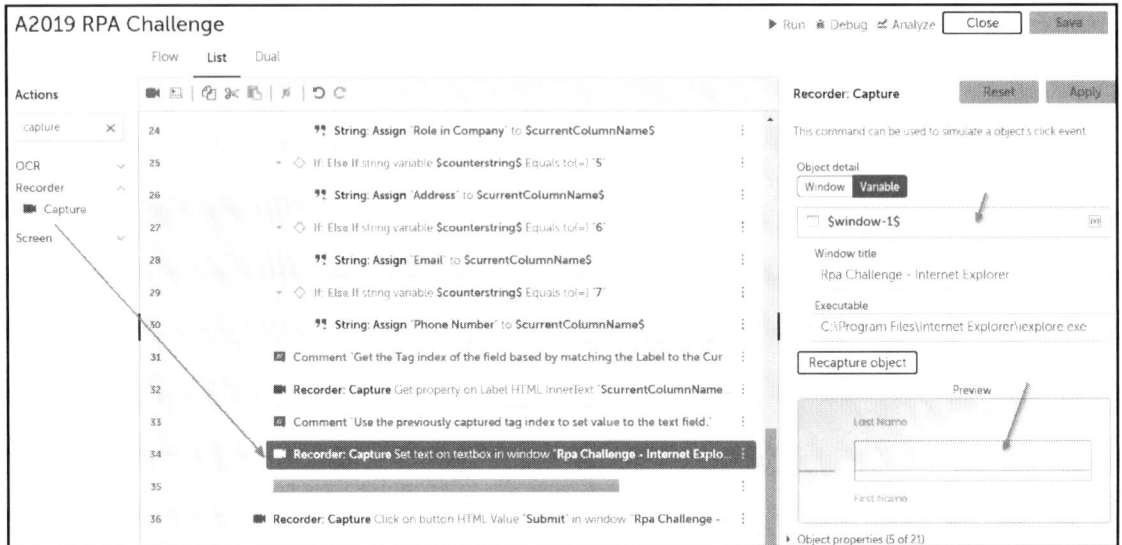

4. Next, we will use the `htmlTagIndex` variable we populated previously to identify the correct input box to populate data. For example, if the variable has a value of 5, we know that we have to input the data from the `Last Name` column. The data is present in the `excelColumn` variable. So, we will use the **Set text** action on the `excelColumn` variable. Ensure that your screen looks like the following screenshot and only has the properties shown here:

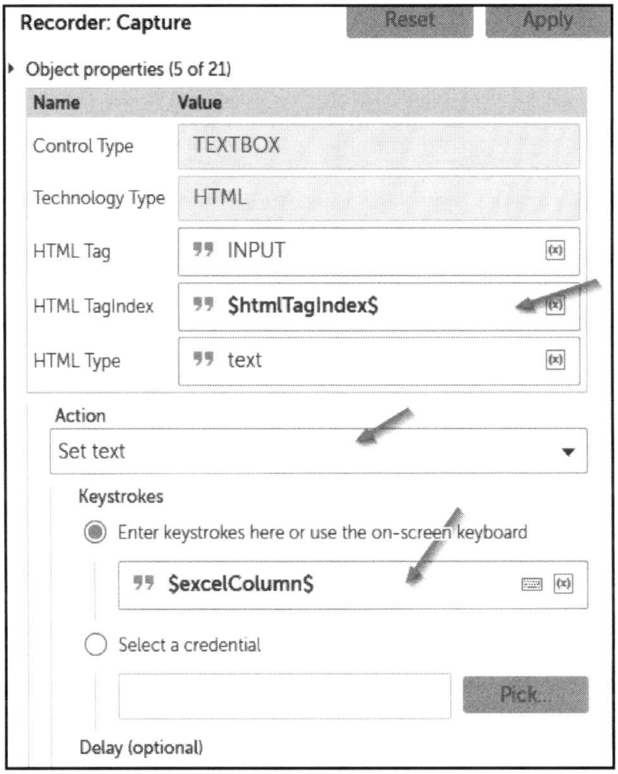

5. To keep the **Record** loop going, let's increment the counter of the currentIteration variable. Add **Assign** for **Number** and set the property value to $currentIteration$+1 for the currentIteration destination variable:

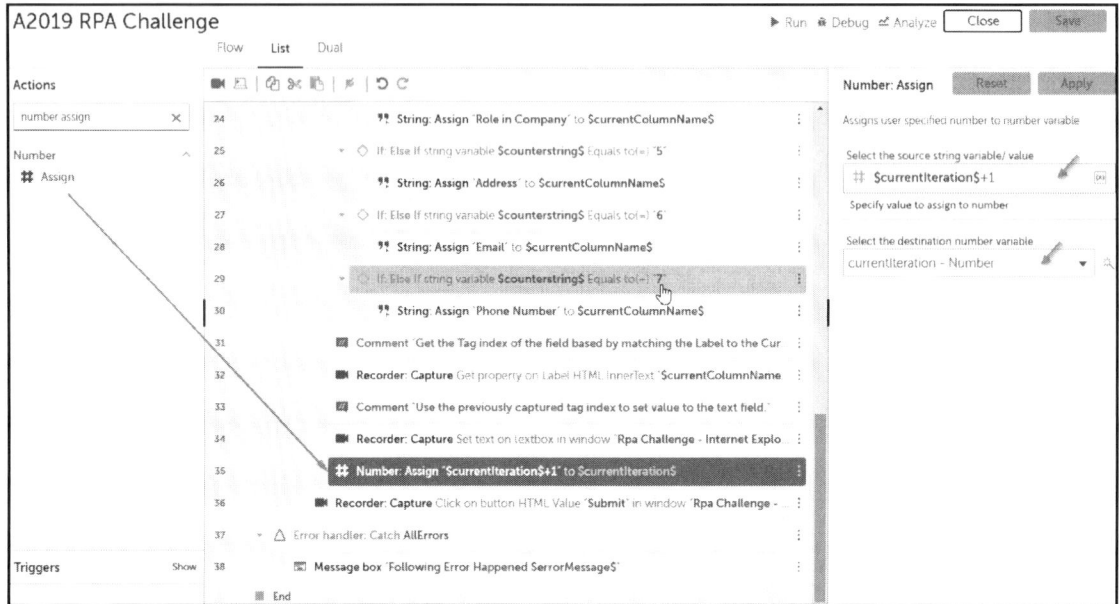

6. Finally, let's click the **SUBMIT** button after each form is filled. Add another **Capture** action outside the **Column** loop. In the **Capture** properties, choose the **Rpa Challenge - Internet Explorer** window and capture the **SUBMIT** button on the RPA challenge page:

7. Ensure that only the properties required for **Capture** are selected, as in the following screenshot. Select **Click** for **Action** to make sure that the **SUBMIT** button can be clicked:

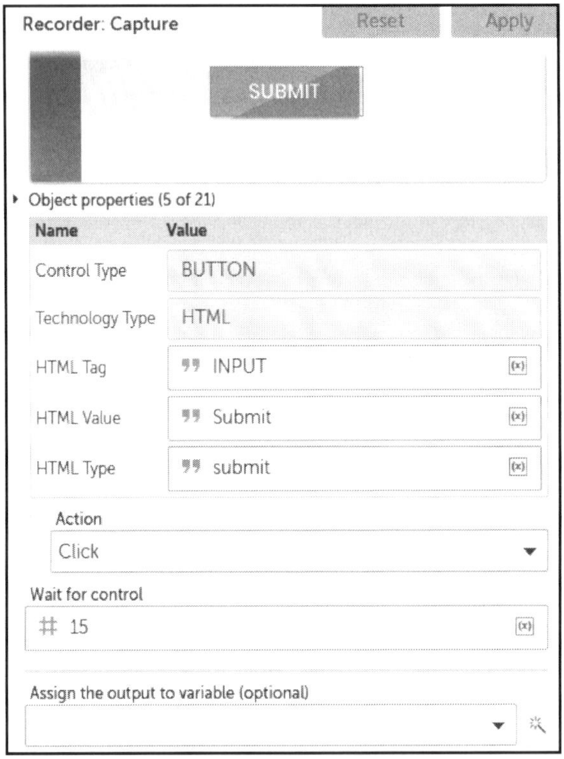

The completed **List** view for the bot should look like the following. We have divided the image in two for clarity. Part one:

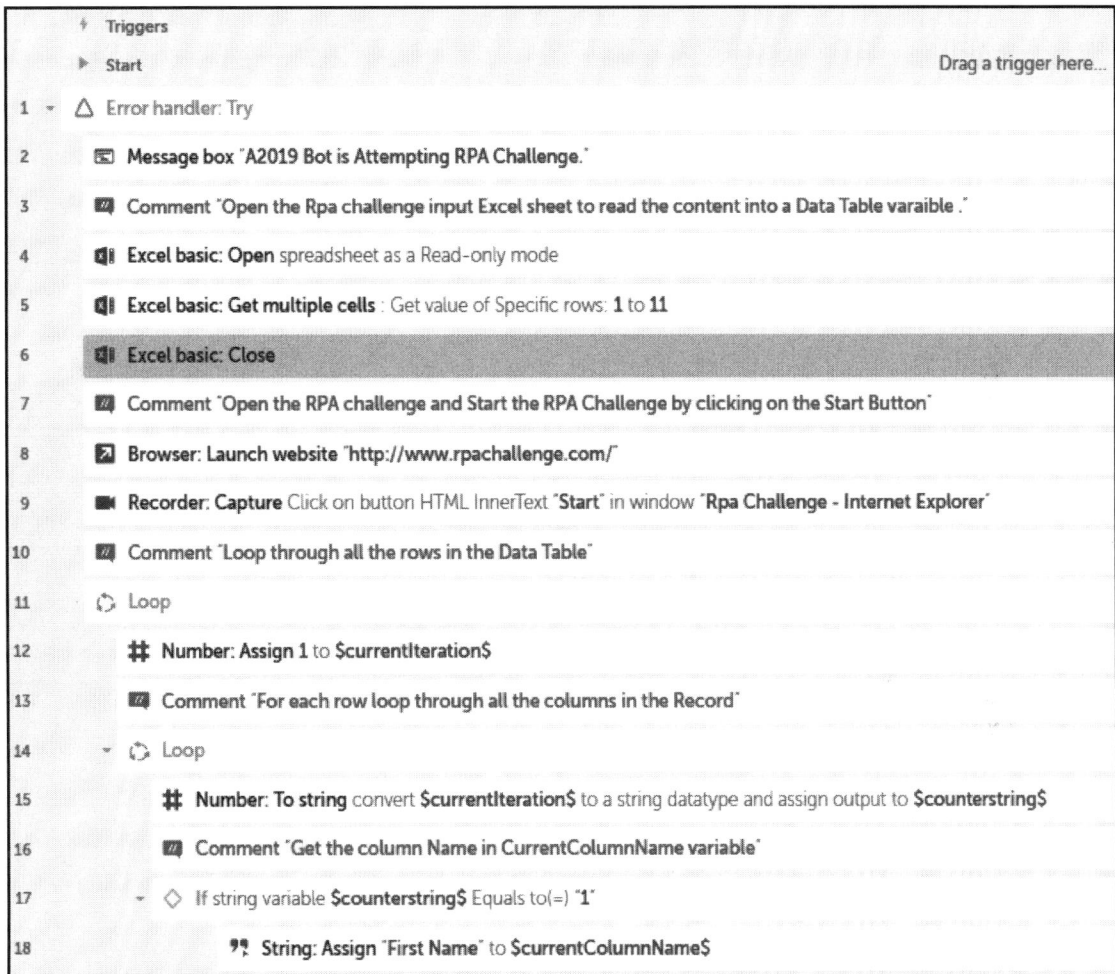

⚡ Triggers	
▶ Start	Drag a trigger here...
1 ▾ △ Error handler: Try	
2 ▣ **Message box** "A2019 Bot is Attempting RPA Challenge."	
3 ▨ **Comment** "Open the Rpa challenge input Excel sheet to read the content into a Data Table varaible ."	
4 ▨ **Excel basic: Open** spreadsheet as a Read-only mode	
5 ▨ **Excel basic: Get multiple cells** : Get value of Specific rows: **1** to **11**	
6 ▨ **Excel basic: Close**	
7 ▨ **Comment** "Open the RPA challenge and Start the RPA Challenge by clicking on the Start Button"	
8 ▨ **Browser: Launch** website "http://www.rpachallenge.com/"	
9 ■ **Recorder: Capture** Click on button HTML InnerText **"Start"** in window **"Rpa Challenge - Internet Explorer"**	
10 ▨ **Comment** "Loop through all the rows in the Data Table"	
11 ○ Loop	
12 # **Number: Assign 1** to $currentIteration$	
13 ▨ **Comment** "For each row loop through all the columns in the Record"	
14 ▾ ○ Loop	
15 # **Number: To string** convert $currentIteration$ to a string datatype and assign output to $counterstring$	
16 ▨ **Comment** "Get the column Name in CurrentColumnName variable"	
17 ▾ ◇ If string variable $counterstring$ Equals to(=) **"1"**	
18 ❝❞ **String: Assign** "First Name" to $currentColumnName$	

Part two:

19	▾ ◇	If: Else If string variable $counterstring$ Equals to(=) "2"
20		❞❞ String: Assign "Last Name" to $currentColumnName$
21	▾ ◇	If: Else If string variable $counterstring$ Equals to(=) "3"
22		❞❞ String: Assign "Company Name" to $currentColumnName$
23	▾ ◇	If: Else If string variable $counterstring$ Equals to(=) "4"
24		❞❞ String: Assign "Role in Company" to $currentColumnName$
25	▾ ◇	If: Else If string variable $counterstring$ Equals to(=) "5"
26		❞❞ String: Assign "Address" to $currentColumnName$
27	▾ ◇	If: Else If string variable $counterstring$ Equals to(=) "6"
28		❞❞ String: Assign "Email" to $currentColumnName$
29	▾ ◇	If: Else If string variable $counterstring$ Equals to(=) "7"
30		❞❞ String: Assign "Phone Number" to $currentColumnName$
31		🗐 Comment "Get the Tag index of the field based by matching the Label to the CurrentColumnName"
32		🎥 **Recorder: Capture** Get property on Label HTML InnerText "$currentColumnName$" in window "Rpa Challenge - Internet Explorer"
33		🗐 Comment "Use the previously captured tag index to set value to the text field."
34		🎥 **Recorder: Capture** Set text on textbox in window "Rpa Challenge - Internet Explorer"
35		# Number: Assign "$currentIteration$+1" to $currentIteration$
36		🎥 **Recorder: Capture** Click on button HTML Value "**Submit**" in window "Rpa Challenge - Internet Explorer"
37	▾ △	Error handler: Catch **AllErrors**
38		🖾 **Message box** "Following Error Happened $errorMessage$"
		▥ End

That completes the Automation Anywhere scripting for the RPA challenge. Let's now carry out a quick test.

Testing the Automation Anywhere challenge automation

Let's now run the RPA challenge automation in A2019:

1. Click on the **Run** option in the top menu.
2. The controller will first deploy the bot to your computer and do some preprocessing.
3. It will then pop up the initial message we added.
4. Once the message is closed, it will open `rpachallenge.com` on Internet Explorer.
5. The bot will then identify each of the input fields and fill in the Excel data.
6. It will fill in the data for each of the 10 input forms on the website.

If there are any issues, Automation Anywhere will generate any error messages, address them, and run again. The challenge should complete with a 100% success rate in 2 minutes or less.

That is it! We have completed the RPA challenge.

Summary

In this chapter, we solved the RPA challenge with both UiPath and Automation Anywhere.

We identified the dynamic input fields in 10 different forms and completed the challenge!

We also had a first look at Automation Anywhere A2019. The RPA challenge is a slightly tough first project but should give you a solid start with A2019.

We will take a look at sales order processing with Automation Anywhere in the next chapter.

7
Sales Order Processing

Let's start with our second Automation Anywhere project. We will automate the sales order processing.

Organizations generate a **sales order (SO)** on receiving a **purchase order (PO)**, which is an intent to buy one or more items. The PO specifies the product or service that a customer would like to purchase. The SO is used for inventory and order management.

For this automation project, we will take order data from an Excel spreadsheet and input it into the Orders app in Apptivo – cloud-based business management software. This will be a step up from the first A2019 project we did in `Chapter 6`, *Completing an RPA Challenge*.

Here is what we will cover as part of this project:

- Automation Anywhere A2019 Excel automation
- Automation Anywhere web automation
- Using the Automation Anywhere A2019 recorder
- Splitting automation into Parent and Child bots
- Exception handling in Automation Anywhere

Technical requirements

Let's look at the hardware and software we need for this project:

- Automation Anywhere A2019 Community Edition. Sign up at `https://www.automationanywhere.com/products/community-edition`.
- A PC with the Automation Anywhere Community Edition A2019 bot agent installed.
- Google Chrome with the Automation Anywhere extension installed .
- Internet Explorer 11.
- Microsoft Excel 2007 or later.

- Check out the following video to see the Code in Action: `https://bit.ly/2zZsKVu`.
- The Apptivo Saas application with the Orders application. You can sign up for free at `https://www.apptivo.com`.
- Make sure customers (Amazon, Uber, and Salesforce) and items (laptop, router, and phones) are added in the Apptivo Order application (you will have done this step in `Chapter 3`, *CRM Automation*, and `Chapter 5`, *Purchase Order Processing with UiPath ReFramework*).

Project overview

As we said, we will create SOs using data from an Excel spreadsheet. Usually, this data comes from POs. For this project, we are assuming that we have an Excel sheet generated from POs. This can be done by the Automation Anywhere IQ bot, which can read POs in PDF format to generate a spreadsheet with data. This IQ bot part is not covered in this initial Automation Anywhere project. We cover the IQ bot in `Chapter 10`, *Using AI and RPA for Invoice Processing*.

In this project, we will have an A2019 bot read the SO details from an Excel sheet, which we will place in the `Input` folder. It will process each row of SO data and input it into the Apptivo Order application. For each order entered into the application, the bot will take the generated SO number and input it into the Excel spreadsheet. Once all the SOs from the Excel sheet have been processed, the bot will move the spreadsheet to a `Processed` folder. Here is a high-level workflow for the project:

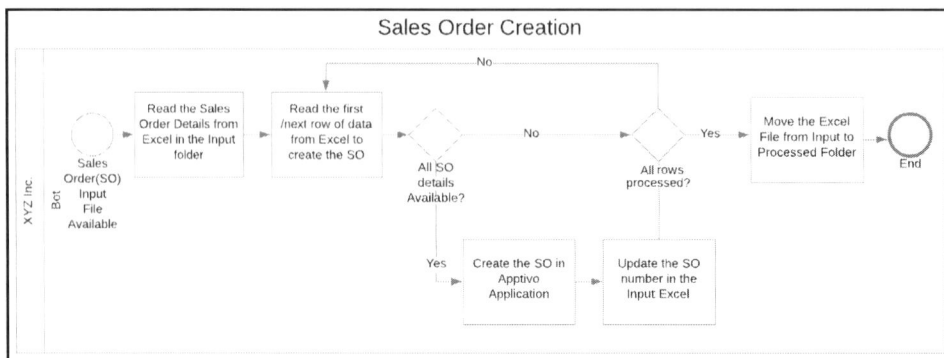

Now that we have a high-level understanding of the project, let's dive into the details and create the automation.

Project details

In Automation Anywhere, we create bots to carry out each task. For this project, we will be creating a Parent bot that will carry out all of the steps. It will invoke a Child bot to create SOs.

As the name indicates, a Parent bot is like the main workflow in UiPath. We will have one main workflow that will then call the other child workflows.

Here is a SO creation sequence diagram with the Parent and Child sequences:

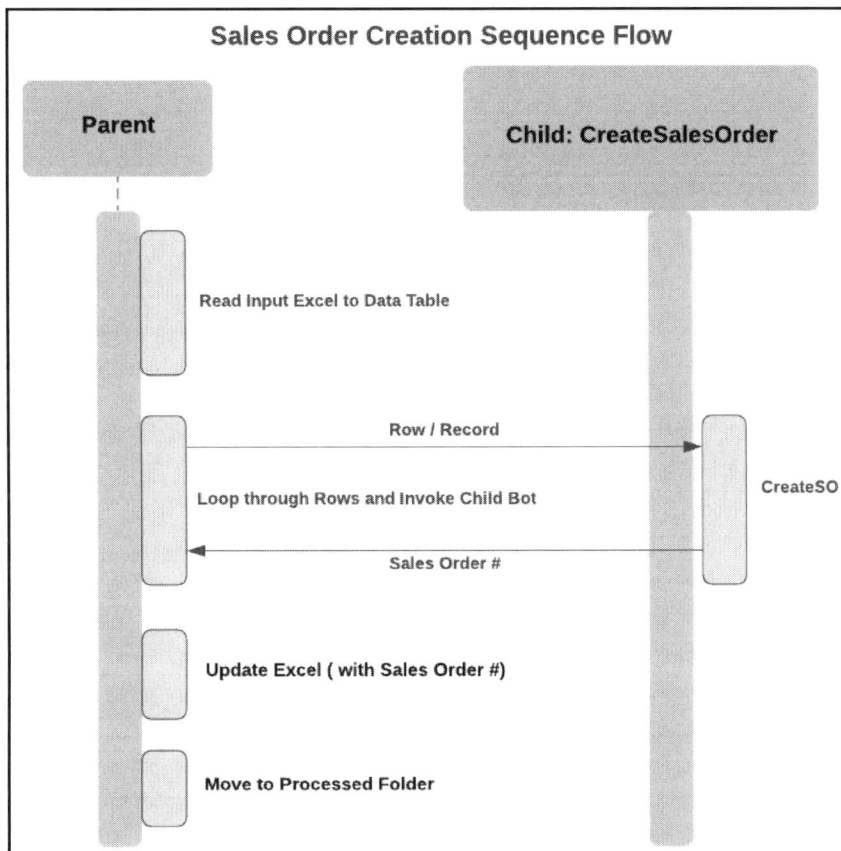

As you can see in the diagram, we start by opening and reading the Excel file in the Parent bot. The data is read and stored in a data table variable. We then loop through each record in the data table and create the SOs by invoking the Child `CreateSalesOrder` bot. The Child bot returns the generated SO number to the Parent bot.

The Parent bot takes this SO number and updates the corresponding row for the SO in the Excel sheet. Once all the data in the Excel sheet has been processed successfully, the Excel file is moved to the `Processed` folder.

We will do some groundwork for the project before building these components for the automation.

Project groundwork

Let's ensure we have some of the supporting material for the project before we build the automation itself. Please follow the steps given here:

1. Let's create an Excel spreadsheet with a few sample SOs to process. The Excel SO file will have **PO #**, **Customer**, **Address**, **City**, **State**, **Zip**, **ItemName**, **Quantity**, and **SO** columns, as shown here:

	A	B	C	D	E	F	G	H	I
1	PO #	Customer	Address	City	State	Zip	ItemName	Quantity	SO
2	202001	Salesforce	1009 Think Pl	Morrisville	North Carolina	27560	Laptop	6	
3	45678901	Uber	2300 E President George Bush Hwy	Richardson	Texas	75082	Router	2	
4	896734	Amazon	4851 Regent Blvd	Irving	Texas	75063	Phones	7	

2. As we did for some of the previous UiPath projects, let's open the Apptivo application at `Apptivo.com`. Please ensure that you log in to the application. If you have not signed up yet, please do sign up and log in.
3. Go to the **Supply chain** option on the menu and then choose **Orders**. We are assuming that you are logged in and on the **Orders** home page as we create this bot.
4. Finally, let's open Automation Anywhere A2019 to create the bots. As we did in `Chapter 6`, *Completing an RPA Challenge*, log in to the A2019 Community Edition in your browser at `https://community.cloud.automationanywhere.digital/#/login`.

Now that we have completed the groundwork, it is time to create the Parent bot.

Creating the Parent bot

Let's first create the main task bot, which we are calling the Parent bot:

1. To do that, we'll go to **My bots** on the left panel and then click on **Create a bot** as shown here:

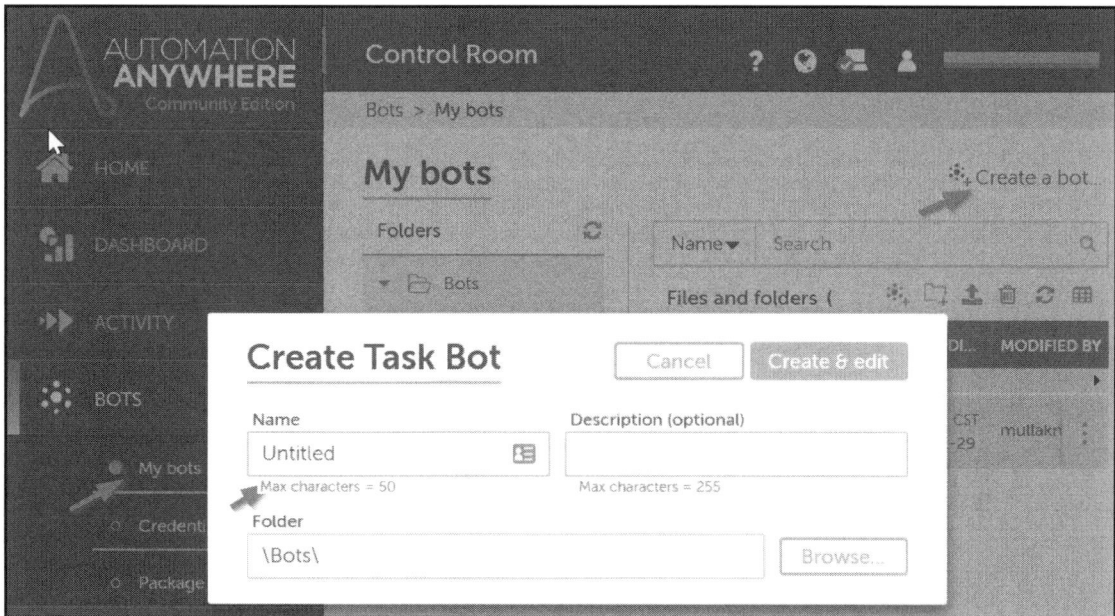

2. In the popup, provide a name for the bot and click on **Create & edit**. This creates the bot and opens the canvas for us to configure the bot's workflow. We will use the **List** view for this project.

> As you use the A2019 **List** view, you may notice that it sometimes becomes difficult to insert actions where we exactly need them. You can switch to the **Flow** view and insert an action where you want it to be and then return to the **List** view.

Let's switch to the **List** view on the Canvas and start with exception handling.

Exception handling

Let's add an error handler try-catch to exit gracefully if there are errors.

1. To do that, look up **Error handler** and then drag and drop the **Try** action. We will add most of the automation steps in this **Try** block in the next few sections.
2. Before we do that, add the **Catch** action below **Try**.
3. In the **Catch** properties, choose an **Exception** type of **AllErrors**.
4. Create a **String** variable called `errorMessage` to store the error message.

5. Click on the wizard icon on the right of the input box to create new variables, as shown here:

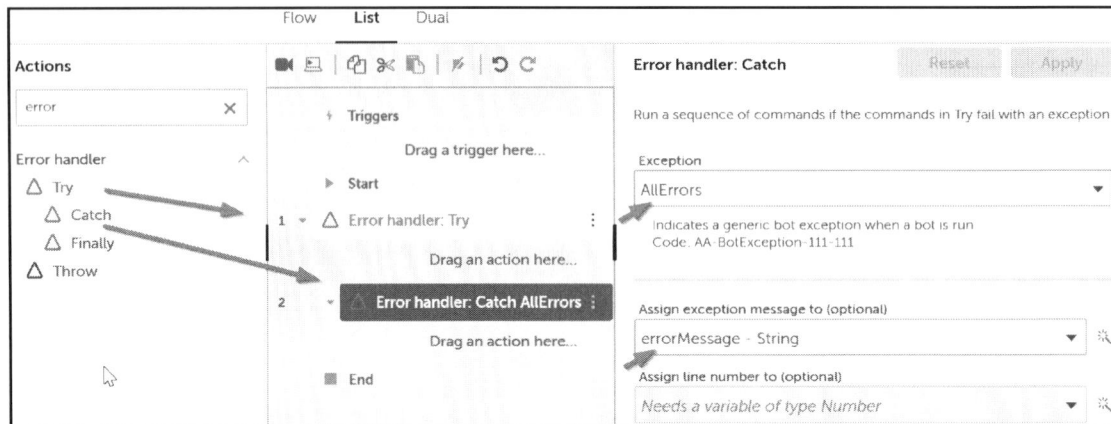

6. Click on **Apply** to apply the properties.
7. Then, within the **Catch**, add a message box with the message `Following error happened $errorMessage$`.
8. Finally, click **Save** at the top to save the bot so far, before we open the SO Excel file.

Opening and reading Excel data

We will start by reading the SO data from Excel and storing it in a data table variable.

Just as we used sequences in UiPath to logically separate a sequence of activities, we will use **Step** activities in Automation Anywhere. We'll add our first **Step** activity for these Excel activities.

Within this **Step**, we will add two commands to open and read Excel data:

1. Add the **Excel basic: Open** action to open the input Excel file. Let's add the following properties:
   - A **Session name** of S1.
   - Choose the **Desktop file** option and then **Browse...** and select your SO Excel file.
   - Open in **Read-write mode**.
   - Check the sheet contains a header option:

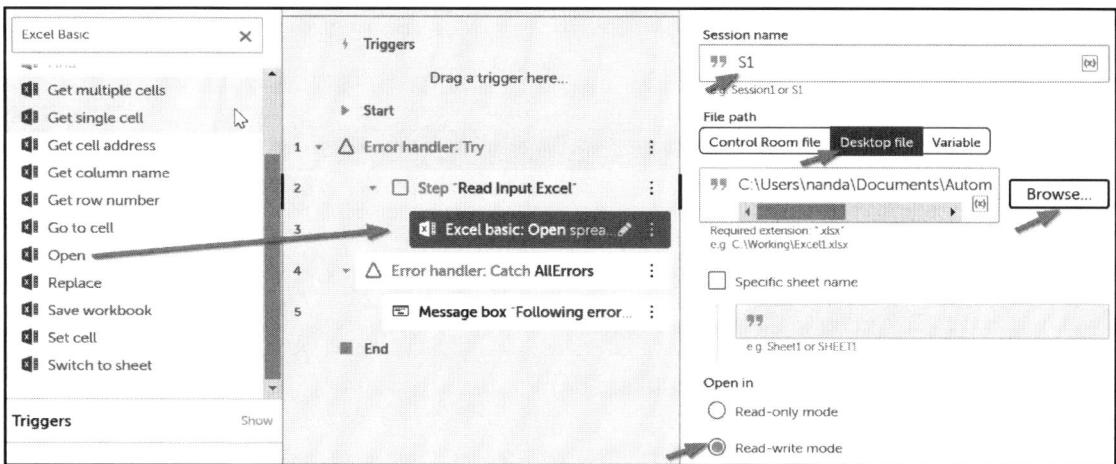

2. Add the **Excel basic: Get multiple cells** action to read and store the Excel records in a data table variable.

3. Add the properties for this action as **Session name**: S1 and **Loop through**: All rows, and create a variable of type Table called excelTable and use it in **Assign value to the variable** as shown here:

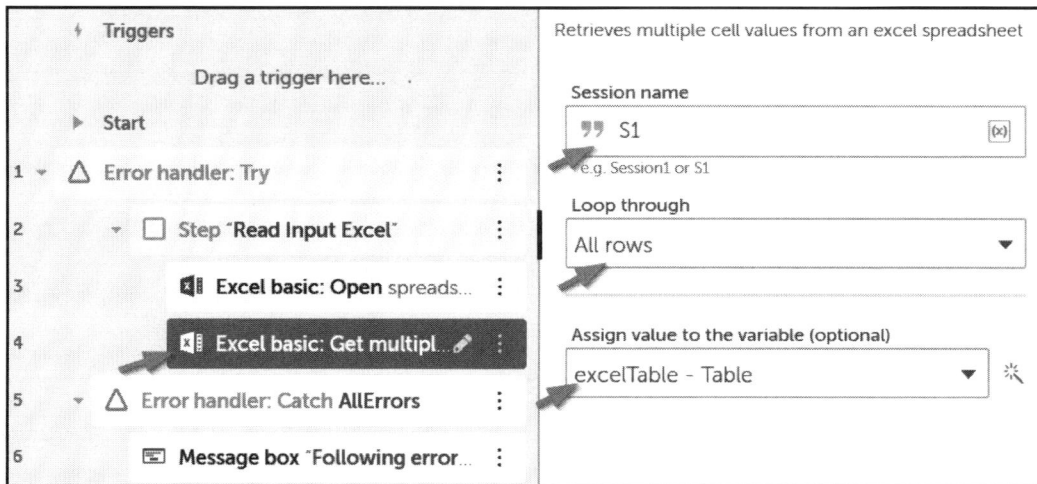

4. Now that we have read the data into the data table, the next step is to loop through each of the records and invoke the Child bot to create SOs. Before we add that loop, let's create the Child bot. Close the Parent bot and create a new bot (click **Create a bot**) from the **My bots** page, as we did with the Parent bot.

Let's now configure the Child bot.

Creating the Child bot for SO processing

We will be using this SO bot to create SOs within Apptivo. Since this mostly involves clicking buttons and inputting data, we will be using many capture actions to click or input data. Let's open Apptivo in the Google Chrome browser, if you have not already done so. Since this mostly involves clicking buttons and inputting data, we will be using the recorder to capture actions.

Using the recorder to capture SO creation

Within the newly created bot, we will add a **Step** action to logically separate out the recorder steps to create SO. Within this **Step** action, we will first click on the **Create** button and then choose the **Order** option on Apptivo. To do that, let's follow these steps:

1. Add a **Record** variable, which we will use to pass data from the Parent bot. Go to **Variables** on the left pane (just below **Actions** and **Triggers**) and click on the plus sign.
2. We will name the variable `RowRecord` of type **Record** and check **Use as input,** as shown here:

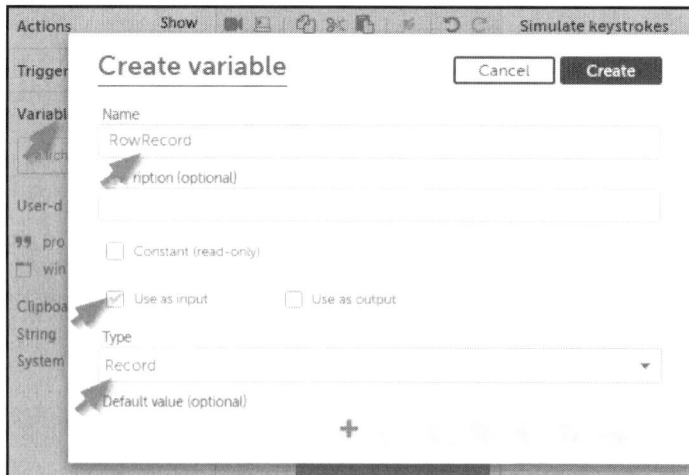

3. Add a **Recorder Capture** action to click on the **Create** button on the Apptivo **Orders** screen.

4. In the properties for **Capture**, choose **Window** for **Object detail**, then refresh the input box by clicking the icon on the right.

5. Choose the **Orders | Apptivo - Google Chrome** window from the dropdown. Click on **Capture object**, as shown here, and point to the **Create** button on Apptivo in Chrome:

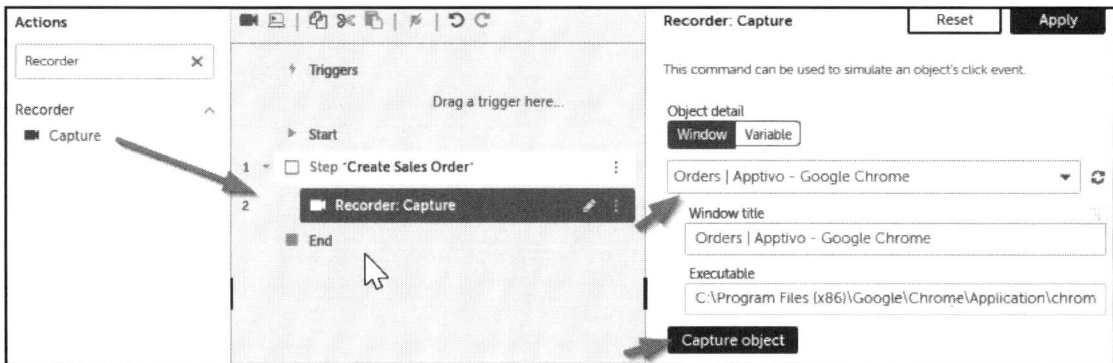

6. Staying with the properties for the preceding **Capture** action, let's ensure that the **Object properties** are as shown in the following screenshot. Choose **Click** for **Action** and then change **Wait for control** to 1,000 milliseconds, as shown here:

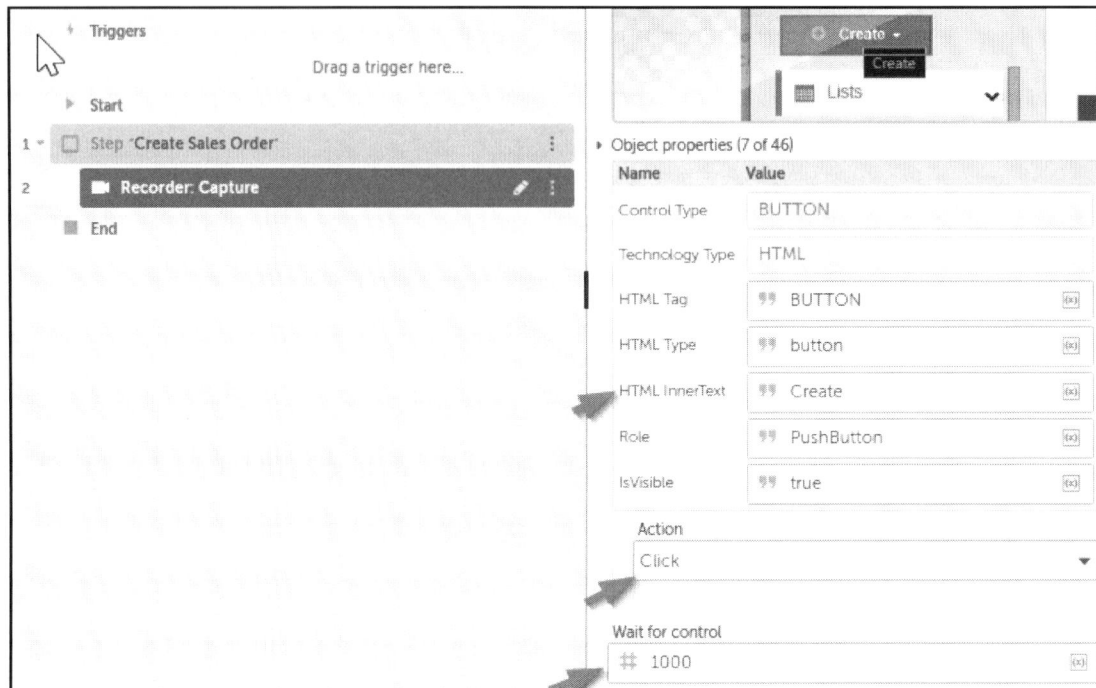

7. Finally, click on **Apply** to apply these property values:

> The object properties have mandatory (which can't be edited) and optional properties (which we can choose). We need to choose these optional properties with care. Please choose the object properties you see in the screenshots. In this case, **HTML Tag**, **HTML Type**, **HTML InnerText**, **Role**, and **Visible**. We can use wildcards and regular expressions as well.

8. Next, let's click on the **Order** option on Apptivo. To do that, we will add another **Recorder Capture** action. Choose the same **Orders | Apptivo - Google Chrome** window in the properties.

9. Click on **Capture Object** and point to the **Order** option on Apptivo. Ensure that the **Object properties** are as shown in the following screenshot.

10. Choose **Click** for **Action** and then change **Wait for control** to 1,000 milliseconds, as shown here:

11. Finally, click on **Apply** to apply these property values. Also, do not forget to save the bot so far.

These sequences of clicks will have opened the **Create Order** form in the right pane. Let's now enter the customer details in this form.

Filling in customer details for an SO

We will remain in the same **Step** action as the preceding subsection. Let's now fill in the customer information:

1. Add a new **Recorder Capture** action.
2. After choosing the same **Orders | Apptivo - Google Chrome** window, click on **Capture Object** and point to the **Customer** input box on Apptivo. Ensure that the object properties (especially **HTML Tag** and **HTML TagIndex** are provided) and **Action** are as shown here:

3. Just below the **Recorder Capture**, let's add a **Delay** Action with **Delay** as 500 milliseconds. This to enable the select box to show up before we enter the value.

> We are assuming that the customer names and item names exist in Apptivo. The sample data in our SO Excel has the same customer and item names as the ones we added in Chapter 5, *Purchase Order Processing with UiPath ReFramework*. If you do not have these customers or items, please add them to Apptivo before proceeding.

4. Let's now enter the value for the customer name. For that, we will add the **Simulate Keystrokes** Action. In the properties, choose the same **Orders | Apptivo - Google Chrome** window. For **Keystrokes**, click on **Insert a variable** in the input box and then choose the variable **RowRecord** with **By index** set to **1**, as shown here:

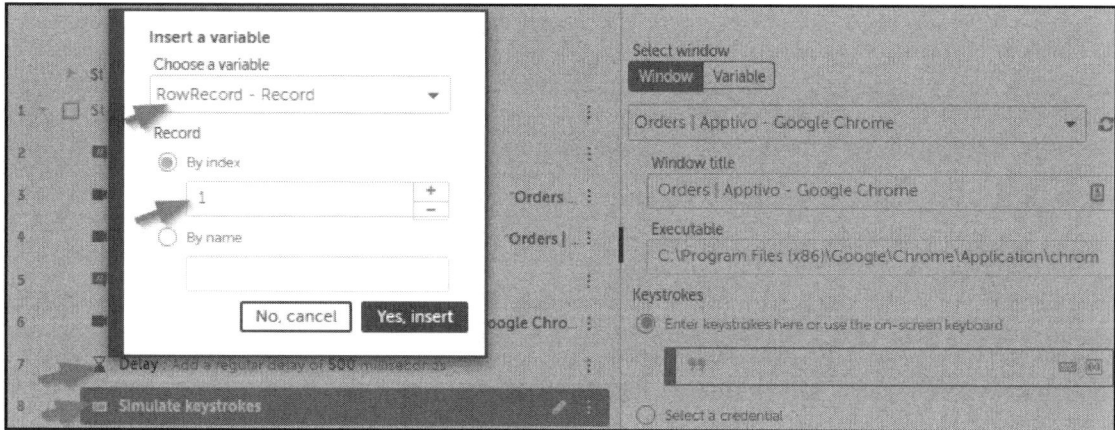

This is because the customer name is recorded index number 1 in the record data that was read from the Excel sheet (the count starts at 0, so PO# is at position 0 and the customer name is at position 1).

5. Add another **Delay** Action with **Delay** as 500 milliseconds. This is to enable the value to be entered fully before we press the **Enter** key.

> You can copy similar actions to speed up the bot configuration process. For example, to add a **Delay**, you can copy the previous **Delay** action and paste it. You can use either *Ctrl + C* or you can click on the options for the action (three dots) and click copy. You can then paste the action where you would like the new action to be.

6. To press *Enter*, add another **Simulate Keystrokes** action. Choose the same **Orders | Apptivo - Google Chrome** window. For **Keystrokes**, click on the keyboard icon in the input box and choose **Enter,** as shown here:

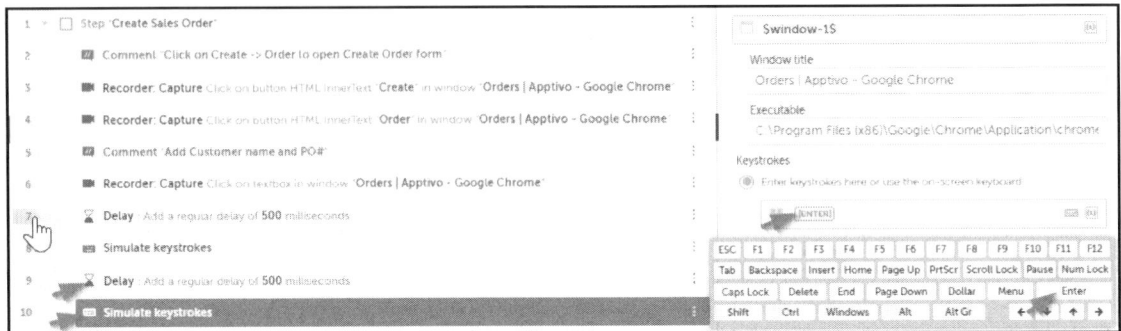

7. Let's now add the PO number within the customer information. Add a new **Recorder Capture** action for the same **Orders | Apptivo - Google Chrome** window.

8. Click on **Capture Object** and point to the **PO**# input box on Apptivo. Make sure that the **Object properties** are as shown in the following screenshot. Choose **Set text** for **Action** and set **Keystrokes** to **RowRecord[0]** (to extract PO#).

9. Ensure you also add a **Delay** of 500 milliseconds in the properties (below **Keystrokes** – not shown):

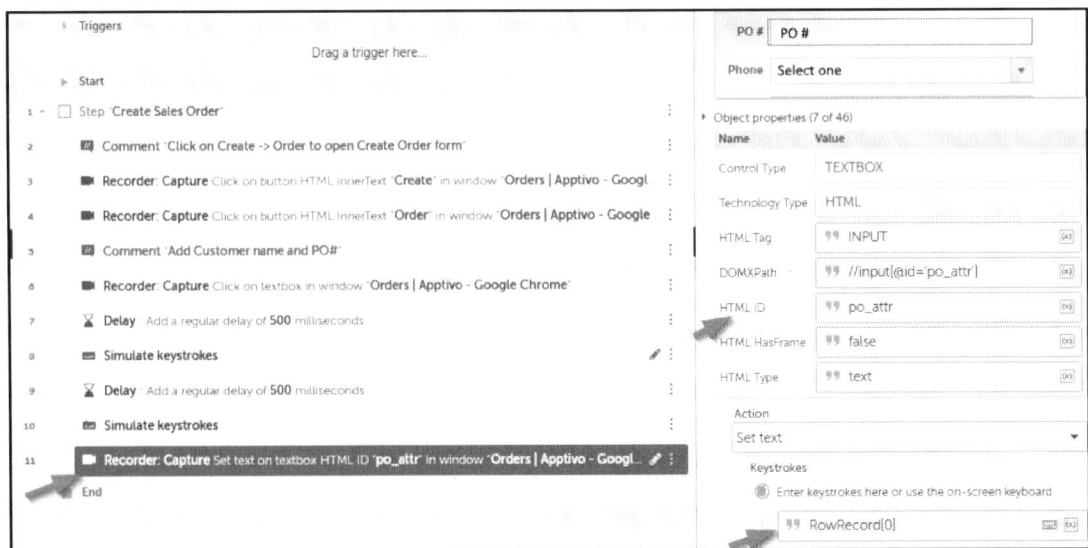

Next, you can optionally fill in the customer address information as well. You can add the billing address, city, state, and zip data similar to the preceding **PO#** by adding four capture actions and setting the respective keystrokes with the correct `RowRecord` index.

We will now proceed to add the item details on the order form.

Filling in item details for an SO

The items are goods that the customer would like to purchase. In our Excel sheet, we added items such as laptop, router, and phones. The item name in Apptivo is a select box just like the **Customer** box we had previously, so we will use the same procedure to enter the item name. We will use a **Recorder** action followed by **Delay**, then **Simulate Keystrokes** to enter the value, another **Delay**, and finally, **Simulate Keystrokes** to press **Enter**:

1. Add a new **Recorder Capture** action to add the Item name.
2. Choose the same **Orders | Apptivo - Google Chrome** window, click on **Capture Object**, and point to the **Item Name** input box in **Products/Items** on Apptivo. Ensure that the **Object properties** and **Action** are as shown here:

3. Next, add a **Delay** of 500 milliseconds, followed by a **Simulate Keystrokes** action, as shown in the preceding screenshot.
4. In the properties, add the variable `RowRecord[6]` in **Enter Keystrokes.** This is to enter the item name, which is at position 6 in the record. Also, add a 1,000 millisecond delay between each keystroke.

5. Add a **Delay** action for 500 milliseconds and then add another **Simulate Keystrokes** action to press the **Enter** Key.

You will notice that we have added ample delays in the workflow. We have delays in **Recorder Capture** actions as well as standalone **Delay** actions. As you run the code, inputs will, therefore, be slow. This is done to make the bot action onscreen reliable. You can experiment with shorter delays.

6. Now, let's add a **Recorder Capture** to add the item **Quantity**. Click on **Capture Object** and point to the **Quantity** input box on Apptivo. Ensure that the **Object properties** are as shown in the following screenshot. Choose **Set text** for **Action** and set **Keystrokes** to RowRecord[7], as shown here. Also, add a **Delay** of 500 milliseconds in the properties (below **Keystrokes** – not shown):

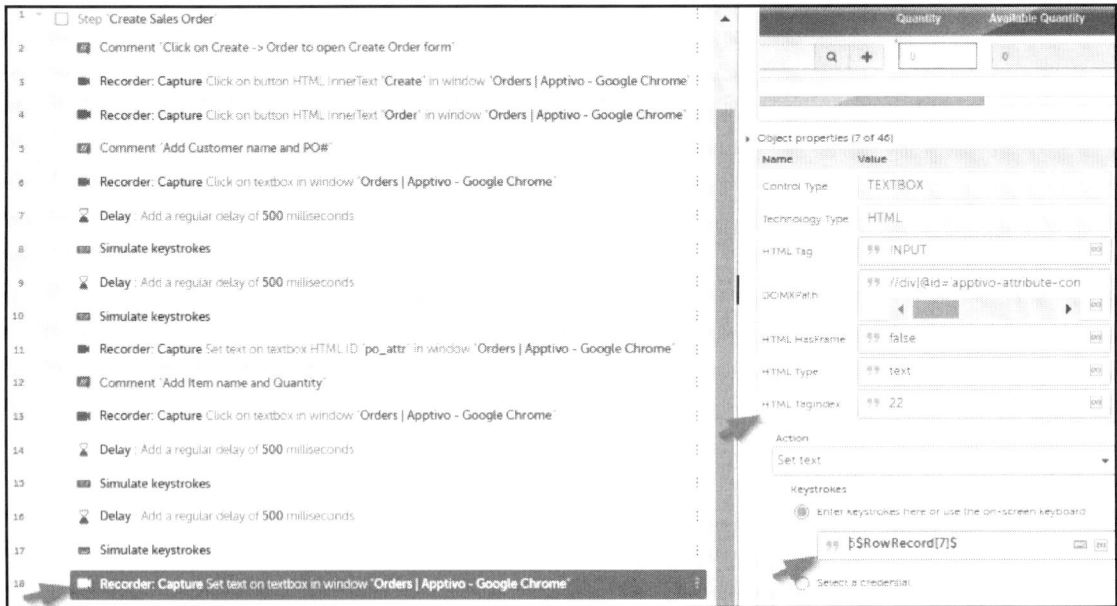

7. Finally, let's add another **Recorder Capture** to click on the **Create** button to create the SO. Ensure that the **Object properties** and **Action** are as shown here:

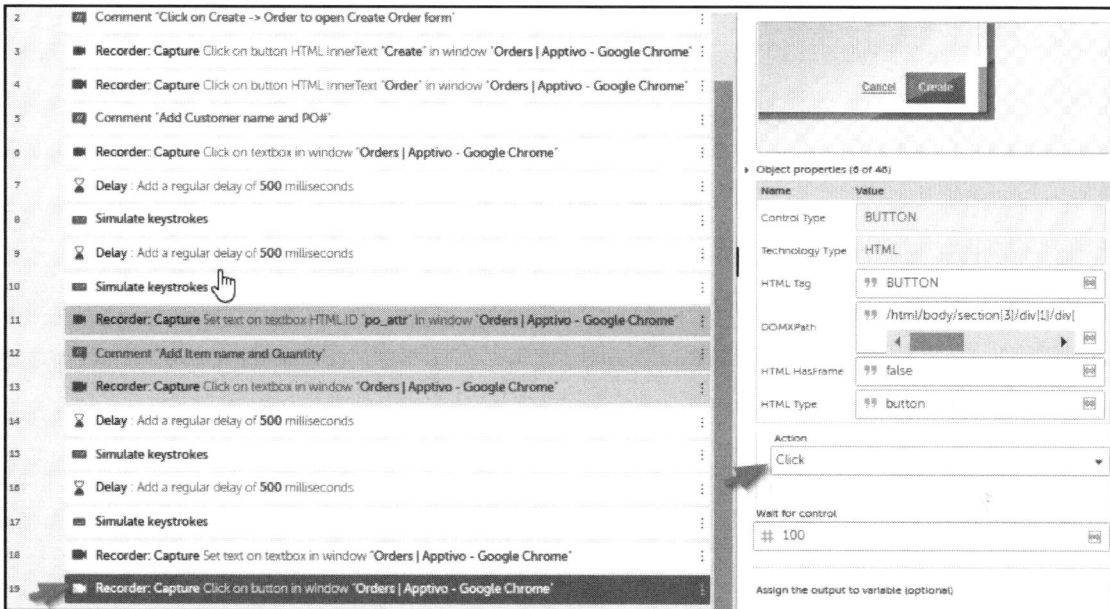

We have now entered the data and created the SO. Now, let's pass the SO number back to the Parent bot.

Passing the SO number

Once the SO is entered in Apptivo, an SO number is automatically generated by the application. Let's capture that number and pass it back to the Parent bot to input in the SO Excel sheet.

There may be instances when the form throws an exception as well. So, let's handle that before we capture the SO number:

1. Go to the Apptivo **Orders** home e page by going to **Supply chain** and then **Orders**. Click on **Create** and then **Order** for a new SO form. Scroll all the way down and click on the **Create** button without entering any data. An error message should pop up on Apptivo. We will capture this dialog box to handle this error.

2. Let's go back to the A2019 workflow. We need a variable to capture the SO number. So, go to **Variables** and create a new variable called `SalesOrder` of type **String**. Check the **Use as output** box as you create it.

3. We will add a new **Step** to group these actions and call it `Capture Sales Order number`.

4. Within the **Step**, we will add an **If** action. In the properties, choose **Object** for **Condition** (under **Recorder**). Let's choose the same window as we did before (**Orders | Apptivo**) and capture the **OK** button on the error dialog in Apptivo. The **Object properties** should look like this:

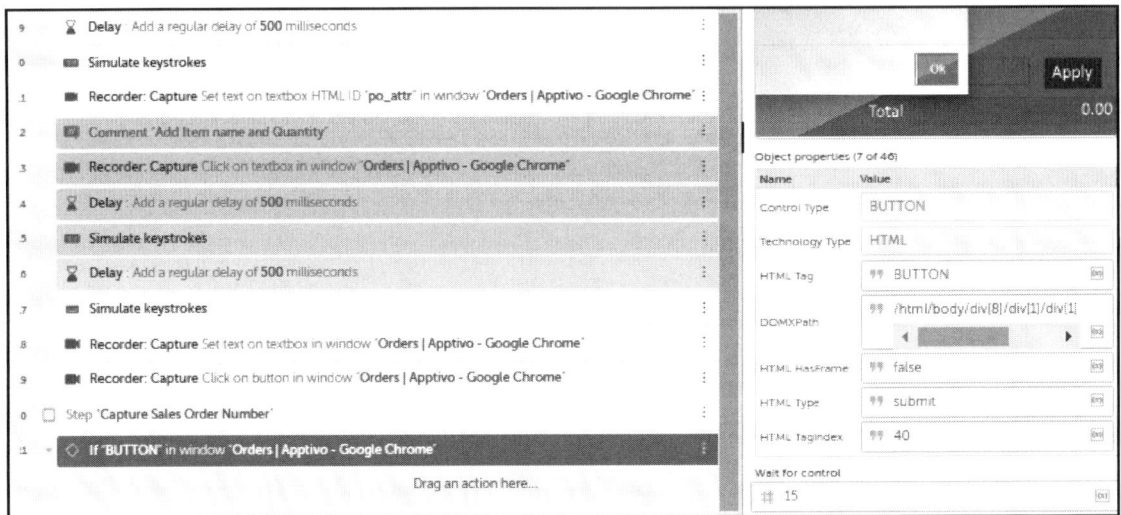

5. Let's now click the **OK** button so that the bot can carry out the next transactions. Add a new **Capture** action for the Apptivo **Orders** window and point to the **OK** button. The object properties will look similar to the ones for the **If** action. Ensure you choose **Click** in the **Action** property.

6. We will also set the `SalesOrder` variable to null as we could not capture it. Add a **String Assign** to set the `SalesOrder` variable as **Null**, as shown here:

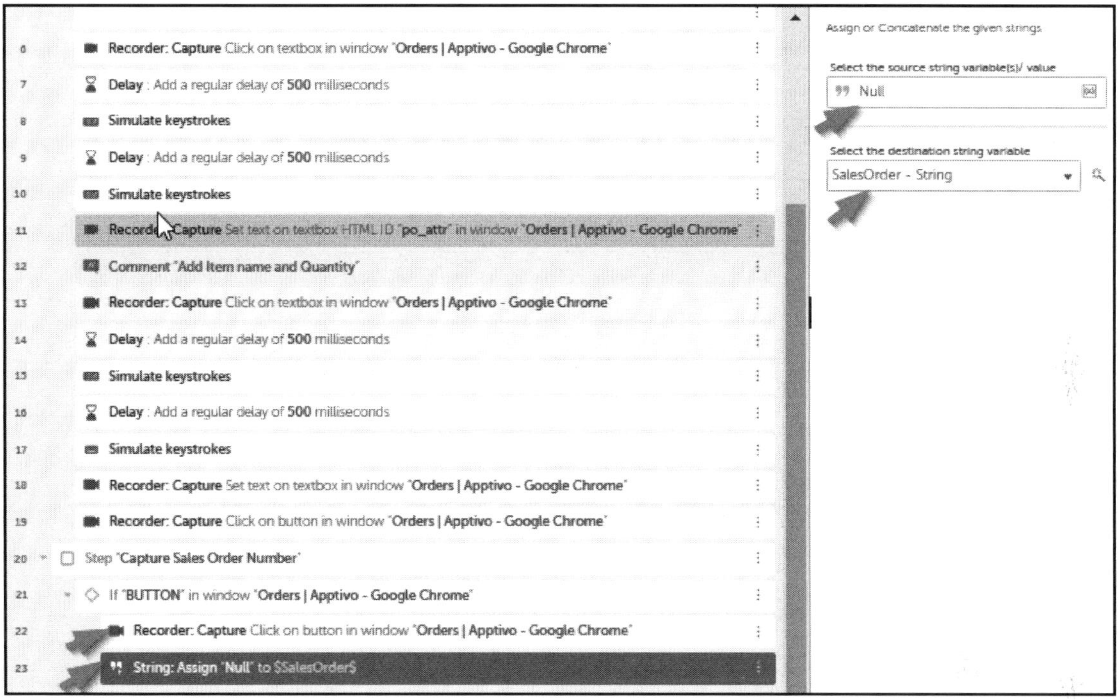

7. In an **Else** condition, when SOs are created without errors, let's capture the generated SO number. Add the **Else** action within the preceding **If**.

8. In Apptivo, enter a dummy order to get to the **Order Created** screen. Add a new **Recorder Capture** action within the **Else**. Keeping the same window, let's capture the input box near the **Order#** label. Set the action as HTML InnerText and assign it to the SalesOrder variable, as shown here:

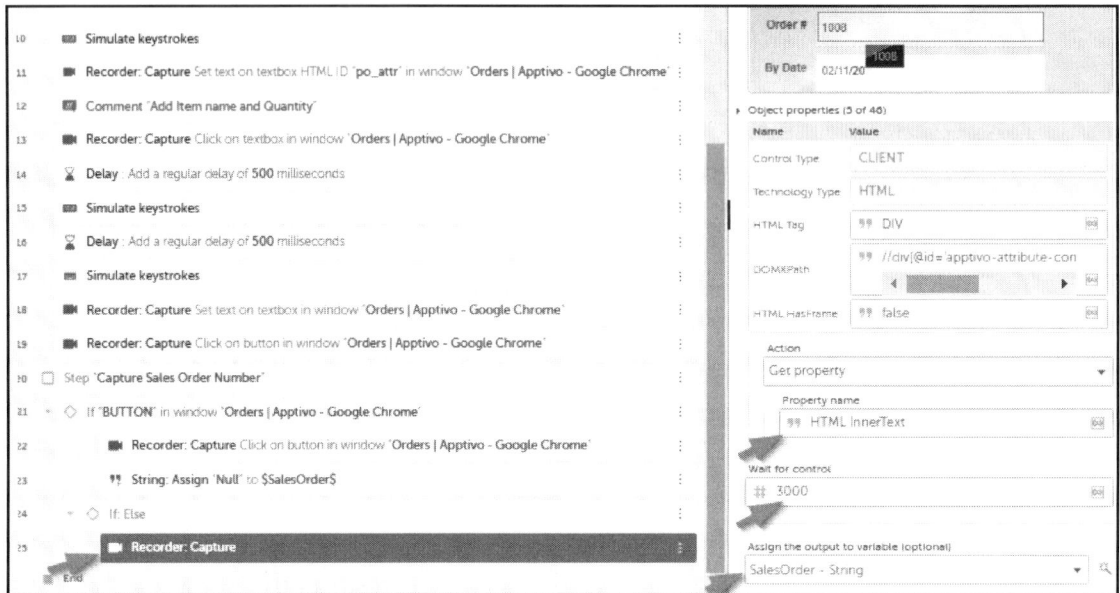

That completes the Child bot configuration. We have now entered the SO in Apptivo and populated the data variable that will be passed back to the Parent bot. Let's get back to the Parent bot for the rest of the steps.

Invoking the Child bot and updating the Excel sheet

We are now ready to complete the automation in the Parent bot.

We will invoke the SalesOrder bot, get the SO number and enter it into the Excel sheet, and finally, move the Excel sheet to the Processed folder. We will start with some groundwork before we invoke the Child bot.

Looping through rows and invoking the Child bot

Let's open up the Parent bot if you do not have it already open. We will continue from where we left off within the **Try** block.

We will add a **Step** action to group together the actions in this section. We have named it `Loop, Invoke and add to Excel`. You can add a title that makes sense to you. Within this step, let's perform these steps:

1. Add a variable to keep a counter as we loop through the data table records. Let's call it `currentIteration` and choose **Number** for **Type.** Check both **Use as Input** and **Use as Output.**
2. Add another variable to store the output we receive from the Child bot. We will call it `dictOutput` and choose **Dictionary** for **Type**. Check **Use as Output**.

> **TIP**
>
> The `dictOutput` **Dictionary** variable stores the key-value pair with all the output variables in the Child bot. In our case, we are using this to retrieve the value of the SO number using the `SalesOrder` output variable defined in the Child bot.

3. Let's add a **Number Assign** action to initialize the variable `currentIteration` to `2` as shown in the following screenshot. This is to start reading values from the second row as our data table has headers:

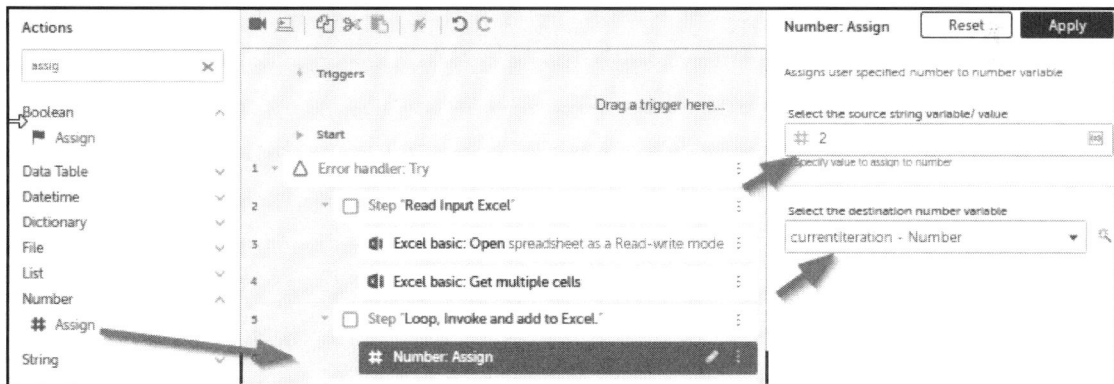

4. Let's now loop through the data table. Add a **Loop** action and choose **For Each Row in Table** for **Iterator**, **excelTable** for **Table variable** and create a new **Record** variable called `currentrow` to assign the current row from the record. When you create the variable, check both **Use as Input** and **Use as Output**. Your workflow so far will look like this:

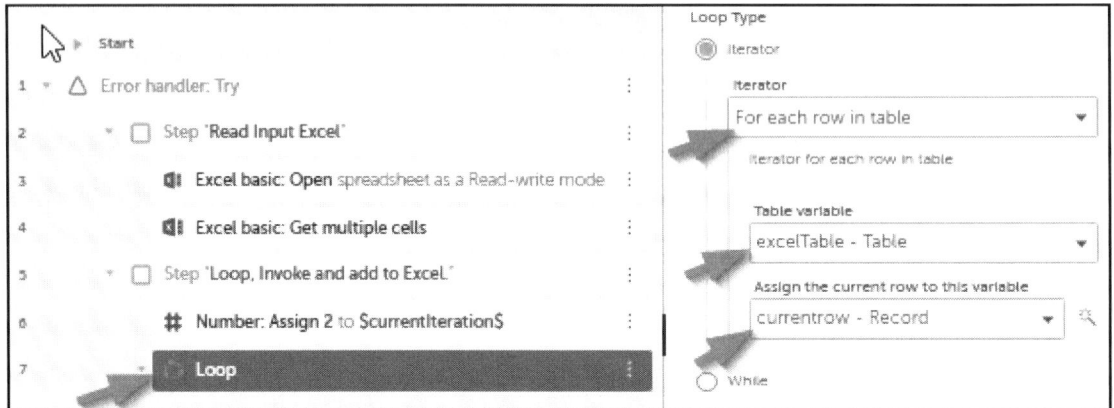

5. As the first step of the **Loop**, let's invoke the Child bot. Add the **Task Bot Run** action. In the properties, choose the `CreateSalesOrder` bot. You will see an option called **Set RowRecord**. If you remember, `RowRecord` is the variable we added in the `CreateSalesOrder` bot to pass data. We will set **Set RowRecord** to the `currentrow` variable so that we pass the current row to the Child bot as shown in the following screenshot. Also, scroll down the properties and **Assign the output to variable** `dictOutput` (not shown):

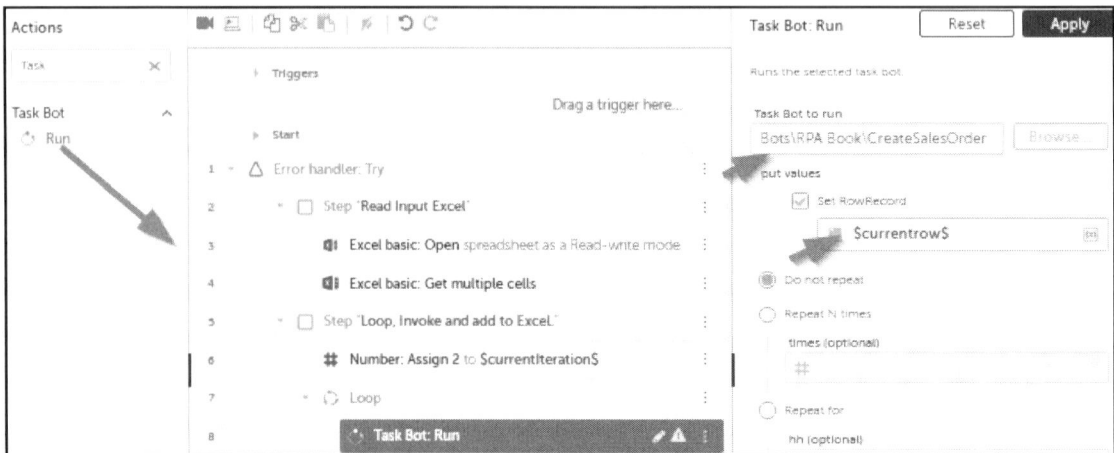

After invoking the Child bot, the bot returns the SO number. Let's take that and update our Excel sheet.

Updating Excel with the SO number

Stay within the loop and add a new **Step** with **Title** as "**Update Excel with SO Number**". Let's add a few steps to update the Excel sheet:

1. To concatenate the current row number and read specific Excel cells, we will convert the number variable `currentIteration` to `String`. Add the **Number To string** action to convert the `currentIteration` variable and assign the output to a new variable called `currentIterationString` that can be used as input or output (create this variable by clicking on the magic wand on the right of the input box). Your workflow should look like this:

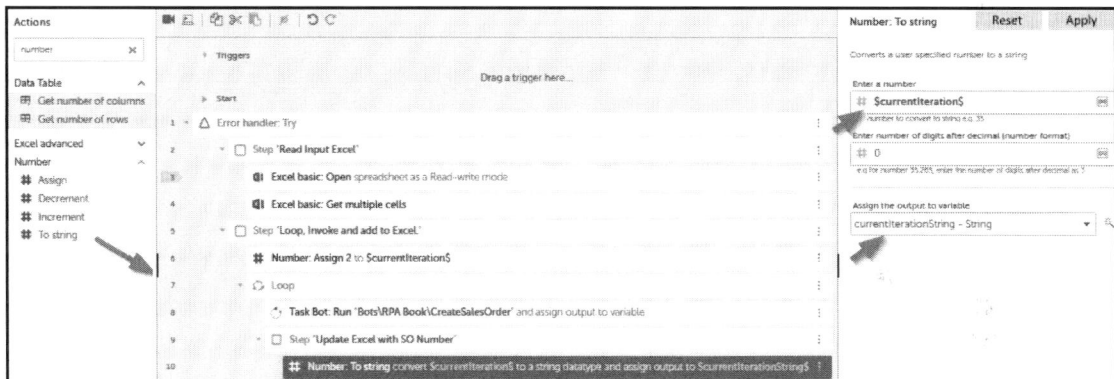

2. Now, let's set column I (**SO#**) in the Excel sheet with the SO number we got from the Child bot. Add the **Excel basic Set cell** action. In the properties, set **Session name** to `S1`, choose **Specific cell** and set it to `I$currentIterationString$`, which would translate to I2, I3, and so on and set its value to `$dictOutput{SalesOrder}$`. `dictOutput` is the output variable from the Child bot and `SalesOrder` is the dictionary key:

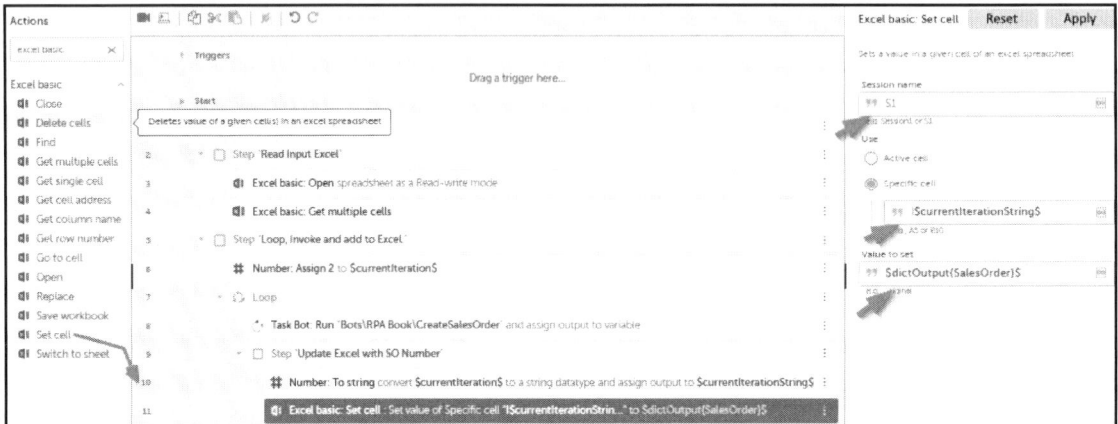

3. Now that we have completed the activities we wanted to carry out in the loop, let's increment the counter. Add a **Number Assign** action and in the **Select the source string variable** box, add `$currentIteration$+1`. Select the destination number variable as the `currentIteration` number variable.

4. Finally, let's close the Excel sheet. Add an **Excel basic Close** activity at the level of **Step "Loop, Invoke and add to Excel"**. Update **Session name** with **S1** – the session name we provided as we opened the Excel sheet.

We are done with updating the Excel file with the SO number. Let's move it to the `Processed` folder.

Moving the Excel file to the Processed folder

We will copy the Excel file that we processed to the `Processed` folder and then delete the original file. Here are the steps to do so:

1. Add a new **Step** action with the title `Move to Processed Folder`.

2. Add a **File Copy** action and choose the **Source file** as your original SO Excel sheet. Choose the **Destination file/folder** as the folder where you want to place the processed files (create one if you do not have one):

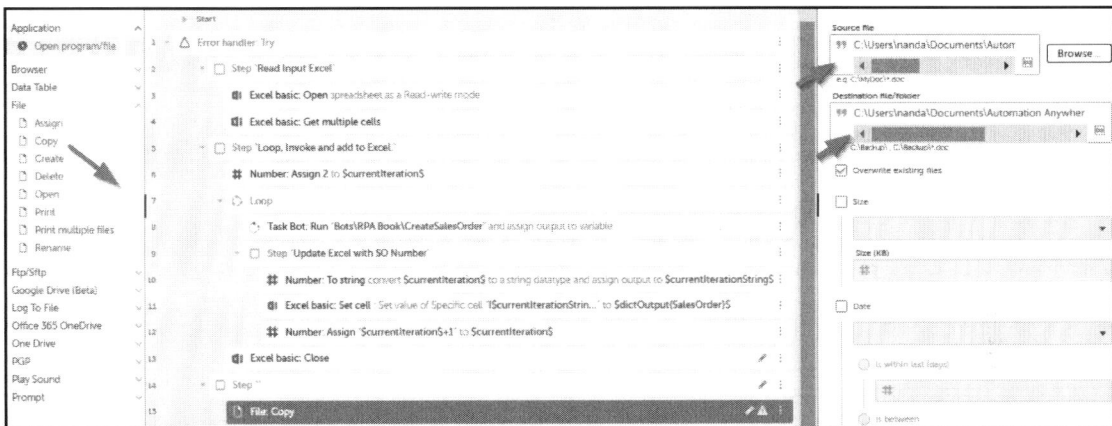

3. We will now delete the original Excel file. Add a **File Delete** action and point the file property to the original SO Excel file.

4. Finally, let's add a success message for the bot to confirm. Add a **Message box** with message to display as `Success! All Sales Orders Created and file moved to Processed Folder`.

That completes the configuration for the automation. Let's now run it.

Testing the automation

It is now time to test the automation we created – both the Parent and Child bots. Before we run the automation, let's ensure the following:

- That all customer names in the SO Excel sheet are also in Apptivo. Try entering the customer names in a dummy order. The **Customer Select** box should show the customer name if it exists. Otherwise, go ahead and add the customer by clicking the plus sign near the input box.
- That all item names in the SO Excel sheet are in Apptivo. Similar to the customer names, try entering the item names in the order form. If the item name is not present, go ahead and add the item name by clicking the plus sign near the input box.
- The SO Excel file is closed.

Once you have ensured these things, go to the Parent bot and click on **Run** from the top menu.

You should receive the success message that we added earlier. You can confirm that the bot ran successfully by checking the following:

1. All the SOs have been added to the Apptivo Orders application as per the Excel sheet.
2. The respective SO column (I) for each PO# row should be updated in the SO Excel sheet.
3. The SO Excel file should now be in your `Processed` folder.

Once you have got all of this right, you will have processed all the SOs successfully.

Summary

That was our first full-fledged Automation Anywhere A2019 project.

We used a Parent and Child bot combination to take SO records from an Excel sheet and enter them into a web-based application. The bots also took the SO numbers generated and updated the Excel sheet.

We hope this has given you a better sense of how you can use A2019 for Excel and web automation. In the next chapter, we will do some system administration with Automation Anywhere A2019.

See you there!

8
ERP User Administration

System administrators perform multiple activities on a typical day, including user administration, installation, monitoring, and troubleshooting. Of these activities, the creation of users and resetting passwords take up the bulk of the average system administrator's day. These repetitive activities take away precious time that could be used to focus on helping with other, more critical activities.

In this chapter, we will build a bot that automates one of these repetitive tasks – creating users. We will look up user information from a user creation request and create the user in a **Software as a service (SaaS)** application.

Here is what you will learn as part of this Automation Anywhere A2019 project:

- Automation Anywhere A2019 PDF automation
- Reading specific fields in a PDF
- Automation Anywhere A2019 email automation
- Automation Anywhere A2019 web automation
- Using Automation Anywhere A2019 Recorder
- Using regular expressions
- Automation Anywhere A2019 triggers
- Logging in Automation Anywhere A2019
- Exception handling in Automation Anywhere

Technical requirements

Let's understand the hardware and software we need for this project:

- Automation Anywhere A2019 Community Edition – you can sign up at `https://www.automationanywhere.com/products/community-edition`.
- A PC with Automation Anywhere Community Edition A2019 Bot Agent installed.
- Google Chrome with the Automation Anywhere extension installed.
- Freshsales Saas CRM Application – you can sign up for free at `http://freshsales.io/`.
- Microsoft Excel 2007 or later.
- Check out the following video to see the Code in Action: `https://bit.ly/2LL8JEz`.

Project overview

We will create a bot that will pick up user requests from an `Input` folder. The bot will read the necessary details to create the user and enter them into a SaaS application called *Freshsales*. If the username or role were missing, and assuming the email ID was present in the request, then the bot would email the user asking for missing details. If the user is created successfully, the bot moves the user creation request PDF to a `Processed` folder. Here is the workflow:

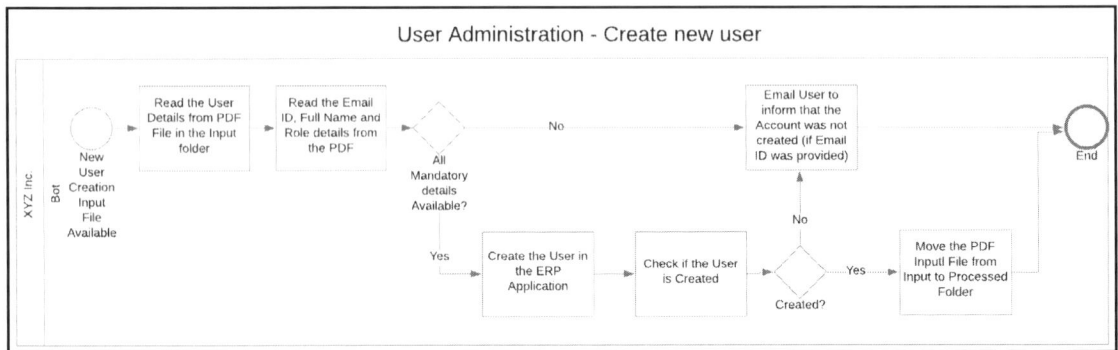

That was a high-level view of the new user creation process. Let's now look at the details and dive into the step-by-step creation process.

Project detail

As with `Chapter 7`, *Sales Order Processing*, we will have a Parent bot and Child bot. The Parent bot will invoke the Child bot to create a new user in Freshsales.

The Parent bot starts by reading the contents of the input PDF file and assigning them to a **Table** variable. We will loop through the **Table** variable, and assign each row in the Table to variables. We will then extract the necessary field values using String operations.

With these details, we will invoke the Child bot, which enters the data in Freshsales and returns a flag indicating success or failure. If there is a failure, we send an email to the user requesting the missing data.

If successful, the user gets an email automatically from Freshsales to activate the account. The bot takes the processed request PDF and moves it to the `Processed` folder.

The sequence of action is as follows:

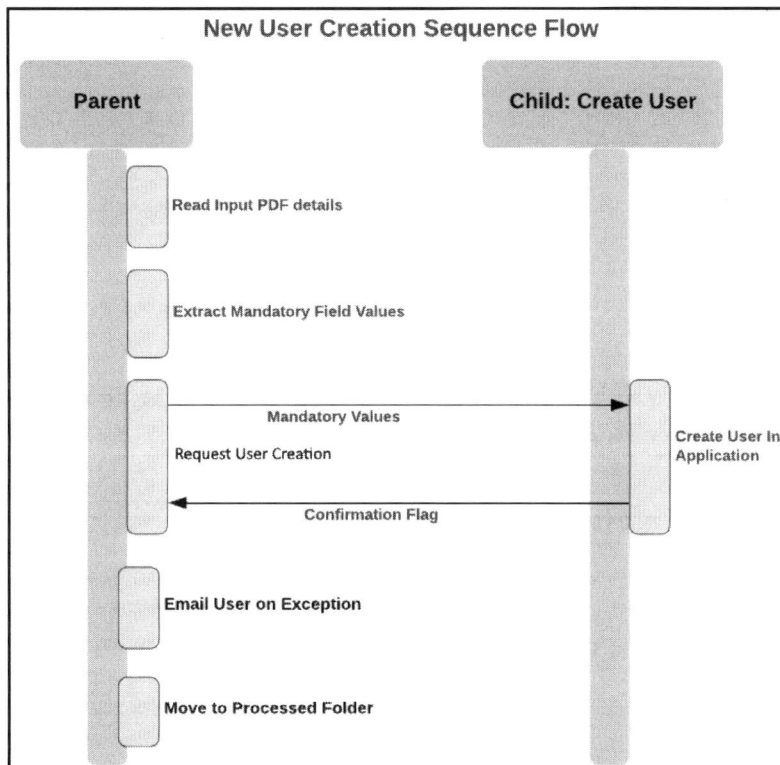

As with our previous projects, let's do some groundwork for the project before building these components for our automation.

Project groundwork

Let's create the input PDF file and set up the Freshsales application before we get busy building on Automation Anywhere 2019. We will start with the user request PDF.

Creating a user request PDF

For this project, we will create a simple input user request PDF. To do that, we'll create a simple Excel file with the following rows:

	A	B
1	Email ID :	john.doe@gmail.com
2	Full Name:	John Doe
3	Role:	Manager

Let's then save this Excel file as a PDF by going to the **Save As** option. This should give you a simple PDF with the following content:

Email ID :	john.doe@gmail.com
Full Name:	John Doe
Role:	Manager

> We are converting and using PDF files since user requests usually come as PDFs. It also helps you understand how you can read PDF files for automation within A2019.

Now that we have the input file created, let's go to Freshsales and ensure that we are set up.

Signing up for Saas application

Go to the Freshsales site at `http://freshsales.io/` and sign up. You will be asked for your details and also a CRM domain name. Provide any unique domain name of your choosing and sign up.

Once you have signed up and logged in, head over to **Admin Settings** on the left panel. We will be using the **Users** option for adding new users:

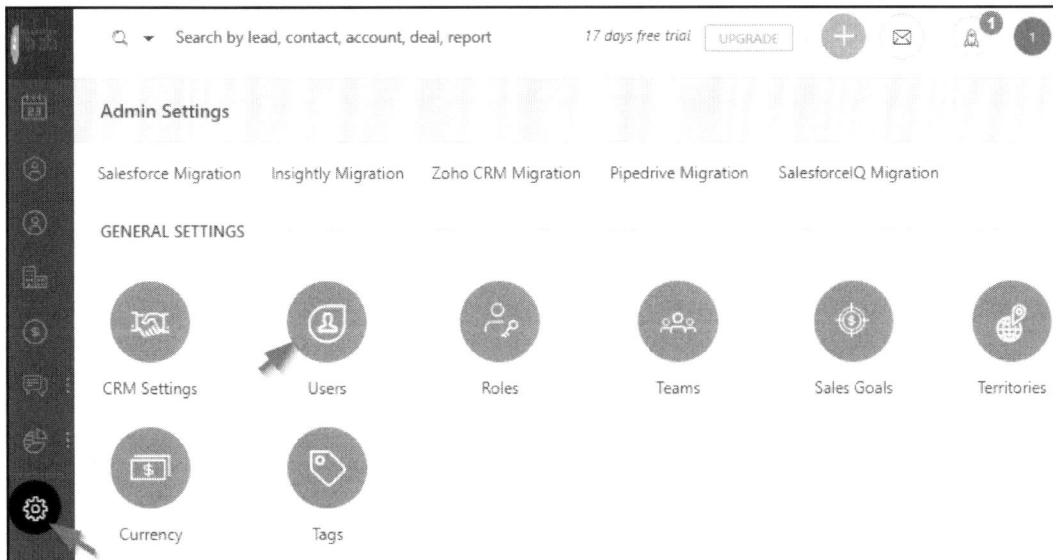

Now that we have the application open and ready to go, let's open A2019 and start building our bots.

Opening the Automation Anywhere A2019 control room

Finally, let's open A2019 to create the bots. Log in to the A2019 Community Version in your browser at `https://community.cloud.automationanywhere.digital/#/login`.

Now that we have completed the groundwork for the project, it is time to create the first bot – the Parent bot.

Creating the Parent bot

As we did in `Chapter 7`, *Sales Order Processing*, go to **My Bots** in the A2019 control room and create a new bot. This creates a new bot and opens the development environment for us to configure the bot workflow. We will use the **List** view for this project.

As with most of our projects, let's start by adding the **Try** and **Catch** actions to handle any exceptions in our Parent bot.

Exception handling

Let's add **Error handler: Try** and **Error handler: Catch** to catch any errors. To do that, look up **Error handler** and then drag and drop the **Try** action. We will add all of the automation logic in this **Try** block in the next few sections.

Before we do that, we'll add the **Catch** action beneath **Try**. In the **Catch** action's properties, set the **Exception** type as **AllErrors**. Create a **String** variable called `errorMesage` to store the error message:

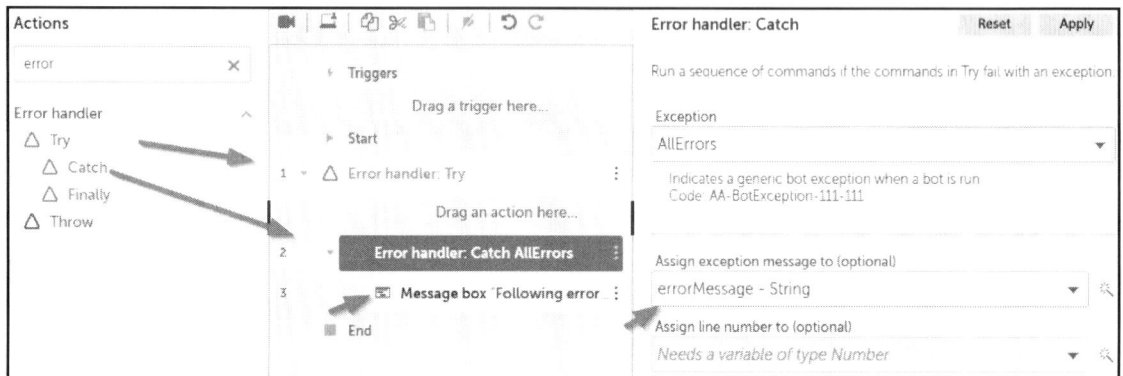

In the **Catch** block, let's also add a **Message Box** with the message `Following error occurred $errorMessage$`. Finally, click the **Save** button at the top to save the bot so far, before we open and read the user request PDF file.

Extracting user details from PDF

We will now extract all the text in the PDF file:

1. We'll start by adding a **Step** action within the **Try** block and call it `Read PDF` to logically separate these steps. Within this **Step** action, extract the text in PDF to a Table variable so that we can loop through the content. To do that, first extract the PDF text to a temporary text file. Add the **PDF Extract text** action and set the **PDF path** to the desktop PDF file that we created. Set the **Text type** to **Structured text** and set **Export data to text file** to `Temp.txt`, as shown here:

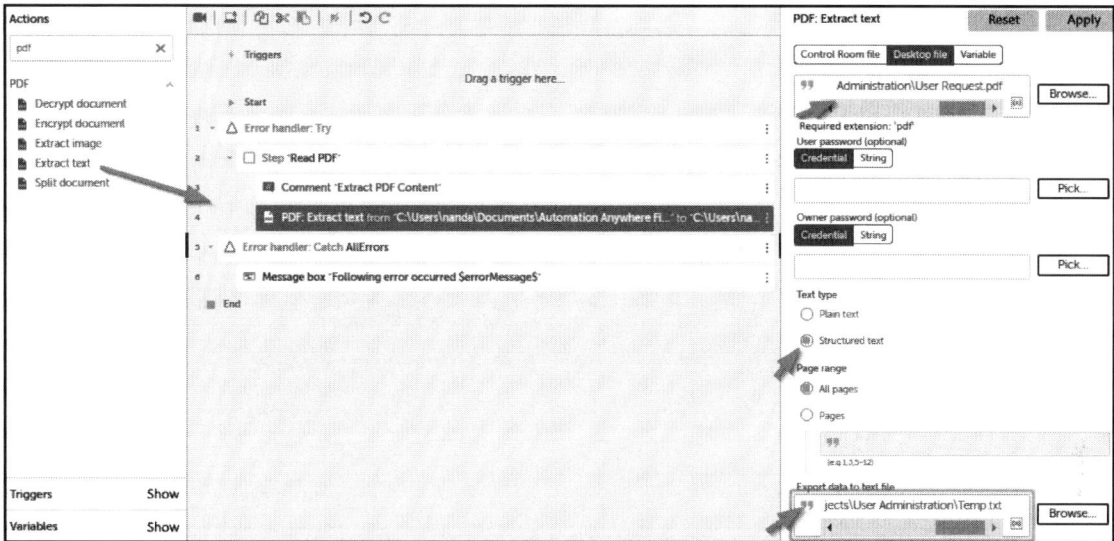

2. Over the next few steps, we will read the data from the temporary text file (**Temp.txt**) and assign it to a **Table** variable. This is so that we can loop through the text data and manipulate it:

   - Let's add the **CSV/TXT Open** action. Choose a **Session name** (such as S1), set the **File path** to Temp.txt, and select **Tab** for **Delimiter**.
   - Next, add the **CSV/TXT Read** action and set **Assign value** to the variable called ExtractedUserData. Create this new **Table** variable using the wizard.
   - Finally, let's close the Temp.txt file by adding the **CSV/TXT Close** action. Make sure that you add the same **Session name** (such as S1) that you used to open the file.

Your workflow after adding these series of actions will look like this:

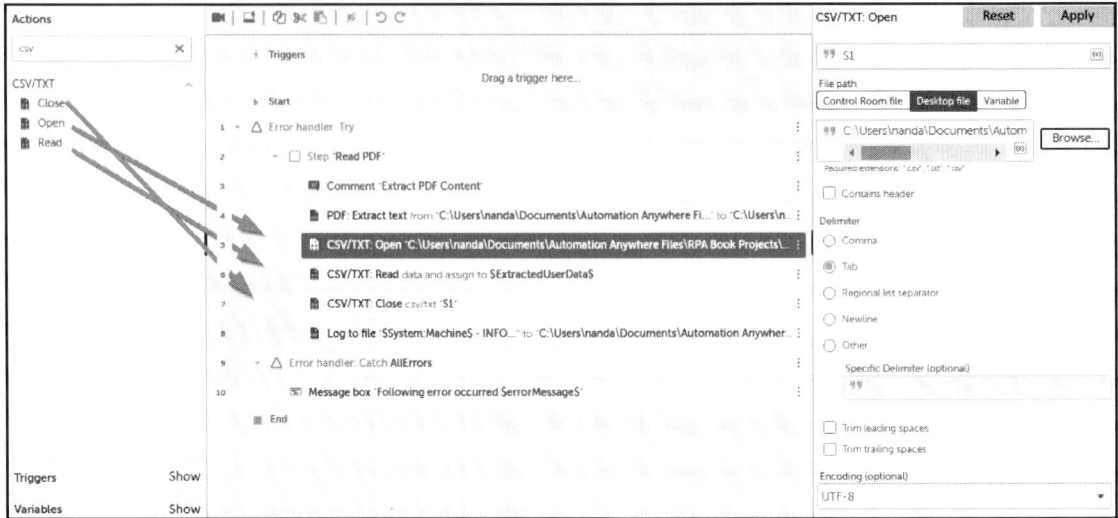

We will be logging the key steps in this project so that we understand how we can log information for troubleshooting. Automation Anywhere A2019 provides an easy way for you to create a log file to track events as the bot executes. We will use the **Log to file** action for that.

3. Finally, we'll log the completion of this step. Create a new log file called ExecutionLog.txt for logging events from this project. Then add the **Log to file** action and set the path to the ExecutionLog.txt file. To indicate we have the data in the **Table** now, let's set **Enter text to log** to $System:Machine$ – INFO – PDF Data Extracted to Table.

When we start logging the execution logs, there are two best practices you can follow:
a) The log filename should follow a good naming convention and you should make sure it has the date tag, for example, AA_UserCreation_Execution_log_02292020.
b) The log file should start with a header; for example, <Machine Name> – <Log Type> – <Details> in the first row.

Now that we have the PDF data in a **Table** variable, let's loop through the data.

Assigning user data to row variables

We will loop through the `ExtractedUserData` variable and delineate each row for String manipulation in the following steps:

1. Add a new **Step** action with the **Title** as `Loop DataTable`. Add it outside the previous **Step**, but still within the **Try** block.

2. Within this **Step** action, add a **Loop** action to step through each row in the **Table**, set the **Table** variable as `ExtractedUserData`, and **Assign the current row** to a new **Record** variable called `CurrentRow` (create this with the wizard), as shown here:

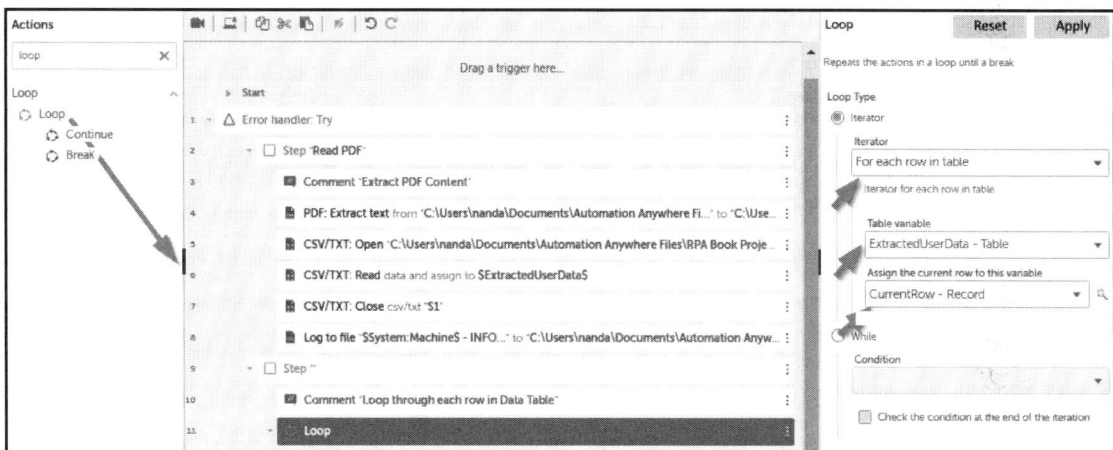

3. Under the previous loop, let's add another **Loop** action to step through each item in the row. For that, we will iterate through each value in the record, set the **Record** variable as `CurrentRow`, and assign the current value to a new variable called `CurrentValue`, as shown here:

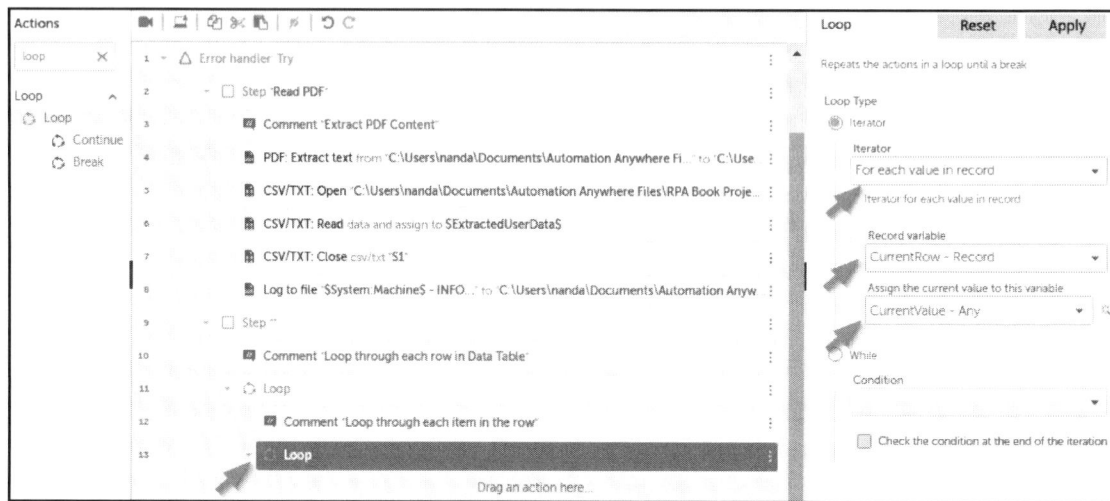

4. Within the second loop, we will check for the row number and assign it to the respective row name. Let's add a `counter` variable of the **Number** type to keep track of the loop iteration and read the rows.

5. To check for the row item being iterated, let's add an **If** with **Condition** as **Number condition**, and **Source value** as the `counter` variable. Set **Operator** to = and **Target value** to 0 to check for the first row, as shown here:

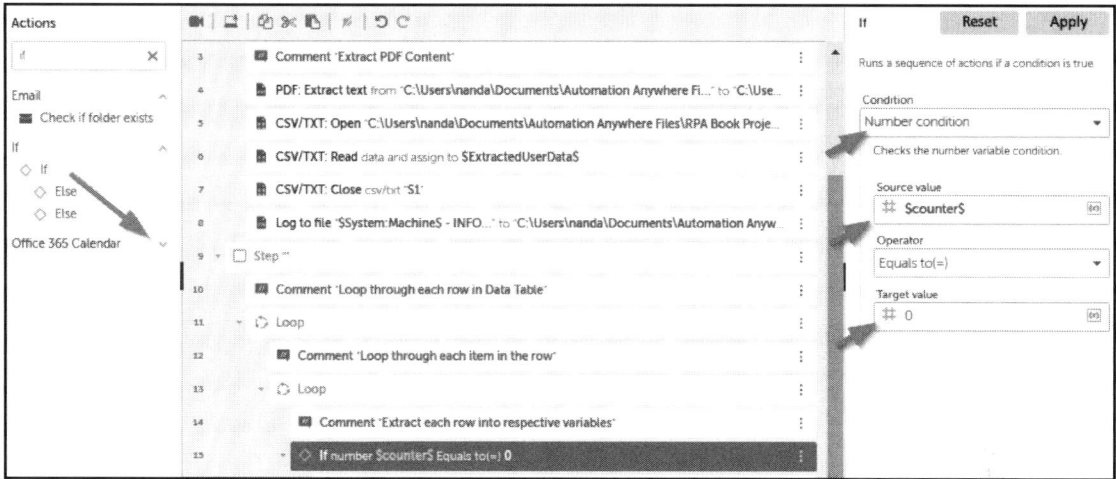

6. We now know that the first row in our user request PDF was the email ID. So, let's assign the **source string variable** value, CurrentValue, to another new **String** variable called EmailRow, as shown here:

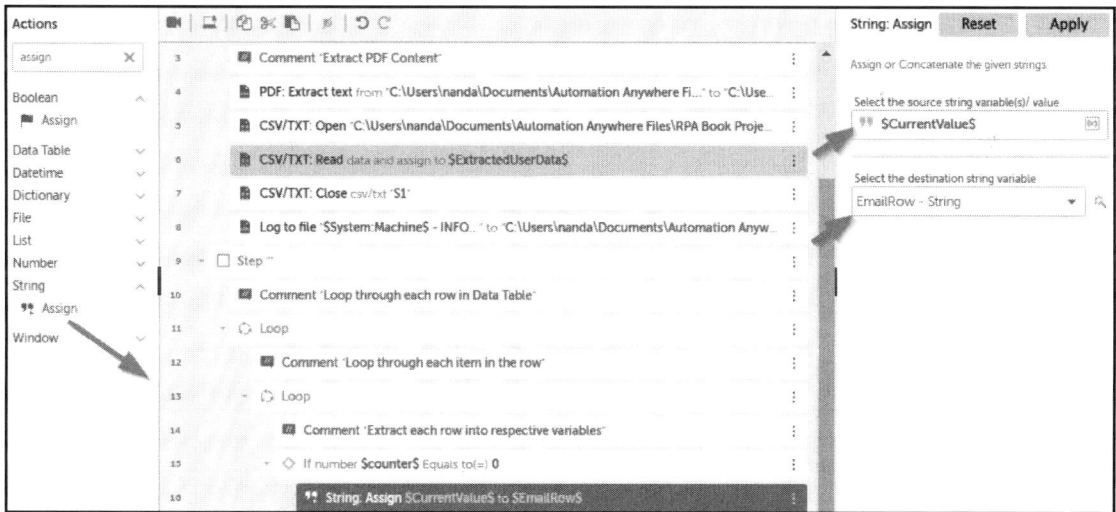

7. Similar to the preceding two steps, let's now assign the other rows to respective variables. We will use two **Else If** conditions for counter, equaling 1 and 2, and **String: Assign** them to the variables, FullNameRow and RoleRow. Your workflow should now look like this:

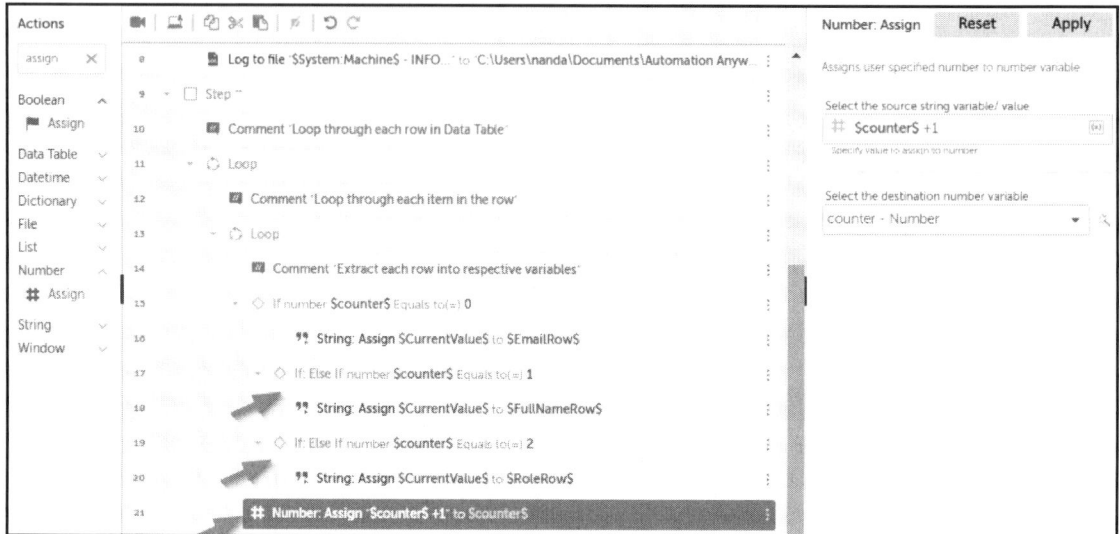

8. Let's also increment the counter using an **Assign Number** action, as shown in the preceding screenshot. Within the **Assign** action, set **Select the source string variable/value** to $counter$ +1 and **Select the destination number variable** as the counter variable.

> Instead of using **Assign** to increment the counter variable, you can also try the increment command under **Number** for the same outcome.

9. You can log the completion of this step by adding the **Log to file** action and setting the path to the ExecutionLog.txt file we created earlier. To indicate we have the data in row variables, we can set **Enter text to log** to $System: Machine$ - INFO - Row Extracted to variable.

Now that we have the rows in respective **String** variables, let's manipulate these variables and read the field values.

Extracting user details with String operations

We will now perform a few String operations to read the values for the respective fields of `Email`, `Name`, and `Role` from the `Row` variables. We will then pass these variables to a Child bot to create the new user. Let's implement the following steps:

1. We'll start by adding a new **Step** action. We can set the **Title** to `String Operations to get Email, Full Name, and Role details`.

2. Within this step, let's add a **String Extract Text** action to extract the email ID. We will use `EmailRow` as the **Source string**, and colon (:) as **Get Characters - Start after text**, as shown in the following screenshot. Assign the output to a new String variable called `EmailID` by scrolling down the properties (not shown here – refer to the next screenshot under *step 3*):

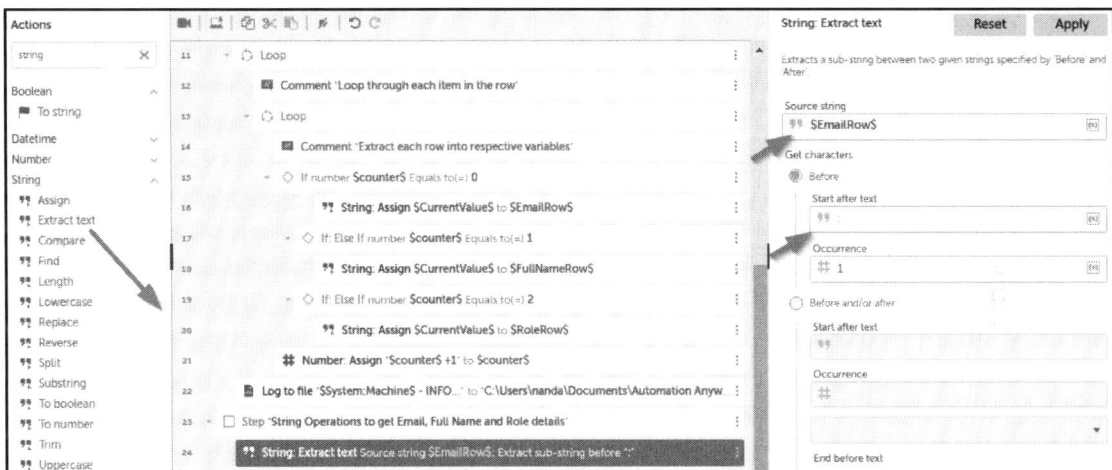

3. Similar to the preceding step, we will use two more **String Extract Text** actions to extract the full `Name` and `Role` details. Use the variables `FullName Row` and `RoleRow` as the **Source string**, a colon (:) as **Get Characters - Start after text**, and assign the output to new String variables called `FullName` and `Role`, respectively. The following are the steps with the new variable for `Row`:

Make sure you check the two checkboxes to **Remove blank spaces** and **Remove Enter from the extracted text**.

4. We can add a **Log to File** action with the `ExecutionLog.txt` file path. To print out extracted data, we can set **Enter text to log** to `$System:Machine$ - INFO - Data extracted: $EmailID$, $FullName$, $Role$`.

We now have the data we need to input into the Freshsales application to create a new user. Let's validate the email before we proceed.

Validating email addresses with regular expressions

We will validate the email address that we just extracted using a regular expression:

1. To create this validation functionality, let's add a **String Find** action. We will use the **Source string** as the `EmailID` variable, and within the **Find string**, we will paste the following standard regular expression to validate emails: `^[A-Z0-9._%-]+@[A-Z0-9.-]+\.[A-Z]{2,4}`. Then we'll assign this output to a new variable called `output`, as shown in the following screenshot:

2. Let's now add an **If** action to check whether we got the email format correct before we invoke the Child bot to enter this data in Freshsales. We will use the **Number condition** to check whether the variable output has a value of 1, which means the email format is good:

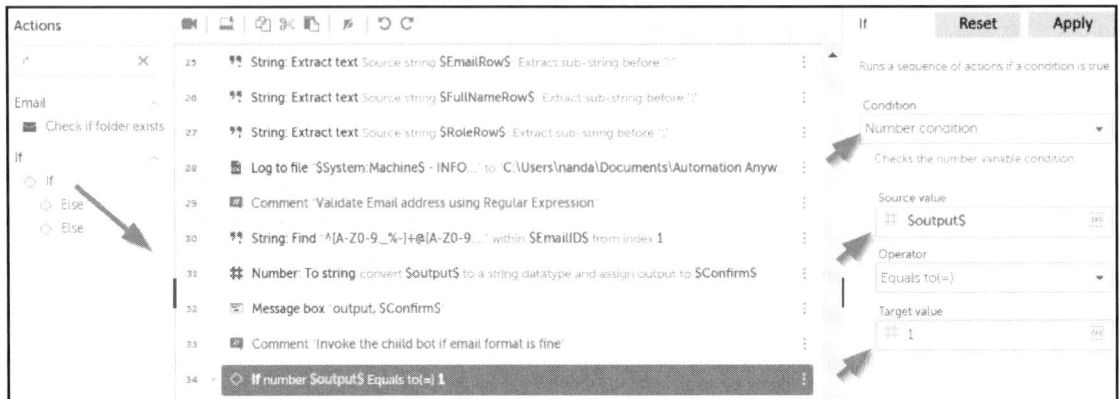

3. Let's also add the **If Else** condition in case the email format is incorrect. We will add a **Log to file** action within this **Else** condition to indicate a bad email format: `$System:Machine$-INFO - Bad Email format. Use Creation Failed`:

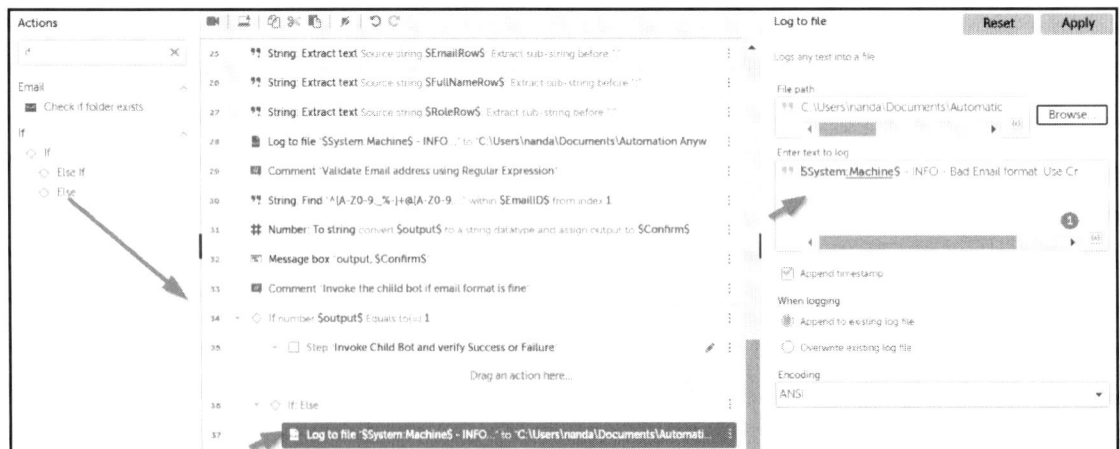

We can now invoke the Child bot within the **If** condition. We will add a **Step** action, as shown earlier. Within this **Step** action, we will add the steps to invoke the Child bot and create a new user in Freshsales.

But before that, we need to create the Child bot. Let's save the Parent bot and close the bot. We are now ready to create the Child bot.

Creating the Child bot for new user creation

Go ahead and create a new bot using **Create a bot** under **My bots** in the control room.

This will open the development canvas for the Child bot. Let's also open the Chrome browser and navigate to the **Admin settings** in Freshsales and then click on **Users** as we did in the *Project groundwork* section. Keep this browser tab open, as we will capture the fields for input from this page and create the new user.

Creating a new user in Freshsales

We will create a new user by inputting the data we got from the Parent bot. To input data, we will use the **Capture** action as we did in Chapter 7, *Sales Order Processing*:

1. Let's start by adding a **Try** block to handle any errors. We will add the **Catch** block toward the end to return a failure flag.
2. Within the **Try** block, add a **Step** action with a **Title** of Create a new user in Freshsales.

3. Let's now add the steps, starting with a **Recorder Capture** action to click on the **Add user** button in Freshsales. In **Object detail**, choose **Window** and then the **User Admin Settings** window from the drop-down. Click on **Capture Object**, as shown in the following screenshot, and point to the **Add user** button on Freshsales:

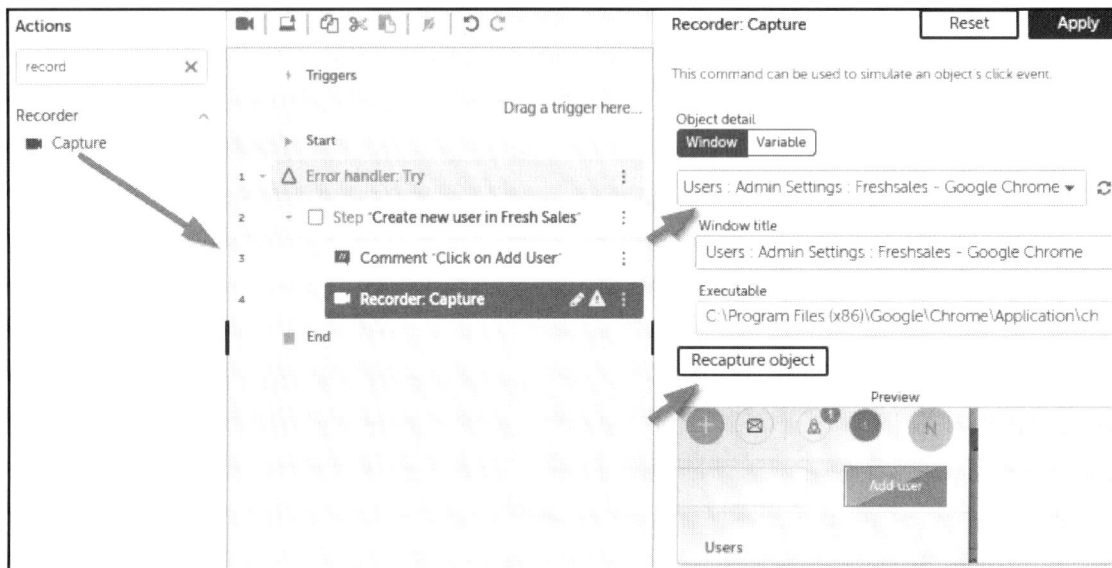

Then, set **Action** to **Click** and set the properties as shown in the following screenshot:

Make sure you choose and use stable object properties. You may need to do some trial and error to figure out the right combination of the properties for all the **Record Capture** actions.

4. We will now add a few more **Record Capture** actions to add email, full name, and role details on the next screen in Freshsales. These are the mandatory fields we need to create a new user. As you may recollect, this is the same information we created the user request PDF with (refer to the *Project groundwork* section). To pass these values from the Parent bot, let's create three new **String** variables in this bot – EmailID, FullName, and Role. Choose **Use as input** as you create these variables. We will map these variables to their respective Parent bot variables when we invoke the Child bot.

5. Let's add a new **Recorder Capture** action and set **Window** to **Add User: Admin Settings: Freshsales**. Note that this is the new window that opened up after we clicked on the **Add user** button. Click on **Capture** and point to the **Email** input box on the Freshsales **Add user** form. Finally, set **Action** to **Set Text** and within **Keystrokes**, add the `EmailID` variable, as shown in the following screenshot:

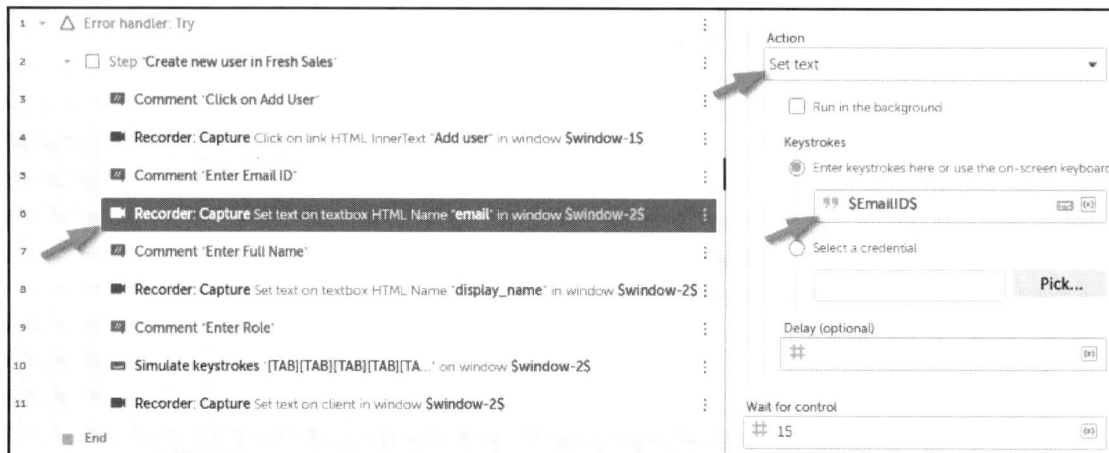

6. Just beneath that, let's add another **Recorder Capture** action and choose the same **Window** - **Add User: Admin Settings: Freshsales**. Click on **Capture** and point to the **Full Name** input box on the Freshsales form. In the **Action** property, choose **Set Text** and add the variable `FullName`.

7. Next, we will input the role data. As you may have noticed, the **Role** field is at the bottom of the form in Freshsales. So let's tab our way to the field. Add a **Simulate Keystrokes** action, choose the same **Add User** window and add eight **Tabs** and an **Enter** as keystrokes (click on the keyboard icon in the input box). Also, add a delay of 500 milliseconds, as shown here:

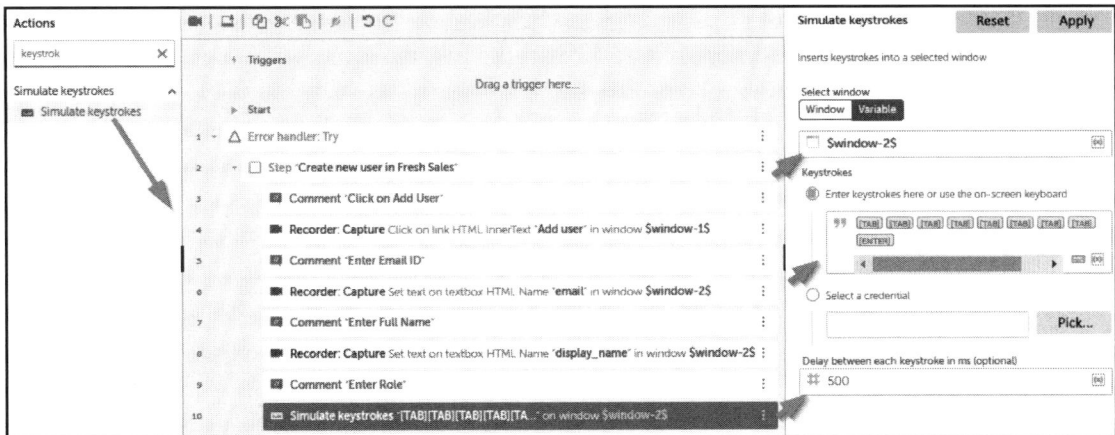

8. To input data in the **Role** field, we have to enter the data in the drop-down box. So, go to the form on Freshsales, click on the **Role** dropdown, and keep the following input box ready to capture:

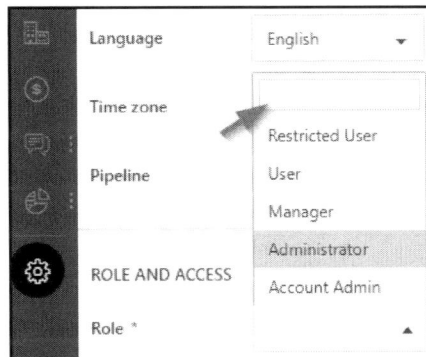

9. Add a new **Recorder Capture** action, choose the same **Add User** window, and **capture** the input box shown earlier. In the **Action** property, choose **Set Text** and add the variable `Role`. Also, add an **Enter** keystroke to register the value in the drop-down box, as shown in the following screenshot. Add a delay of 500 milliseconds as well:

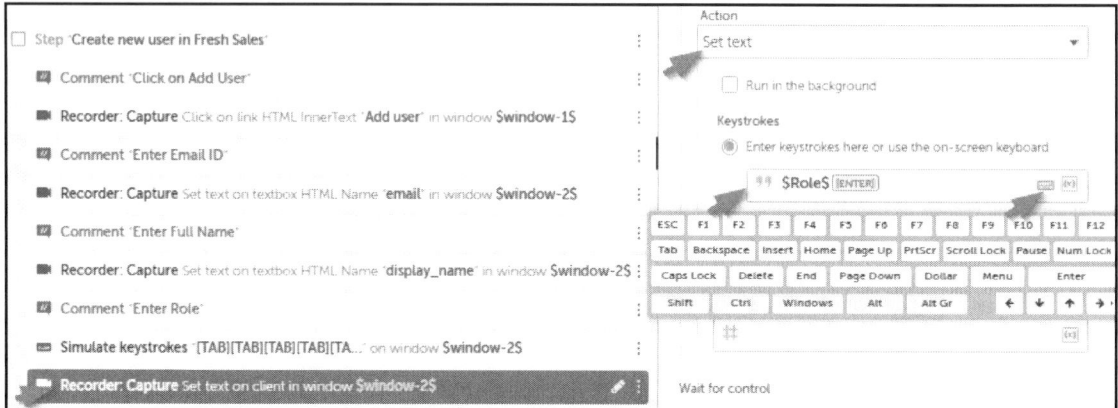

10. Finally, click on the **Submit** button to create the user with the entered data. We will add another **Recorder Capture** action, choose the same **Add User** window, and **capture** the **Save** button. Set **Click** to **Action**. This will create a new user if all goes well.

There may be instances when some of the data is not present or there is an error. Let's handle such situations before we get back to the Parent bot.

Handling form validation errors

Let's handle two scenarios here – form exceptions, such as data not being present or being incorrect, and then any other errors that may come up:

1. If there are any issues with creating a new user, the form does not advance to the next page. So what we will do is check whether the **Save** button is still present on the page. In that case, the user addition failed and we have to return a failure flag, or else we return a success flag. To do that, let's add a **Delay** action for 2 seconds. Then, add an **If** action and set **Condition** to **Object**. **Capture** the **Save** button in the **Add User Window** we used in the last step, as shown in the following screenshot:

2. As we said, if the **Save** button is still around, it is a failure and we return a "No" flag. Let's add a **String Assign** action and set **Select the source string variable(s)** to No. In the **Select the destination string variable** property, create a new variable called `SuccessFlag` and set it to be used as **Output**.

3. Let's set a click of the **Cancel** button to return to the **Admin Settings** page, to be used when we could not create the user. Add a new **Recorder Capture** action and set **Window** to **Add User: Admin Settings: Freshsales**. Click on **Capture** and point to the **Cancel** button on the form. Finally, set **Action** to **Click**, as shown in the following screenshot:

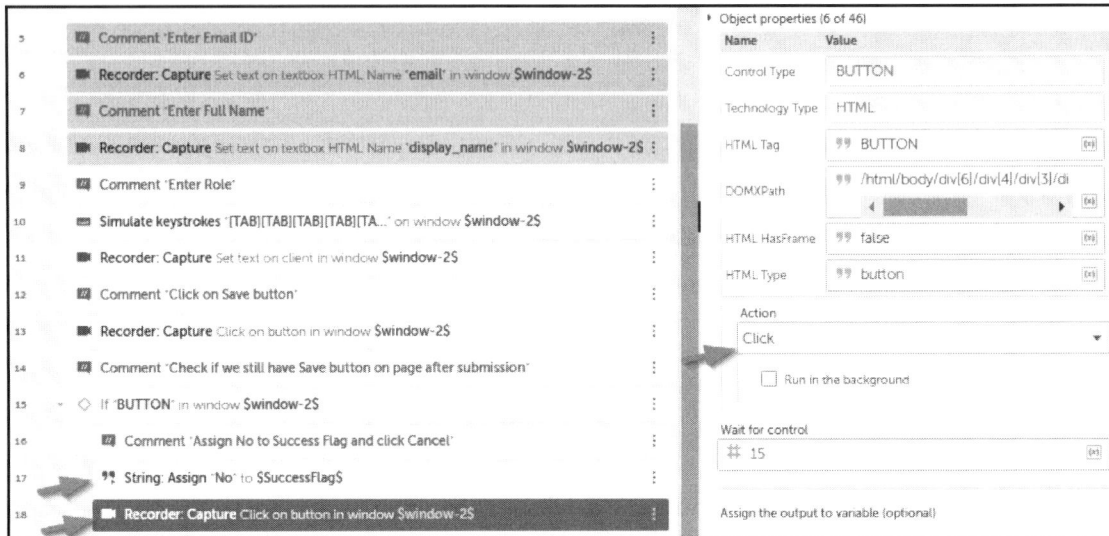

4. If the **Save** button is not there, let's set the `SuccessFlag` as `Yes`. Add an **If Else** Condition and within it, add a **String Assign** action and set **Select the source string variable(s)** to `Yes`. In the **Select the destination string variable** property, add the variable called `SuccessFlag` that we created:

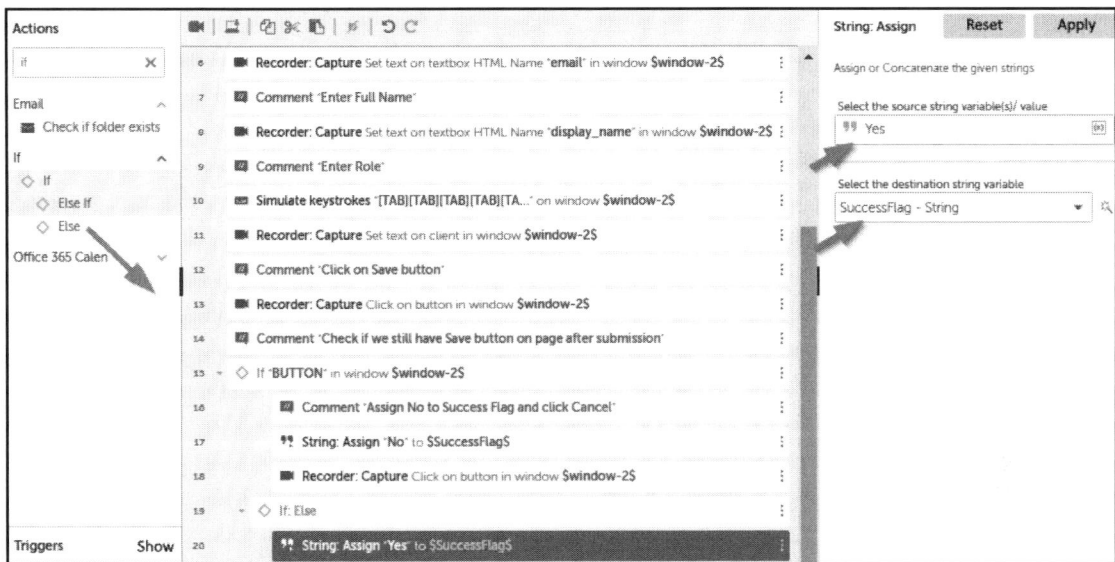

We have now handled the form validation errors. Let's now handle the system errors to complete the Child bot.

Handling exceptions

Let's now add the **Catch** block for the **Try** block we added at the start of the bot workflow:

1. Add the **Catch** action at the same level as the **Try** action. In the **Catch** properties, set **Exception** type to **AllErrors**. Create a String variable called `errorMesage` to store the error message.
2. We will set the success flag to `No`. For that, add a **String Assign** action and set **Select the source string variable(s)** to `No`. In the **Select the destination string variable** property, add the `SuccessFlag` variable.

3. Let's also log the error by adding a **Log to File** action with the `ExecutionLog.txt` file path. To print out the extracted data, we can set **Enter text to log** to `$System:Machine$ - ERROR - Child bot execution failed with $errorMessage$`:

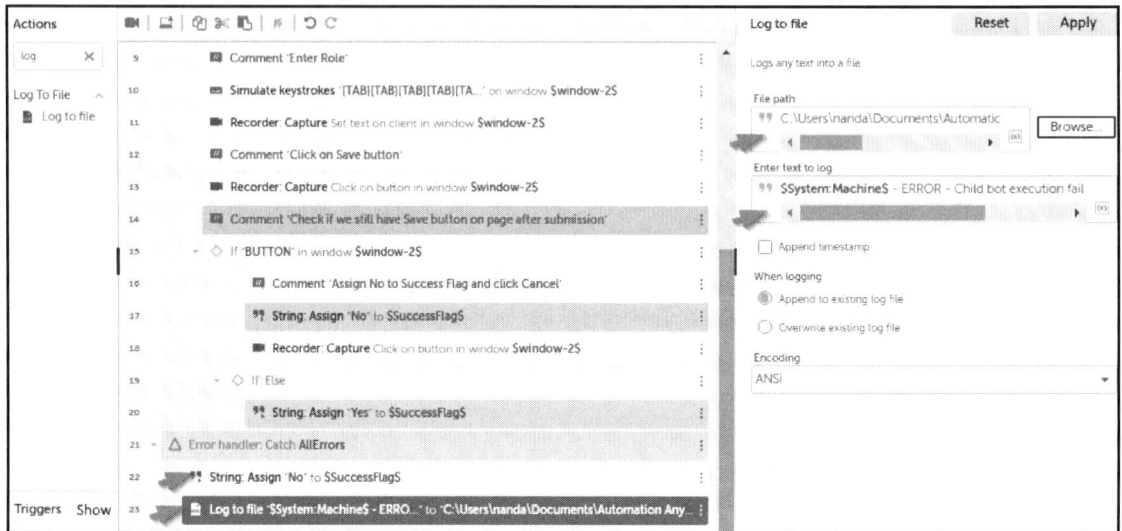

That completes the Child bot configuration. We have now created a new user in Freshsales and populated the flag that is passed back to the Parent bot. Let's get back to the Parent bot for the remainder of the steps.

Invoking the Child bot and creating the new user

We are now ready to complete the automation in the Parent bot:

1. Open the Parent bot if you do not have it open already. We will add a variable to store the flag we will receive from the Child bot. We will also add a new dictionary variable called `ChildOutputDict`.

2. Let's then get back to where we left off after the section *Validating email addresses with regular expressions*. We had created a **Step** to invoke the Child bot. Now that we have the Child bot, we'll go ahead and add the action to invoke it. We will also add a **Task Bot Run** action. Select the Child bot we just created for the **Task Bot to run** setting using the **Browse** button. Within the **Input values**, you will already see the variables we passed from the Child bot. Map them to the respective variables in the Parent bot, as shown in the following screenshot. Also, assign the output to the variable we created earlier - `ChildOutputDict` (not shown here; scroll down and add it yourself):

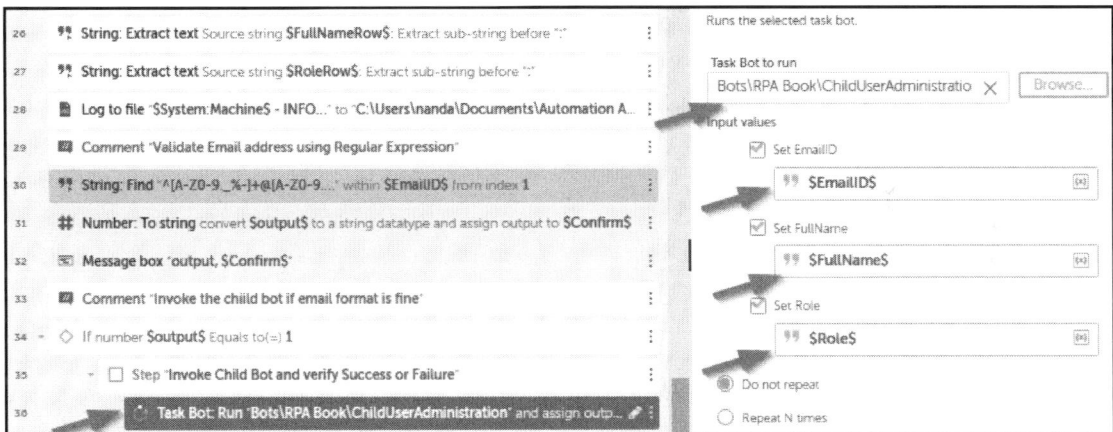

3. Let's read `SuccessFlag` from the `Flag` variable that was passed. For that, add a **String Assign** action and set **Select the source string variable** to `$ChildOutputDict{SuccessFlag}$` (we are reading `SuccessFlag` from the `Dictionary` variable). Then, set **Select the destination string variable** to **Confirm**, as shown here:

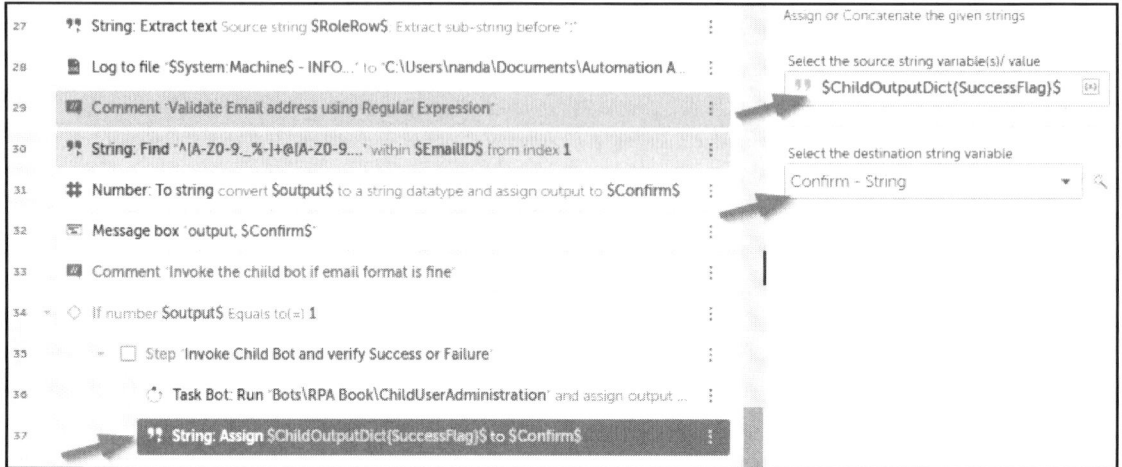

We now have the success flag. Based on this, let's process for success or failure.

Moving the PDF to the Processed folder on success

If the flag is `Success`, the new user was created and we can move the request PDF to the `Processed` folder:

1. Let's check the `Confirm` variable for the flag. To do this, add a new **If** action with **String condition** set to the variables given in the screenshot:

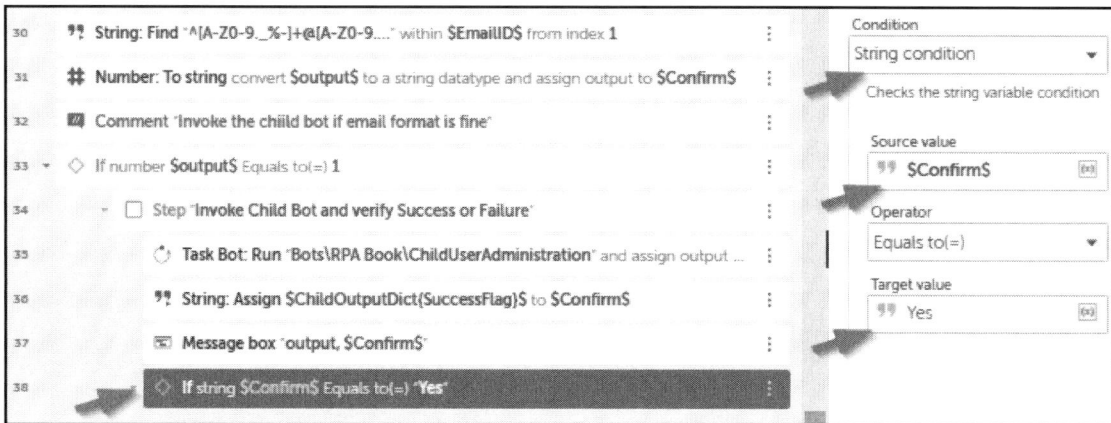

2. Within this **If** action, let's first log a success message. We'll add a **Log to file** action and indicate that the new user was added, as follows:
   `$System:Machine$-INFO - New User Creation was successful.`

3. Since the new user was added successfully, let's move the request PDF file to the `Processed` folder. For that, we will copy and delete the file by means of the following steps:

   - Add a **File Copy** action with the source file as the PDF and the destination folder as the `Processed` folder. You can choose to overwrite existing files.
   - Add a delay of **2 seconds** by adding a **Delay** action.
   - Then, delete the original file by adding a **File Delete** action. Set the file to be deleted as the original PDF file.
   - Add a **Log to file** action and indicate that the file was moved, as follows: `$System:Machine$-INFO - File moved to Processed folder.` Your code for this block would now look like the following:

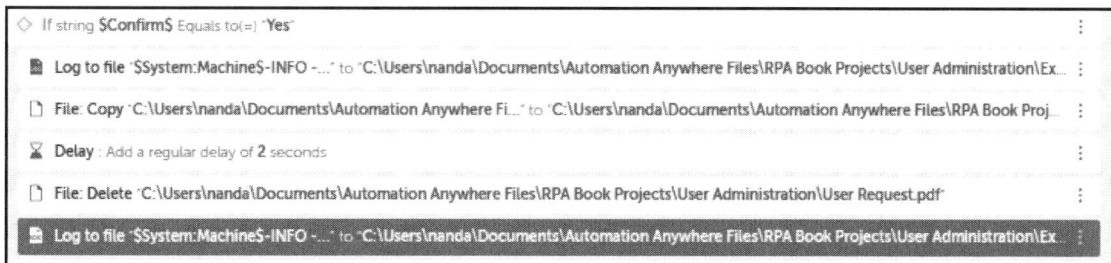

Those were the steps for success. If the new user could not be created, let's email the user and request the missing information from them.

Notifying the user in case of insufficient data

We will email the user if we have a valid email ID:

1. Let's add an **Email Send** action. In the **To address** field, we add the `EmailID` variable and a **Subject** and **Message** body, as shown in the following screenshot. In the **Send email as** property, choose **Outlook** (not shown). You must have **Outlook** on your machine for the bot to be able to send an email with this option:

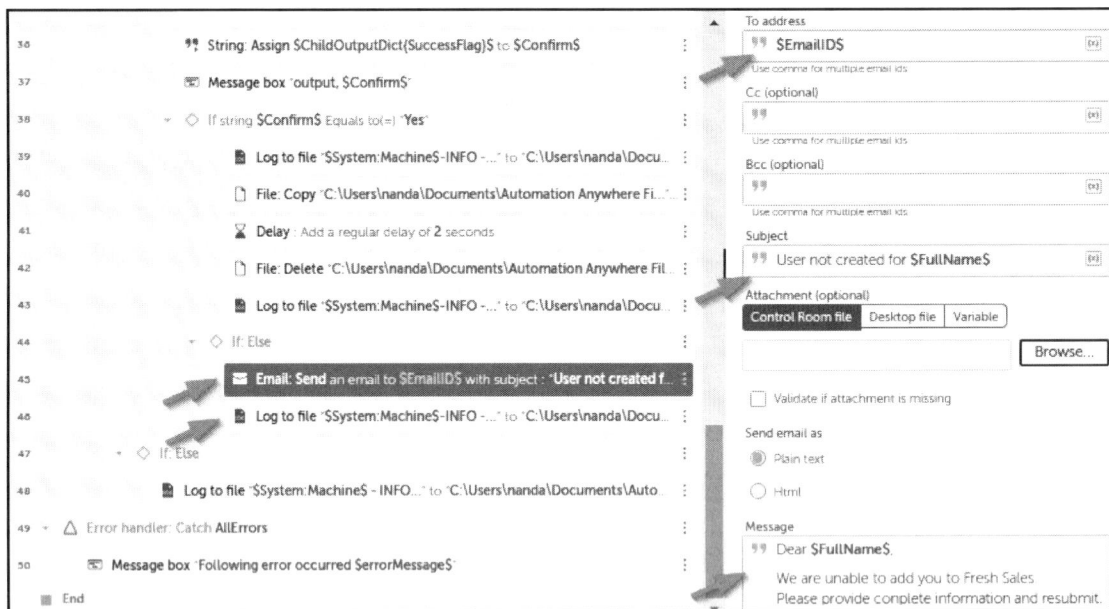

2. Let's also add a **Log File** action to the `ExecutionLog.txt` file path with the text `$System:Machine$-INFO - User Creation failed. Email sent to User.`

We are mostly done with our automation. Let's now add a couple of steps to the **Catch** block we created at the beginning.

Logging errors and sending email notifications

Let's log the error, as well as email the user in case of errors. To do that, copy the log and email steps from the section *Notifying the user in case of insufficient data* or add new ones as follows:

1. We will add a new **Email Send** action. In the **To address** field, we add the EmailID variable, along with a **Subject** and **Message** body, as shown in the following screenshot. In the **Send email as** property, choose **Outlook**:

2. Also, add a **Log File** action to the `ExecutionLog.txt` file path with the text `$System:Machine$- Error- $errorMessage$. User Creation Failed`, as shown in the following screenshot:

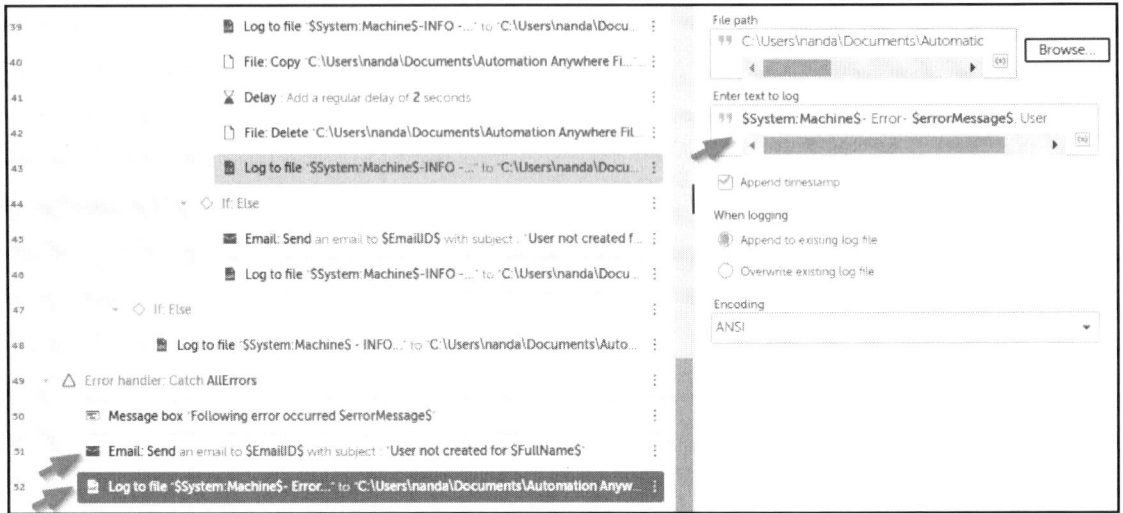

That completes the configuration for the automation. Let's now run it with a file trigger.

Triggers

We can run the automation by itself or by using riggers. Triggers enable you to run a task automatically in response to an event; for example, running the process when there is a change to a file or folder. For this project, we will use **File Trigger** to run the process when the input `UserRequest.pdf` file is created (placed in the input folder).

To do this, use the **File trigger** action from the **Triggers** menu (below the action panel). Provide the properties of the filename and set the **Start the bot when the file is...** field to **created**:

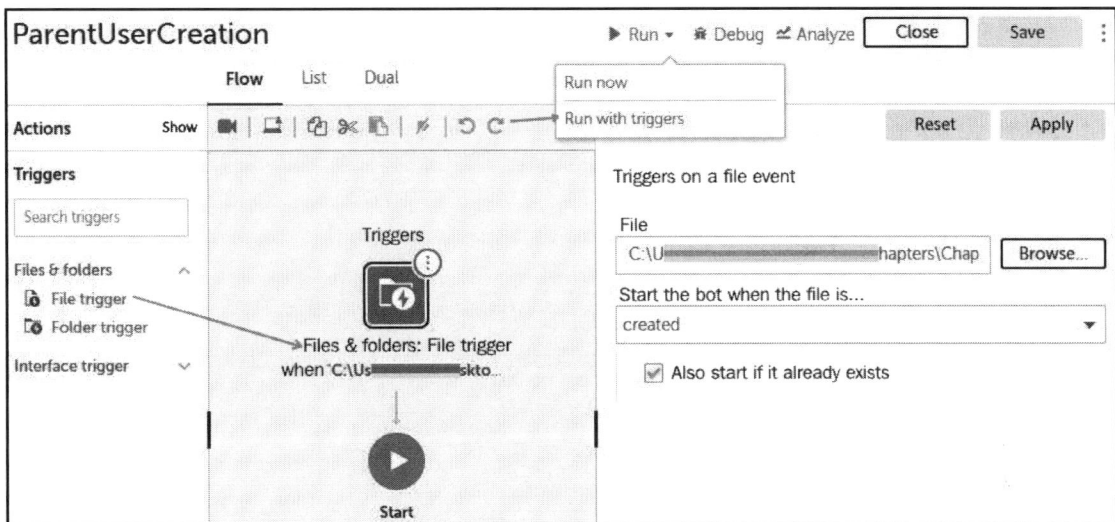

We will now test the automation using this **Run with triggers** option (shown in the preceding screenshot).

Testing the automation

It is now time to test the **User Administration - Add new user** automation. Before we run the automation, let's ensure the following:

- You have a PDF file with the user request information, as we saw in the *Project groundwork* section.
- The email address was never added to Freshsales before. (Please refer to the following info box for more on this.)
- In the Freshsales browser window, ensure that you are on the **Users: Admin Settings** window.

> Note that you have to change the email ID every time you run the test. Freshsales remembers all the emails added. If it sees an email that was already assigned to a user even if the record was deleted.

Once you have got all this right, run the Parent bot using the **Run with triggers** option and specify the input file as `UserRequest.pdf`. Once the file is created, the bot will process the request, add a new user, and place the request PDF in the `Processed` folder.

You can also run for exception scenarios with a role that is not present in the Freshsales **Role** dropdown. The bot should send an email to the user at the email provided (check your Outlook sent folder). All these success- or error-related activities should be logged in your `ExecutionLog` text file as well.

Summary

In this chapter, we automated the administration activity of adding a new user. Our bot took data from a user request PDF file, parsed and validated the data, and added the new user in a web-based application. If the data was insufficient, we emailed the user to ask for more information. In the process, we explored a few new and important concepts – triggers, PDF automation, email automation, using regular expressions, and logging in to a text file.

We thus took another important step with Automation Anywhere A2019. In the next chapter, we will implement a slightly more complex project for a **Human Resources** (**HR**) team to notify employees in case of emergencies.

Employee Emergency Notifications **9**

You may have come across many situations where your organization needs to reach out to employees urgently.

At the time of writing, the world is going through the Covid-19 pandemic. A virus is one such scenario where an emergency notification needs to be sent to employees. Other such scenarios include hurricanes, floods, wildfires, active shooters, and more.

With **Robotic Process Automation (RPA)**, you can look up your HR system, identify the employees by specific criteria (for example, office, region, and so on), and send mass messages. Since RPA looks up the HR system as it sends messages, it will have up-to-date information regarding the employees that need to be notified.

In this chapter, we will be simplifying this by looking up a list of employees and sending them a mass text (SMS) message. We will cover the following topics:

- Twilio
- Automating with A2019 REST actions
- Invoking Twilio APIs to send text messages
- Automation Anywhere A2019 Excel automation
- Using log files in Automation Anywhere A2019
- Exception handling in Automation Anywhere

Technical requirements

The following are the technical requirements you'll need for this chapter:

- Automation Anywhere A2019 Community Edition. Sign up for free at `https://www.automationanywhere.com/products/community-edition`.
- A PC with the Automation Anywhere Community Edition A2019 Bot Agent installed.
- Google Chrome with the Automation Anywhere extension installed.
- Twilio Communication API. Sign up for free at `https://www.twilio.com/`.
- A mobile phone with a carrier service so that you can receive text messages.
- Microsoft Excel 2007 or later.
- Check out the following video to see the Code in Action: `https://bit.ly/2WSgyPj`.

Project overview

We will be sending employee notifications by looking up a list of employees in a spreadsheet. The bot will loop through the employee list, read their names and phone numbers, and send **Short Message Service** (**SMS**) notifications using the Twilio API. This API will log whether the message was sent successfully or not before moving on to the next employee. The bot continues with this process until all the employees on the list have been processed. The following diagram shows the flowchart for this process:

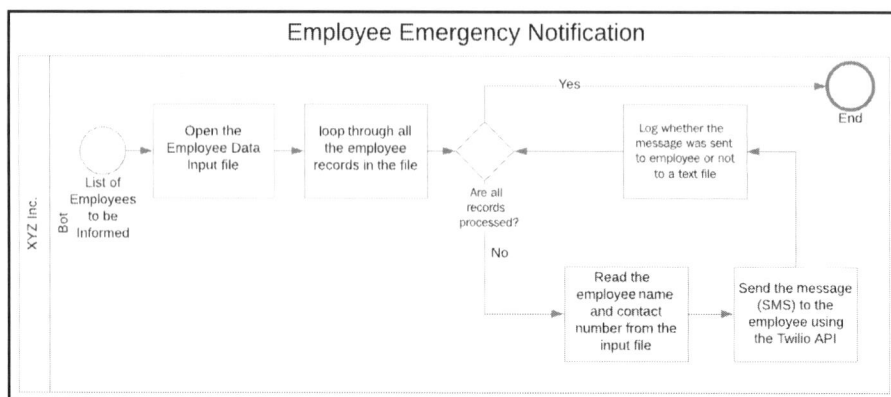

Now that we've provided a quick overview of what we will do in this project, let's take a closer look at the components we'll be using.

Twilio

In this chapter, we will be sending employees text (SMS) messages using a communication API called Twilio.

Twilio is a cloud-based service that enables you to make calls and send and receive texts programmatically. It provides a modern cloud communications platform that your applications can leverage quickly and easily. The key capabilities of the platform are as follows:

- **Voice**: You can use APIs to call landlines and mobile devices from your web and mobile applications.
- **Text/SMS**: You can send and receive SMS and MMS from your web and mobile applications.
- **Video**: You can embed video collaboration into your web and mobile applications.

You may have most likely used Twilio when using apps such as Uber, Airbnb, Netflix, and so on. These apps use Twilio to send you notifications over text or phone. It enables communication for more than 40,000 businesses around the world.

We will be using the Twilio API to send mass text (SMS) messages to employees.

Now, let's take a look at the automation components and complete the project.

Project details

In this section, we will create a Parent bot that will read the employee spreadsheet and invoke the Child bot so that it sends a text message to each employee on the list.

In the Parent bot, we will initialize the variables required to invoke Twilio. Then, we will open the employee Excel sheet, loop through each detail regarding the employee, and invoke the Child bot with the necessary parameters.

The Child bot will take these parameters and invoke the Twilio REST web service in order to send the text message. The Child bot will return a success or failure response to the Parent bot.

In the Parent bot, we will check this response and log it to a file if the message was sent successfully to each employee. A high-level sequence flow showing this process can be seen here:

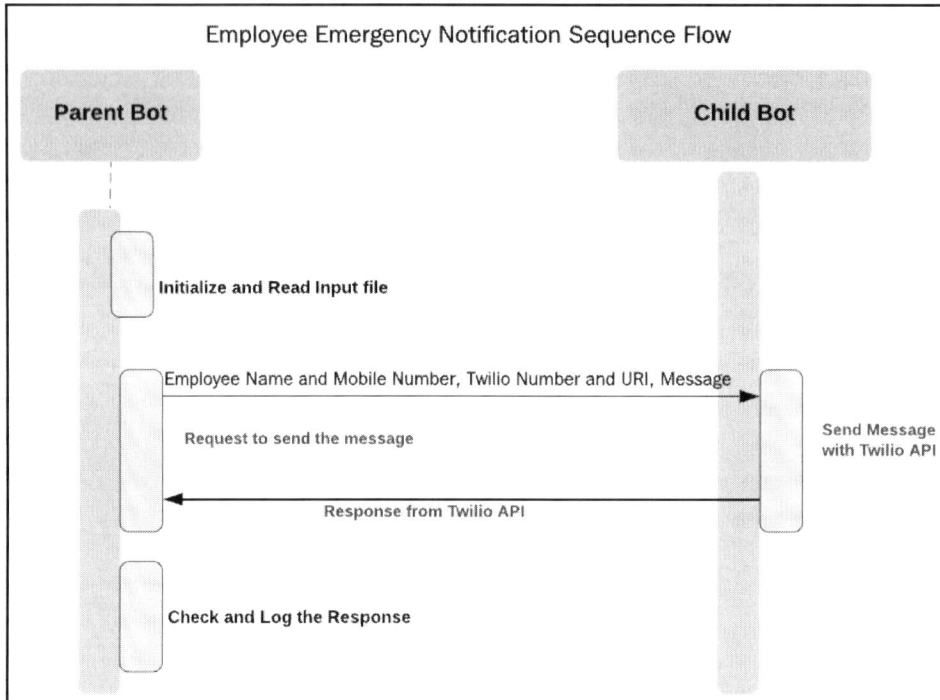

Now, we will start configuring the project. We will do this by covering some project groundwork.

Project groundwork

Before we start creating the bots, let's create the employee spreadsheet, set up Twilio, and open the Automation Anywhere Control Room.

Creating the employee spreadsheet

First, we will create a list of employees that we need to notify in case of an emergency.

Let's build a new Excel spreadsheet with two columns – **Employee Name** and **Mobile Number**. We will keep this simple and only add two rows for testing purposes:

	A	B
1	Employee Name	Mobile Number
2	Arun	150
3	Nandan	15

Now, let's sign up for the Twilio service.

Signing up for Twilio

As we mentioned previously, the key component we will use to send text messages is Twilio.

Follow these steps to sign up for Twilio:

1. Sign up for a free account by going to `Twilio.com`. Provide your details on the sign-up page and submit them.
2. Once you've submitted your details, you'll need to verify your email address. You will also need to validate yourself via phone. A text message containing a verification code will be sent to your phone; simply use that to complete the verification phase.
3. You can skip the next set of screens until you get to the Twilio console dashboard. Once there, get a trial number by clicking on the respective button.
4. On the next screen, you will be asked to confirm the number Twilio has chosen for you.
5. Once confirmed, your trial number will show up on the dashboard.

6. On the dashboard, we need to take note of a few things we'll need for our automation – the trial number, the account SID (user ID), and the auth token (password), as shown in the following screenshot:

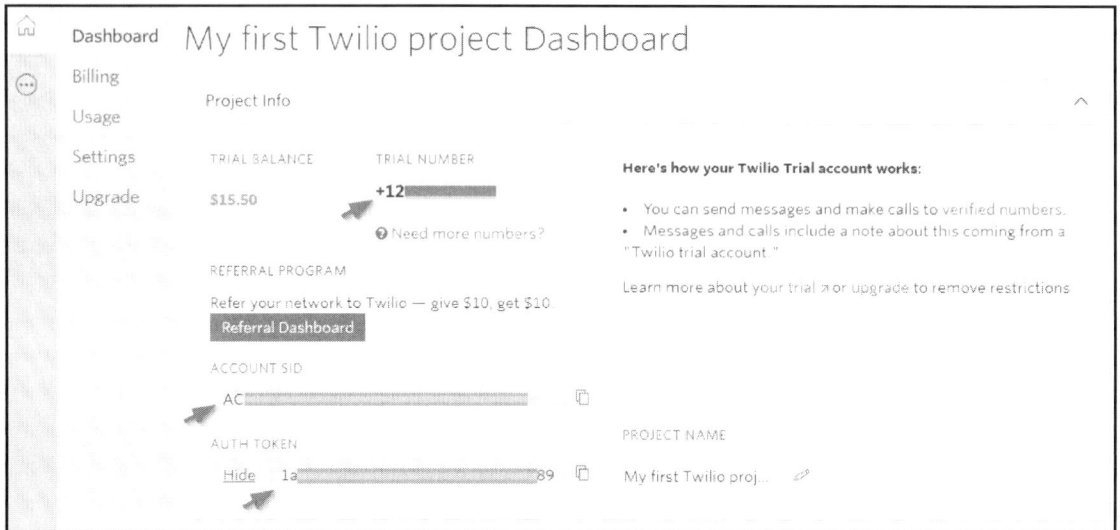

7. Next, we need to configure Twilio so that it can send text messages. First, go to the **Programmable SMS** product option on the left panel. Then, go to the **Messaging Services** option and click on **Create new Messaging Service**, as shown in the following screenshot:

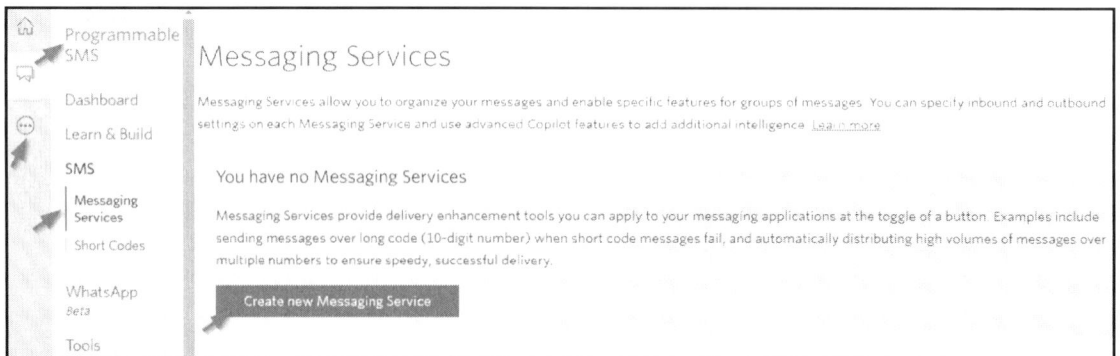

8. On the next screen, choose a name for your new messaging service and set the use case to **Marketing, Outbound only** since we will only be sending one-way text messages for this project:

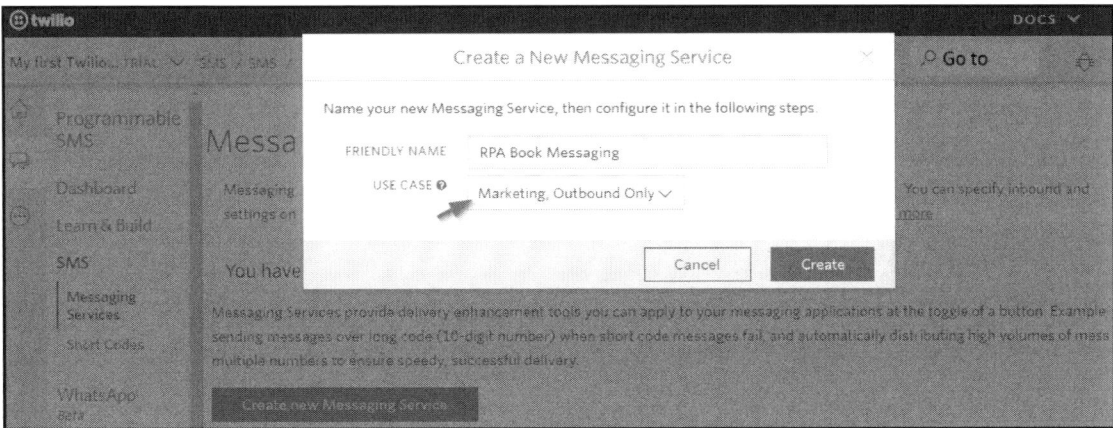

9. Next, we need to associate the trial number with this SMS service. Within the new messaging service we added, go to the **Numbers** option and click on **Add an Existing Number**, as shown in the following screenshot:

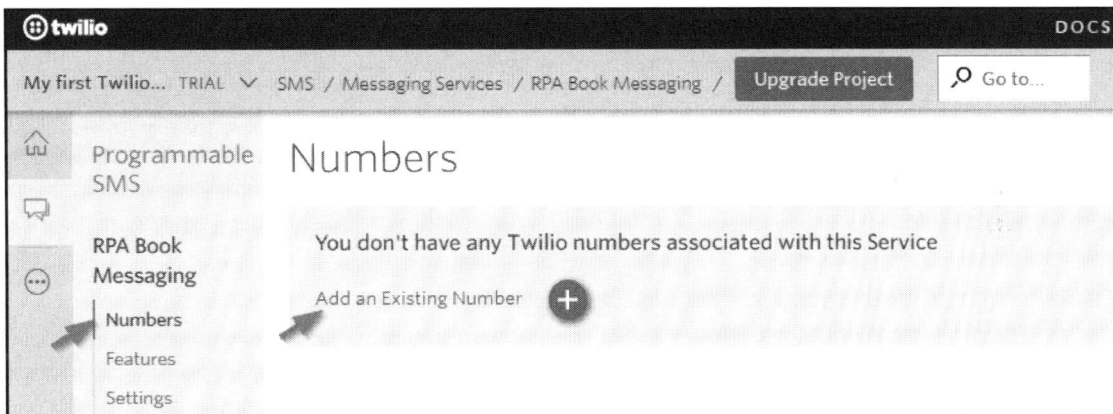

10. On the following screen, choose your trial number and click **Add Selected**:

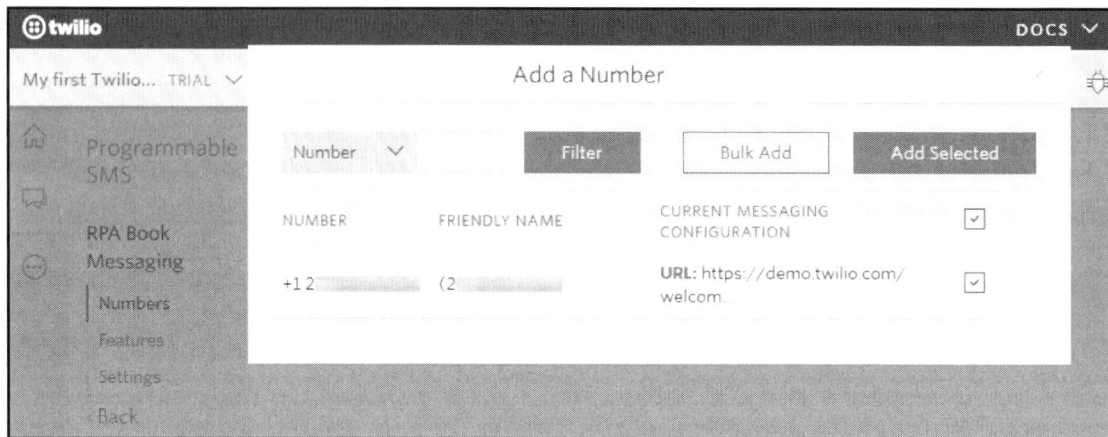

Now, the number will show up under the numbers you have for the service. With that, you have set up the Messaging Service within Twilio.

Since we only have a Twilio trial account, we can only send text messages and make calls to numbers that have been verified through our account. The number that you added at the signup stage will be one of your verified numbers. If you want to send text messages to more numbers, you will have to add and verify them as well. To do that, go to the **Phone numbers** option on the left panel and go to **Verified Caller IDs**. Use the add numbers symbol (the plus sign (+)) shown in the following screenshot to add new numbers and verify them:

> You can purchase the paid version of the Twilio service if you'd like to send messages to any mobile number without having to verify them.

That's all the setting and configuration we need to go through regarding Twilio. Now that we have set up Twilio and are ready to go, let's open A2019 so that we can start building our bots.

Opening the Automation Anywhere A2019 Control Room

As in prior 2019 projects, let's log in to the Automation Anywhere Community Edition Control Room at `https://community.cloud.automationanywhere.digital/#/login`.

Now, we can start creating our bots. For this project, we will create the Child bot first and then build the Parent bot.

Creating a Child bot to send messages

Let's create a Child task bot so that we can invoke the Twilio API and send text messages. We will invoke this from a Parent bot, which will loop through employee names and send employees text messages using the Child bot.

As we did in the previous A2019 projects, let's go to **My Bots** in the A2019 Control Room and create a new bot. We'll start by handling any exceptions.

Exception handling

Let's add an error handler so that we can catch any errors:

1. Look up `Error handler` via the search bar and then drag and drop the **Try** action. We will add all of the automation logic to this **Try** block in the next few sections.

2. Before we do that, we'll add the **Catch** action below the Try one. In the **Catch** action's properties, set the **Exception** type to **AllErrors**.

3. Create a String variable called `errorMessage` to store the error message:

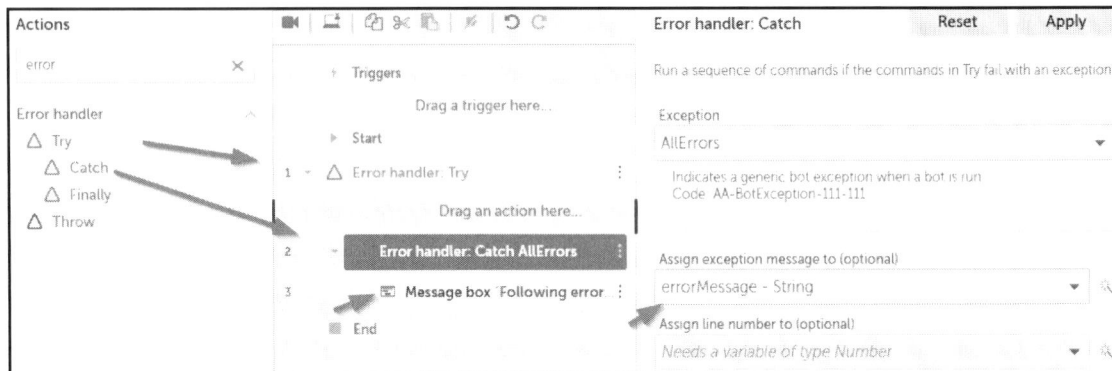

4. In the **Catch** block, also add a message box with the message `Following error occurred $errorMessage$`.

5. Finally, click the **Save** button at the top to save the bot so that we can set up the credential locker.

Saving Twilio credentials

We will save our Twilio ID and password in a secure Automation Anywhere locker in the Control Room. Follow these steps to do so:

1. Go to the **Credentials** option under **Bots** on the left panel.

2. Go over to the **My Lockers** tab and add a locker, if you don't have one already.

3. Choose all the default options. Then, under **Locker consumers**, ensure that you add **CE_user**, as shown in the following screenshot:

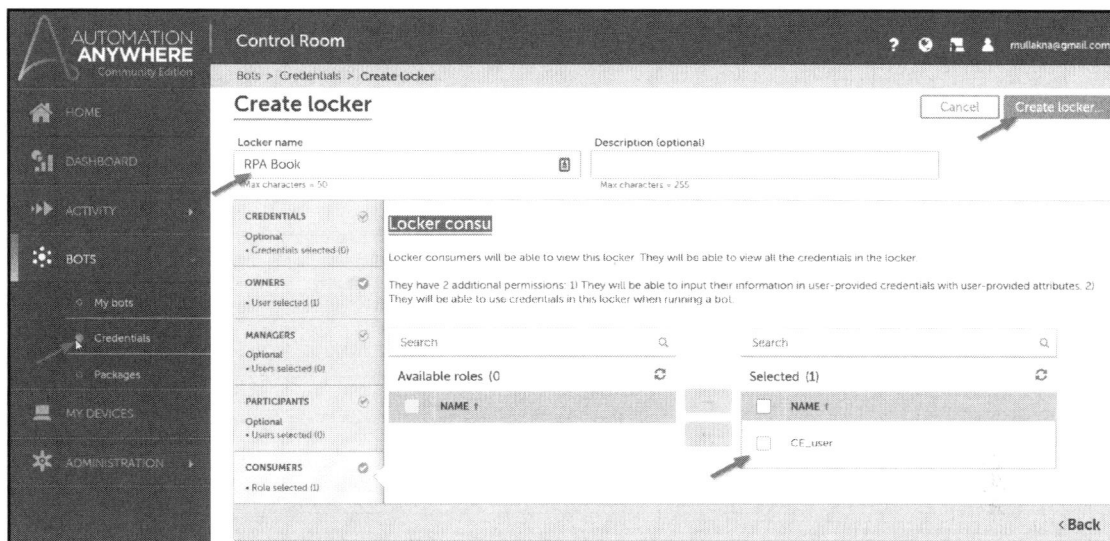

4. Now, let's add the Twilio credentials to the locker we created. Head over to the **My Credentials** tab and click on **create a credential**. We will name our credential `TwilioCredentials`.

5. Under the **General section**, add the **Locker** that we created previously.

6. Under **Attributes**, add the `TwilioID` and `TwilioPassword` attributes. The type should be set to **Standard**, as shown in the following screenshot:

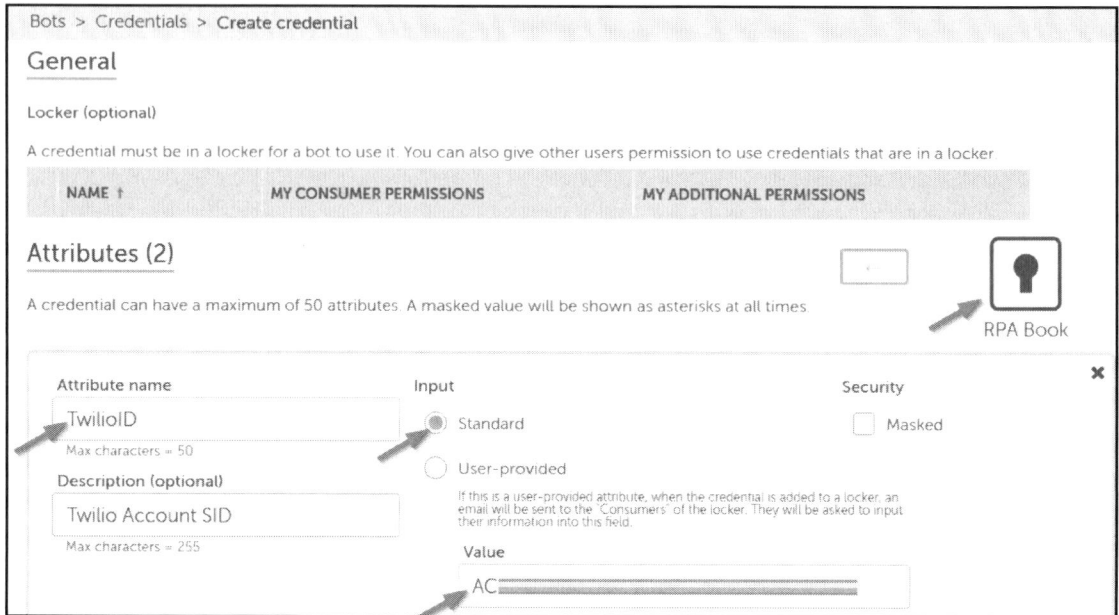

> ℹ️ **TwilioID** and **TwilioPassword** are the Twilio account SID and Twilio account auth token that we noted when we created the Twilio account.

Now that we've added the Twilio credentials to the locker, let's add the variables that are required for this Child bot.

Adding variables for the Child bot

Let's start by creating the variables we will use to populate and invoke the Twilio API. We will also create a variable that will send the response back to the Parent bot.

For the variables that need to receive data from the Parent bot, select the **Use as input** option. For the ones that we need to send back, we will select the **Use as output** option.

Let's add the following variables, which we'll pass from the Parent bot in order to invoke Twilio. Choose the **Use as input** option for all these variables:

- `SenderPhoneNumber`: This is a **String** variable that will be used to hold the phone number we will use to call employees.
- `RecieverPhoneNumber`: This is a **String** variable that we will pass employee phone numbers through.
- `RecieverName`: This is a **String** variable that will be used to pass the employee names.
- `MessageContent`: This is a **String** variable that will be used to pass the emergency notification message body.
- `URI`: This is a **String** variable that will be used to pass the request URI for the POST method.

> The URI should be in the following format: `https://api.twilio.com/2010-04-01/Accounts/ACXXXXXX XXXXXXXXXXXXXXXXXXXXXXXXXXX/Messages.json`. Note that `ACXXXX...` is where you need to place your Twilio SID.

Finally, let's add the response flag we will send back to the Parent bot. Choose the **Use as output** option for this variable:

- `Response`: This is a **String** variable that we will pass as either `Good` or `Bad` to the Parent bot.

Now that we have the necessary variables, we are ready to invoke Twilio.

Invoking the Twilio REST post method

Now, we will use the credentials and variables with the values from the Parent bot and invoke some Twilio REST web services:

1. Within the **Try** block, add the **REST Web Services Post method** action. Let's add the URI variable we added as the **URI** property. Next, set **Authentication Mode** to **Basic**. For the **Username**, pick TwilioCredentials, TwilioID from the credential locker that we created previously. For the **Password**, pick TwilioCredentials, TwilioPassword, as shown in the following screenshot:

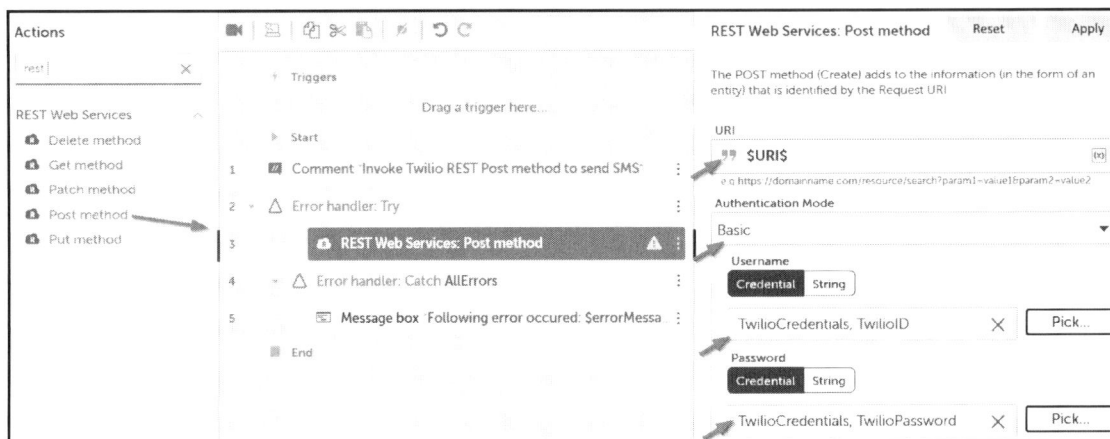

2. Staying on the REST action properties, let's scroll down and set the content type to **application/x-www-form-urlencoded**. Now, add the following **Custom parameters**:

Name	Value
Body	Hello $RecieverName$ $MessageContent$
From	**$SenderPhoneNumber$**
To	$RecieverPhoneNumber$

3. Finally, let's assign the output to a variable. Click on the wizard near the input box and create a new dictionary variable called **output**. Your REST properties will look like this:

Now that we have our output from the REST action, let's read it to check whether the message was sent successfully and take the appropriate action.

Returning a response flag to the Parent bot

We will return a Good or Bad flag to the Parent bot based on the output we get back from Twilio. Follow these steps to do so:

1. First, let's read the Connection property from the output dictionary variable. This contains the Twilio REST response. We will use the **String Assign** action to assign the value of $output{Connection}$ to a new String variable called OutputResponse:

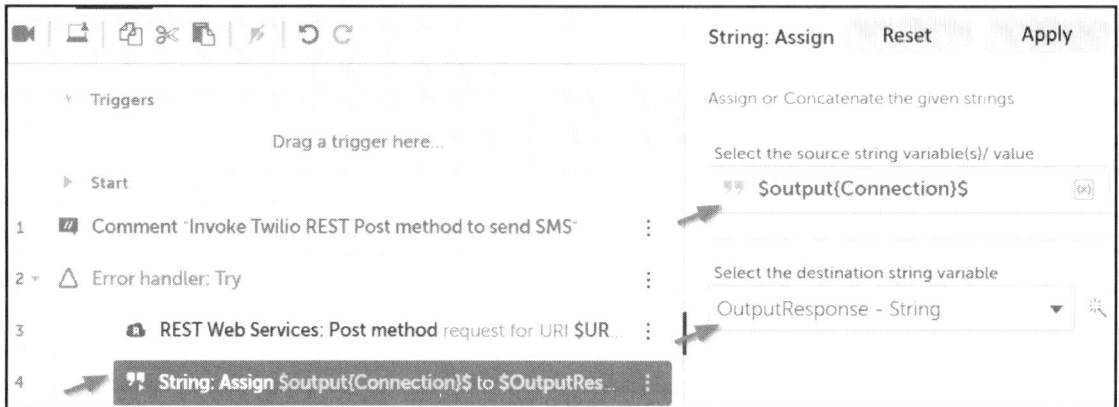

2. Now, we'll use an If condition to check this OutputResponse and set the return flag for the Parent bot. We will check $OutputResponse$ for the **target value** of keep-alive. Within the If condition, since the response is good, we'll use **String Assign** to assign a value of Good to the Response output variable, as shown in the following screenshot:

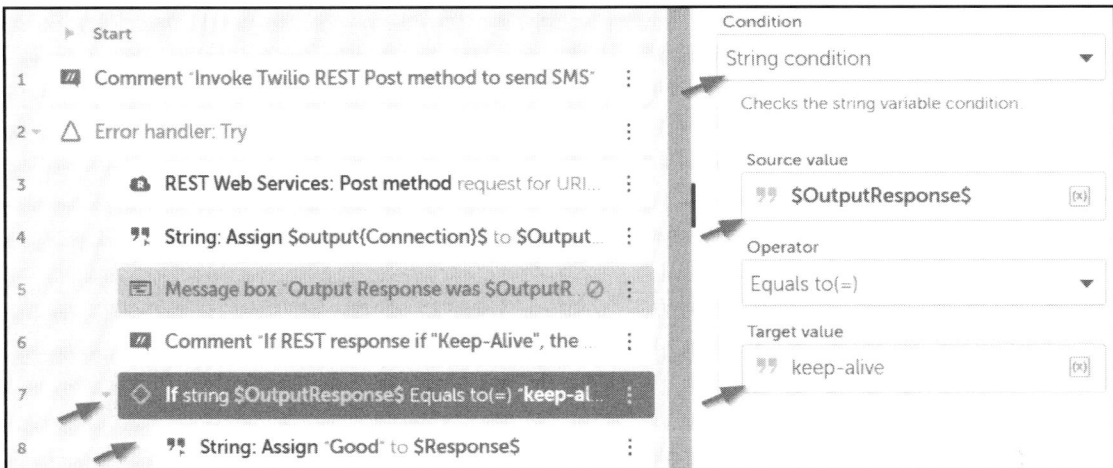

3. If the response isn't good, then we'll need to send a bad response within the **If Else** action. Let's add another **String Assign** so that we can assign a value of `Bad` to the `Response` output variable, as shown in the following screenshot:

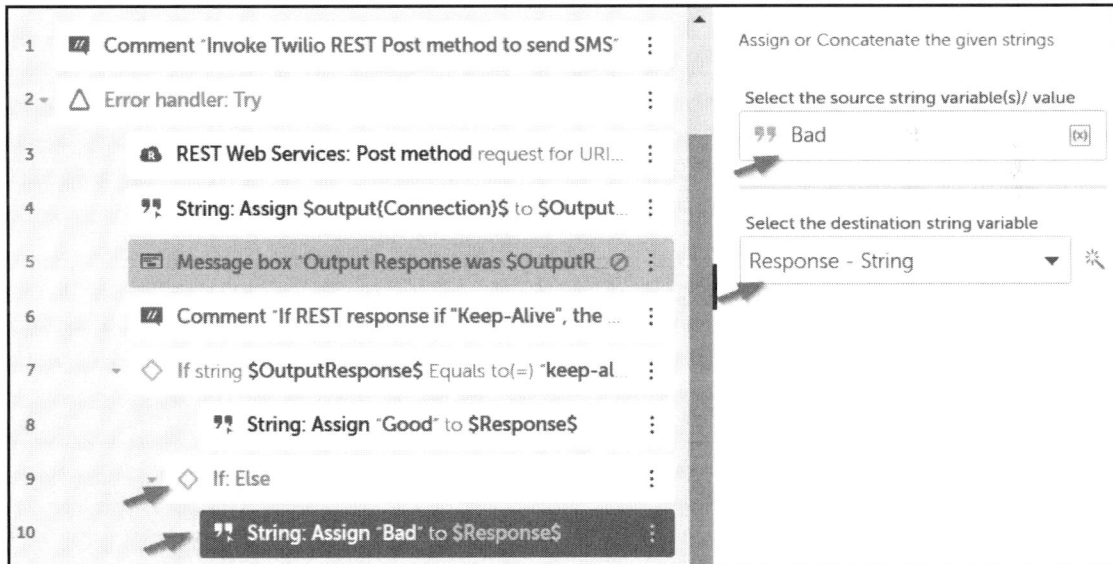

4. Finally, we'll also return a bad response if there are any errors. So, within the **Error handler** we added earlier, let's add another **String Assign** and assign a value of Bad to the Response output variable, as shown in the following screenshot:

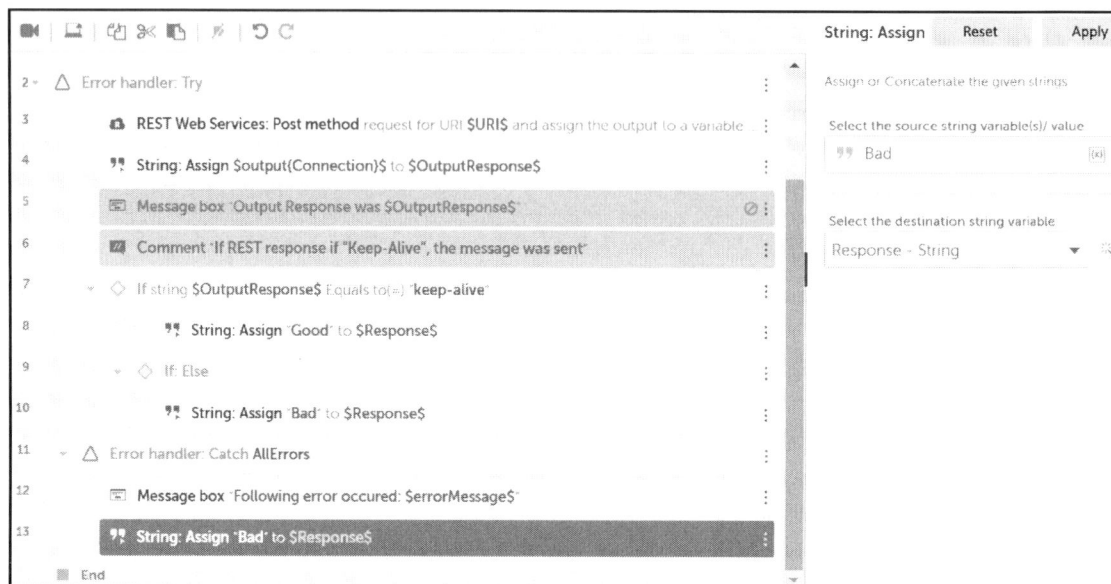

Now that we have finished configuring the Child bot, let's unit test it.

Unit testing the Child bot

This is an optional step before we build the Parent bot. We can unit test the Child bot and check if it is sending the messages as intended. To do so, follow these steps:

1. Let's add two log messages so that we can check whether the bot sent the message successfully or not. We will add these within the **If** and **If Else** conditions we added in the previous section. Add two **Log to file** actions and point them to a text file. This is where we'll be storing log messages. Your log messages can be in one of the following formats:

    - For success (Within an **If** condition): $System:Machine$ – INFO – Message Successfully sent by Child Bot
    - For failure (Within an **If Else** condition): $System:Machine$ – INFO – Message send failed in Child Bot:

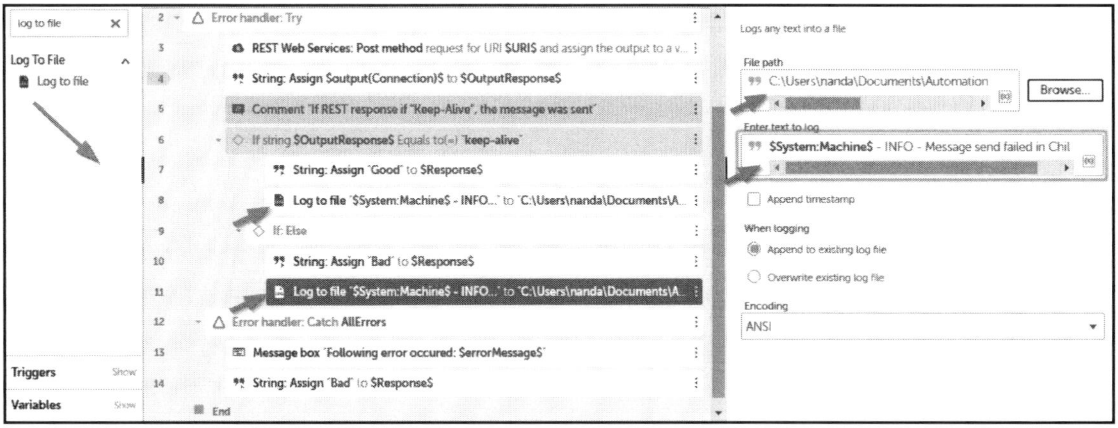

2. Next, go ahead and **Run** the Child bot from the top menu. The A2019 Control Room should appear and provide you with input boxes, as shown in the following screenshot. Provide your values from the Twilio console for the obfuscated areas. Note that in the URI, the obfuscated area is the Twilio account SID. **SenderPhoneNumber** is the trial number from Twilio, while **ReceiverPhoneNumber** can be any of your Twilio validated caller IDs:

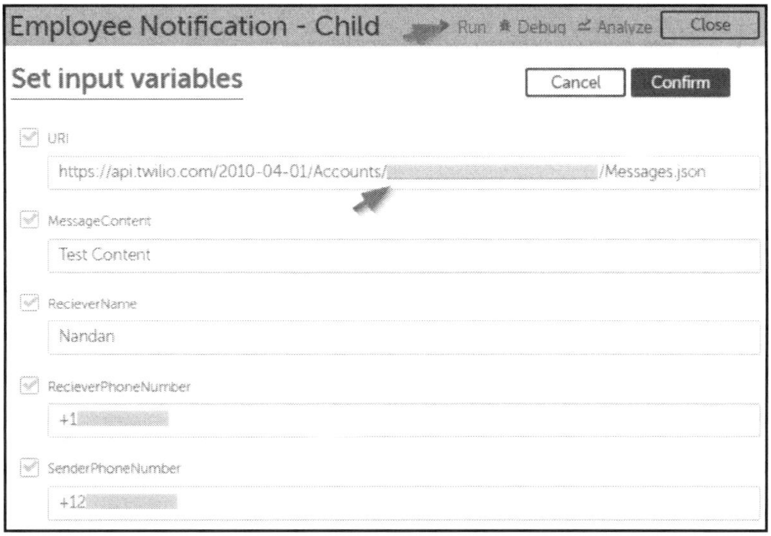

If all goes well, the Child bot should run successfully and your log file will have an entry stating that the message was sent successfully by the Child bot. You should also receive an SMS on your phone with the message that you sent.

Now that the Child bot is ready and we can send messages with it, let's create the Parent bot.

Creating the Parent bot

Our Parent bot for this project will read the employee list from Excel and invoke the Child bot in order to send a message. Then, we will need to log the response from the Child bot and handle any errors.

We'll start by initializing the variables for Twilio.

Initializing Twilio and opening the employee Excel file

First, we will initialize the common Twilio data and open the employee Excel file so that we can loop through the list of employees:

1. We'll add a **Step** action and name it `Initialize and Open Excel File`. There are two Twilio values that are constant for this bot as they are not based on the Excel data. Let's initialize these variables first:
   - We'll use **String Assign** to assign the trial phone number we received from Twilio to a new **String** variable called `SenderPhoneNumber`. You can use the wizard at the end of the input box to create the new variables.
   - Similarly, we'll also assign the Twilio Account SID to a new **String** variable called `TwilioID`, as shown in the following screenshot:

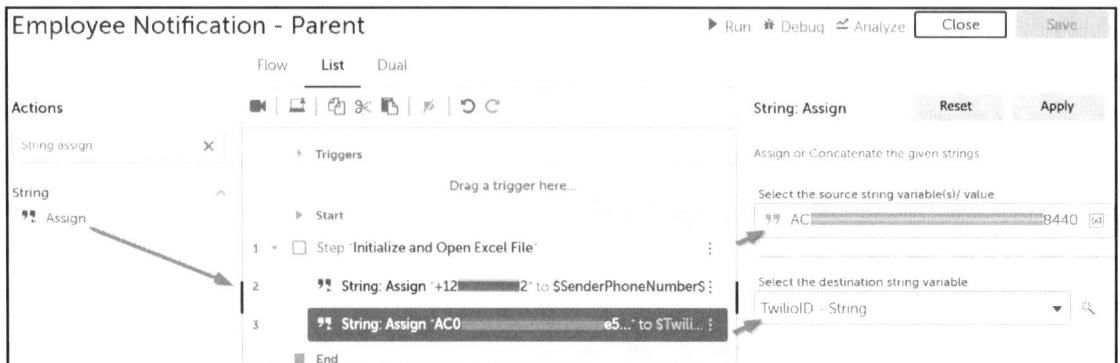

2. Now, let's open the Excel file so that we can loop through and read employee details. Add the **Excel basic Open** action and provide a desktop **File path** for the employee Excel file. You can provide a **Session name** and open the sheet in read-only mode, as shown in the following screenshot:

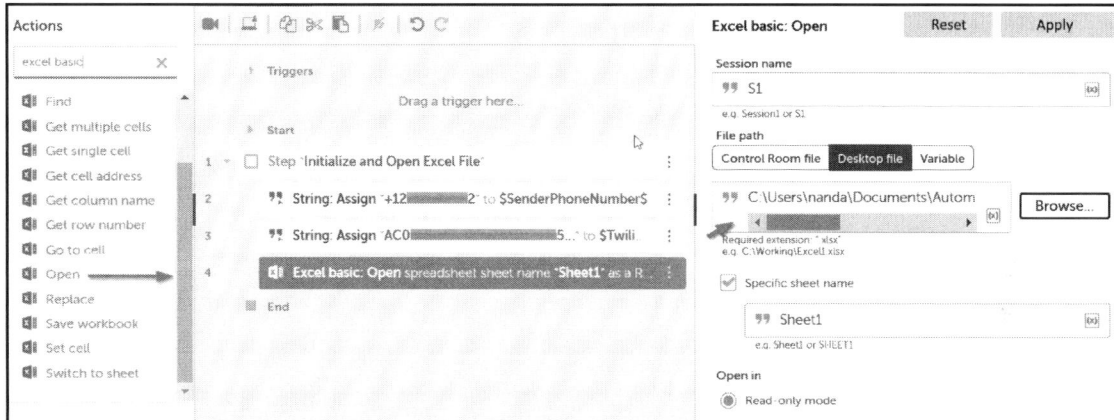

Note that the **Sheet contains a header** (not shown) since our Excel file has a header.

Now that we have opened the Excel file, we are ready to loop through and send messages to each employee.

Looping through the employee list and sending text messages

In this section, we will read each of the Excel rows and invoke the Child bot so that we can send messages to employees on the list:

1. Let's add another **Step** action so that we can logically separate out this block. Add a **Step** Action and name it `Loop through Employee List and send Text Messages`.

2. Within this Step, add a **Loop** Action. We will iterate for each row in the worksheet and assign the current value to a new **Record** variable, which we will call CurrentRow, as shown in the following screenshot:

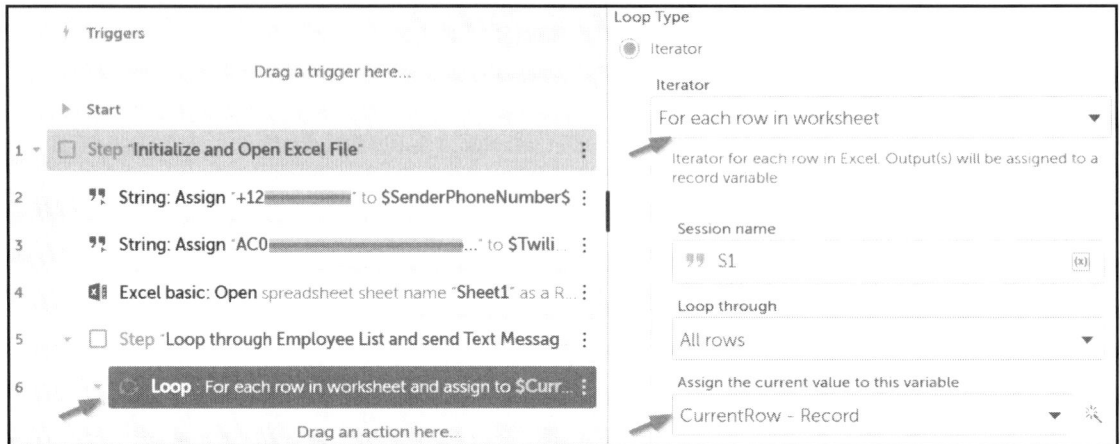

3. Now, we can get the employee name and number from this record variable. As you may recall, Employee Name was in the first column and Employee Number was in the second column. Let's assign them to two new variables:
   - Use **String: Assign** to assign $CurrentRow[0]$ (the first column) to a new **String** variable called ReceiverName.
   - Also, add another **String: Assign** to assign the next column, $CurrentRow[1]$, to another new **String** variable called ReceiverPhoneNumber, as shown in the following screenshot:

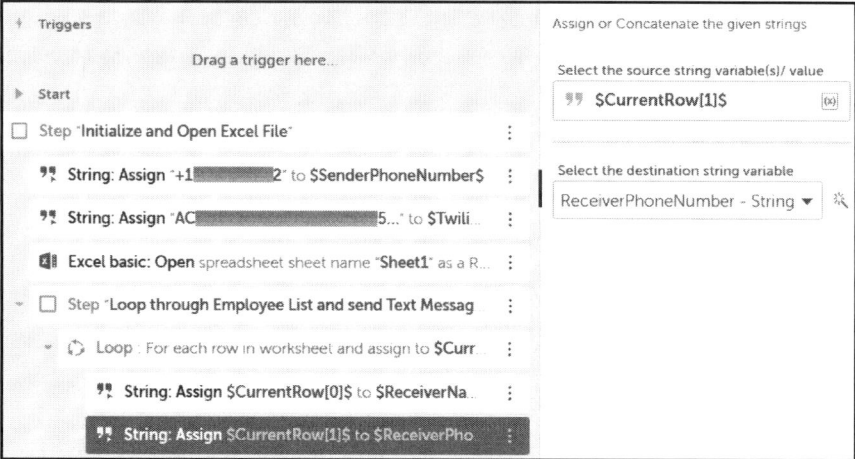

4. We'll add a message that we need to send. You can send any message you like; for example, we added `Due to Virus outbreak, please work from home. Thanks, HR`. Then we'll assign this to a new variable called `MessageContent`.

5. Let's also assign the URI that we need to invoke the Twilio REST API. It is of the following format: `https://api.twilio.com/2010-04-01/Accounts/<Your Twilio Account SID>/Messages.json`. Note that you need to add your Twilio account SID to the URI, as shown in the following screenshot:

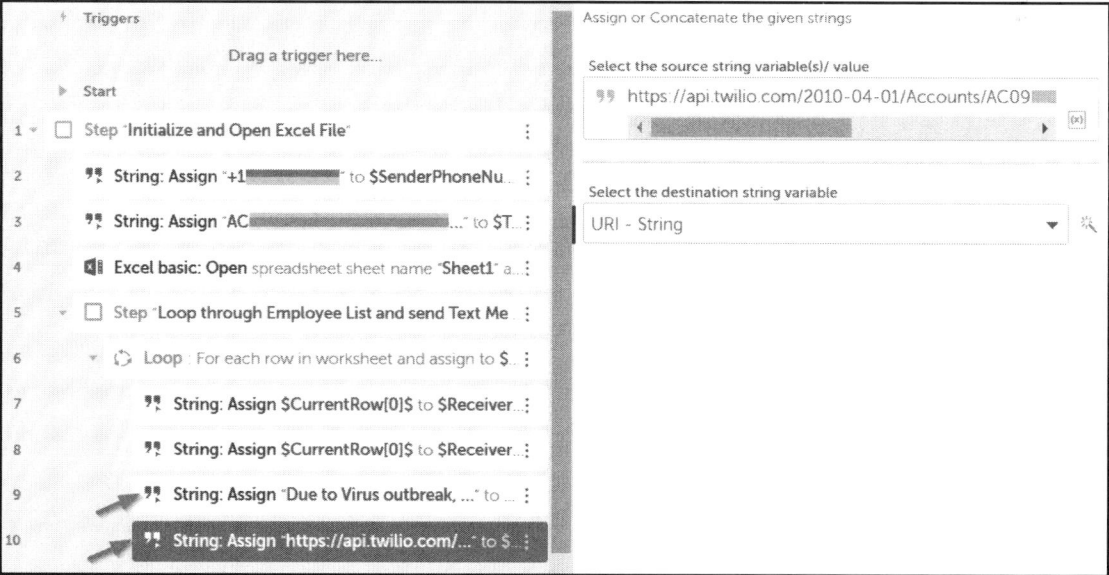

The current edition of A2019 does not allow us to invoke credential attributes in normal variables. Therefore, we have to hardcode the Twilio SID in the URI.

6. Finally, let's add a **Dictionary** variable so that we can capture the output we will get when we invoke the Child bot. Call it `TaskOutputDictionary`. Set it to **Use as output**, as shown in the following screenshot:

7. Now, we have populated all the necessary variables so that we can invoke the Child bot. Let's add the **Task Bot Run** Action. Browse to the Child bot we created for this project and select it as the Task Bot to run. Map each of the **Input values** from the Child bot to the respective variables we created previously, as shown in the following screenshot:

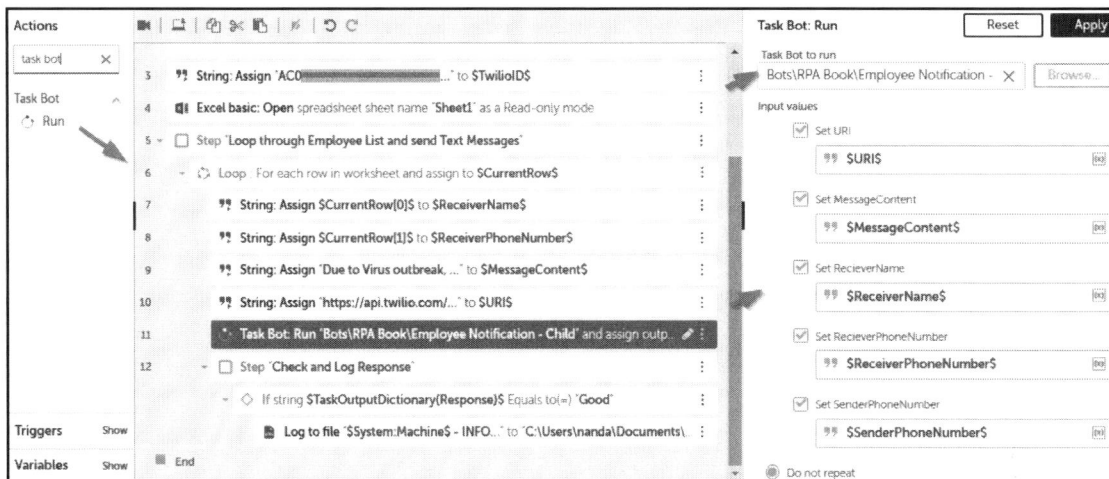

Scroll down and check **Upon error, continue with next repeat**. Also, **Assign the output to variable**, that is, `TaskOutputDictionary`, we created previously (not shown).

Now that we have invoked the Child bot with the required parameters, let's check the response.

Checking and logging responses from the Child bot

Now, we will read the response from the `TaskOutputDictionary` variable and log the response that we sent from the Child bot:

1. Let's add another **Step** Action called `Check and Log Response`.

2. Within this **Step**, add an **If** condition to check whether the response is Good. Add an **If** Action with the **String Condition**, that is, $TaskOutputDictionary{Response}$, equal to Good, as shown in the following screenshot:

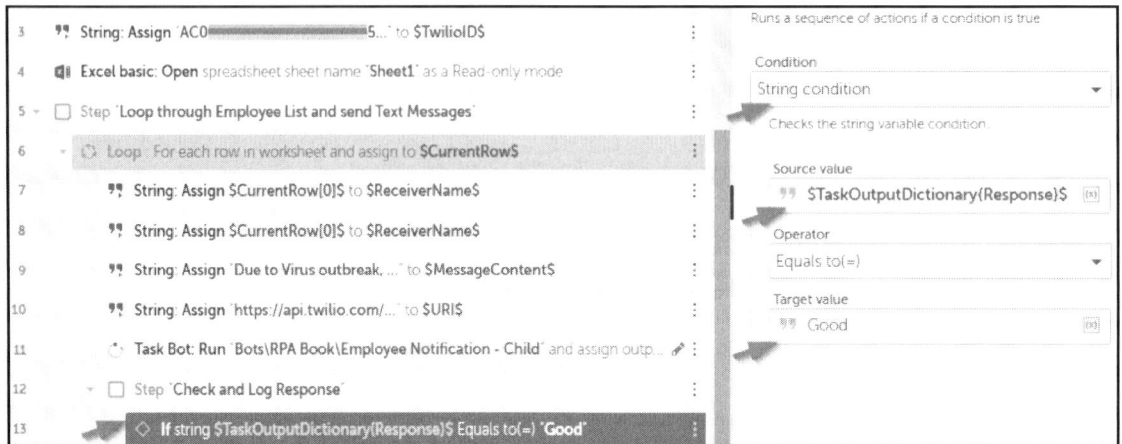

3. If the response you receive is Good, we can log that the message was sent successfully. Let's add a **Log to file** Action and provide the **File path** of the text file where we'd like to log messages for this bot. For the text we wish to log, we can add $System:Machine$ - INFO - Message Successfully sent to $ReceiverName$. We'll also use **Append Timestamp** and choose to **Append to existing log file**, as shown in the following screenshot:

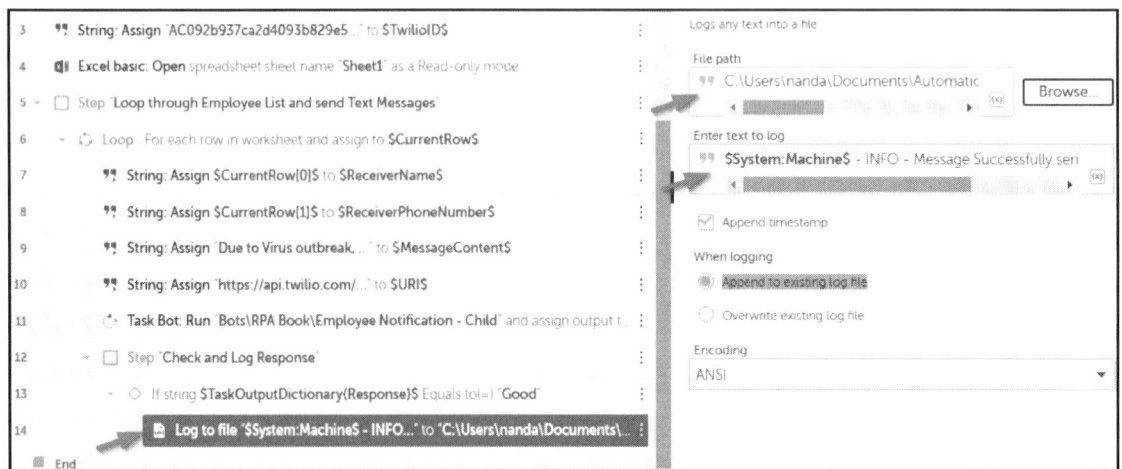

4. If the response is `Bad`, we need to add a log entry. Add an **If Else** action and another **Log to file** Action below it. Log to the same file we logged to previously with **text to log** set to `$System:Machine$ - INFO - Message could NOT be sent to $ReceiverName$`.

5. Now that we have finished messaging the employees on the list, we can close the Excel file. Add an **Excel Basic Close** Action and choose the session we just used, as shown in the following screenshot:

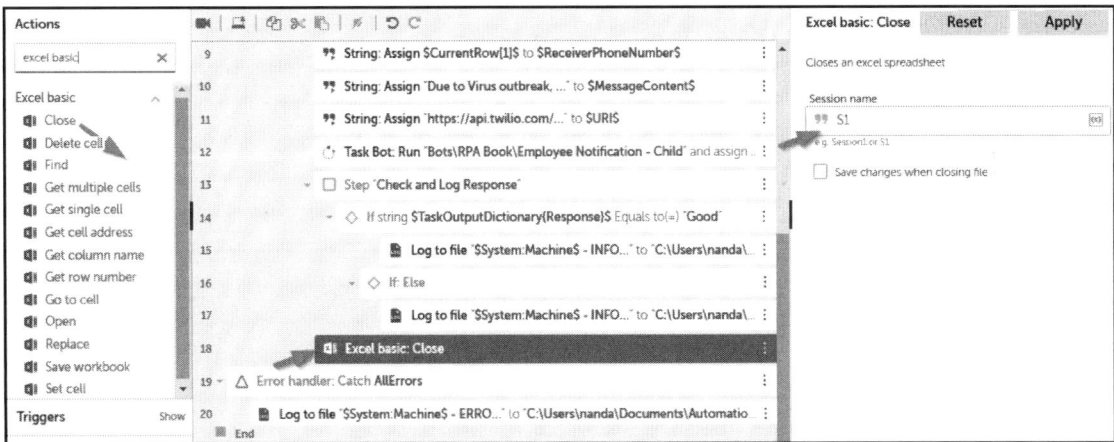

Now, let's add some exception handling to this bot before we perform end-to-end testing.

Exception handling in the Parent bot

We can add the Try-Catch block and log any errors by following these steps:

1. Let's add the **Error Handler Try** Action at the beginning of the code as shown below. Move the steps we have completed so far into the Try block. Just drag the first **Step** Action into the Try block; all the steps will move into the Try block.

2. Next, we'll add the Error Handler Catch block at the end. In the Catch properties, set the **Exception** type to `AllErrors`. Create a String variable called `errorMesage` to store the error message.

3. Within this Catch block, let's log errors. To do this, add a **Log to file** Action with a message stating `$System:Machine$ - ERROR - Bot failed with exception: $errorMessage$`.

Your overall configuration for the Parent bot, including exception handling, will look as follows:

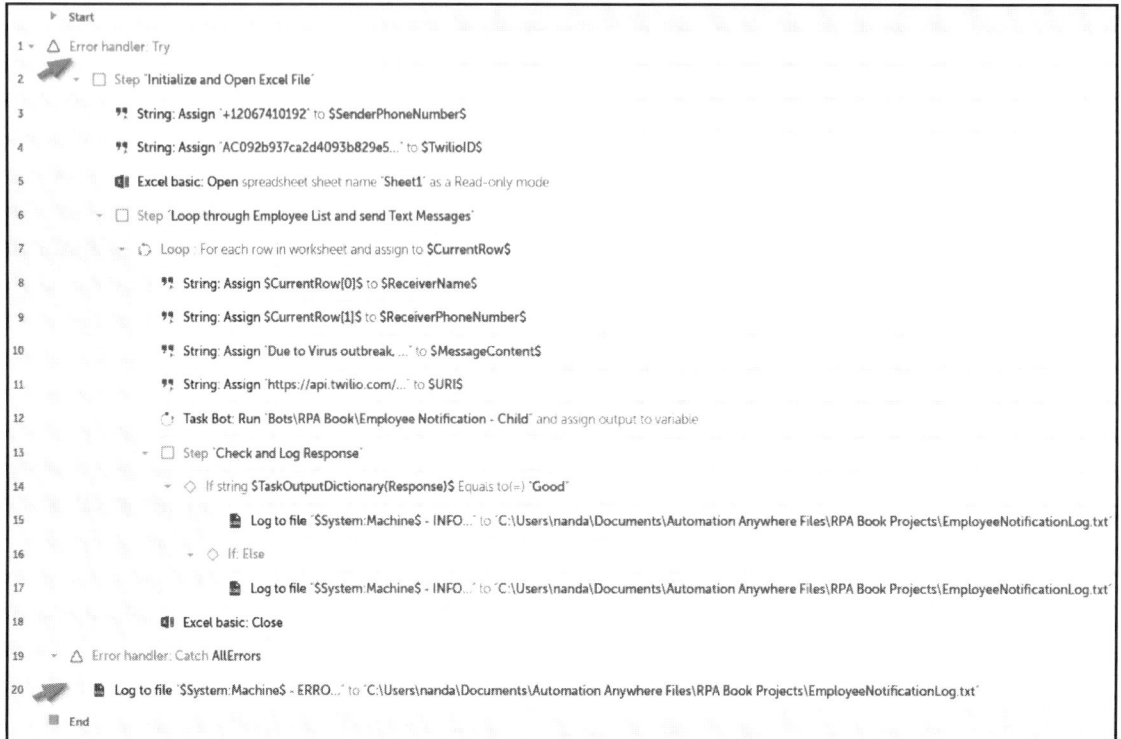

Now that we have finished configuring the Parent and Child bots, let's test them.

Testing the automation

Now, it's time to test the Employee Notification project.

Before we run the automation, we need to ensure that we have the Excel sheet containing the list of employees in the specified location. The receiver phone numbers must be the ones on your Twilio Verified Caller IDs list, as we discussed in the *Project groundwork* section.

Go ahead and run the Parent bot. If all goes well, you should receive text messages at the numbers you had on the sheet. You will also see success messages in the log file.

If you run into any errors or the bot couldn't send text messages to any of the numbers, they will be logged in the log file. You may have to troubleshoot and debug any errors you come across.

Summary

In this chapter, we've completed a relatively complex project so that we can send text messages with Twilio using the REST API. We hope you found this project easier to complete since you have a few A2019 projects under your belt.

In the next chapter, we will learn how to use **Artificial Intelligence** (**AI**) with RPA to process documents.

See you there!

10
Using AI and RPA for Invoice Processing

In this chapter, we will complete our first project with Automation Anywhere RPA and **Artificial Intelligence** (**AI**).

We will use the Automation Anywhere IQ Bot to convert invoice data from an unstructured format into a structured format that we can use for automation. IQ Bot is an intelligent document processing platform from Automation Anywhere that can be used to classify, extract, and validate content from documents. IQ Bot allows us to process unstructured data using AI technologies such as computer vision, **Natural Language Processing** (**NLP**), **Machine Learning** (**ML**), and text classification.

More than 80% to 90% of data in organizations is placed in documents and forms. So, processing documents is one of the common requirements for most automation use cases.

We will learn about basic document processing and more in this chapter. More specifically, we will cover the following topics:

- Using basic AI with RPA
- Document processing using IQ Bot
- Creating learning instances for document processing
- Invoking IQ Bot with the A2019 Task Bot
- Downloading unstructured data from IQ Bot

Technical requirements

The following are the technical requirements you'll need for this chapter:

- Automation Anywhere A2019 Community Edition. Sign up at `https://www.automationanywhere.com/products/community-edition`.
- A PC with the Automation Anywhere Community Edition A2019 Bot Agent installed.
- Google Chrome with the Automation Anywhere extension installed.
- Sample invoices to process. You can download this from the A2019 IQ Bot.
- Microsoft Excel 2007 or any program that can be used to view CSV files.
- Check out the following video to see the Code in Action: `https://bit.ly/3cOZCi0`.

Intelligent document processing

When we started using RPA in our organization, one of the major difficulties we faced was the need to process a large volume of documents. Since these documents and forms contribute to a bulk of the data in the enterprise, this is the experience of many early RPA practitioners.

The traditional way to process documents with RPA was to use **Optical Character Recognition (OCR)**. This technology has many limitations when it comes to different document formats, interpreting natural language, and detecting blurred and scanned text. Without intelligence, OCR is not accurate and impedes straight-through processing.

Now that we can use AI with RPA, we have the ability to perform **Intelligent Document Processing (IDP)**, which uses ML to read, classify, and extract the data in these documents into structured data. The documents that usually need processing include emails, forms, PDF documents, and scanned documents. With IDP, we can use the generated structured data to automate more processes end to end.

We will be looking at this option of using AI for IDP and enabling straight-through processing for our automation. Also, RPA with AI – Cognitive Automation - is one of the most promising areas in RPA. This is the reason we have included this topic – so that you can some experience in this evolving area.

Both UiPath and Automation Anywhere offer IDP solutions. Let's take a look at them.

UiPath – Document Understanding

The Document Understanding offering from UiPath can be used to extract data from a wide range of document types.

The major phases of this solution are as follows:

- **Load Taxonomy**: This is the form and fields hierarchy and will be used for classification and extraction.
- **Digitize**: Uses different OCR engines to digitize the document into a machine-readable format.
- **Classify**: Classifies document types; for example, claims, invoices, and receipts.
- **Extract**: Extracts data from forms, such as name and date of birth.
- **Validate**: Validates and corrects the extracted data against the data in the document.
- **Export**: Exports the data as an output file; for example, Excel.

There are different OCR engines that are shipped with this package that can be used to digitize the documents in different formats, such as PDF, TIFF, JPEG, and so on. Classifying and extracting the content is done with position-based form extractors.

ML extraction is also available for specific formats such as invoices, receipts, and purchase orders. Custom machine models can be built for specific cases too. An interesting aspect of this solution is that it allows us to mix and match available form extractors and machine leaning extractors at the field level of the forms.

Automation Anywhere – IQ Bot

The IQ Bot offering from Automation Anywhere uses machine learning to extract structured or semi-structured data from documents.

IQ Bot uses AI technologies such as machine learning, computer vision, and NLP to learn and extract information from business documents and emails.

The main features of IQ Bot are as follows:

- **Classification**: IQ Bot uses AI-based learning algorithms to recognize and classify content.
- **Digitization**: It does not rely on traditional OCR. Instead, it uses the latest computer vision technologies to intelligently digitize documents.
- **Continuous learning**: It learns from user feedback and validation, thereby improving its classification and extraction accuracy over time.

There are five key phases of the IQ Bot process:

- Create a learning instance
- Review and update field mapping
- Load documents to classify and extract data
- Output the extracted data
- Validate forms with issues

And if necessary, retrain the learning instance. We will be covering most of these phases in this chapter.

Now, let's look at the project components and how we can perform intelligent document processing for invoices using the Automation Anywhere IQ Bot.

Project overview

In this project, we will create a bot that will use RPA and AI to process invoices.

First, we will create an IQ Bot learning instance so that we can classify invoices and extract invoice details from PDFs and place them in a CSV file. The IQ Bot will learn our invoice format using AI and process them.

Then, we will use an A2019 Task Bot to feed the invoices that we'd like to process. We will loop through each file in the Invoice inputs folder and upload them to the IQ Bot Learning instance we'll create.

Once the Upload bot has run successfully, we will be able to download the CSV files from the IQ Bot. We will use another Task Bot to download the CSV files and verify the data contained within them. If there are any shortcomings, we can retrain the IQ Bot.

The overall workflow is as follows:

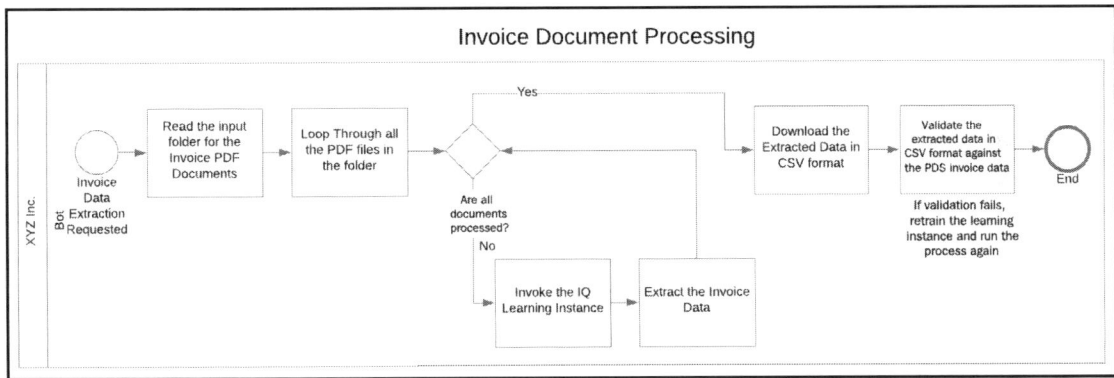

What we are doing here is intelligent document processing using AI. This is an important area where RPA is making a difference in enterprises. Now, let's take a look at the project's components.

Project details

Processing invoices containing unstructured data in PDF files and changing them into structured data in the form of CSV files involves two steps. Let's take a look:

1. **Creating a learning instance**: We need to create a learning or training instance by feeding a few sample invoice documents for the AI (IQ Bot) to learn from. Then, we need to review and confirm or correct the mappings so that the AI learns the fields correctly. The IQ Bot is then ready to process invoices that are uploaded to it and convert them into structured CSV files. This can be seen in the following diagram:

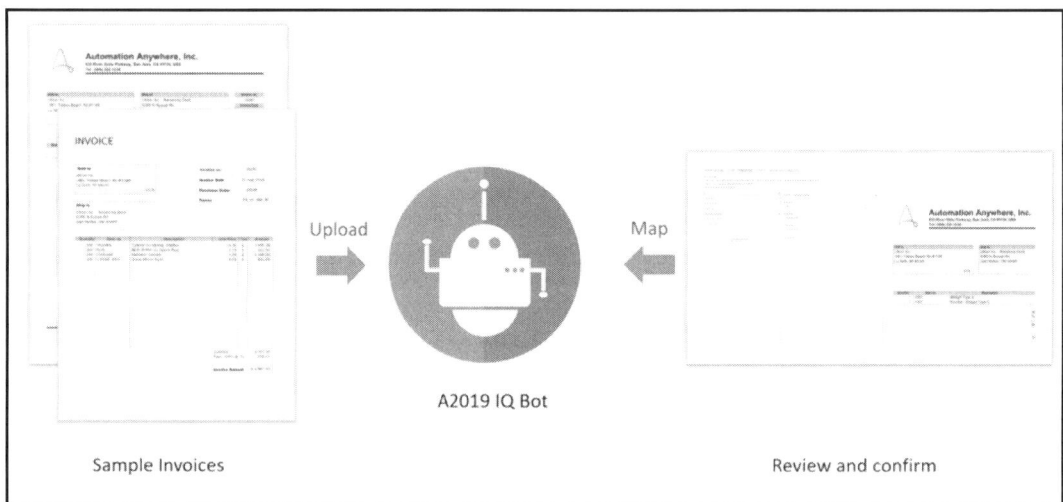

2. **Upload and download from IQ Bot**: Once we have the learning instance, we can use a Task Bot to upload the invoices that we'd like to process to the IQ Bot learning instance. The IQ Bot processes the PDF documents and provides structured data in CSV format. We will use another bot to download those CSV files. Here is a sequence diagram showing this process:

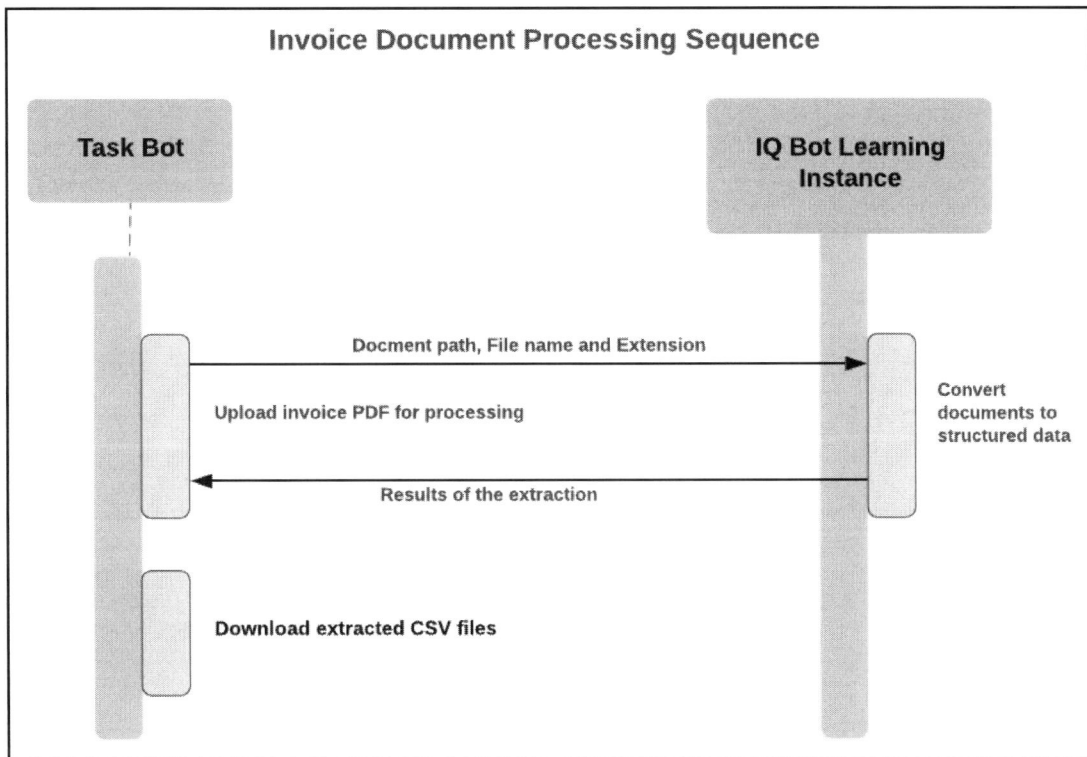

Now, let's go through the project, starting with some groundwork.

Project groundwork

Let's set up a few things before we start working on the project. We will open Automation Anywhere A2019 and download the sample invoices that we will learn and process.

Opening the Automation Anywhere A2019 Control Room

We will be creating an IQ Bot learning instance and some Task Bots so that we can invoke IQ Bot using the A2019 Control Room. So, open the A2019 Community Edition in your browser at `https://community.cloud.automationanywhere.digital/#/login`. Please log into the Control Room so that you end up on the Control Room's home page.

Now that we're in the A2019 Control Room, we can go to IQ Bot and gather the invoice samples.

Downloading sample invoices

We will download and use the A2019 IQ Bot invoice samples so that it's easy for you to follow along:

1. To download Automation Anywhere samples, click on the **Launch IQ Bot** button from the Control Room home page, as shown in the following screenshot:

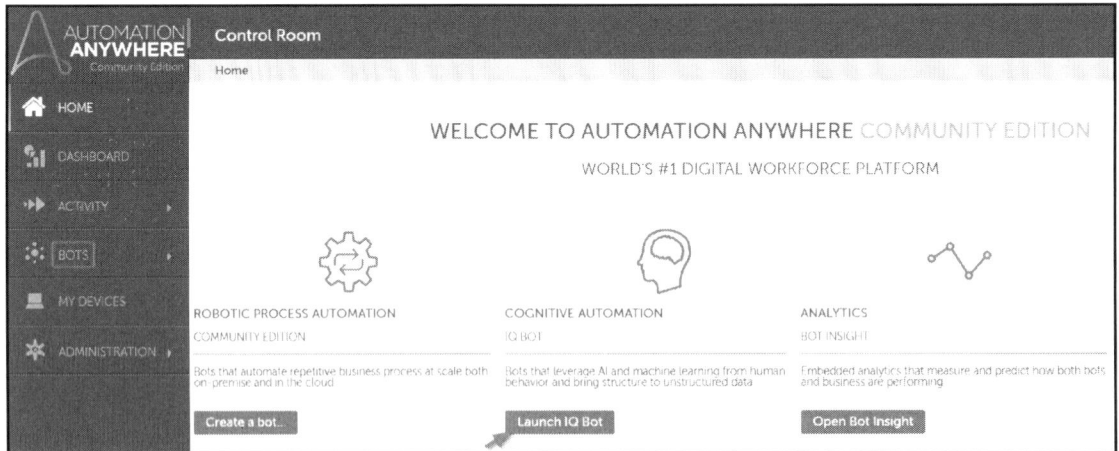

2. A2019 will open the **IQ Bot home** page in a new browser tab. Click on **Get Started** on the IQ Bot home screen to advance.
3. On the next screen (**Create**), you should find the option to **Download sample documents**, as shown in the following screenshot:

Click on the **Download sample documents** button. This will download a ZIP file containing all the document samples.

4. Extract the ZIP file and look for the **Invoices** folder. Copy that folder over to the project area.

5. Within this **Invoices** folder, create two folders – **Train** and **Test**. We will put the invoices that we want to use for learning in the **Train** folder and the ones we want the bot to process in the **Test** folder. We can choose three typical formats and put them in the **Train** folder and place seven in the **Test** folder. You can choose different combinations and test the combinations for yourself.

Now that we have the sample invoices for the project, we can start creating the IQ Bot learning instance.

Creating the IQ Bot learning instance

As we discussed in the introduction, IQ Bot uses AI to learn the format of the invoice. It uses what it's learned to process the rest of the invoices.

So, the first step is to create an instance that has been trained using the necessary invoice formats. Once we have the learning instance, we can upload the invoices to IQ Bot and convert them into structured data. Let's start by setting up the IQ Bot instance.

Setting up the initial IQ Bot learning instance

As part of the groundwork process, we opened the IQ Bot and went to the initial screen to create the learning instance. Go back to that page and pick up from where we left off:

1. On the **Create** screen, under **General information**, choose a name for the instance. Next, we have to provide a **Document Type**. We use this to tell the IQ Bot what type of documents we will be processing. Let's choose **Invoices** as we want IQ Bot to process invoices.

2. Under the **Upload your documents** section, we have to upload a few sample invoices for IQ Bot to learn from. Click on **Browse** and upload the invoices we put in the **Train** folder previously.

3. Finally, under **Fields to extract**, you can leave the default selected fields for the invoice as is. Click on **Create instance and analyze**:

It will take IQ Bot a few minutes to analyze the documents and create the learning instance. After doing this, it will present us with a screen where we can review these changes and make any updates to the training process.

Reviewing and updating field mappings

IQ Bot presents us with a **Review group** with the mapping it has so far for the invoices we uploaded for training. This mapping is a starting point based on typical invoice formats. It is up to us to review and ensure that the fields and values are mapped correctly. Let's look at the steps:

1. Here's what the review screen looked like for us. This may vary based on the training invoices you chose, though not by much if you also choose the Automation Anywhere sample invoices:

2. Look at each field and check whether the **Field Label** and **Field Value** options match with what is on the invoice on the right. For example, in the preceding screenshot, we have pointed out the fields and data to check for **Invoice Date**.

IQ Bot may classify the documents into different groups if there is more than one distinct format. We chose three similar types, so there is only one group. If there is more than one group, an extra button will appear at the top, near **Save and close**, so that you can review the other groups as well.

3. Next, click on the **See extraction results** button to verify that the data is being extracted as intended. You will see a screen similar to the one shown in the following screenshot so that you can verify whether the data is being extracted to the right fields. You can navigate to the results for the three invoices using the buttons at the top of the screen. Once you are satisfied with the extraction process, you can go **Back to training** by clicking the button shown in the following screenshot:

4. Once you are back on the **Review group** screen, click on **Save and close**. You will see a popup, asking whether you would like to save what you have trained currently. Go ahead and click on **Save** if you are satisfied with the training and the extraction you've done.

5. IQ Bot will then show you the learning instance and its group(s), as shown in the following screenshot. For us to use IQ Bot, we need to send to production using the toggle button shown in the following screenshot:

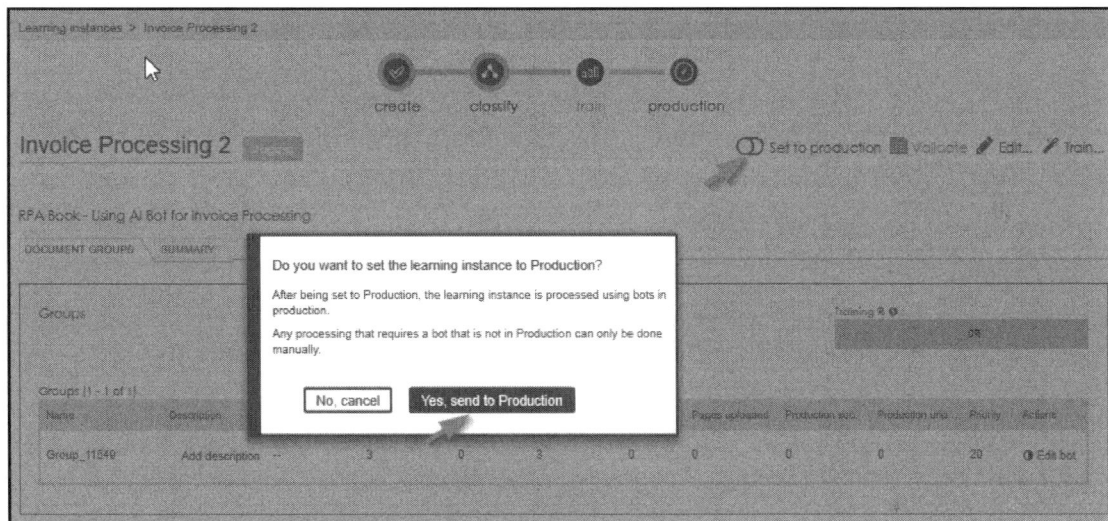

After some time, training will be at 100%. Now that we have a learning instance in production, we can upload the invoices we 'd like to process in IQ Bot.

First, let's create a Task Bot so that we can invoke and upload the invoices to IQ Bot.

Uploading invoices to IQ Bot

Now, we are ready to process the rest of the invoices we placed in the **Test** folder. We will create a Task Bot that will loop through the **Test** folder and upload all the documents to IQ Bot. Follow these steps:

1. Let's go back to the Automation Anywhere A2019 Control Room home page. Note that this is different from the IQ Bot home page. Go to **My Bots** and then **Create a bot**, just like we did for our past A2019 projects. Name the bot **Invoice Upload** (or any name that you'd like to use to identify the bot):

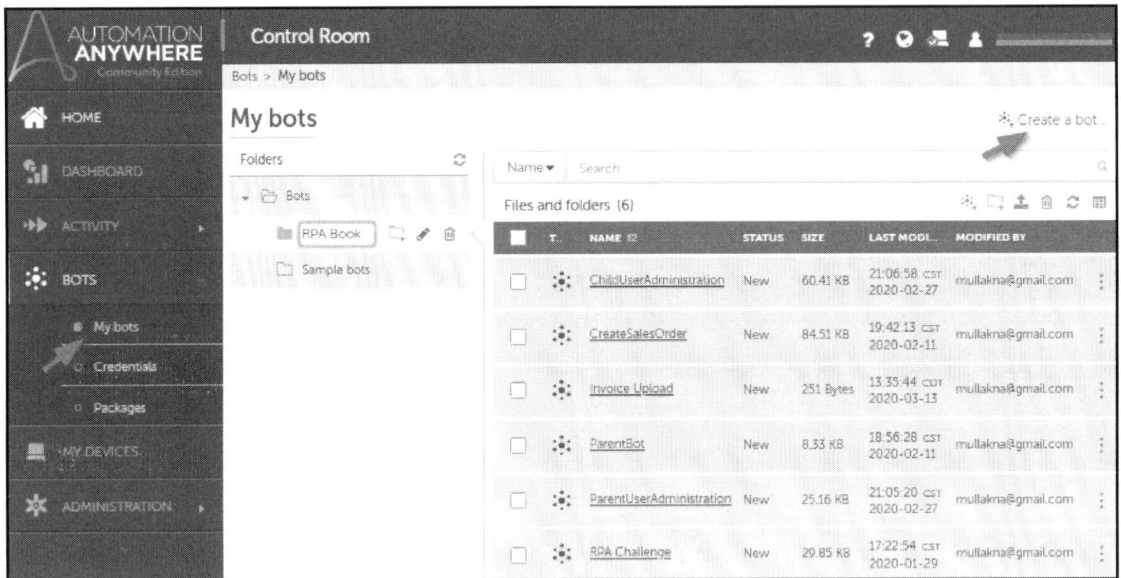

2. On the new bot canvas, add a **Loop** action. Since we need to loop through each file in the **Test** folder, we'll set **Iterator** to **For each file in folder**. Provide the **Folder path** as the complete path to the **Test** folder. Finally, choose the wizard and add a **Dictionary** variable called `File` for the **Assign file name and extension to this variable** input box:

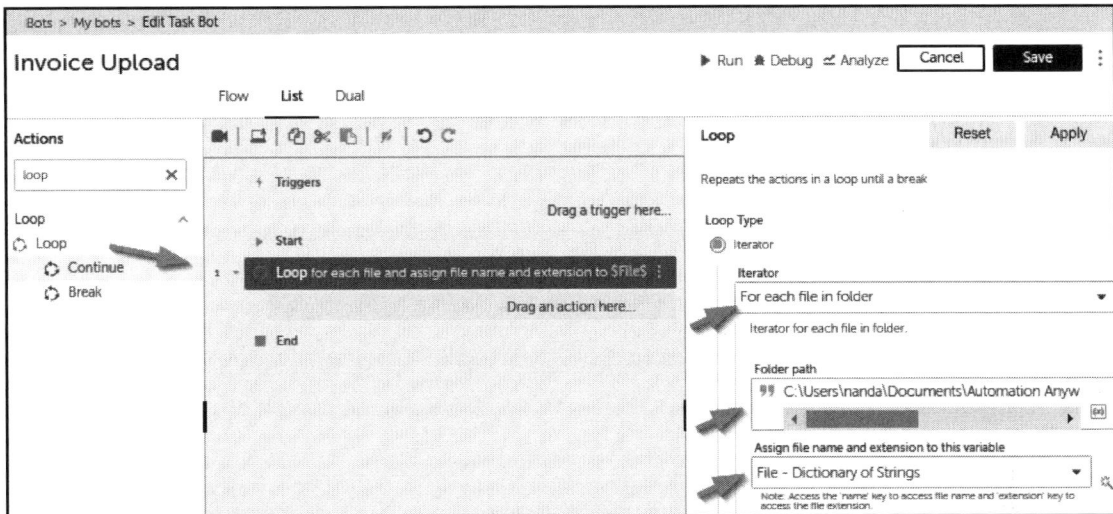

3. Next, add an IQ Bot step so that you can upload each of these documents. Choose the **IQ Bot Upload Document** Action. In the properties, choose the learning instance that we set to production in the previous section:

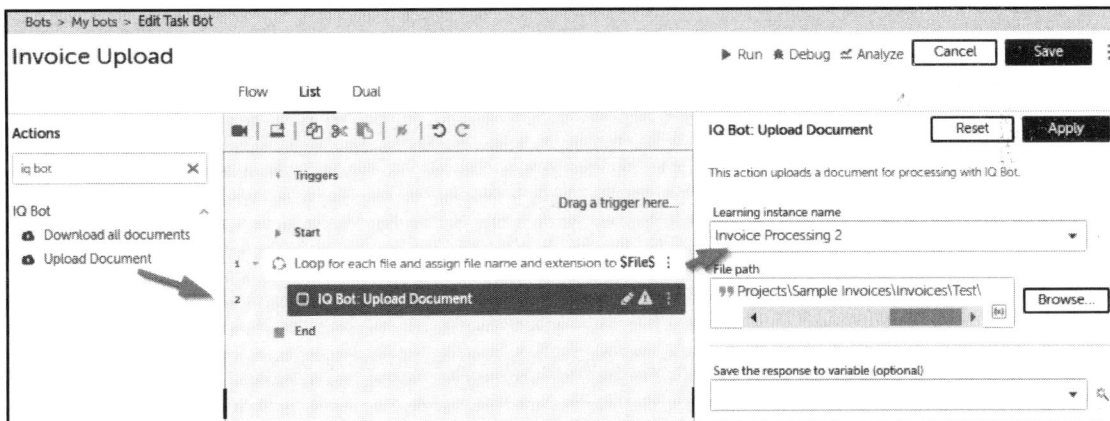

4. For the **File path** property, we need to construct the filename and append it to the path. To do so, we need to add the path to the `Test` folder, followed by a "\", and then click on the insert variable within the input box. Choose the `File` Dictionary variable and then type in `name` for the **Dictionary key**. Since we are constructing a filename with an extension, we'll need to add a "." after the **File name** variable. Click the insert variable again, choose `File`, and add a **Dictionary key** called `extension`. Your **File path** will be in the following format: `<Your File Path>\$File{name}$.$File{extension}$`. This can be seen in the following screenshot:

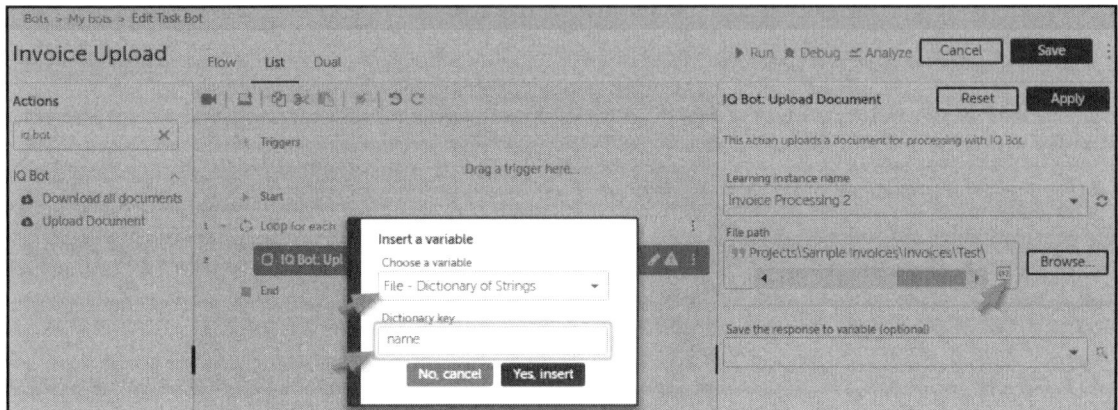

> You can also add a variable to capture the response from IQ Bot using the **Save the response to variable** option in the **Upload Document** activity, as shown in the preceding screenshot. Then, you can check whether the response is positive before uploading the next document.

5. Your uploaded Task Bot is ready. **Save** the bot and run it using the **Run** button. This will upload all the invoice documents we'd like to process with IQ Bot. If all goes well, you will receive a message stating that your bot ran successfully:

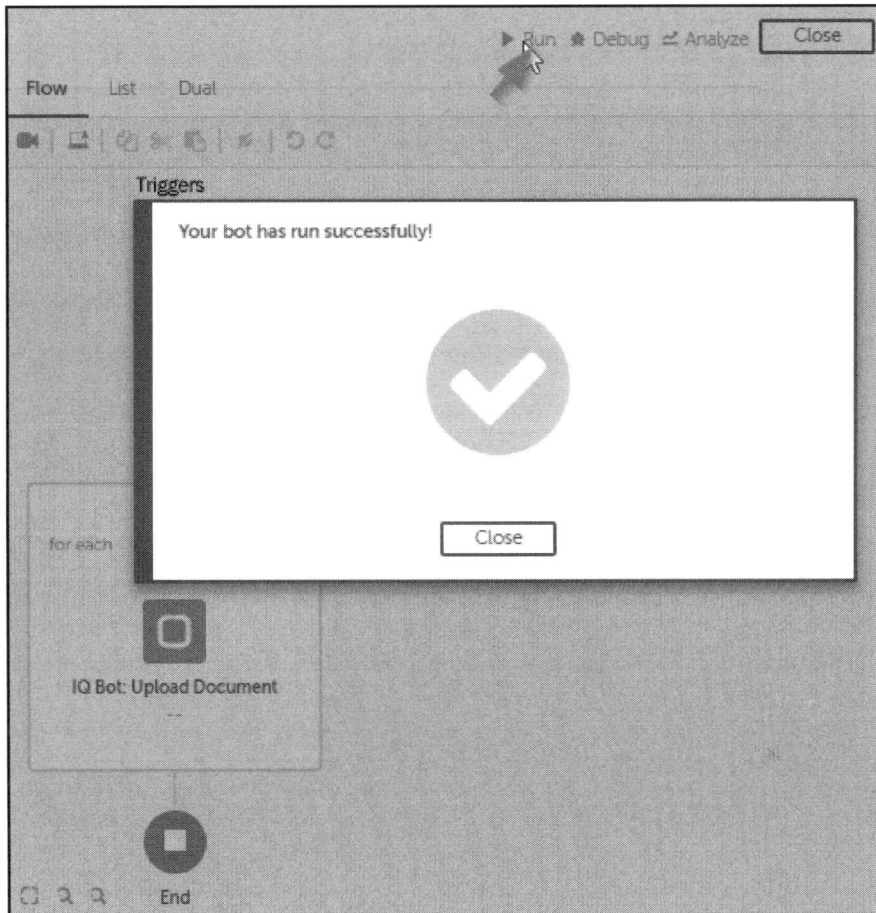

So far, IQ Bot has taken all the invoices from the `Test` folder and converted them into structured data. Now, we need to download them.

Downloading structured data from IQ Bot

Now, let's download the CSV files that were generated by IQ Bot. These CSV files contain the invoice data from the mapping we created in the learning instance. To create this Task Bot, follow these steps:

1. Go to **My Bots** on the left panel and select **Create a bot**, just like we did in the previous section. Name it `Invoice Download`.

2. We just need one Action to download the files from IQ Bot. Let's look up and add the **IQ Bot Download all documents** Action. In its properties, choose the learning instance we created earlier. For the **Local output folder**, add the path where you'd like the bot to place the processed CSV files:

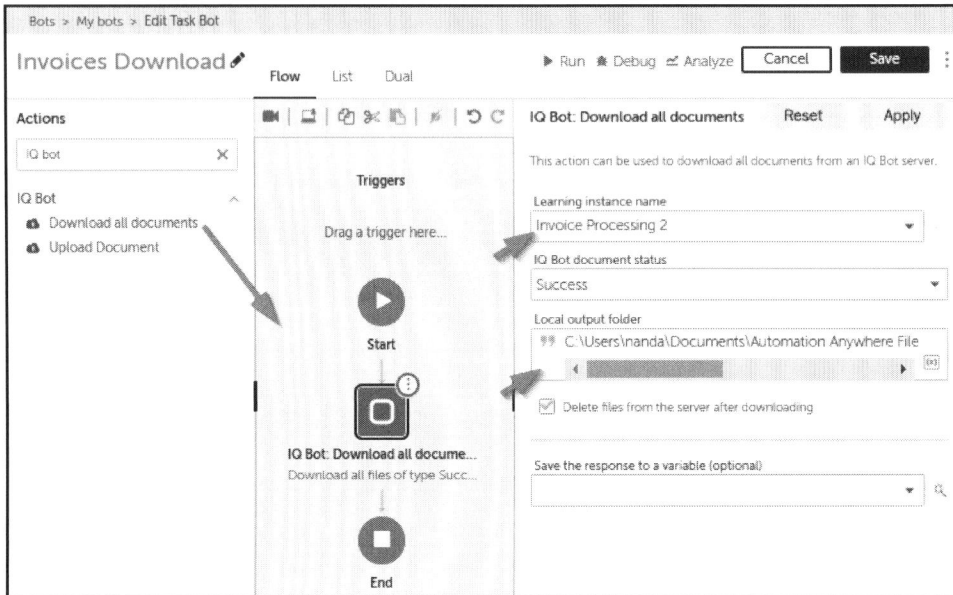

3. Save the bot and run it. Once the bot has run successfully, go to the processed CSV files folder and check whether you have the files. The bot will have processed all the invoices that matched the format that we trained it on.

Now that we have the structured data downloaded, let's verify the data with the corresponding invoices.

Checking the automation

Let's compare the structured data output from the bot with the unstructured data from the invoices. This way, we can test that our project works.

Open the CSV file from the processed files folder. Also, open the corresponding invoice. The bot will have named the CSV file so that the invoice's filename is at the end. Place them side by side to compare them, as shown in the following screenshot:

You can compare each of the invoice fields to the columns in the CSV file. Do this comparison for the rest of the files that were generated. If all goes well, all the fields should match perfectly.

These CSV files can now be used as input for an automation process that needs to use the invoice data. IQ Bot Community Edition can process many standard document formats such as invoices, purchase orders, bank statements, credit memos, and utility bills. There are many more formats in the Enterprise version.

So, if we were to repeat these steps for purchase orders using a sample format, we could take the structured data and put it in a purchase order application, just like we did in `Chapter 5`, *Purchase Order Processing with UiPath ReFramework*.

This was our last project with Automation Anywhere. Let's do a quick recap.

Automation Anywhere projects – recap

With this project, we completed five projects with Automation Anywhere A2019 that have increased in complexity. Here is what we've covered:

- We started with the Automation Anywhere A2019 platform by solving an RPA challenge. This included performing basic automation, along with handling dynamic elements in forms.
- Then, we learned how to use web automation by creating sales orders in the Apptivo application.
- Next, we learned about how to perform user administration with bots by creating new users in a SaaS application.
- Then, we completed an exciting project that sent emergency text messages using the Twilio API.
- In this final project, we learned how to use AI to extract meaningful data from scanned documents using Automation Anywhere IQ Bot.

With that, we have covered five different projects using Automation Anywhere and UiPath!

Summary

In this chapter, we learned how to use AI with RPA for document processing.

Processing documents such as purchase orders and invoices is one of the common yet difficult problems that arises when it comes to automation. So, in this chapter, we looked at how to crack that problem with AI.

Once AI has processed these documents into structured data, it opens up many automation use cases for downstream processing. For example, invoice data output could be entered into the Apptivo application, which we used previously in this book.

Now that we have come this far, we encourage you to try out what you've learned for yourself. In fact, there are many more use cases that you can automate based on the projects we completed in this book.

This is the last chapter in this book. We had great fun creating these projects and have included provided the code on GitHub. We hope you've enjoyed working on the projects as much as we've enjoyed guiding you through them. We're sure you've faced some difficulties but have come out the other end as a better RPA practitioner.

Hopefully, we will get to write more books on this subject. When we do, we hope to see you there – or somewhere on the web!

Appendix A and B for UiPath

Appendix A – Connecting UiPath Robot to Orchestrator

As we discussed in Chapter 1, *Getting Started with RPA*, UiPath Orchestrator is the central place to deploy and manage our bots.

To deploy the processes you build in Studio to Orchestrator, you have to connect the local UiPath Assistant (Robot) that we installed in Chapter 1, *Getting Started with RPA*, to your Orchestrator account in the cloud.

Let's learn how to connect a standard Assistant/Robot to the UiPath cloud platform containing Orchestrator.

Getting started

Let's start by doing some groundwork.

First, we will access Orchestrator on the cloud. To do so, perform the following steps:

1. Access the UiPath cloud platform (go to platform.uipath.com).
2. Log into the platform if needed.
3. Click on **Services** on the left-hand panel.
4. You should be able to find a default service. Click on its name.
5. This should open up Orchestrator's home page.

Next, let's get the machine name from UiPath Assistant. To do so, perform the following steps:

1. On your Windows PC, locate the **UiPath Assistant** application (go to **Start** and search for it).
2. Open up the Assistant application and click on **Settings** (the gear icon at the top) and choose **Orchestrator Configurations**.

3. Take note of the **Machine Name** in the Orchestrator configuration, as shown in the following screenshot:

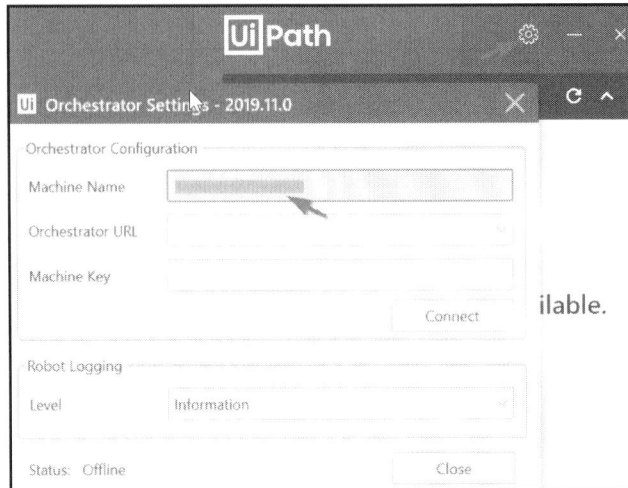

Now that we have the machine name, let's create the Orchestrator Robot.

Creating a Standard Robot in Orchestrator

Head over to Orchestrator, which we opened in the first set of steps in the previous section. Now, let's create the Robot:

1. Click on **Robots** on the left-hand panel.
2. On the right-hand panel that opens up, click on **Add** (the plus (+) sign) and then choose **Standard Robot.**
3. In the form that pops up, enter the following information:
   - Machine: Enter the machine name from the local Orchestrator configuration (we took note of this previously).
   - Click on **Provision machine...** under the **Machine** field to provision the machine.
   - **Name**: Type in any name for the Robot.
   - **Type**: Select **Studio** as the Robot type since we want to connect to Studio.

- **Domain\Username**: Add the username that you use to log into your PC:
    1. Go to your Command Prompt (from **Search** or **Start**).
    2. Run the `whomai` command.
    3. Take note of the name and use it as the **Orchestrator Username**.
- **Password** (optional): Type in the Windows password for the specified username.
- Click on **Create** to create the bot in Orchestrator:

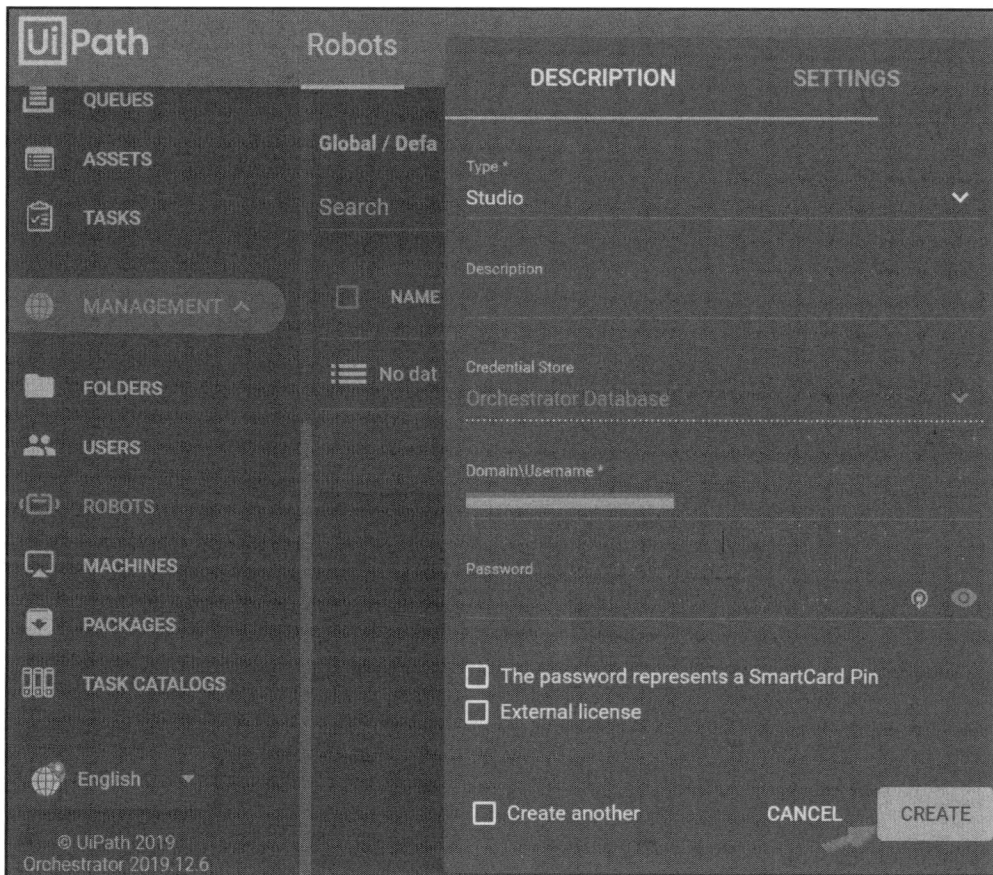

Adding an environment for the Bot

We will now choose an environment for the Robot to run in:

1. Within the **Robots** option, from the left-hand pane, click on the **Environment** tab in the top blue ribbon.
2. Click on **Add** (the plus (**+**) sign).
3. On the **Create Environment** form, provide a name for your environment.
4. Once created, choose the environment options (use the three dots on the right-hand side) and choose **Manage**.
5. Choose your Robot from the list and click **Update**.

Connecting Orchestrator to the local Robot

We are now ready to connect to our local Robot. To do that, we need some information from Orchestrator.

First, let's take note of the **Machine Key** from the **Machines** page on Orchestrator. To do that, perform the following steps:

1. Head over to **Machines** on the left-hand pane.
2. Choose the machine you provisioned (while adding the Robot) from the right-hand pane and choose **Options**.
3. Choose **Edit** (the three dots on right).
4. Copy the **Machine Key** value.

Next, let's also take note of the Orchestrator URL. In any web browser with Orchestrator open, copy the URL.

Finally, go back to **Orchestrator Settings** in the UiPath Assistant/Robot tray in your local machine. Fill in the URL and **Machine Key**, as shown in the following screenshot:

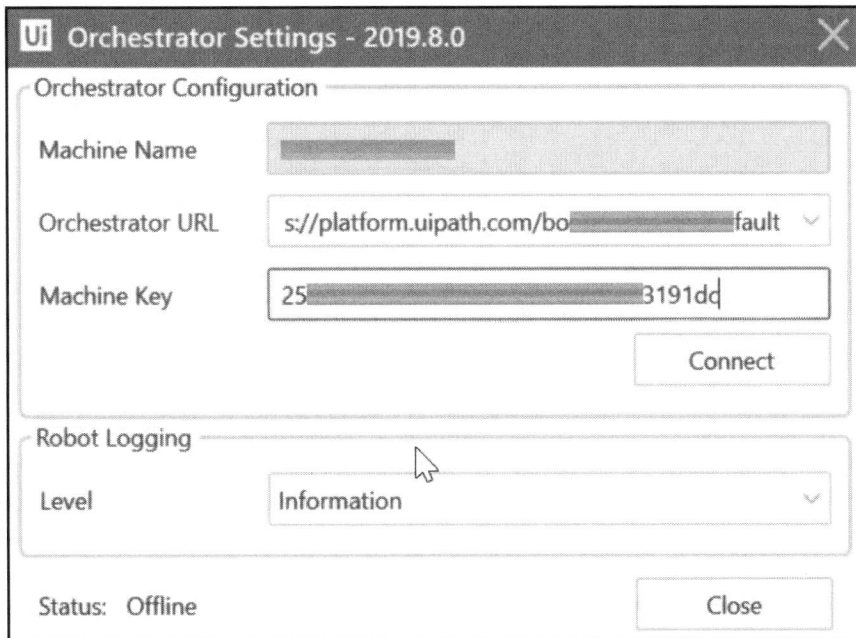

In the local Assistant/Robot Orchestrator settings window, the status should show **Connected, licensed**. In Orchestrator, within the **Robots** section, the Robot that you just added should have a status of **Available**, and there should be a green checkmark alongside the Bot's name.

Your Robot is now connected to Orchestrator.

Appendix B – Publishing to Orchestrator

Make sure Orchestrator and the Assistant/Robot are already connected. Please follow the steps detailed in Appendix A to do this.

Publishing to Orchestrator

Once the Assistant/Robot is available in Orchestrator, click on **Publish** in UiPath Studio and choose **Orchestrator**, as shown in the following screenshot:

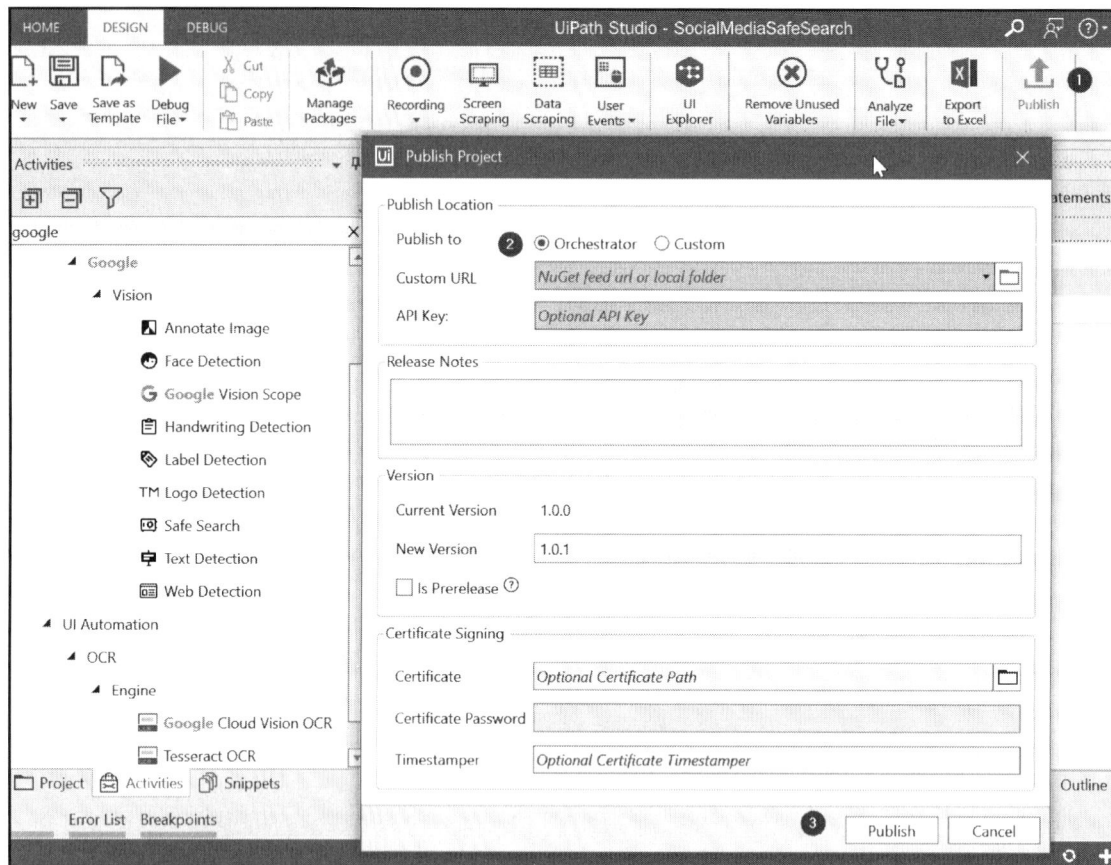

Once the package has been published, we will get a confirmation message, similar to the one shown in the following screenshot:

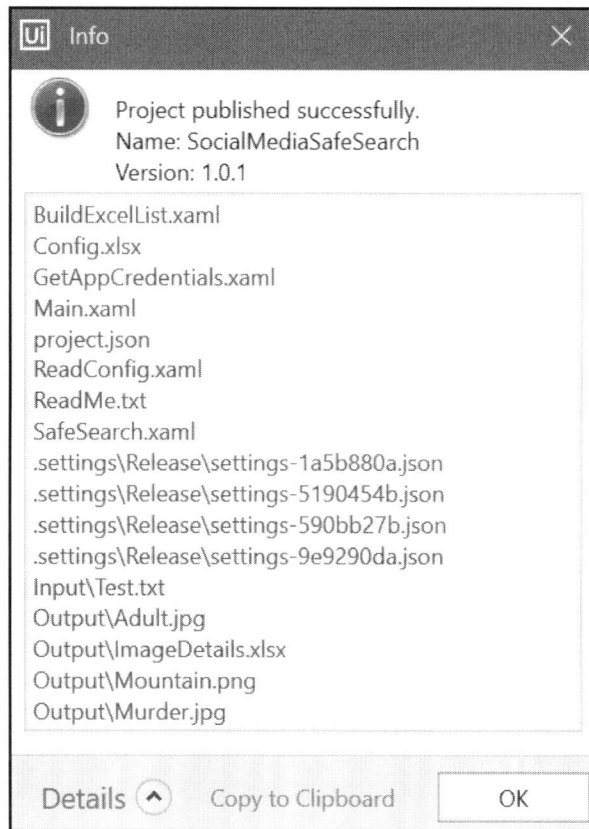

Creating a new process

Once you've received the confirmation message, log in to Orchestrator and use this package to create a new process. To do this, perform the following steps:

1. Go to **Processes** and click **Add** (the plus (+) sign).
2. Choose the package you want to run from the dropdown.
3. Leave the version that is displayed.
4. Choose the environment you want the process to run in.
5. Click on **Create.**

These steps are depicted in the following screenshot:

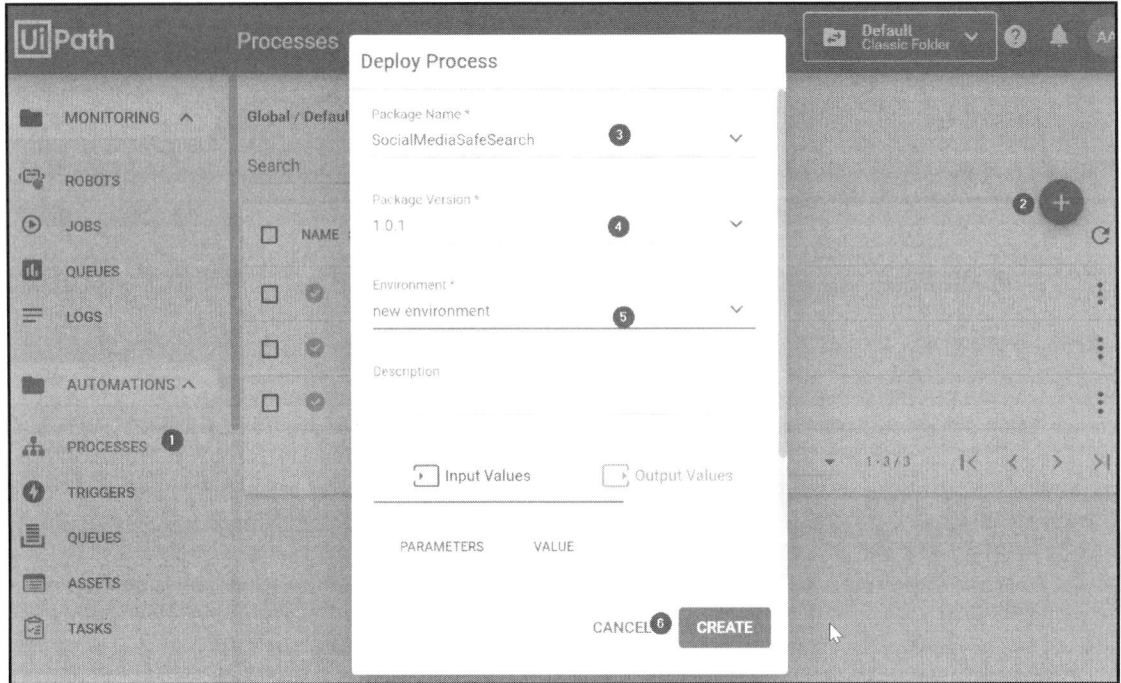

Running the process

Once the process has been added, we need to create a Job in order to run it. Perform the following steps:

1. Click the **Jobs** option on the left-hand panel.
2. To start a Job, click on the **Start** (play) button.
3. In the pop-up form, do the following:
   - Choose a process that you want to run.
   - For **Execution Target**, choose an active Robot.
   - Click on **Start**. The Bot will start executing in the system:

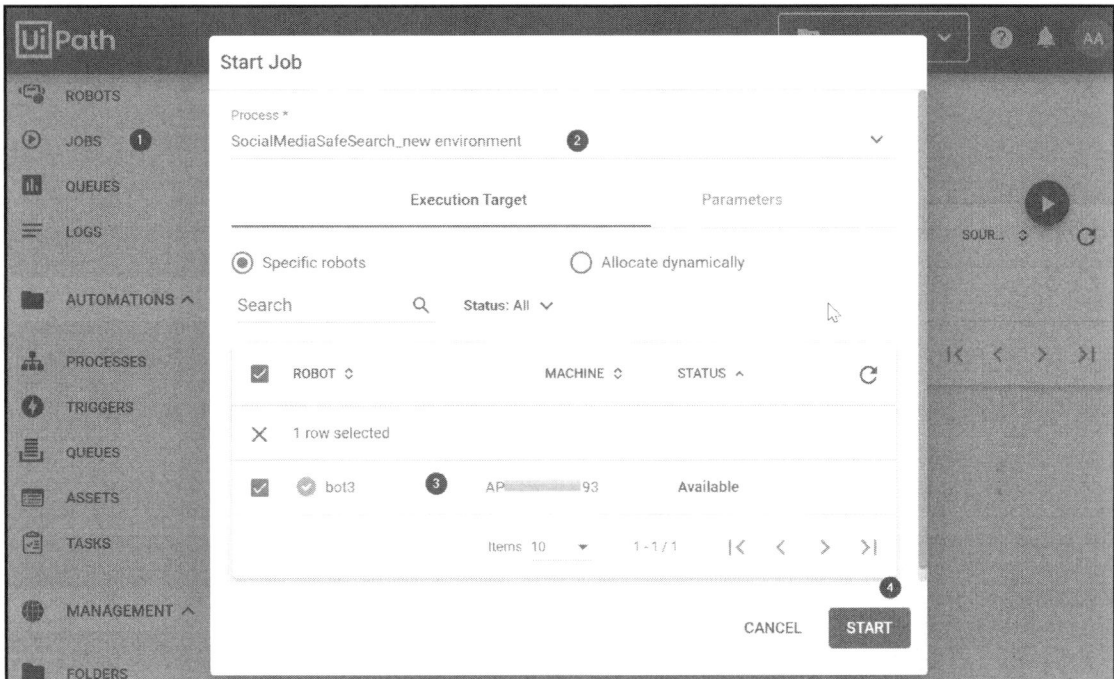

Once the job has run successfully, you will see that **State** is **Successful**, with a green checkmark next to it.

Scheduling the process

You can also create a trigger so that the process runs at scheduled intervals. To do this, perform the following steps:

1. Click on **Triggers** from the left-hand pane.
2. Click on **Add** (the plus (+) sign) and choose **Time** on the next screen.
3. Provide a **Name** for the trigger.
4. Choose your timezone.
5. Choose the **Process** you like to schedule.
6. Choose your specific Robot.
7. Select the schedule you'd like the process to run (for example, you can schedule as `Daily` and add a specific time).
8. Finally, click on **Add** to schedule the process.

This is how you publish to Orchestrator and run or schedule a Robot. You can do this to run any of the UiPath projects in this book.

Appendix: Looking Forward and Next Steps

Robotic Process Automation (**RPA**) is a rapidly advancing field and is going through exponential change due to several internal and external factors.

Since the beginning of the Information Age, we have gone through many waves of process automation. We started with the computerization of lines of businesses led by **Management Information Systems** (**MIS**) groups within each organization. Once the businesses were computerized, we started looking for ways to optimize the business processes through **Business Process Management** (**BPM**). While BPM focused on end-to-end processes, RPA emerged as a way to automate discrete tasks using existing user interfaces.

Now, with significant capital being invested, we can see that RPA platforms are expanding, with the inclusion of technologies such as **Artificial Intelligence** (**AI**), **Computer Vision** (**CV**), **Optical Character Recognition** (**OCR**), process mining, chatbots, and many more. The RPA platforms are also morphing into enterprise-scale platforms with marketplaces, which we will explore in this appendix. This is leading to rapid changes and an RPA market that is much more advanced than the task automation that RPA started with.

Even as we wrote this book, a new version of Automation Anywhere A2019 was released. UiPath also came up with a new platform with products for each phase of the automation life cycle. We had to adjust to include the changes as they came up.

We are sure there will be many more rapid developments in this field. As we write this in March 2020, here is what we can see.

Future of RPA

RPA tools have emerged and are used as part of an enterprise-grade automation platform to connect processes with comprehensive controls and security. With advancing automation requirements, RPA vendors have added additional technologies to enable the automation of tasks that could not be automated with simple RPA.

With the addition of these new technologies, all the top RPA tools now offer a platform for automation. Each platform offers an "operating system" that can be used to build and manage Bots. You can then add additional components such as AI-ML, which you need for your automation, using components provided by the vendors themselves, their partners, or community members. So, RPA is becoming a gateway technology to using new or advancing technologies and paradigms for automation.

Most RPA software vendors are adding to the core RPA function in a few common areas. These areas include the following:

- Artificial intelligence (AI-ML)
- Process mining and/or process discovery
- Intelligent document processing (OCR/ICR/ML)
- Conversational AI (Chatbots)
- Advanced analytics

Gartner has come up with the term **hyperautomation** to refer to this approach of using a basket of technologies, including RPA for automation.

Hyperautomation

Garner stated the following about hyperautomation:

> *"Hyperautomation refers to an approach in which organizations rapidly identify and automate as many business processes as possible. It involves the use of a combination of technology tools, including, but not limited to, machine learning, packaged software, and automation tools to deliver work."*

Hyperautomation is the first and one of the most important trends in Gartner's "Top 10 Strategic Technology Trends for 2020." Gartner suggests using a wider spectrum of tools beyond RPA for automation. Along with RPA, Gartner recommends using **intelligent Business Process Management Suites** (**iBPMSes**), **integration Platform as a Service** (**iPaaS**) platforms, and decision management systems. Including these tools, which provide an orchestration layer, Gartner suggests using technologies such as process mining, ingestion engines, OCR, computer vision, analytics, user experience, and **Machine Learning** (**ML**).

If all this seems a bit confusing to you, the key idea of hyperautomation is to build the plumbing to drop in emerging technologies (such as AI-ML) to enable better and wider automation. While we still do not know which tool will end up being the tool of choice to provide the orchestration layer, we can say that RPA is still one of the best choices.

Here is an example of what hyperautomation can look like:

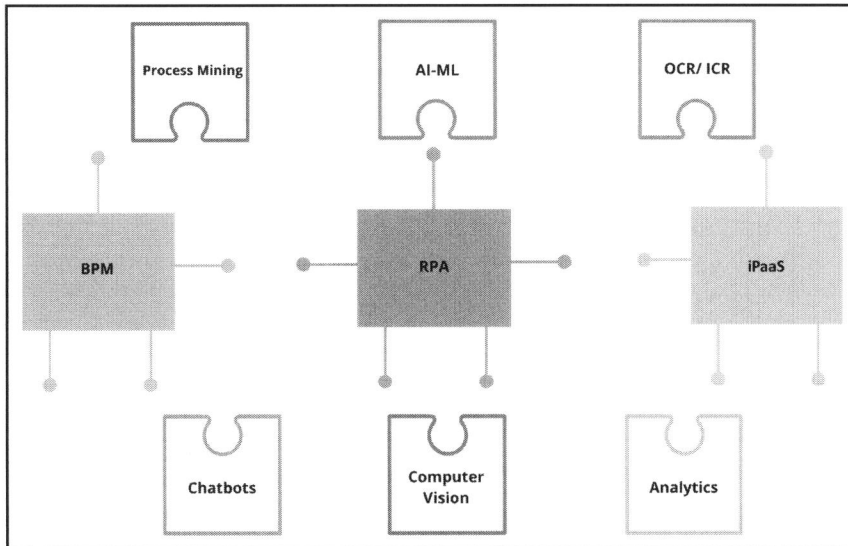

Considering these developments, let's look at a few rapidly emerging technologies and trends to watch out for.

Future technologies and trends

As the heading suggests, let's look at some of the technologies and trends we'll see in the future.

Artificial intelligence (AI)

Everyone looking to get to the next stage of RPA implementation is adding different aspects of AI to their automation initiatives. As per Deloitte, initiatives that scale are more likely to use a combination of RPA and AI. According to their study, almost half (45 percent) of organizations scaling automation combine RPA and AI. The automation programs also report whether the automation initiatives meet or exceed their expectations.

Among AI, we are seeing lots of implementations with ML, computer vision, and **Natural Language Processing** (**NLP**). These are being used in specific use cases where AI is enabling smart detection, prediction, and execution; for example, to read emails (NLP), image or video processing (computer vision), and sentiment detection. As per a study conducted by Deloitte, the most popular AI solutions being implemented are ML-based solutions, expert or rule-based systems, and NLP-based solutions.

Let's look at two key areas where AI is being used with RPA other than ML.

Document processing

By most estimates, more than 70% to 80% of data in enterprises are in documents – mostly PDFs, scans, and forms. Digitizing this information opens up many use cases for automation.

With AI, document processing has been able to overcome many challenges, as noted in `Chapter 10`, *Using AI and RPA for Invoice Processing*. The IQ Bot project we completed in that chapter gave you a glimpse into the document processing capabilities that are being added to RPA. You can also add document processing to RPA using Cloud AI (for example, Google, Microsoft, and Amazon) or use dedicated OCR/ICR vendors such as Abbyy, Hyland, Kofax, or Hyperscience.

Conversational AI

RPA Bots are using NLP and **Natural Language Understanding** (**NLU**) to interact with customers and employees through voice or text. With RPA and chatbots, users can converse with automated processes in natural language.

Through these conversational AI solutions, enterprises are expanding in terms of the variety and complexity of the use cases that are being automated. You can expose this automation to customers and employees through these conversational channels. End users can now interact with your automation through mobiles, the web, and even social apps. The inclusion of these conversational journeys improves end user experiences.

Process mining and process discovery

Process mining is a set of techniques that enable enterprises to understand the actual processes that are followed in organizations. Most end users visualize these processes as simple workflow diagrams. The reality is that the actual processes being followed by people on the ground are much more complex. Process mining helps you visualize and analyze these complex processes.

While we do RPA, we usually come back from looking at end users with simple workflows. We discover the complexity of the process as we progress through the automation. End users point out the branches that have been missed, one by one. Process complexity and identifying processes for automation and prioritizing them are some of the challenges for RPA.

Process mining and process discovery come to the rescue here. We can now add process mining with RPA. Both UiPath and Automation Anywhere have their own offerings in this area that can be used. There are also dedicated process mining vendors who have tailored their offerings to help with RPA process discovery and prioritization. You can also analyze and track the impact of your RPA automation.

Like RPA, process mining vendors have been adding more features as there is increasing interest and investments coming into this space as well. Some of the process discovery tools even allow you to generate an RPA **Process Definition Document** (**PDD**) automatically. Some of the RPA vendors claim that process mining or discovery can generate and provide you with skeleton RPA code that you can customize. This is an evolving field and some analysts are predicting that with more data, we will see that the creation of Bot scripts can be automated to a large extent.

RPA as a service

As we mentioned earlier, Automation Anywhere came up with a new version – A2019 – as we wrote this book. We pivoted to completing all our projects in A2019, which is a good example of delivering RPA from the cloud as a service.

As we saw with A2019, all the development, testing, deployment, and monitoring phases are carried out from a web-based control room. We downloaded and installed an agent on the desktop that the control room connected to in order to execute the automation locally. With this approach, you now have the ability to create automation from anywhere and across multiple operating systems. You can even start your automation on one device and finish it on another device.

We may also see new RPA models, such as pay as you use licensing RPA platforms, which will reduce the licensing cost of bots as competition intensifies in this product space.

RPA marketplaces

As we saw, RPA vendors are providing a way for us to plug in emerging technologies. These technologies are included as components that are provided by the RPA vendors themselves, partners, and even people like you. These components are usually available on a marketplace. Here are the marketplaces from the top RPA vendors:

- **UiPath Connect Marketplace**: An extensive library of reusable RPA components
- **Blue Prism Digital Exchange** (**DX**): A central place to find and include pre-built "skills"
- **Automation Anywhere Bot Store**: Includes digital workers (Bots) that can automate tasks

All these platforms allow you to automate better by enabling you to add a wide variety of technologies to solve business problems. These components can usually be added to your automation through drag-and-drop interfaces for easy configuration.

As these RPA platforms grow, we should see more participation and a greater variety of components that we can include in our automation. You could soon find pre-built components for the most typical automation scenarios.

Conclusion

These are the technologies and trends we can see as of now. RPA has played an important role in operating core processes during the COVID-19 pandemic period, and the adoption of RPA and hyperautomation is going to be accelerated by these global disruptions, so it would be prudent to master these key technologies to stay relevant in the job market. Also, stay on top of these and other evolving trends as you look to automate business processes.

Good luck!

Other Books You May Enjoy

If you enjoyed this book, you may be interested in these other books by Packt:

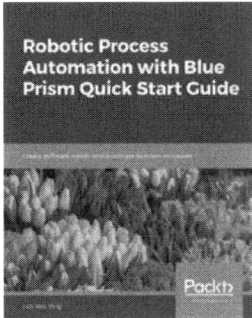

Robotic Process Automation with Blue Prism Quick Start Guide
Lim Mei Ying

ISBN: 978-1-78961-044-4

- Learn why and when to introduce robotic automation into your business processes
- Work with Blue Prism Studio
- Create automation processes in Blue Prism
- Make use of decisions and choices in your robots
- Use UI Automation mode, HTML mode, Region mode, and spying
- Learn how to raise exceptions
- Get the robot to deal with errors
- Learn Blue Prism coding best practices

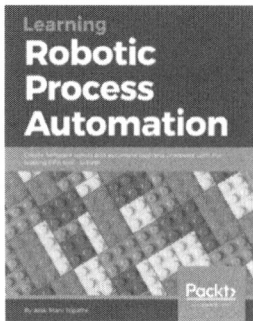

Learning Robotic Process Automation
Alok Mani Tripathi

ISBN: 978-1-78847-094-0

- Understand Robotic Process Automation technology
- Learn UiPath programming techniques to deploy robot configurations
- Explore various data extraction techniques
- Learn about integrations with various popular applications such as SAP and MS Office
- Debug a programmed robot including logging and exception handling
- Maintain code version and source control
- Deploy and control Bots with UiPath Orchestrator

Leave a review - let other readers know what you think

Please share your thoughts on this book with others by leaving a review on the site that you bought it from. If you purchased the book from Amazon, please leave us an honest review on this book's Amazon page. This is vital so that other potential readers can see and use your unbiased opinion to make purchasing decisions, we can understand what our customers think about our products, and our authors can see your feedback on the title that they have worked with Packt to create. It will only take a few minutes of your time, but is valuable to other potential customers, our authors, and Packt. Thank you!

Index